Joseph Mullens

**The religious aspects of Hindu philosophy stated and discussed**

Joseph Mullens

**The religious aspects of Hindu philosophy stated and discussed**

ISBN/EAN: 9783337234218

Printed in Europe, USA, Canada, Australia, Japan

Cover: Foto ©Lupo / pixelio.de

More available books at **www.hansebooks.com**

THE

# RELIGIOUS ASPECTS

OF

# HINDU PHILOSOPHY

STATED AND DISCUSSED.

A Prize Essay.

BY THE

## REV. JOSEPH MULLENS,

MISSIONARY OF THE LONDON MISSIONARY SOCIETY,
AUTHOR OF "MISSIONS IN SOUTH INDIA,"
AND "RESULTS OF MISSIONARY LABOUR IN INDIA."

LONDON:

SMITH, ELDER AND CO., 65, CORNHILL.

———

M.DCCC.LX.

TO

# MY MISSIONARY BRETHREN IN INDIA,

OF ALL BRANCHES OF

## THE CHURCH OF CHRIST,

### This Essay,

WRITTEN WITH SPECIAL REFERENCE

TO SOME OF

OUR COMMON DIFFICULTIES,

IS

RESPECTFULLY INSCRIBED.

# CONTENTS.

---

Part Second.

## THE CHIEF RELIGIOUS ERRORS OF THESE SYSTEMS.

### PART FOURTH.
## AN OUTLINE OF SCIENTIFIC AND RELIGIOUS TRUTH.

# PREFACE.

THIS work was first suggested by the following proposal :—

" A prize of 300*l.* is offered for the best Statement and Refutation, in English, of the Fundamental Errors (opposed to Christian Theism) of the Vedánta, Nyáya, and Sánkhya Philosophies, as set forth in the standard native authorities, in the Sanskrit language, treating of those systems; together with a demonstration (supported by such arguments, and conveyed in such a form and manner as may be most likely to prove convincing to learned Hindus imbued with those errors) of the following fundamental principles of Christian Theism, viz. :—

" *First.*—Of the real, and not merely apparent or illusory distinctness of God from all other spirits, and from matter ; and of the creation (in the proper sense) of all other spirits, and of matter, by God, in opposition to the Vedánta.

" *Second.*—Of the non-eternity of separate souls, and their creation by God, in opposition to the Nyáya and Sánkhya.

" *Third.*—Of the creation of matter, in opposition to

the tenet of its eternity in the shape of atoms (as maintained in the Nyáya and Vaiseshika Schools), or in the
shape of Prakriti (as maintained by the Sánkhya).

"*Fourth.*—Of the moral character and moral government of God; and of the reality and perpetuity of the
difference between moral good and evil; with reference
to such dogmas of the above systems as are opposed to
those doctrines.

"The refutation of the above-mentioned Hindu errors
should (as it seems to the proposer) proceed upon a
double basis, viz.:—First, the disproof of the grounds
on which the native authors claim divine authority for
the founders of the several philosophical schools; and
for the Vedas, in so far as those schools profess to
be founded thereon.   Secondly, a demonstration of the
contrariety of these doctrines to reason, or to the best
conclusions to which reason leads.

"The erroneous systems in question embody the best
solutions which Hindu philosophers have been able to
frame of the mysteries of human existence.   When,
therefore, these theories are controverted, the difficulties which they were considered to neutralize, will
again occur to the Hindu's mind, as demanding solution.
Thus: their theory of the eternity of souls, and of the
present state being one of retribution for good or bad
deeds done in former stages of existence, obviates, in
their idea, the charge of partiality to which they conceive the Supreme Being would, on the other hypo-

thesis, be obnoxious, on account of the unequal distribution of his gifts in the present life. Hence the objections (founded on the above or other difficulties) which Hindu writers or reasoners raise to the non-eternity and creation of souls, and other doctrines of Christian Theism, must be encountered as they arise.

" With the view of doing the fullest justice to the subject, and ensuring most effectually the end proposed, viz., the conviction of the acute adherents of the errors in question, whose belief is founded on the reasonings as well as the authority of their own writers, the Essay must bear constant reference to the specific grounds on which the native authors base their doctrines, and to the arguments and illustrations by which they defend them. All important statements should be supported by references to the native authors.

"As native authors make use of frequent illustrations, either to set their tenets in a clear light, or to defend them, it might be useful that the same practice, in so far as it answers the former purpose, should be employed by their opponents, to illustrate their own views.

" The treatise should be so constructed as to show the English reader, in detail, what those grounds, arguments, and illustrations are, by which the Indian authors support their systems.

" In spirit, the treatise should be most kind and conciliatory, recognizing cheerfully every merit and every true principle which may be justly ascribed to the native authors, and encountering their errors with the utmost gentleness which may be compatible with a clear indication of their pernicious tendency.

" The subject is limited as above defined, because the points which have been indicated above, form the peculiar difficulties of the Hindu controversy; and are the points with which those missionaries who may be distinguished by no remarkable metaphysical acumen, and devoid of any accurate acquaintance with the Indian philosophies, (though they may know the main features of that which is popularly current,) are least capable of dealing successfully. When such difficulties have been cleared away, the remainder of the argument, comprising the positive proofs of our holy religion, and the answers to objections which are not peculiar to Indian thinkers, or connected with their distinctive tenets, does not call for the same acuteness, or depth of Indian learning, on the part of the Christian advocate."

The task assigned in this proposal is of a high character, and very hard to execute. It is difficult for one brought up in England to get away from our own well-proved systems of philosophy and science, and stand upon an entirely new platform, with a complete set of systems, based upon new notions, in many respects consistent with each other, and hanging together with great tenacity. For a full understanding of these systems, one ought to get at the exact meaning of every term employed, and give to each not the

breadth of meaning which many bear in European
science, but a force no greater than the original teacher
attached to it.    To do all this thoroughly, to meet
these Hindu philosophers on their own ground, to think
only as they thought, and see the world with their
eyes ; one must almost forget all the principles we have
been learning from childhood, one must almost become
un-English, un-Baconian, and un-Christian.    In order
to meet their errors, one has to evolve from their systems principles on which they agree with us, and
thence, without employing the authority of the Christian system, to bring forth a system of truth.    To have
failed in accomplishing so difficult a task can be thought
nothing strange : though the attempt has been made.
A half share of the Prize above offered was awarded
to this work : the other half being given to the Essay
recently published by Dr. Ballantyne of Benares,—
" Christianity contrasted with Hindu Philosophy."

In the following pages Sanskrit words, technical terms, and the like, have been written in English letters, according to the system of Sir W. Jones, as modified by Trevelyan. The vowels bear the Italian pronunciation; and the inherent vowel *a* is pronounced like the *u* in the English word *but*.

# HINDU PHILOSOPHY.

## Introduction.

HINDU philosophy, though known to only a small class of European scholars, deserves, on several grounds, the most attentive study. Tracing back its origin to the earliest ages of civilization, preserved during a long series of centuries, and taught by numerous admirers even in the present day, it presents to us the singular spectacle of the old world standing side by side with the new, and exhibits speculators like Empedocles and Democritus continuing their ill-based inquiries, while surrounded on every hand by the inductive philosophy of recent years. The curious notions it has defended, the singular compactness of the forms it has assumed, the length of time it has endured, increase its claims to attention. The classical scholar, as he learns its different views of the origin of the universe, the cases of the soul, the wanderings of transmigration, the primary elements, or the relation of inferior divinities to

B

the Supreme, finds himself transported to the schools of
Greece and Alexandria, and cannot fail to observe how
far the philosophies of the East run parallel with those
of classic lands, and in how many points the mode of
inquiry adopted, and the results attained, by the former
systems are identical with those belonging to the latter.
But apart from the mere interest attaching to its speculations, and the light they throw on the progress of the
human mind, there are circumstances connected with
them which render some portions of Hindu philosophy
matters of vital importance. Several of its most prominent doctrines lie at the very root of the religious
faith now current among the Hindus ; and these, in the
discussions aroused by Christian missionaries, are defended by their advocates with all the earnestness which
reverence for ancient authority and the deductions of
reason can place at their command. It must then be
manifestly desirable to know what these doctrines are,
what is the evidence adduced in their favour, and what
are the arguments by which they are defended.

To the various branches of this philosophy the most
celebrated names in the Hindu world have largely contributed. Including the later sections of the Vedas
themselves, a large proportion of their ancient literature is conversant about that philosophy, either in its
more speculative or more religious aspects. The poets
of India are comparatively few ; the authors of history
are still less numerous ; even the writers of the Vedic
hymns are almost unknown, except in name ; but the
philosophers of India are numerous and renowned.

Amongst all the sages of the land, none bear a more honoured name than VEDA VYÁSA, or KOPILA, or GAUTAM.

The subjects embraced within its boundaries are of the most extensive kind. They include all those fundamental inquiries into the nature of the universe, the origin of matter, the nature and history of the soul, the origin of virtue, and the chief end of man, which have engaged the attention of the wisest from the dawn of civilization to the present hour. They are, however, all regarded from a particular point of view, and are all placed upon a religious basis. Philosophy, cosmogony, and religion, the laws of logical method, the structure of plants, and the number of the vital airs, all find a place within these systems; and all these varied objects of inquiry are represented as having a religious character, as connected with religious aims, and as leading to religious rewards. Nothing can more clearly show the erroneous notions which have prevailed among the Hindus from the earliest ages respecting the nature and sphere of true religion, than the fact that its highest rewards are promised to those who attain to a correct knowledge of these different systems of learning.

Formerly the systems of Hindu philosophy were little known beyond their native soil. In European " Histories of philosophy " slight references were made to them: the notices of their doctrines were brief, partial, and frequently erroneous; and an English reader could obtain from such second-hand sources but very imperfect information as to what they really taught.

This is not the case, however, in the present day.
Numerous works, published by able scholars, are now
available to those who wish to inquire what the systems teach; and the merest outline of their doctrines
and general plan will show at once how worthy they
are of careful study.  Many of their conclusions, especially on questions of physical science, will raise a
smile in those who have been taught the well-proved
deductions of modern philosophy.  But smiles are not
all that they deserve.  The systems were formed when
the human race was in its boyhood; and they exhibit
the Hindu mind, even in that early age, as active in
the extreme.  Some of their results are very striking.
Though the Hindus were isolated amongst the nations of
the world, high generalization was carried on, and
broad principles of inquiry were adopted.  The Sánkhya
and Nyáya systems, for instance, even at that remote
period, distinctly advocated the very uncommon doctrine of a perfect separation between human souls and
the Divine.  The Nyáya system possesses elements and
advocates theories of which Aristotle might be proud.
Could we but catch all the finer shades of meaning
which the teachers of these systems attached to the
nomenclature they employed, and could we limit the
technical uses of terms simply to those ideas which they
were accustomed to convey, we might be able to understand the systems better than we now do, and perhaps
might find as large an amount of truth beneath their
surface as some enthusiastic scholars would lead us to
believe exists within them.  All technical language,

especially that which relates to the branches of mental science, is difficult, and requires to be accurately defined. How much more difficult is that of the Hindu systems, which purposely concentrated their doctrines in the most narrow compass, and employed a language which, till the days of Sir W. Jones, scarcely one European had ever studied. The spirit of the Hindu students was anything but childish; the aim they kept in view was the highest which men of their knowledge could possibly adopt; and the course of discipline prescribed to them was both painful and long continued. To ridicule those systems, or to contemn them on account of their absurdities, is to expect from the world's boyhood the experience of ripened age; to expect from the men who were groping in the gloom of unaided reason the finished conclusions which have been reached by the philosophic world in ages enlightened by the homely lessons and majestic doctrines of the revealed Book of God. One may rather find interest in the fact, which these systems fully confirm, that apart from a special revelation from heaven, the mind of man meets with insuperable difficulties in the constitution of the universe; that it moves within a narrow sphere of speculation, shut up to one or another class of errors; and that, left without Divine teaching, it roves like Noah's dove, not finding solid land whereon it may rest in confidence, and whence it may take a higher and farther flight to regions which are still unknown.

A further obstacle to the study of this philosophy is found in the form in which it has been presented.

Since better materials have become available for an examination of what Hindu philosophy really is, its study has appeared, even to willing scholars, peculiarly dry and repulsive. It must be confessed, that to master the great dogmas of the system, to observe their differences, and familiarly compare them with each other, is a task of no ordinary magnitude. The difficulty lies chiefly in two things. On the one hand, so far as present inquiries have extended, we have gathered scarcely any materials for securing a history of the notions which the systems develop, or personal notices of the individuals by whom they were advocated. Singularly complete in themselves, it is difficult to determine with exactness in what age they arose; which system was first in time; what was the order of progress in the development of each, or in the doctrines which are common to them all. On all these points, so useful in rendering such systems clear, we are only beginning to acquire information. The books survive, with their bare abstractions, a few names of learned adherents and commentators are added, a few isolated facts connect the philosophical with the political world, and the rest remains to the internal evidence of the systems themselves. Future researches may at least partially remove this difficulty.

On the other hand, the manner in which the systems are drawn out, and their notions expressed, is peculiarly uninviting. The chief books of authority are written in a very curt and oracular style, having been constructed with the special purpose of hinting the largest amount of instruction in the fewest possible words; and, as if this were not enough, the systems are all constructed in the synthetical form. The reader pursues, therefore, the course of study without any idea of the doctrines he will arrive at, or the turn which the inquiry will take. Though, like the philosophy of Greece, the systems of India are conversant much more about the structure of the mind than the phenomena of matter, yet the modes in which the two are presented differ most widely. The former is wonderfully individualized to us; we identify the philosophers as individuals like ourselves, moving in the society of their fellows; subject to human passions, engaged in public pursuits, and involved in the many vicissitudes of human life. Some of them are historical personages: they discuss common affairs; and from them take occasion to develop some recondite truth, that throws light on the structure and government of the world. Hindu philosophy, on the contrary, presents us with none of these pleasant accessories to abstract study. It gives us nothing like the dialogues of Plato, or the more familiar recollections which Xenophon recorded of his great master. It gives us only the dry abstractions, tells the names of its sages, and leaves us to find all the interest of the study in the theme itself.

The SUTRAS, which constitute the earliest works in which the various systems were drawn out on a settled plan, are short treatises in the Sanskrit language, of very compact form. So complete are they, and so concisely expressed, that it seems evident that the subject they treat of must have been thoroughly examined and discussed previous to their time, and all their branches and divisions properly developed. These Sutras have been the great standards of instruction in later times, and have formed the basis both of commentaries in which their tenets are expounded, and of other treatises in which native scholars have arranged their doctrines, according to their own judgment, with new illustrations and perhaps greater breadth of plan. Their brief aphorisms and concise style were intended to assist the memory, although they necessarily render the meaning obscure. Containing important truth expressed, or rather implied, in the fewest possible words, they received from the first the exposition of the living teacher, who clearly elucidated the meaning of each expression and exhibited its connection both with the context and the general course of the argument. Such is apparently the origin of the commentaries of various kinds with which the Sutras have been ever accompanied. The original author was most probably the first commentator, and stamped each aphorism and each word with the full meaning which he intended it to bear. The best commentaries have been written down, and again commented on by others. Thus have the systems been handed down from age to age and from one generation of students to another; and thus it is, that without new light from more correct systems, the same dogmas have been advocated in the schools of Hindu learning, with the same arguments and almost in the same terms, as were employed hundreds of years ago.

It will not be inappropriate to add here a few words concerning the general mode of student-life in India. The manner in which students were gathered in ancient Greece, and instructed in one or more branches of learning by individuals of note, resembles, to some extent, that in which Hindu students have been brought up during several hundred years. Considering the differences in the religious notions of the people, and in those ordinary habits which have depended much on differences of climate, the similarity appears very striking. India has no splendid colleges, like those of the European universities; no ancient corporate bodies, sustained by ample landed endowments, from which the expenses of students and the salaries of professors are annually provided. Yet its schools and seats of learning are numerous; the number of brahmins who are able to expound its ancient books of philosophy, is large; its courses of study are as extensive as the students can desire; and, like the universities of Europe, its learned men confer degrees of honour upon their successful scholars. At the present day, if a brahmin, fond of such pursuits, with a reputation for scholarship acquired during his own studies, and with a title of honour conferred by his teacher, wishes himself to become the teacher of others, he will open a *tola* or college, and invite students to attend his lectures. If he have a wealthy patron, he will assemble them in one of the halls of his patron's house; and lecture there upon his chosen theme. If he prefer it, he may secure a respectable house, in

some well-known seat of learning, as Nuddea, and
erect accommodations for his scholars within its premises.    Unlike the disciples of the Sophists, the
scholars pay no fees for their education: on the contrary, the teacher will furnish them with food, lodging,
and instruction gratuitously: and they will provide
whatever else is needed, as their clothes, books, paper,
ink, and oil, out of their own resources: their expendi-
ture, however, on these accounts, frequently amounts
to only eight or ten rupees a year.    The income of the
teacher is acquired in a manner quite different from
that of our European professors.    Learned brahmins
are always much respected by Hindu men of wealth:
and numerous are the occasions on which it is customary to give them presents.    At the time of festivals,
weddings, and feasts for the dead, they are invited to
the houses of the wealthy, are feasted, treated with
honour, and on their departure receive gifts of value.
These presents vary with the branch of science in
which they excel, with their reputation for learning,
the public esteem in which they are held, the number
of their scholars, and the fame of their school.    The presents include dresses, gold and silver vessels, ornaments
of numerous kinds, food, and also money.    A man of
learning often takes one or more of his scholars to such
assemblies, both to enhance his own reputation, and to
accustom them to respectable society: and the students
also obtain a share of the presents.    From gifts of this
kind the larger number both of teachers and students
in the Hindu schools of learning are supported, their

food procured, and their house accommodation provided. *Tolas,* or native colleges, of this kind, are scattered all over the province of Bengal; and one or more may be found in all the great villages. The zillah of Burdwan, for example, though not particularly celebrated for learning, contained, a few years ago, 190 Sanskrit schools and 1,350 students. Some places are more celebrated as seats of learning than others. In North India, for instance, Nuddea, Santipur, Tirhoot, and above all Benares, contain a large number of "colleges:" in South India, they are chiefly found in the provinces of Tanjore and Madura.

These schools are divided into three classes: those wherein general literature is studied; the schools of law ; and those of philosophy. In the first the subject matter of study embraces grammar, lexicology, poetical works, and rhetoric. In the law schools, the Dáya Bhága, Mitakshara, and especially the Institutes of Raghunandan, are the principal books of authority : though the latter is studied with an especial view to a knowledge of the ritual ceremonies of the Hindu religion. The students who enter these law schools almost always pass through the classes of literature first: the students of philosophy, also, generally spend years in the same preliminary pursuits, before they enter on a full consideration of the great philosophical systems. The study of these systems ranks the highest of all in general estimation : and those who thoroughly master the best works are comparatively few in number. They are men who must have spent many years in study of one kind or another before they could attain such knowledge. The systems are not held in like estimation everywhere. In South India the Vedánta is frequently studied; in Bengal the Nyáya seems most popular; in Upper India, though the Nyáya is very popular, the Sánkhya and Vedant find numerous adherents, the Vedant holding the highest place of all. In Benares followers of all these systems may be found, including the most accomplished of the learned men in Hindustan.

In the present day there are influences at work which will probably diminish the study of the ancient systems very considerably. In the great cities and towns of India, and chiefly in Lower Bengal, there has sprung up an intense desire to learn English, both for the pleasure which it gives and for the valuable appointments to which a knowledge of that language leads. This desire is drawing away the minds of the young brahmins from that Sanskrit learning, which in former days was their great path to wealth and honour; and on which they spent half their years. The *Káystha*, or writer caste, a most intelligent race, forbidden to study Sanskrit, have eagerly embraced the new opportunity offered for their advancement, and are competing with the brahmins for the fruits of real learning. The village Sanskrit schools are being deserted for English institutions: the brahmins, who taught in the former, can acquire better incomes by entering the latter. The demand for a sound vernacular education, now made by all true friends of the native population, will operate in

the same direction. Intelligent teachers are required
as pundits, and as the remuneration is good, it will pay
far better to prepare for such labour than to carry on,
for years together, those studies to which the class once
gave so much heed. At the same time, the spread of
better knowledge, and more correct notions, prevents
the brahmins from being so much honoured, and
receiving so many gifts at weddings and festivals as
they once enjoyed. They must therefore exchange
their study for a life of toil. Under these varied
influences, which will be the means of spreading sound
education and the practical results of true philosophy
over the country at large, the older systems will probably, ere long, disappear from their high platform of
authority, and be regarded only as ancient curiosities,
which few will care to preserve.

# PLAN OF THE WORK.

In view of the special aim of this work, viz., to expose the religious errors of Hindu philosophy, it will be well, at the outset, to give a general outline of the chief systems, that the place held in them by the religious errors may be fully understood ; next, to state clearly and fully the errors themselves, with the texts in which they are asserted, the arguments by which they are defended, and the illustrations by which they are made plain: and then to set forth the grounds upon which, even on their own showing, these dogmas must be objected to, as great and dangerous errors.   The essay thus naturally divides itself into three parts :—

PART FIRST : The Systems of Hindu Philosophy surveyed.

PART SECOND: The Religious Errors of these Systems stated.

PART THIRD: These Errors discussed and exposed.

# PART I.

## General View of the Systems.

———•◦•———

### THE VEDIC AGE.

RIGHTLY to appreciate the notions current amongst a people, it is necessary to learn in some degree the customs of their daily life; to consider, not only the deep religious emotions which stirred the depths of their nature, but the amusements of their idle hours; to see them at home, to hear their bazar talk, to know the objects by which they are daily surrounded; in a word, to realize those circumstances, objects, customs, which mould the thoughts, the habits of each generation, and gradually determine the current and the course in which their human life shall run. It will be well, therefore, at this point, briefly to consider that state of society in which Hindu philosophy first began to germinate, in which it was gradually reduced to a settled system, and by which those systems were determined and illustrated. To do this thoroughly would require a large volume. Puránic religion, notions, legends, and customs are passing before our eyes, and have been discussed and exposed again and again. Some of the most tenacious of these notions have been defended among the ancient philosophies of the land; but these again everywhere rest upon the primary rock of Vedic religion and Vedic life. The last controversy with the Hindu system must deal with these; and the man who shall specially provide the material for showing in a complete, satisfactory and convincing form, that Vedic life, Vedic sages, and Vedic authority were erring and human, instead of divine, will confer upon the agencies of Christianity in India a boon of incalculable worth. A far more summary view of these subjects will suffice for our present purpose.

The ARYAN race, from which the modern Hindus have sprung, had long since quitted the valleys of Media and Bactria, found their way across the snowy passes of the Hindu Koosh, and settled along the margin of the Punjab rivers and of the plains which they inclose. Successive emigrations increased their numbers, and enlarged their territory. They found on their arrival a native population, of Tartar origin, occupying the soil. They were of another lineage and spoke a different tongue: while the Aryans belonged to the great shepherd race which gave the Pelasgians to Greece and Italy, and the Teutonic tribes to Northern Europe. Their progress was so disputed, and the tribes of Dasyus which they drove back were so pertinacious in their resistance—they yielded so slowly to their conquerors, and so frequently plundered them— that long after the tribes had been swept away, their

name was employed as the common term to describe
a prowling robber.

When the Aryans first appear to history in the
pages of the oldest Veda, we see them a sturdy race,
active, intelligent, and warlike, of simple habits; living,
to a large extent, upon their flocks and herds; yet
dwelling in small towns and villages, and cultivating
with cereals and fruits the fields and gardens which
they have wrested from the earliest holders of the soil.
They continue to increase their numbers and their
territory; and to push southward and eastward across
the plains of Sirhind to the head waters of the Ganges
and Jumna, which they were destined to render so
famous in future days. Their settlements are evidently
greatly scattered; the land and the people are broken
up into sections, to a great degree independent of each
other, and often involved in quarrels. In some parts
arid plains spread out for miles; in others, thickets and
tangled jungle cover the country, in which live the wild
elephant, the tiger, the bear, the wolf, and many kinds
of deer.

With diligent hand they cultivate their fields and
gardens, watering them from the stores gathered in
tanks and ponds, covered with the horned singhara and
the blue lotus. Their wealth consists principally in
cattle, goats, horses, and sheep; and everything which
can tend to secure the retention or the increase of
these blessings is an object of intense desire. Their
petty wars and contests, whether with their kindred,
or with the aborigines, occupy a large share in

their anxieties. Their rivalries are numerous, their contests frequent, and their victories, as in other lands, are celebrated in the most spirited and joyous songs. They are living a natural active life, divided by the ordinary distinctions of society, and absorbed in the ordinary employments which shall defend their settlements and supply their wants. They possess many striking features of character, and are peculiarly distinguished by family attachments and ties. To them home is a sacred place, and the hearth the centre round which their affections most strongly twine. Affected by so many pressing wants, all the aspects of nature, on which they are dependent, impress them in the profoundest degree. The three seasons of the year, the cold bracing winter, with its sky of brilliant blue, the hot season, with its blinding glare and its terrific dust storms, and the rainy months, when the refreshing showers clothe the parched earth in carpets of richest green, are objects of vital interest.

Their religion naturally bears the character of their daily life. It has few objects of worship, and the rites that are paid to them are few and simple. The " One Great Creator," almighty, all-sufficient, has nearly passed from their view; mere remnants of tradition, in their most ancient songs, are all that speak his praise.

Their deities have a direct relation to the circumstances in which they dwell. AGNI, the god of light and fire; INDRA, the god of the firmament; VARUNA, the god of order; USHAS, the dawn, " the daughter of the sky," " whom age cannot touch;" the Maruts, the whirlwinds, the attendants of Indra; the Ashwins, the sons of the Sun, and a few others, thirty-three in all, are the deities whom they reverence.

To them light and fire in all their forms, applications, and uses, were objects of intense interest. Whether on the household hearth, on the sacrificial altar, in the brilliant day, or the terrific blazing of the kindled forests, they saw their mighty genial god AGNI, " the ever young " " Agni of the golden eye and golden hand." His praises therefore are frequent, the epithets applied to him are endless, and petitions for earthly objects of desire are unceasingly renewed. To INDRA, likewise, who rules the firmament, and bestows the blessings dependent upon rain and sunshine, they turn with longing eye. To him, the warrior god, they appeal for victory over enemies and the huge spoils that follow a successful raid. In the burning months of the hot season, when they see the arid plains cracking with the fierce heat, the trees losing their brilliant green, the herbage parched before their eyes, and all their cattle failing for thirst, they turn to him. It is Vritra, his enemy and theirs, that withholds the refreshing showers for which all eyes long. And when at length along the western horizon the vapours thicken, and the desired storm bursts in grandeur—when they see the blinding dust whirling in lofty columns on its mighty march, and the swift scud flies low along the ground—when they see the blue flashes which pierce the clouds, and hear the crashing peals of the awful thunder, it is Indra and his Maruts that are fighting the celestial battle on their

behalf. And when the driving rain pours from the heavy
clouds, and the earth drinking it in, all nature renews
its life, fresh verdure clothes the fields, and the birds
carol their joyous songs, it is to the mighty Indra, the
Conqueror, that their thanks are paid, and from him
that fresh blessings are humbly craved. The worship
paid is exceedingly simple, and is offered especially,
though not exclusively, on the family altar. In order
due, the rites are paid; thrice in the day, the sacred
log is laid upon the fire; each father of a house pours
upon its blaze the offerings of butter, repeats the prayers
or sings the sacred song. They speak to the gods on
most familiar terms, as to a petted child; pat them on
the back with praises, and because of their gifts express
a strong hope that the gods and they will be friends
again. They cry aloud at times for mercy, and plead
human infirmity as the cause of their errors. "It was
not our own doing, O Varuna! it was necessity, an in-
toxicating draught, passion, dice, thoughtlessness; even
sleep brings unrighteousness."

In those early days offerings of the soma-juice to
Indra were very frequent, and the *soma-yága* was celebrated in public by the village community in general.
The plant was gathered specially at the appointed hours,
its juice expressed, prepared and fermented; part was
poured upon the fire for the god, and the rest drunk by
the worshippers. It is evident, however, that the exhilara-
tion produced was by no means regarded with the feelings
with which modern Hindu society looks on drunken-
ness. The soma was taken in their worship and offered

to their god; and the excitement of mind and nervous elevation it produced were evidently regarded as a divine afflatus deepening their religious feelings, intensifying their fervour, and bringing them into closer communion with their deity. They attributed the same elevation to Indra himself, prayed him to drink deeper draughts, that his strength might increase; and little understood the moral character of their offering, when they praised him for securing his victory over Vritra by the noble [Dutch] courage with which the soma had inspired him. This was one of the earliest forms of rites, like the Dionysiac ceremonies, or the ceremonies by which the Marabout, the dancing Dervish, and the Shaker have endeavoured to attain artificial excitement in their outward worship: an excitement mistaken for that fervour of religious principle which ought to spring only from the heart within.

Expressing themselves thus naturally, holding a close communion with their various gods, and offering new prayers and praises as circumstances dictated, the hymns in which their litany was embodied gradually increased, and at length, apparently about a thousand years before Christ, seem to have been collected from among the scattered settlements in which they were honoured, and brought together in the form in which they now appear in the RIG VEDA. Writing was entirely unknown; they were transmitted from generation to generation entirely by memory, though special care was taken to transmit them with great correctness. There was no exclusive priesthood, as in later days, or at least only the germs of that exclusiveness had been avowed and were beginning to appear. Kshatriyas could offer worship, or receive fees; and even one sprung from the Dasyu race was permitted to contribute hymns to the worship of the Vedic gods.

Hundreds of years passed on. On every side the Aryan nation, with their Sanskrit speech, increased in number, extended their authority, and enlarged their territory. Their civilization rose to a higher level; their notions were enlarged, their habits were developed. Powerful kingdoms were established; and when their systems of philosophy appear, the nation at large, and the learned classes in particular, had reached perhaps the highest point of civilization and of mental vigour which they were ever permitted to attain. When Alexander entered the Punjab, all Upper India was in their hands. The vast plain of the Ganges to the hills of Rajmahal, the valley of the Soane, the rich lands of Oude and of Tirhoot; from the jungle slopes of the Siwalik hills, with the deadly Terai at their feet, to where the basaltic masses of the Vindhya range o'erhang the loamy plains watered by the swiftly-flowing Nerbudda; from the open fertile provinces on the Ganges to the hilly valleys and recesses of Guzerat and Rajputana, ARYA VARTHA, "the land of the Aryas," included them all. The Hindu kingdoms were numerous, and probably only a few were powerful. Kanouj, Benares, 'Awadh (Oude), Avanti, Indraprastha, Vesali, Sravasti, were the centres of independent principalities. The powerful kingdom of Magadh, or Behar, had its

capital at Rajagriha, and subsequently at Pataliputra.
Central India contained many such independent states.
The kingdoms in the Ganges plain, in Oude, and
Magadh seem to have been most completely Hindu,
and most subject to brahmin influence, custom, and law.
In Central India there existed much more freedom, and
other influences held considerable sway. Great changes
had passed over the country. As the Aryan race advanced in numbers and in territory, it seems clear that
they by no means exterminated the original inhabitants:
but when the latter submitted, permitted them to occupy
their villages and cultivate their fields: they were glad,
doubtless, to avail themselves of their services as la-
bourers. Though they lost their languages, and adopted
the language of their conquerors, many traces of such
original inhabitants exist throughout the provinces down
to the present day. Besides these, subdued and in a measure mingled with their conquerors, a border of native
tribes everywhere fringed the Hindu kingdoms, living
independent and free upon the hills, in the dense forests
and the pathless tracts; protected by swamps, or by hill
fastnesses, that their enemies could with difficulty approach. Small in stature, dark in features, living
hardly, of rude manners, limited in knowledge, fond of
drink, afraid of demons, seeking protection in charms
and spells, bound together in clans, they have remained
to this day, ill-treated by successive conquerors, but
really tamed by none; prepared to plunder all, when-
ever fit occasion should arrive.

Great changes had passed over Hindu society at

large.  The brahmins, ambitious of retaining the priesthood exclusively in their hands, and of ruling all classes
through their superstitious fears, had carried their efforts
for that purpose successfully through; had maintained
fierce contests with the Kshatriyas, and in the eastern
portion of the Aryan land had all but exterminated
them.   They stood, therefore, at length at the head of
Hindu society, and their authority was maintained with
a firm hand.   The caste system had been fully developed, and in it all ranks of society now found their
place.   A large body of Sudras had been formed,
partly, we presume, from the intermixture of the
Aryan with the native races, and partly from the degraded families of the purer castes.   In the west,
crippled though not exterminated, the Kshatriyas held
the states of Central India, filling the high plateau
watered by the Chumbul and the Betwa; mingled
largely with the native races, the Bhils and Mairs,
from whom they had wrested the many fortresses that
crown the isolated hills, amongst which, eminent above
all, stood the noble mountain of Abu, with the " Jewel
Lake" upon its lofty brow.   Even here, however, while
retaining more fully an independent rule, for religious
ordinances and the due performance of public festivals,
they were compelled to look to the brahmins, with
whom they had contended.

Occupied and cultivated, the country appeared probably the same as it does now.   In the villages and
along the high roads were seen the wide-spread banyan,
with its pillared walks, the home of the monkey, the

bat, and the "flying-fox;" the peepul, with its green, glossy, and pointed leaves; the caotchuc; the umbrageous tamarind and the bitter neem; the soft, pointed, feathery clusters of the bamboo; the mango, with its abundant wood; the clumsy jack-tree, with its ugly, lumpy, and far-scented fruit; the cotton-tree, with its silky fibres, the wonder of the Greeks; the tall, straight palmyra and date trees; the betel palm, with its slender trunk and feathery crown; and near the sea, the cocoa-nut, with its rich store of fruit. In the gardens, both rich and poor loved to look on the thick foliage of the asoka, with its heads of orange, crimson, and scarlet flowers; upon the sacred kusa grass; the purple, and orange, and red hibiscus. They loved to scent the fragrant lemon-grass, the bokul, with its white, sweet flowers, and the gondhoráj, "the king of scents." A profusion of vegetables and fruits filled their gardens and the public markets: the trailing cucumbers, gourds, and melons lay thick upon the cottage roof: the plantain, the custard-apple, the betel-creeper, and all classes of peppers and spices, beans and pease, yielded their stores for the comfort of all classes. These gardens were watered from the numerous wells with which the land was filled, or from the tanks, covered with water-lilies and bordered with green turf and shady trees: dense jungle ran along the mountain bottoms and sprang from the feverish swamps; while, over all, stood the mighty range of Himavat, clad with dense forests of the feathery pine, and crowned with the ever-glistening fields of stainless snow: a mighty range,

beheld from afar with speechless awe, and believed in
after ages to be the abode of the mighty Siva, who
through his streaming hair is fabled to have poured the
goddess Gunga, that, bursting through the rocky bar-
riers below, she might carry life, health, holiness, and
immortality to their millions of votaries in the burning
plains.

The villages were few and far between, built of mud
huts, or cottages of bamboo and mat, surrounded by
mud walls for self-defence, and governed by the little
fraternity which has maintained the municipal element
down to the present day.  The towns held the most
civilized portion of the community: some were large
and comparatively wealthy, containing houses of brick
and stone.  No temples were to be found in them:
their noblest buildings were the palaces of kings and of
the chiefs that surrounded them.  While in the country
a skilful agriculture produced abundant crops of wheat
and barley and rice, in the towns the various arts and
trades were in a flourishing condition: and from their
operation the brahmin teacher drew many an illustration of the principles he taught.  The smith could produce iron and steel of the finest temper, and work them
into swords and arms of the best kind.  The weaver
provided, of cotton and silk, dresses, both coarse and
fine, with plain or figured patterns, and of various
colours.  Precious stones and pearls were set by the
jeweller in earrings, bracelets, and other ornaments for
women; in caps, and arms, and tiaras for warriors and
kings.  Pottery of all kinds; vessels of brass and bell-

metal; embroidery of gold and silver thread, were all readily produced and highly prized. The wealthy rode in cars drawn by bullocks; the umbrella was borne only over the heads of kings; and the fine yák-tails of Tibet were carried before them in their honour. All warriors, high and low, sought to excel in archery: they rode in chariots, on horses, or on elephants: they defended themselves with bull-hide shields or fought with inlaid swords. Camels and elephants carried their camp equipage and supplies.

The amusements of the people were found in listening to the legends of their race; in gambling, for which houses were specially provided; in ram-fighting and cock-fighting; in exhibiting feats of strength; in riding, driving, and shooting with bows of strange strength at a peculiar mark.

The Hindu women in this earlier period of their history evidently enjoyed far greater freedom than was given them in later times. They could walk and ride abroad, were openly present at public festivals and shows, at the great marriages, and at great trials of skill and of strength, in which their own hand was the victor's prize. The oldest legends of the people, which are worked up as episodes in the Mahabhárat, and other authorities, relate the most interesting and attractive stories of their excellence; and show both men and women at times exhibiting an earnestness of principle, an amount of self-sacrifice that would not be expected in modern days. The faithful, unwearied search of Damayanti for her ruined husband; the bright in-

telligence of Maitreyi, and her desire to know all that
can be taught of the soul's future: the purity and faithfulness of Sita; the filial reverence and self-renuncia-
tion of Nachiketa; the high self-respect of Sunahsepha;
the intense fondness of all classes for family and home,
exhibit the Hindu character on a higher platform, and
as able to attain a higher excellence than in modern
and degenerate days.   Signs of that excellence exist
still.   In spite of the degradation of ages, in spite of
the lying, deception, and cringing subservience produced by centuries of oppression, the Hindus have
some noble traits of character remaining still.   Morally
ruined, often left the victims of passion which their
religion supplies no principles to control, in cooler hours
they are courteous, gentle, kindly, hospitable; and display an active intelligence, and a desire for knowledge,
which gratify all who are willing to instruct them.   As
compared with Mahomedans, they have always been a
favourite race with missionaries; and few can doubt
that, under the sanctifying influence of the gospel, they
will become one of the noblest races in all the eastern
world.

It is perfectly clear from these ancient legends, that
in the long series of years of which we now speak, the
claims of brahminism, though steadily pressed, were by
no means speedily settled; and the institutions and
manners of the people were by no means confined
within the limits which brahminical law subsequently
set around them.   The Kshatriya Visvamitra long
resisted with success the exclusive claims of the brah-

min order, and was at length admitted amongst them. King Janaka offered a similar resistance. A most striking illustration of the difference between earlier and later customs is seen in the fact that the Princess Draupadi was the wife of the five Pandu brothers, the chief of whom were Arjuna and Judhishthira; and that Vyása, their grandfather, married his brother's widows. In the different families and clans the household ceremonies and customs differed considerably from one another; and so sacred was ancient custom allowed to be, that even Vedic rule was not strong enough to set it aside. Families differed from each other in the braids of their hair, the shaving of their heads, the colour of their priestly dress, or in the materials employed in worship; and, as in Bengal to the present day, great families adopted different gods as the favourite objects of their reverence.

While retaining, however, very largely the ancient Vedic gods and ancient modes of worship, the whole nation developed to a much larger degree than at first that love for metaphysical speculation and for a life of contemplation for which they have become celebrated. Their religious system assumed a broader shape and occupied a wider field. Their ritual, confined almost exclusively to the elements provided by antiquity, was thoroughly settled, and its different portions classified and arranged. Their household ceremonies, administered by parents and priests for their children and scholars; the solemn sacrifices; the duties which every householder had to discharge, or every student had carefully to observe, were clearly and succinctly detailed. The four classes of priests required by Vedic service had their distinct duties assigned, and rules were adopted to assist them in the punctilious discharge of even the most minute service. The *adhváryus*, aided by the ritual prescribed in the YAJUR VEDA, prepared the place of ceremony, provided the materials, led up the animal, sacrificed it, and performed all the harder labour, muttering as they proceeded the usual invocations. The *udgátris*, directed by the SÁM VEDA, sang the sacred hymns. The *Hotri*, acquainted with the whole, as taught in the RIG VEDA, recited at the appointed times, in loud, clear tones, the holy texts, invocations, and prayers. While the brahmin superintended the whole, watched that mistakes were corrected, and saw that the entire rites were performed in due order. On all these topics explanations arose, minute directions were given; and as time went on, and the original import of particular ceremonies and sacrifices became lost, other explanations, even of the most puerile kind, were suggested, confirmed, and adopted. For instance, the great sacrifices, the *Aswamedha* and the *Purushamedha*, in which no doubt at first, in the early history of the race, horses and men were literally sacrificed, entirely changed their character; substitutes were provided for the victims, and the original custom and meaning entirely passed away. These explanations and minute directions became the nucleus of the BRAHMANAS of the Vedas, which contain many of them to the present day.

In this age, also, the first attempts were made to philosophize about the world at large. The laws of thinking, the laws of causation, were but dimly understood: thought wandered free and unrestrained; and it can be no matter of wonder that inquiries should be incomplete, facts ill-examined, explanations crude and puerile, and conclusions utterly unsound. Still the process was original; it was entirely unguided by the thinkers of other lands; it had to develop not only its object-matter, but the rules by which its own methods should be conducted; and it is, therefore, in the highest degree interesting as an exhibition of the modes in which the unaided reason of man carries on its inquiries, of the objects of contemplation which it chooses, and of the results at which it is able to arrive.

One of the strangest facts connected with this matter is, that the whole of these discussions were carried on, and those long and extraordinary treatises formed, without the aid of writing. Slowly weighed, prepared and thought out in the author's own mind, they were taught with infinite pains to students; by them learned by heart, together with the running commentary which expounded them; and were subsequently taught to others. The extent to which memory was taxed and developed was infinitely greater than anything exhibited in these latter days, when books may be weighed by tons and paper measured by the mile.

The earlier settlements of the Aryan race were scattered and much separated from each other; and even in their most flourishing days, the want of good roads,

the frequent occurrence of jungle tracts, of arid plains
and undrained swamps, must have greatly hindered
their mutual intercourse.  But wherever they went,
however far they spread, they carried with them the
hymns of their fathers and the religious rites transmitted to them from ancient days.  All were preserved
by memory alone, and all the ceremonies and customs
in which they had been trained were regarded with the
highest veneration.  While their faith and their life
were fresh and natural, new hymns were composed and
adopted in the various clans, or separate families, spread
over the country.  The ancient songs also were preserved with the greatest care; and at length the whole
were gathered, as we have seen, about a thousand years
B. C. into the collection known as the Sanhita of the
RIG VEDA.  Within three or four hundred years more
the ritual collections of the other Vedas, and the explanations and speculations of their Brahmanas were also
produced.  All were transmitted from generation to
generation.  The fact that they were so dependent
upon the memories of men who were continually dying
away, led them to make extraordinary efforts to master
the minutest detail, to learn each passage with the
greatest exactness, that they might be taught without
error to the generations that should follow them.
Many years, varying from twelve to forty-eight, were
spent by individuals in learning these works by heart;
and it is not improbable that the care employed for this
purpose by the brahmin families, the large amount of
learned lore to be transmitted, the necessity of having

a class devoted solely to its acquisition, and the consequent high authority they obtained, contributed to
secure the fulfilment of those high aims which their
ambition had formed, to be religiously the masters of
their entire race.    Besides, amongst the Hindus of
those remote ages, an amazing reverence existed for
literary compositions.    They thought nothing of mere
conventional rules; they fancied there was something
divine in these communications; and they reverenced
not merely the sentiments or the authority of the com-
posers, but regarded with profoundest awe each syllable,
each letter; and the very tones and emphasis with
which each should be pronounced.    The mispronoun-
cing of a single accent might mar the power of a
prayer !

In spite, however, of all their care, the circumstances
in which they were placed naturally produced in the
course of time various differences in the text of their
hymns and the proceedings of their ceremonies.    Different localities naturally acquired different " editions " or
" recensions " (*sákhá*) of the Veda: the families and individuals that followed a particular *sakha*, or " branch,"
were called a *charana :* and among the various charanas
there existed, in most places, *parishads*, or coteries of
well-qualified individuals, who were regarded as refe-
rees on all disputed questions of the reading of words,
syllables, or sentences of the sacred text.    As the compositions of various kinds increased, and the population
spread, these sakhas and charanas increased also.    There
were *charanas* that varied in their reading not only of

the Rig Veda Sanhita, the oldest of all, but of every Sanhita, of every Brahmana, and of the different compositions of which the collections were composed. And in spite of all precaution, through the deaths of individuals, the decay and extinction of different families, nothing would seem to be more clear than that, in some cases, hymns, rites, customs, and treatises, that were once well known, became obsolete, and eventually were entirely lost. So that the Vedas and other ancient works, including the oldest legends, are but a portion, though a considerable one, of the literary compositions which the fertility of the Hindu intellect and imagination put forth in ages when they received not the slightest aid from that art of writing which, in modern days, is deemed of essential importance to the existence of civilization itself.

Such were the people, such the land, such the attendant circumstances from which these ancient systems of philosophy sprang. Such was the history of their thinking; such the hard training, the painful toil with which their knowledge, their science were slowly gathered. Whatever be the character of their attainments, the results are entirely their own. Their scholars enjoyed few of those helps for attaining truth which so largely abound in modern days. They had none of the practical common sense education which surrounds a Protestant Saxon child from his cradle: they breathed all their life long a different atmosphere. They were not aided by the accumulated wisdom, experience, and conclusions of earlier civilizations. They knew no country but the Aryan land, and the broad border of rude native tribes, which cut them off from other portions of the globe. The material of their thinking, the rules of inquiry, they had to provide for themselves. They could start only from that platform of primeval civilization, with its remnants of Biblical tradition, which their fathers had brought with them from the Chaldæan plains. Their systems, therefore, are native and original ; and so far are objects of peculiar interest. It is not strange that their first attempts at philosophy should be loose, free, and unsatisfactory : that they should often fail to hit the mark at which they aimed ; that the research should be partial, the reasoning inconclusive ; and that to the eyes of a wiser age, both the processes and the results should appear puerile and ridiculous. The schoolmen of the middle ages, with all their great advantages, their masculine vigour, and their sometimes grand results, were not free from a like charge. And the failure was less unnatural, in an age when the teachers and thinkers were brahmins, who had pressed with unceasing vigour their claims to the exclusive priesthood, had fought with success the most desperate contests on behalf of their order, and now stood triumphant, the spiritual lords of the Hindu race. Teaching with high and undisputed authority, they dealt out with careless hand a great deal of what the world calls rubbish ; for true philosophy flourishes only when sifted by honest opposition.

The time for sifting at length arrived. About six hundred years before the Christian era a new class of

speculations in philosophy, and new theories respecting
the shortest mode of "liberating the soul," began to
find currency.   Existing notions were freely examined :
greater system, therefore, became the order of the day.
An artificial system of expressing the largest amount of
knowledge in the fewest possible words was invented,
and seems to have been received with enthusiasm.   The
brief aphorisms so formed were termed SUTRAS.   They
were constructed on peculiar principles, to which a key
was furnished; they rather hinted at knowledge than
expressed it; and, from the first, required the explanatory commentary which should declare all they were
intended to convey.   With a view to aid the priests in
their severe toil of learning by heart all the formulæ
necessary for their official duties, the directions conveyed in the Brahmanas of the Vedas were reduced to
a system termed *Kalpa Sutras;* and so easy did the process become, that many were induced to neglect the
Brahmanas, and study the Sutras alone.

The objects of philosophy were treated in the same
way.   The thinking became more clear; the principles
of inquiry more defined; reasons, arguments, and illustrations were brought forward in defence of the tenets
advocated; controversies became numerous and sharp;
and apparently, within a period of two or three hundred
years, the great systems which have come down to us
were sifted, arranged, and settled.   The order in which
they were started is not distinctly known; and to ascertain it is not a matter of vital consequence.   Most
probably the system now termed the SÁNKHYA was the

first that left the beaten track of the old Bráhmanas ;
and by its novel theories, so contrary to the current
brahmin notions, became the occasion of stimulating to
new inquiries, and rendering the arguments respecting
them more satisfactory and sound.    While exceedingly
free in its speculations, and on many important points
differing from ordinary Vedic doctrine, it partly saved
its position by not directly questioning the authority of
the Vedas, or of the brahmin priesthood.    As a matter
of doctrine and argument, the Vedánta system seems to
have been formed in direct reply to it.    The other systems were likewise propounded ; and at one time the Sánkhya, Yoga and Vaiseshika were denounced as heretical.
Brahminism, however, was very lenient where mere
speculation was concerned.    It was only a denial of its
authority that roused all its ire and called forth its most
active opposition.    This spirit was conspicuously exhibited in the case of Buddhism ; which, as it grew in
strength, directly attacked it in its most vital seats.

When that system was first formed, the strength and
the pretensions of brahmin exclusiveness had reached
their culminating point.    That class had driven the
Kshatriyas and all others from the priesthood.    They
excluded all knowledge of sacred books from the lowest
castes ; even those who sought to acquire that knowledge with a view to their elevation in another world
had to spend years in painful toil, in weary studies, and
in self-mortifications of the most bitter kind.    Practically, the lower castes were shut out from all such
aspirations ; and the spirit in which the priests desired

to deal with them is well exhibited in those cruel
" Laws of Manu," which were already partly current
among the Taittiriya clans for whom they were compiled.     Buddhism was the natural, popular reaction
from this grinding tyranny.   Its founder, SAKYA SINGH,
a Kshatriya prince, had studied deeply brahminical lore :
and at length prepared a system of his own, which, to
much of Kopila's Sánkhya doctrine, added a simpler
theory of relief from the ills of transmigration than
the Vedic system taught.   On the courses of transmigration, past as well as future, he dwelt very fully :
and laid it down that all classes, without those years of
weary study, could carry on the works of virtue, which
should infallibly end in final annihilation.   Apparently
pitying, with a large-hearted benevolence, the ignorance
of the lower orders, he encouraged them to attend his
teaching; preached his discourses in plain language,
with repetitions and explanations that made his doctrine
more clear and more impressive : and sought in every
way to render his instructions not the privilege of a
lordly few, but the heritage and the purifier of the most
despised.   Indirectly, therefore, he attacked the Vedas,
the brahmin priesthood, and ancient brahmin learning,
in their very heart; by showing that if his system were
adopted, the whole of them might be neglected without
harm.   Controversies of course arose, the brahmins
tenaciously defended their views.   But large numbers
enrolled themselves as his disciples : the system spread,
including brahmins as well as others within its pale : its
followers became exceedingly numerous ; and when at

length, under the great Asoka, it became a political power, it not only brought about the one great crisis in the history of brahminism, but at one time even threatened its extinction. After severe contests the tide of opposition was rolled back ; brahminism, once more triumphant, was considerably popularized, and the Puranic system was rapidly developed. Henceforth in Hindustan, all knowledge, all philosophy were confined to the brahmin caste. But little was the author of Buddhism aware that he was founding an awful system of religion; which when completed and carried into other lands by his successors, should subjugate the minds of half the human race for many, many centuries ; an awful system of fatal error, which while denying the existence of the Supreme God, should lead its disciples to take as their model, and the support of all their future hopes, an utterly ANNIHILATED MAN.

## NAMES AND CHARACTER OF THE HINDU SYSTEMS.

The various schools of Hindu philosophy which were formed under the circumstances we have now described are distinguished from each other by names expressive of their origin or of the opinions which they advocate. As we have seen, the doctrines of some are taken from the Vedas, or are at least consistent with the tenor of brahmin teaching, and the maintenance of brahminical authority. The speculations of others directly and indirectly tend to destroy that authority. The former are declared to be orthodox ; the latter, heretical. The

system of the Buddhists, and that of the Jains which
sprang from it, are the most ancient of the heretical
schools, and have been most largely followed : but
others have arisen and contended with brahminism in
later days. The schools which are reckoned peculiarly
orthodox are SIX in number, and are well known by the
names of the SÁNKHYA and YOGA ; the NYÁYA and
VAISESHIKA ; the PURBBA and UTTARA MIMÁNSÁ. These
systems, termed DARSANAS, always occupy a conspicuous place in any enumeration of the sacred shastres :
and inspiration is claimed for their respective authors,
who enjoy the highest reputation as men of learning.
Jaymini and Veda Vyása, the authors of the two
Mimansas, are reputed to have taken an important
share in the compilation and arrangement of the Vedas.
The six systems are not totally different from each
other. Owing to the great similarity in doctrine
and purpose existing between some of them, and the
contrast which therein they present to others, the systems form themselves into three groups or pairs ; and
their followers into three great schools. The VEDÁNTA
and PÚRBBA MIMÁNSÁ constitute one pair, as correlative
to each other and working to the same end. The
Púrbba Mimánsá expounds the "earlier" portion of the
Vedas, and describes the ritual ceremonies and acts of
devotion by which religious merit may be acquired.
The Uttara Mimánsá or Vedánta, expounding the
"later" books, the ·Upanishads, develops the higher
mode of meditation on the nature and attributes of the
Supreme Brahma, by which absorption into his essence

can be more speedily and effectually attained. The
SÁNKHYA in its structure and tenets differs widely
from the VEDÁNT: but is closely followed by the YÓGA of
PÁTANJALI. The NYÁYA and VAISESHIKA are also alike
in doctrine; the former being occupied chiefly with the
principles of investigation; the latter with the physical
inquiries which form the main purpose of its treatises.

All the systems deal with those familiar topics which
lie near to the surface of human life and human reflection. They all discuss the constitution of man; the
point in existence from which he starts; the aim of his
mundane life; the course he runs; and the sphere
awaiting him in another world. They examine his
relation to the Supreme and to the system of nature;
the structure of his frame; the universe in which he
dwells; the elements of which it is composed; the
beings with which it is peopled; the regions into which
it is divided; the heavens above, the worlds of dread
and punishment below.

The three pairs of systems, however, deal with these
problems differently; and are strongly contrasted with
each other in their fundamental positions, as well as in
the modes by which they account for the origin of all
things. The NYÁYA, giving special heed to the cause
of our sensations and the pursuits to which they lead,
looks outward to the world, whose varied objects produce those sensations, and stir the thoughts of the soul
within: and observing in the human organism five
channels of information respecting external objects in
the five senses, adopts unquestioned the theory of the

five elements, and develops all its consequences. Apart
from its excellent principles of investigation, it is a
more natural system than the others: it embraces a
wider range of topics; classifies them more correctly;
enters more deeply into their constitution; and arrives
at sounder conclusions respecting them than either
or both those systems have done. In its doctrine concerning God, the substratum of matter, and the operations of the human soul, it comes much nearer to
modern philosophy than they. The SÁNKHYA, arrested
by our emotions, which are of three kinds, and which
continually disturb the soul's " quiet," searches for that
which " enslaves" the soul, naturally free, and passing
by the active agency of a Supreme Lord, educes everything from the union of an eternal matter and eternal
souls acting by themselves. The VEDÁNTA, passing
below the surface of both external appearances and
internal emotions, looks at the question of Being, asks
What is, What is real: and, leaving everything that is
mediate and apparent, decides that there is but one
Existence and one Substance in the universe, the Supreme
Brahma. This explanation of their fundamental principles will render it easy to understand the details, now
to be presented, in which each of the systems has been
worked out. Having surveyed them separately, and
instituted a comparison between them, we shall be
better prepared to judge of their peculiar characteristics;
and to enter more deeply into their view of those all-
important religious questions of which they principally
treat.

It may be thought that the systems are in several essential points so completely opposed to each other, that they may well be left to that mutual destruction which such contradictions should involve. But the vitality of Hindu errors is not so easily destroyed. These errors have fought against each other for two thousand years, and live still. Stern consistency in the search after truth rarely belongs to any but the disciples of Bacon; to those who have been trained under the common-sense philosophy which governs countries where the Bible gives health to the intellect as well as to the heart. In the present day, these systems are by no means regarded as irreconcileable antagonists. However great their differences may have been thought in former ages, however fierce may have been their many discussions, however earnest their rivalries, their modern followers have long since adopted the comfortable conviction that the differences are reconcileable, and have arranged the various glosses and interpretations by which that reconciliation is secured. A mere reference, therefore, to the discrepancies between their systems is insufficient to silence the advocates by whom they are defended. In respect to their religious position, likewise, these native scholars are all at one. All are orthodox brahmins, who, whatever be their systems, honour the Vedas above all other books, pay complete respect to the current Hinduism of the day, perform the daily ceremonies, and observe the usual caste rules. Even the great doctrine of Kopila, which gave to his system the name of the *Nireswara Sánkhya,* "the Sankhya

without a God," can be held by his followers without
any suspicion that such speculations injure their religious standing; for they now argue that he does not
deny the existence of a God, he merely asserts that,
in the arguments he is discussing, that existence is not
proved.   The followers of all the systems fully recognize the divine origin and authority of the Vedas; and
they are, therefore, thoroughly at war only with those
who, like the Buddhists and Jains, dispute that authority.   Their philosophical creed is matter of opinion:
their daily life is ruled by the Puránic Hinduism
around them.   Their systems may furnish material for
study in quiet hours, or for the pleasant discussions
which whet the appetite at a funeral-feast.   But they
have little to do with them as men; and guide them
but little in the details of ordinary life.   Making, however, full allowance for these things, it is clear that
certain fundamental doctrines of the systems do differ
essentially from one another; and if truth be sought
as the result of sound and earnest inquiry, it is foolish
to give up the advantage secured by the fair exhibition
of such discrepancies.   Any accommodation in such
cases is impossible; and its adoption must tell both
against the systems and against the spirit of inquiry by
which their followers are guided.

# CHAPTER I.

## THE SANKHYA.

THE Hindu system termed Sánkhya was apparently the earliest formed among those which introduced the really philosophic age. Its author is said to have been the great sage, KOPILA: but though his learning and acumen must have been great, and his name is still highly honoured, very little is known of him except his name and his opinions. Legends declare that he was a son of Brahmá; an incarnation of Vishnu, or of Agni, whose name, like his own, denotes " fire;" he is numbered among the seven great rishis, or saints, and many marvels are ascribed to him. He was evidently a clear and independent thinker. Though a brahmin, and taught probably the vague theories current before his time, he struck out a path for himself; and no longer following the puerile comments and loose unsatisfactory philosophies of the Aranyakas and Brahmanas, he formed a compact system of his own, intended to explain the world around us in a broader fashion, and with greater consistency than any one had previously attempted. While largely using Vedic notions and materials, he quitted Vedic theories; and in important particulars reaches conclusions the very opposite of what the Vedas teach. It is probably both from the spirit and method adopted in his inquiries, that his

system is named Sánkhya. This term is derived from
the Sanskrit word *sankhyá*, which denotes " number,"
also " judgment," " discrimination." The doctrines of
the system are pre-eminently sought and defended by
" Reason," in opposition to mere authority, of which
the Brahmins at that period were very fond. " They
exercise judgment," says the Bharat, " and are therefore
termed *Sánkhyas*."

The question of its position among the other systems
is by no means settled, and is very difficult to determine. It has been argued that the Vedánt is later than
the Sánkhya because it acknowledges its tenets and
endeavours to refute them. M. Cousin, in reply, points
to the fact that all the systems quote each other, imply
each other, and argue with each other; the authorities
having been re-touched and interpolated in later times;
until it would seem that they all sprang into existence
on the same day. M. Cousin endeavours to find a
test of age in the nature of the doctrine. He argues
that the system which discusses only a particular point,
is later than one which treats of truth in general; and
that a system, which is more free in its principles of
inquiry, and pushes them to a higher range of truth, is
later than one which cleaves to authority, and merely
repeats opinions already formed. On these grounds he
places the Sánkhya at a later period than the Vedánt.
The argument will apply to the Sánkhya as against
the Upanishads, but not to the other systems: and it
has been argued, that the Sánkhya was prior in time;
it took the Upanishads and erroneously represented

their texts as concurring in the doctrines of its own system; the Vedánta was called forth to show what the true system of the Upanishads was, and prove that the views of the Sánkhya were misrepresentations. The latter opinion seems to be the more popular among European scholars.

The Sánkhya system contains two grand divisions, which differ on the vital question of the existence of a God. One is termed the *Seswara* Sánkhya, the *Sánkhya cum Deo;* the other is named *Niréswara Sánkhya*, the *Sánkhya sine Deo.* The latter is Kopila's system: the former is the YÓGA of Pátanjali. On general doctrines the two coincide. The oldest authority of the system is the work entitled *Sánkhya Pravachan Sútras.* It is attributed to Kopila, and is evidently a work of great value; all its positions are well discussed, and an ample store of material is provided for the student of the philosophy. This work, as usual, has been commented on and annotated in the *Kopil-Bhásya*, or *Sánkhya Pravachan Bhásya*, written by Vigyána-Bhikshu. The most valuable authority of all is the SÁNKHYA-KÁRIKÁ, a collection of memorial verses by Iswar-Krishna, in which the system is embodied. This most admirable work is based upon the Sutras of Kopila; it takes up all their doctrines, arranges them in perfect order, reproduces their arguments and illustrations, avoids controversy, and gives a clear, complete, and logical view of the system and of the mutual bearing of its several parts. The work is very brief, and contains only seventy-two slokas. Its great value has caused other

works to go out of use, including even the original
Sutras on which it is itself based. It has been commented on by learned scholars, especially by Gaurapád,
who has written the oldest and best commentary.

Both these works on the Sánkhya philosophy are
now available to students who know but little of
the Sanskrit language. Of the two, the more valuable,
from its completeness, is the translation of the Sánkhya
Kárika, by Professor H. H. Wilson. This book is a
quarto volume, most handsomely printed; it contains the
Sanskrit text of the Karika, and of the Bhasya of Gaurapád; a complete translation of both, and a comment
by Professor Wilson himself, containing numerous elucidatory extracts from other native authorities that
throw light on the subject. Every student of the
system should reckon the complete study of this work
a duty of the first importance. Colebrooke's Essay on
the Sánkhya describes the system most completely, from
the Kárika, with additions from other authorities. Dr.
Ballantyne has lately published a translation of Book I.
of Kopila's Sutras, with the commentary; and thus made
another valuable contribution to the list of original
works. After the completion of these Sutras, which
are most admirably arranged, and go fully into the
subject, there will be little to desire, on the side of
Kopila's division of the Sánkhya system. Dr. Ballantyne has also translated Books I. and II. of the Yóga of
Pátanjali, with a brief commentary. These books
bring out clearly the great questions upon which their
author and Kopila differ.

Kopila's philosophy was entirely new. The Upanishads had been gradually developing in a clearer form
the pantheist doctrine that the Supreme Brahma was
not only the author of the universe, but that he is the
universe, including human souls. Kopila taught that
in that universe there are two primary agencies, Nature
or matter (Prakriti) and Souls; but there is no Supreme. Souls have existed in multitudes from eternity;
by their side stands this Prakriti. For eternal ages the
two remained separate: at length they became united,
and the universe in all its forms was developed from
their union. The products of that union are twenty-
three in number; so that twenty-five principles explain
everything; of which soul and nature are the chief.
He proceeds to explain how by the union first is produced the individual man in his germ and his full development; and then how the world and universe
around are aggregated. The great evil of human
existence is this union between soul and nature; it
causes all the pains of life; and the endless transmigrations which the soul makes from one gross body to
another. The soul which knows the Sánkhya system
can secure the separation, and transmigration will at
once cease. To all this the Yóga system adds, that
besides the two primal agencies, there exists a Supreme Lord, and that intense devotion to him will
secure the same desired end. A brief outline of the
systems will show how these doctrines are laid down
and defended. The SÁNKHYA KARIKA embraces eight
distinct topics.

E

§ 1. The *object* of the Sánkhya, as well as of the other
branches of Hindu philosophy, is the removal of human
pain by the final and complete liberation of the individual soul.　This pain is of three kinds; it proceeds
from one's self, either by bodily disease or anxiety of
mind; from some fellow creature; or from the accidents of divine providence.　Temporal means merely
alleviate these pains in the present life, and they frequently return.　Even the revealed mode of religious
worship, which has final liberation in view, which en-
joins sacrifices and prayers, is ineffectual.　For it is
impure, because it requires the sacrifice of animals; it is
defective, since even the gods, who have attained its
highest rewards, perish at the appointed period; and it
is excessive, because the happiness of one being is
secured at the expense of the good of others.　These
means are all insufficient.　True wisdom alone gives
a permanent deliverance, and secures an absolute termination to all the ills of human existence.　This wisdom
consists in a true discrimination between the principles
and elements of the material world and the sensitive
and cognitive principle in man, the immaterial soul.　To
secure this discrimination, and to show how it may be
attained, is the distinctive aim of the Sánkhya.

§ 2. *Principles of investigation.*—In order to obtain
wisdom, three kinds of evidence are admissible, viz.,
*perception, inference,* and *affirmation.* [*Analogy,* added
by Gautum, is included in inference; and the *Tradition*
of Jaimini belongs to affirmation.] Intuition is the
only other legitimate source of knowledge, but it is con-

fined to superior beings.   The *perception* of the senses
is allowed as the first kind of evidence.   *Inference* is of
three kinds : (1.) Inference of an effect from seeing its
cause in operation.   " It will rain, because clouds are
gathering."   (2.) Inference of a cause from observation
of its effects.   " There is fire on that hill, for I see
smoke."   (3.) Inference from a relation different from
both.   The colour of a flower is inferred from perception of its scent.   The saltness of the sea is inferred
from that of some of its waters.   This is the inferring
the existence of some correlatives, from the known
existence of others.   *Tradition* or *affirmation* denotes
the authority of the Vedas, whose texts are reckoned
inspired by Brahmá : also the recollections of those who
remember events in their former births.   More generally it includes all oral communication, especially if it
comes from those who are celebrated teachers.   From
all these sources, then—the direct perceptions of sense,
the indirect inferences of reasoning, and the *dicta* of
inspired or celebrated authority—this wisdom, which is
to liberate the soul from pain, may be derived.   The
last is held by the Sánkhya very much in subordination
to the second, and comparatively little weight was at
first allowed to the Vedas, in a system which, in several
important points, flatly contradicts them.

§ 3. *The twenty-five principles.*—The Sánkhya system
next considers the various categories or objects of knowledge to which the soul must apply itself, and in respect
to which true wisdom is to be acquired.   These principles are *twenty-five* in number.   They are stated in

the order of their origin, and are all regarded in relation to causality.

The first and chief is *Nature* (*Prakriti*), the plastic
origin of all things. It is termed *pradhán*, or chief,
from being the universal material cause, the prime
cause of all things. It denotes not ordinary matter,
which is reckoned gross; but the eternal matter,
whence the latter has sprung. It is without beginning,
without parts, inferrible from its effects: itself unpro-
duced, but productive of other things. We shall consider this principle at greater length hereafter.

The second principle is *Intelligence* (*mahat* or *buddhi*).
It is the first product of nature: increate, prolific, itself
productive of others.

The third is *Self-consciousness* (*ahangkár*); its peculiar
function is the recognition of the soul, the *self*, in its
various states. In perception it declares that objects of
sense concern *me*. It is the product of intelligence, and
produces principles which follow.

The next five principles (4-8) are the five subtle
particles, or atoms of things (*tanmátra*). These are
imperceptible to the gross senses of human beings, but
may be cognized by superior intelligences. Consciousness is their origin, and from them spring the gross
elements.

*Eleven organs* (9-19), (*indriya*), follow next in order,
the organs of sense and action: of which ten are
external and one is internal. The organs of *sense* are
five: the eye, nose, tongue, ear, and skin. The organs
of *action* are also five: voice, hands, feet, the termina-

tion of the intestines, and the organ of reproduction. The mind (*manas*), which denotes (as in the Nyáya) the sphere of living and present consciousness, serves both for sense and action. These eleven organs, with intelligence and self-consciousness, constitute thirteen instruments of knowledge. They are likened to three warders and ten gates in the human constitution. An external sense perceives: the internal one examines: self-consciousness applies itself to the recognition of its state; intellect resolves: an organ of action executes.

*Five elements* (20-24) are produced from the five subtile particles. (1.) *Ether* has the property of audibleness, being the instrument of sound. (2.) *Air* has two properties; it is audible and can be touched. (3.) *Fire* has three, audibility, tangibility, and colour. (4.) *Water* has four, adding to the three last-mentioned the quality of taste. (5.) *Earth* has five, having that of odour in addition.

The last principle (25) is *soul* (*purush, puman, átman*). Like nature, it is not produced, but is eternal. But, unlike nature, it produces nothing from itself. It is multitudinous, individual, sensitive, eternal, immaterial. The Yóga ascribes these qualities also to God, the Iswar, who is the ruler of all.

In relation to causality, these principles are thus described in the Káriká, sutra iii. "Nature, root all, is no product. Seven principles (*buddhi, ahangkar,* and the five subtile elements) are products and productive. The sixteen following are products only. Soul is

neither a product nor productive." These are the
principles about which the system is conversant.

A few words must here be added in respect to the
three principles which lie at the root of Kopila's
system. His views seem most strangely to confound
the products of matter and mind; and it is difficult for
those who have been taught from the cradle to think of
intelligence and consciousness as purely mental states,
to understand how he can have fallen into such serious
errors. But the explanation is near at hand. It must
first be clearly understood that by *Prakriti*, his primal
agency, Kopila does not mean ordinary matter. In his
view it is an extremely refined essence, an undefinable
something, different from soul, and yet capable of
bringing forth the very universe. To this essence and
primary agency soul is united. What happens?
Tracing back the soul's most active life, in the daytime
as contrasted with night, in manhood as contrasted
with infancy, Kopila seems to have hit upon the idea
that until it is united with body in some form, the soul's
powers lie in a dormant state. Those powers are not
exerted until adequate occasion calls them forth. He
then teaches that when soul is first united to rudi-
mentary matter, intelligence, the first dawning of
mental life and power, begins to appear. But mis-
taking occasion for cause, he calls this intelligence the
product of "nature," instead of the product of soul,
*occasioned* by the union between the two. As intelligence continues to act, there springs up within the
sphere of its activity the thought of *self*. Farther on

within the sphere of self-consciousness are produced the
germs or subtle particles (notions) of the five elements :
notions of the organs of which the body is constructed ;
and farther on, as Berkeley thought, the notions of an
outer universe. It is not improbable that, from some
conviction like Berkeley's that every man had his
own universe in his own mind, Kopila, by tracing the
process of intelligence and thought back to its first
steps, arrived at the doctrine expressed in these first
principles.

§ 4. *The object of soul* and the *means of accomplishing
it.*—This most important branch of the system is next
discussed ; and herein one of its radical deficiencies is
exhibited. Soul, it is declared, existing alone with
primeval nature, but itself unable to produce anything
whatsoever, is united to nature in order to contemplate
it and be abstracted from it. Neither can accomplish
the end by itself; both therefore join together, just
as the lame and the blind join together for mutual
guidance and locomotion in a journey. How the union
begins, and when it begins, are circumstances not at
all satisfactorily explained. By that union *creation* is
effected, and all the objects in the universe are developed. This creation, as we have already mentioned,
has respect to two things ; first, to the residence of the
soul, and secondly, to the sphere in which its existence
is to be passed.

(*a.*) As to the soul's *residence.*—It obtains for itself a
*subtile body,* composed of seventeen principles, of the
finest rudiments. They include intellect, self-conscious-

ness, and mind (2, 3, and 19), with the other organs
and instruments, conjoined with particles of five sorts,
all in the most elementary and refined form. This body,
which the Vedas declare to be of the size of a thumb, is
called the *Linga Sarír* or *Sukhma Sarír.* It is the first
creation; it is primeval, produced at the very earliest
development of principles from the original *prakriti.* It
is unconfined, too subtile for restraint, swift as the wind,
and cannot enjoy till it has a grosser body. This subtile body is the abode of the soul so long as it does not
obtain absorption; and it travels with the soul in all its
migrations. The *grosser bodies* through which they
migrate are composed of the fine elements. They are
perishable, while the subtile body endures. It is doubtful whether Kopila speaks of a third body between
these two; some of his commentators consider that he
does, others that he does not.

(*b.*) The *sphere* in which the soul resides is also produced with a view to subserve its purpose of contemplating nature and being freed from it. The *corporeal
creation,* different from man, includes eight orders of
superior beings, and five of inferior ones. These thirteen classes, with man, are distributed in three worlds.
The eight orders of *superior* beings include the gods,
demigods, demons, and evil spirits well known in Hindu
mythology, Brahmá, Prajapatis, Indras, Pitris, Gandharvas, and the like. The *inferior* orders comprise
quadrupeds, birds, reptiles, fishes, and insects, with all
vegetable and inorganic substances. The three *worlds*
are these. Above are the abodes of the superior beings,

in which virtue and happiness prevail. Below are the
abodes of darkness, in which dulness and gloom abound.
The human world of misery lies between, in which
foulness, activity, and passion prevail. Through the
three the soul wanders, suffering or enjoying till it is
liberated. Much of this doctrine is taken directly from
the Upanishads.

(c.) An *intellectual creation*, interior to the soul, is also
justly recognized, as well as its own body and the
universe, the external abodes which it occupies. This
is called *pratyay-sarga* or *bhāb-sarga*. It consists of
the affections of the intellect, its sentiments and faculties. Described as to their effects upon the soul's object, these affections are divided into four classes, and
are fifty in number. Of these, five *obstruct* the soul.
They are error, conceit, passion, hatred, and fear.
Twenty-eight *disable* it in its progress, owing to defects
in the organs of the body. Nine *content* the soul, five
internally and four externally. Eight species tend to
*perfect* it by preventing the evils both in it and around
it. Five of these are external means, and include
reasoning, oral instruction, study, amicable intercourse,
and purity. These are minor parts of the system, and
show how ingeniously all things are introduced into
the account of the condition and engagements of the
soul.

(d.) Connected essentially with this creation are the
three great *qualities* (*guna*) which occupy so large a
space in Hindu philosophy, and by which the ancient
sages endeavoured to account for the admixture of good

and evil in the world. The description of them and of their tendencies does not differ from that presented by the Vedánt. They tend upwards or downwards, or retain the soul in the middle sphere of passion and activity, encouraging its course towards greater purity and ultimate success in its pursuit of absorption, or drawing it lower and lower into wickedness, gloom, and despair. These qualities enter into the very composition of nature, from the first development of created objects, and co-operate together by a union of opposites; as a lamp is composed of oil, wick, and flame. They are compared to the rope which prevents a horse from running off. Taking up one meaning of the word *guna*, viz. a cord, the commentator, in language more striking than polite, says, " These ' qualities ' are the cords which bind the *purush-pasu*, the brute-like soul."

(*e.*) The *intellect* has eight kinds of disposition: four good, four evil. The four good are virtue or merit, knowledge, disposition, and power. The four evil are their opposites, vice, ignorance, passion, and weakness. These dispositions abide in the intellect, and according to their influence will be the history of the soul. These are connected again as intellectual and corporeal, in which they are respectively cause and effect. Virtue, knowledge, and the like, are efficient causes of the bodily conditions. The corporeal include the different periods of life, viz., embryo, infancy, youth, and old age. According to the admixture of these dispositions will be the end with which the soul meets. Thus, for instance, the soul which possesses dispassion without knowledge, obtains only absorption into nature (*prakriti laya*). It obtains a resolution of its constitution into the eight primary elements. It does not get real liberation, and the soul migrates afresh. *Devotion to God* is declared by the Yóga to be the best means of obtaining beatitude through absorbed contemplation. The devotee will repeat the divine syllable OM, and meditate upon its meaning. Thereby he will propitiate the deity and receive liberation as his reward. This is the doctrine taught by the Yóga; and much care is spent in showing the scholar how the process may be rendered complete, and the reward perfectly secure.

§ 5. Hitherto nothing has been discussed beyond the elements of the creation, from which the categories of the science are derived. Nothing has been taught concerning the *existence* and *attributes* of *God*. This important topic will be treated in the Second Part of this essay. It will suffice here briefly to state, that in the Sánkhya of Kopila, that existence is altogether denied; though he allows a kind of inferior divinity with limited powers, produced, like other elements of the universe, on the first development of nature. Pátanjali, on the other hand, in the Yóga system, fully acknowledges the existence of an Omniscient and Eternal God, whose name is GLORY (OM).

§ 6. The *manner* in which the principles or categories of the Sánkhya may be *discovered* is another of the subjects of which it treats. " Sensible objects are known by perception: things beyond the sphere of sense are learned by inference; a truth which cannot be learned from perception or inference may be communicated by revelation. Nature, owing to its subtilty, cannot be perceived, but is inferred from its effects. Intellect and the other derived principles are effects; something must be their cause, and that is set down as Nature." This introduces the subject of *causation*, on which the Sánkhya teaches a peculiar theory. The Sutras of Kopila speak very distinctly respecting it.

In aphorism 79, he lays down the great doctrine of antiquity: "A thing is not made from nothing." (*Návastuno nastu siddhih.*) (81.) "The product of something is something, and of nothing, nothing." (115.) "A nonentity cannot be developed into an entity; like a man's horn, it is an impossibility." Effects, therefore, are educts, not products or creations of new things. Oil is in sesamum before it is pressed; milk, in the udder before it is drawn; and rice, in the husk before it is shelled. (116.) "There must be a material from which the new product comes." (117.) "Else might anything occur anywhere at any time," without a reason. It will be seen hereafter that, although this principle may be made to bear such an interpretation as to include the Christian notion of sufficiency of power for creation existing in an Almighty God, by Hindu philosophers it was interpreted as teaching that for every material effect there must exist a *material cause*. That God, "who is a Spirit," should in any way produce a material universe was by them regarded as an utter impossibility. The very principle stated above (Sutra 79) would be brought against the doctrine.

Sutra 79, therefore, equals in its force Sutra 116. The Greek principle, τὸ γιγνόμενον ἐκ μὴ ὄντων γινέσθαι ἀδύνατον, seems to have been applied in the same way.

Again (b), he says (118), "A thing possible is made from that which is competent to produce it." Causes, whether material or efficient, must be adequate to the object they produce. Cloth, not pottery, is made from yarn. Milk, not water, is taken to make curds. A potter does not weave cloth, but makes jars and vessels from his clay and wheel.

(c.) A more important principle laid down is (119): "The product is nothing else than the cause itself." A piece of cloth does not differ essentially from the yarn of which it was woven: as an ox does differ from a horse. Barley, not rice, is grown from barley-corns. (120.) "Production is only manifestation" of what previously was. As the whiteness of white cloth is manifested on the removal of dirt, so, by the operation of the potter, the pot is manifested; so oil is manifested from sesamum by pressure: a statue, from stone by the operations of the sculptor; and rice, from the husk, by threshing. (121.) "Destruction," he adds, "is only the resolution of a destroyed thing into its causes." [Násah Kárana layah.] The wise may sometimes trace out the resurrection of an object after such destruction. Thread becomes earth: earth is changed into a cotton-tree; the cotton-tree gives cotton; thence thread is again woven. So is it with all entities.

(d.) Concerning the ultimate cause, the following principle is laid down: "There is a general cause which is undistinguishable ;" and many arguments are adduced to support it. Thus, it is said, specific objects are finite ; they are multitudinous, not universal : there must, *therefore*, be an all-pervading cause. " Homogeneousness denotes cause." A lump of clay is implied by an earthen jar; a gold crown implies the bullion from which it was shapen ; and a rigidly abstemious novice implies that his parents are brahmins ! The great argument is, the issuing of effects from causes and the re-union of the universe with its original cause. The tortoise puts forth his legs and draws them in again : so at the general destruction of all things, the five elements, of which the three worlds are composed, are re-absorbed in the inverse order of that in which they were developed ; returning, step by step, to their first cause. It is singular that, with so much that is true in this theory of causality, Kopila should have steadily adhered to his dogma that lifeless, inert matter was that primary cause ; and that, in spite of all this reasoning, the existence of a GOD could not be proved.

§ 7. The *existence of soul*, and its *attributes*, form another prime topic in the Sánkhya system. (*a.*) The first argument is this : " The assemblage of sensible objects is for another's use." A bed is for a sleeper ; a chair, for a sitter : the person who uses these things must be a sensitive being, of a nature opposite to theirs. So the universe is full of sensible objects, that are endowed with the three qualities, and are inanimate. The converse of them must exist, and must discriminate them from itself: the being which does so is SOUL.

(*b.*) Another argument is: "There must be superinten-
dence" in the three worlds; as there is a charioteer
to a car: the superintendent of matter is the soul.
(*c.*) "There must also be one to enjoy;" a spectator
of the universe, who can derive pleasure from its contemplation. (*d.*) "There is a tendency to abstraction;"
both the wise and unwise desire a termination of their
wanderings, their incertitudes of pleasure and pain.
The only being that can feel this desire, or make efforts
to realize its object, is soul. Soul, therefore, on these
several grounds, must be reckoned a separate and distinct entity or class of entities in the universe, whose
history alone can explain why that universe exists as it
now is and has been.

About its existence, however, there is little dispute.
The question is rather about its attributes. Kopil in
his discussion of it first declares, that soul is something different from body; and adds, that as light does
not pertain to the unintelligent, it must be the essence
of the soul. The great doctrine of the Sánkhya, however, is that soul is multitudinous. The Vedánta
teaches that all souls are emanations from Brahm, and
there is but one soul, the great soul, in the universe.
All the great systems of philosophy in ancient days
held something of this view. But Kopil clearly lays
down the doctrine that the souls of all beings are separate, individual, co-ordinate, perhaps, in their nature,
but independent of one another. There is not one soul
pervading all bodies, which are placed on it "as precious gems upon a string" (Vedánt). (*a.*) " Birth,

death, and the different stages of life are allotted individually." If one soul animated all bodies, one being
born, all would be born; one dying, one being blind
or deaf, one seeing, hearing, or speaking, all would die,
be blind, or see, or speak. Birth is not a modification
of the soul: that is unalterable. Death is the abandonment of its organs by the soul, not its own extinction.
(b.) "Occupations are not at one time the same universally." If one soul animated all beings, all would be
stirred by one impulse. Whereas, some follow virtue;
some, vice; some restrain passion, some indulge it;
some live in error, others seek "wisdom." (c.) Qualities also affect differently. Some are happy; some are
miserable. "The gods are happy; men unhappy: the
lower animals, dull." In discussing these points Kopil
argues against the Vedánt theory distinctly; and endeavours to adduce Vedic evidence for his own doctrine;
of course, unsuccessfully. "The soul," he adds, "is
altogether free: it is a witness, while united to body.
It is really indifferent to pain and pleasure; its nature
is constant freedom."

§ 8. The last topic of the Sánkhya is a *comparison* of
the *attributes* of the several principles. In this the two
great principles, the material and the immaterial, the
discrete and undiscrete, the perceptible and imperceptible, are contrasted with each other. *a.* A " discrete "
principle, one of the products of " nature," is causable.
Hence it is un-eternal: it is also inconstant; at one
time it appears, at another, not. It is unpervading,
does not enter into all, and is confined to its local

sphere: it is also mutable, and changes from one to another. Again, the "discrete" products are multitudinous; there are as many minds, intellects, self-consciousnesses, and so on, as there are souls in bodies. They are supported, resting each on its cause; they are involvable, merging into one another; conjunct, consisting of parts, as sound, taste, &c.; and they are governed, being dependent upon another's will.

*b.* The "undiscrete" principle is the opposite of all these, and exhibits none of these relations of dependence and inferiority. Both the discrete and undiscrete possess the "three qualities." The latter, Nature, has them of its own right; the former derive them from the latter, whence they are themselves drawn: just as black yarn makes black cloth. They are undiscriminating or indiscriminate. Nature is not distinct from itself, nor are the "qualities" separate from it: indeed Nature is their aggregate. They are objects of apprehension to every soul external to the other, but subjects of that one. They are also common; they are irrational and unsentient, just as insensible clay produces an insensible pot. They are prolific, inasmuch as they produce. Nature produces intellect: intellect, self-consciousness, and so on.

Soul has no "qualities:" it is discriminative; it is no object of enjoyment; it is several or peculiar; it is sensitive; it is unprolific, and produces nothing. In these respects it differs from the other principles. From the contrast between it and them, it follows that soul is not an agent, but " witness, bystander, spectator,

F

solitary and passive." It is only through its union with insensible body, that the latter seems sensible; though its qualities be active, it is the soul that appears as the agent. For its great work of seeking deliverance, Nature, though inanimate, prepares the soul, "just as it is the function of milk, an unintelligent substance, to nourish the calf." Nature in its dealings with soul is finally likened to a female dancer; she exhibits herself to soul as an audience; and is reproached with shamelessness for so frequently exposing herself to the spectator's gaze. When she has been seen and understood, she desists, having sufficiently shown herself. He desists, because he has seen her; there is no further use for the world; yet the connection between the two still subsists. In all this discussion, the fact that mind in the world is the great source of power, and the efficient agent in causation, is totally forgotten. The chemical action of substances upon one another is also wholly lost sight of. The connection between soul and nature, the mode in which it originates, and the reasons for which it occurs, are exceedingly weak points in the Sánkhya system.

The following is the conclusion of the whole. By attainment of spiritual knowledge, through the study of the twenty-five principles, from the conviction that the whole universe is ideally produced from self-consciousness, and has no real existence apart from it; from the acknowledgment also that Nature, the root of all, is simply the congeries of the three "qualities," the eternal matter of which they are the component parts, the conclusion, incontrovertible upon such reasonings, is reached and proclaimed—" NEITHER I AM, NOR IS AUGHT MINE, NOR DO I EXIST!" Possessed of this self-knowledge, soul contemplates, at ease, nature thereby debarred from prolific change, and precluded therefore from every other form and effect of intellect, but that special saving knowledge. Yet soul remains awhile invested with body (unless a man dies immediately after the attainment of such knowledge), just as a potter's wheel continues whirling after the pot has been fashioned, by force of the impulse previously given to it. When a separation of the informed soul from its corporeal frame takes place, and nature in respect to it ceases, then is absolute and final deliverance accomplished. " Thus this abstruse knowledge, adapted to the liberation of the soul, wherein the origin, duration, and termination of beings are considered, has been thoroughly expounded by the mighty saint. The sage compassionately taught it to Asuri, who communicated it to Panchasikhyá, and by him it was promulgated to mankind."

The YÓGA of Pátanjali adopts the scientific views of the Sánkhya, as a whole, but runs a course of its own in relation to that distinctive end which all the systems aim at, the freedom of the soul from the burdens of transmigration. The first two books, published by Dr. Ballantyne, are treated in the following way. The first book contains fifty-one Sutras, in which is developed, very systematically, the doctrine of the author

F 2

as to the special mode of securing such deliverance.
This doctrine is far more religious in its tone and spirit
than the purely scientific method taught by the Sánkhya; it adopts, in fact, very much the Vedántic theory
on the subject, and turns to its own account the asceticism so prevalent when the system was taught.   Start-
ing with a quotation from the Katha Upanishad, in
which Náchiketa is declared to have attained the
Supreme Soul by observing the rules of the Yóga,
communicated to him by Yama, Pátanjali avows that
the teaching of those rules, and of the method which
they contain, is the aim of his instructions.   The evil,
with which men have to contend, lies, according to his
views, in the various phenomena which are produced in
the mind, whether in its waking or sleeping hours, by
the perceptions of sense, the deductions of reasons, and
the dogmas of authority; by incorrect notions; by fancy;
by the dreams of sleep and the recollections of former
items of knowledge called up in memory.   In other
words, to get rid of the process of thinking, on which
the soul seems to be employed from birth till death, at
all hours, compelled thereto by the objects which affect
it both within and without, is the *summum bonum* to be
secured.   This great end is to be gained by concentrating the mind.   " Concentration (*yóya*) is the hinder-
ing of the modifications of the thinking principle "
(Sutr. 2): if successful, the soul will be like a spectator
without a spectacle, earnestly engaged in thinking of
nothing!   For this purpose, exercise and dispassion are
necessary: efforts must be made to exclude thought,

stedfastly and perseveringly; and all desire after terres-
trial or celestial objects of every kind must be subdued.
The meditation engaged in is of two kinds—that in
which there is distinct recognition, and that in which
such recognition is lost. The former is the fixing of
the mind upon one selected object, and concentrating
all thought upon that alone; the latter, which is of a
higher character, is without an object, and is confined
to the act of thinking alone. This meditation is preceded by faith, perseverance, intentness, and a thorough
knowledge of the object pondered. All the aspirants
after absorption are not alike: they are divided into
nine classes, according to the impetuosity with which
the object is pursued; the mild, the mediate, and the
transcendent, constituting three chief divisions: all are
exhorted to strive for the transcendent method, and
warm impetuosity is recommended in carrying it out,
that they may be the sooner successful.

The sage points out distinctly that to this severe
course of self-restraint there are many obstacles.
" Sickness, languor, doubt, carelessness, laziness, regard
for objects of sense, erroneous perceptions, failure to
attain any stage of abstraction, and instability" in the
state when attained, all cause distraction of mind, and
hinder the progress of the ascetic. Besides those hin-
drances arising from a diseased body or an undisci-
plined mind, external circumstances bring their obstacles. " Grief, distress, trembling, and sighing are
accompaniments of those distractions." But there are
remedies by which these difficulties can be met. In

order to concentrate attention, and abstract it from
other objects, " let ONE truth be dwelt upon." The
mind also may be pacified by the " exercise of benevolence, tenderness, complacency to the virtuous, and
indifference to the wicked." These methods are external to the Yóga, and are useful in preventing un-
steadiness of thought. Another expedient, a favourite
one in Hindu asceticism, is that of " forcibly expelling
and restraining the breath;" a process similar to some
recommended in mesmerism. He may further fix his
attention by taking up some object of sense, and exclusively regarding that; or, he may reflect on the
inner light of the heart; or, he may call to mind the
example of one who was devoid of passion; or, have
recourse to the dreams he has experienced. In other
words, a Yógi, to steady his mind, may, according to his
own taste, take up any object of thought that he prefers
and ponder it well, until all else is excluded from his
perceptions and his consciousness.

So far, Pátanjali confines his instructions to the mode
by which the concentration of attention may be secured.
He does not touch upon the place or the external
circumstances by which these contemplations may be
aided, the shady grove and the running stream, such
as are described in the Upanishads and the Gita; nor
does he enumerate the various methods (sannyás) by
which ascetics have been accustomed to subdue their
senses, and compel the passions to lie still within them.
He closes with a statement of the fruits of such contemplation. The mind of the ascetic will master all

objects, from the minutest atom to the great ether : he will gradually lose all distinctive perception of the "qualities" of objects ; he will attain spiritual clearness ; his knowledge will be perfectly free from error ; every object of thought will finally disappear ; and his mind will be like the pure rock-crystal, which seems tinged with the red of the hibiscus behind it, but is really unspotted, and will become perfectly free from contamination, by the phenomena and modifications with which it has been ever occupied.

In the SECOND BOOK, the subject of concentration is continued ; the various "afflictions" that have to be met are pointed out ; the mode of meeting them is discussed, and the various fruits of concentration, which result in perfect meditation and the complete subjection of all sense, are enumerated. In the remainder of his treatise, Pátanjali describes the range of transcendental powers to which this asceticism leads, powers which were universally attributed by the superstitious to those meditating denizens of the forests. In addition to knowledge of various kinds, knowledge of his former states of existence, of invisible objects, of the future both of himself and others, the Yógi will acquire invisibility of form, perfect strength, freedom from hunger and thirst, the power of entering other bodies, living and dead, of hearing sounds even in other worlds, of transforming himself into any of the elements, of penetrating anywhere, and even of changing the course of nature. All this resembles the talk of the clairvoyant carried to the extreme, and indicates the extent to which, in fact, mesmerism and clairvoyance were practised in certain ways, and brought to bear upon religious and philosophical attainments in ancient India.

Pátanjali was not, however, a mere mystic. While receiving as a whole the Sánkhya system of Kopila, he opposes in strong and clear terms one of the greatest of Kopila's errors, the rejection of a God. In book i. sutra 23, he refers to the religious mode of attaining contemplation taught by the Vedánta, and says that the ascetic may attain this state of abstract meditation " by profound devotedness towards the LORD." The commentator adds, that by this devotedness is meant a peculiar serving of him, " by giving up all desire for the enjoyment of objects of sense, and by making over all actions to Him as the pre-eminent guide." It is at this point that Pátanjali introduces his view of the existence and attributes of God, which will be quoted in a future chapter.

M. Cousin, in his *History of Philosophy*, has pointed out with great truth the strong resemblance which exists between the YÓGA Shástra and the BHAGAVAT GITA. The system of the latter is, in fact, an eclectic system, which combines the scientific principles of the Sánkhya, with the asceticism of the Yóga and the Pantheism of the Vedánta. The spirit of religious contemplation inculcated, the exclusion of all external objects, the thinking away the various notions of the mind itself, are the same in both the latter, but have different aims. In the Yóga, the contemplation is to be practised in order to produce perfect abstraction from

all thought: in the Gita, it is intended only to secure
a more complete concentration of the mind upon
Krishna or Brahma, the Spirit Supreme.  There can be
little doubt that the Gita was written long after the
other systems had been formed, and that the form which
the poem has assumed is a dramatic device of the
author to give his system currency.  We shall refer to
the poem again.

# CHAPTER II.

## THE NYAYA.

THE Nyáya system is divided into two parts, which
agree to a considerable extent with each other, yet
differ on certain points; each supplying most valuable
elements for supplementing the other, and for securing
one great system combined from both. The NYÁYA,
properly so called, considers specially, though not exclusively, the true mode of inquiring after truth; it is,
therefore, occupied to a great extent with logical questions, and has surveyed the whole field of argument
far more exactly and completely than any other of the
Hindu systems. In doing so, it has pointed out the
true constituents of a sound argument, and the variety
of fallacies, accidental and dishonestly intended, which
lead to wrong conclusions. For these discussions it
is greatly valued and extensively studied by the followers of all the systems down to the present day.
The VAISESHIKA, on the other hand, takes up for its
consideration, chiefly physical inquiries, and surveys,
classifies and endeavours to account for the various
objects existing in the universe, more extensively and
more exactly than others have done. In doing so, it
asserts that all substances have an atomic origin, and
that the atoms are eternal. These atoms, however,

have not been discovered by any chemical analysis, but are purely hypothetical. They are, in size, the sixth part of the smallest visible object, the mote in a sunbeam. Both systems advocate the existence of a Supreme Soul, excelling all other souls in being almighty and all-wise. Souls of a lower rank, whether of gods or men, are not parts of him, but are eternal. The great evil of human existence is found in the restless activity of the soul, which leads to its endless transmigrations. The cure offered is a thorough knowledge of the principles of the system, by which a perfect quietism will be produced.

The Nyáya system is attributed to GAUTUMA; and is described in a collection of Sutras written by him. They are divided into five books; the first of which sketches out the subject-matter of the whole. The Vaiseshika is also recorded in Sutras, by its author KANÁDA, and contains ten lectures. Each of these original works has been commented on again and again, and their doctrines have been arranged in original treatises by other writers. The English reader will find the fullest account of the system in both divisions in Colebrooke's celebrated essay. Dr. Ballantyne has published the first two books of the NYÁYA SUTRAS of Gautum; the first lecture of the VAISESHIKA; and a compact little treatise, the TARKA SANGRAHA, with elucidatory commentaries. The BHÁSHÁ PARICHHEDA, a favourite work among native scholars, which gives a clear outline of the whole system, has also been recently translated into English by Dr. Roer for the Asiatic Society of Bengal, under the title of

*Categories of the Nyáya Philosophy.* All these authorities are of the greatest value.

§ 1. GAUTUM sets out, like the founders of the other systems, with the inquiry, What is the way to attain perfect beatitude (*nisreyasa*) : and then asserts that that deliverance is only to be secured by a knowledge of the truth. This knowledge embraces many topics, but is directed chiefly to the true condition of the soul as separate from body : he who obtains this knowledge, which it is the object of the system to communicate, will be delivered from the evils and pains by which he is now beset. KANÁDA, in his first Sutra, lays down the same dogma : emancipation is to be secured by abstinence from all kinds of works ; and that abstinence is to be attained by the study of his system and the acquirement of its several objects of knowledge. The steps to be followed in the process are enumerated by Gautum with great clearness. The pains to which the human soul has been subjected by its connection with matter are owing to and suffered in its frequent births. These births arise from the soul's constant activity, which requires rewards for its meritorious actions. This activity has sprung from the fault of dislike, or desire, or stupidity, which inevitably leads to it. Their origin, again, is traced to false notions (*mithyá-gyan*) of what men are and may be. Now the Nyáy by its sound instructions will communicate right notions, instead of wrong ones, concerning the soul and the universe. These will destroy the *fault* (*dosha*) of desire and dislike : with that will pass away the *activity* (*pravritti*) which so

erroneously looked for the fruit of its actions: new *births*
(*janman*) and migrations will henceforth cease; and the
original *pain* (*du'kha*) be entirely removed. The removal
of that pain, and the restoration of the soul to its original condition of perfect rest, is the *beatitude* (*apavarga*) promised. Absolute quiet, therefore, is the
*summum bonum* at which the system aims.

§ 2. Gautum next describes the *instruments* (*pramán*)
by which these right notions are to be acquired. He
mentions four: perception (*pratyaksha*); inference (*anu-
mána*); comparison (*upamána*); and testimony (*sabda'*).
Dr. Ballantyne translates them: (1) the deliverance of
sense, the knowledge acquired by a contact of the senso-
rium with its object: (2) the recognition of a sign; this
" inference" is of three kinds; *à priori* inference; *à
posteriori;* and from analogy: (3) the recognition of
likeness, that by which similarity is detected between
different objects: (4) worthy precepts or authority.
By means of these instrumentalities correct knowledge
may be obtained of things as they really are.

§ 3. *Causality* occupies an important place, especially
in the Sutras of Kanáda, and may be most appropriately
mentioned here. A cause (*kárana*) is declared to be
that which is efficacious in the production of something
which otherwise could not be. By its existence or non-
existence, the existence or non-existence of that something, the effect (*kárya*), is rendered necessary. Hence
it follows, that if there be no cause, there is no effect:
if there be no effect, there is no cause. Again: the
quality of the effect depends upon the cause. " If there

be no thread, there is no cloth : if there be no conjunction of the two halves of a jar, there is no jar: if there
be no virtue, there is no happiness."

Three kinds of causes are enumerated : (1.) The *intimate* or *substantial* cause (*samaváyi*), by which an aggregation is produced.   Two atoms make a bi-atomic compound : threads make up cloth ; two halves make a jar.
(2.) *Non-intimate* or *non-substantial* cause (*asamaváyi*);
this is connected with the direct cause: thus the conjunction of two atoms is the proximate cause of the
resulting bi-atomic compound : the putting together of
thread is the proximate cause of the resulting cloth.
(3.) The *instrumental* cause (*nimitta*) is that by which
the conjunction is produced : as the loom of the weaver :
the wheel and stick of the potter.   Kanáda says:   The
cause which refers to substance is intimate cause : and
action is a non-intimate cause.   Of these the first is
usually termed the material cause ; the second, the efficient ; the third, the instrumental cause.   Beside these,
God, the Omniscience of God, desire, endeavour, time,
space, virtue and vice are reckoned general causes.   The
rest are special causes.

§ 4. With these instruments and on these principles,
the various *objects* of knowledge ( *prameya*) are to be
examined.   But as the bare mention of these objects
does not secure a correct knowledge of them, the Sage
takes up the subject of *doubt* (*sansaya*) as one intermediate between hearing and believing: and proceeds
to argue it in the most systematic and logical manner.
In order to get out of doubt, the scholar must have a

*motive* (*prayojana*) for inquiring further. Possessed of such an incentive to inquiry, he will endeavour to enter new regions of truth. But he must start from that which is known, from some established facts or tenets, which are well received and acknowledged. If known among the unlearned, they are called familiar facts. Other facts are scientific, known among the schools of philosophy. Of these, some are dogmas of all the schools; others are peculiar to an individual school: some are hypothetical, and some are implied as inevitable corollaries requiring no special proof. All of them furnish data, on which, as a foundation, further inquiry may be based, and new conclusions be established. Passing from these data, Gautum proceeds to describe the mode of demonstrating a new conclusion. He teaches that every demonstration contains five members: the *proposition* (*pratigyá*), which states what is about to be established: the *reason* (*hetu*), by means of which its establishment is secured: the *example* (*udáharana* or *nidarsana*), which furnishes some familiar case of the fact: the *application* (*upanaya*) of the example to the case to be established: and the *conclusion* (*nigaman*), in which the original case is declared to be proved. These five elements are members of the Nyáya syllogism. It will be seen at once that they are reducible without difficulty to the three propositions of the modern syllogism, and that the mode of demonstration taught by Gautum is that now adopted as the true one. The *proposition* and *conclusion* are of course identical (as he himself says): the same truth being first stated as hypothetical, and at

last as proved.   The *reason* again is only a statement of
the proof employed for the second time in the *application.*   The five elements are thus reduced to the *example*
(or major premiss): the *application* (or minor premiss):
and the *conclusion.*   This is the form in which Jaymini's
syllogism is presented in the Mimansa.   Thus:—

| | | | | |
|---|---|---|---|---|
| Proposition : | . | . | . | The hill is fiery : |
| Reason : | . | . | . | For it smokes : |
| Example : | . | . | . | What smokes is fiery : |
| Application : | . | . | . | The hill is smoking : |
| Conclusion : | . | . | . | The hill is fiery. |

Dr. Ballantyne very justly points out* that this syllogism, though not the strictly logical one, is yet most
valuable regarded from a rhetorical point of view.
The proposition is laid down and the reason assigned.
Presuming a doubt in the mind of the hearer, the case
is then argued logically ; and the final conclusion comes
out the same as the original proposition.   Were the
scholar to confine his attention to that which is required
to convince himself, the last three propositions would
be sufficient.   When he passes onward to the effort of
convincing others who may doubt his first assertion, the
rhetorical process stated by the Nyáya will probably
be adopted.

Should an argument not be clearly apprehended, the
hearer is directed to look at it from an opposite point of
view; to take a simple case, and show the absurdity
involved in a denial of one of the premises.   Thus, sup-

* *Tarka-Sangraha*, pp. 45-47.

pose a person admits that there is smoke in the hill, after allowing that where there is smoke there must be fire, and yet denies the conclusion that the hill is fiery, he is confuted by the proposition that if there were no fire there could be no smoke. This process is called *Tarka*; it is equivalent to the *reductio ad absurdum*; proving a point indirectly by showing the absurdity of its contradictory, the only possible way of proving a negative. The result of these processes, in which evidence is offered, and reasons are given both for the proposition and against it, is the certain ascertainment of a truth (*nirnay*).

So far Gautum has provided for hearing both sides fairly; but even then there may be many who do not accept the conclusion as true. He therefore takes up the subject of controversy, and describes the various classes of disputants which controversy calls up. Three classes are more or less honest; those who enter into candid discussion in order to arrive at truth, then unknown; the wranglers, who aim only to get victory as material for self-gratulation; and the caviller, who only finds fault with the arguments of others, without settling anything himself. Five classes beyond these furnish only apparent reasons, which are really fallacies, and thus deceive both themselves and others. Others, again, employ arguments dishonestly, solely with the intent of deceiving and thwarting their opponents. Some employ objections, miserably futile, that can mislead no one. The lowest rank of reasoners contains only the absolute blockheads, who, though they

doggedly oppose the truth, are too stupid to understand it.

§ 5. Having cleared the way for inquiry, by defining
the instruments of knowledge, and exhibiting in all its
phases the mode of discussion both with friends and foes,
as well as the different classes to whom it is applied, the
Nyáya takes up in order the various *objects* of *knowledge*
(*prameya*) which are to be proved and known. These
are twelve in number: "Soul, body, sense, sense-object,
knowledge, the mind, activity, fault, transmigration, fruit,
pain and beatitude," are the subjects fitted to supply
"right notions," and thus secure the entire removal
of all human pain.

(*a.*) Of these, *soul* (*átman*) is stated justly as first in
importance. The soul is reckoned as the site of knowledge or sentiment. It is distinct from the body and
from the senses. It is different for each individual and
co-existent person. It is perceived by the mental organ,
*i.e.*, its phenomena are learned within the sphere of
consciousness. Its existence is proved by its peculiar
attributes, intellect, self-consciousness, and the like.
This existence is implied by six special signs, viz., desire (*ichchhá*), aversion (*dwesha*), volition (*prayatna*),
pleasure (*sukha*), pain (*du'kha*), and knowledge (*gyána*).
They are only qualities or characteristics of the soul,
and therefore imply a distinct substratum which underlies them. They are, again, not universal attributes,
which belong to space, time, and mind, but particular
attributes apprehended by one organ exclusively. Souls,
again, are multitudinous. In these views Gautum

concurs in the doctrine of the Sánkhya of the separateness and independence of numerous souls in the universe: but differs from the Sánkhya, and is more
correct, in holding that the universe is not merely a
development of the soul's notions, but possesses a real
substratum of an entirely different kind.

Gautum advocates, like the other great sages, the
eternity of souls, and also declares them infinite; they
are eternal in consequence of being infinite. (The *mind*
(*manas*) has an atomic origin, its capacity of retaining
knowledge being very limited; but the " mind " also is
eternal and multitudinous.) Souls are of two kinds, the
animal soul (*jivátmá*), and the *supreme soul* (*param
átmá*). The peculiar qualities and functions of the
latter will be specially described hereafter.

§ 6. (*b.*) The second object of proof is *body* (*sarira*).
Body is an ultimate compound; it is composed of parts,
and has been developed from atoms. Associated with
the soul it enjoys fruit. It is distinguished as being the
site of muscular action, of the organs of sensation, and
of the sentiments or feelings of pleasure and pain experienced by the soul. In its constitution it is earthly,
and has the qualities which belong to earth; it is not
composed in part of the other elements, they being
heterogeneous, which the body is not.

Besides human bodies, Gautum enumerates other
bodies distributed through this and other worlds. Like
the Upanishads, he describes them as aqueous, igneous,
and aërial. Earthly bodies are generated and ungene-
rated. The former include the viviparous or uterine:

the oviparous; the insects engendered in filth and hot moisture: and the plants which germinate from the soil. The third class include worms, maggots, and the like, to which the Vedas and all the Schools ascribe a spontaneous origin.

§ 7. (*c.*) The third object are the *organs of sensation* (*indriya*). "The organs of sense originating from the elements are smell, taste, sight, touch, and hearing." "The elements are earth, water, light (*tejas*), air, and ether." These organs belong to the body; they are not modifications of "Consciousness," as the Sánkhya teaches, but material organs, derived from the elements respectively. The Bauddhas say that the pupil of the eye is the organ of sight, and the outer ear the organ of hearing. But the Nyáya controverts this opinion, declaring that a ray of light proceeding FROM the pupil towards the object viewed is the visual organ; and that ether, contained in the cavity of the ear, communicating by intermediate ether with the object heard, is the organ of hearing. As a torch is not seen at mid-day, so that ray is not usually visible: but in the dark it is visible, as in the eye of a cat! The organs possess qualities derived from their origin. The organ of vision is lucid: that of hearing is ethereal: that of taste, aqueous, possessing saliva: that of feeling, aërial; that of smell, earthy. The site of the visual organ is the pupil of the eye: that of the auditory organ, the orifice of the ear: and so on. The objects apprehended by the senses are qualities of the elements or their products, and they are cognized by the organ cognate with them. Thus odour, which is earthy, is apprehended by the nose; and colour, which is from light, by the eye. These organs are proved to exist by their uses, as that of a knife is proved by an act of cutting. Besides the five external organs, an internal organ, the *manas*, or mind, is also allowed. The five organs of action, in the other philosophies, are not reckoned so here.

This sixth and internal organ, the *mind* (*manas*), equivalent in modern philosophy to the sphere of consciousness or internal perception, is the instrument which apprehends pain, pleasure, and the internal sensations: it apprehends external objects by its union with the five external senses. Its existence is proved by the fact that our sensations occur only one at a time. If apparently several sensations arise in the soul, it is only from their rapidity; just as a lighted torch, when swung round quickly, seems a ring of fire. It is in itself single: each soul has only one. It is limited, not infinite: otherwise it might be united with everything at once, and all sensations and notions be cotemporaneous. Still it is eternal, and conjoined with soul as with body, but has a separate existence from it. Kanáda reckons both Mind and Soul among the substances, and ascribes to them qualities such as substances possess.

§ 8. (*d.*) The fourth object of knowledge in Gautum's list are the *objects of sense* (*artha*). These objects are the qualities of earth, water, light, air, and ether, viz. odour, savour, colour, tangibility, and sound. This branch of the Nyáya is the one which Kanád has so fully developed in the Vaiseshika system, and has described in his six categories: it is sufficient to note that they are included, though briefly, in Gautum's scheme of knowledge: we reserve a special mention of them till his categories are concluded.

§ 9. (e.) The *fifth* of Gautum's twelve objects is *understanding* (*buddhi*). " Understanding, apprehension, and knowledge have all the same meaning." It is that which makes matter known. It is twofold: apprehension and memory. Apprehension is of two kinds: right and wrong. Right notion is incontrovertible, being derived from demonstration, and from the various instruments by which knowledge is produced. It arises, therefore, from perception; as when a jar is properly seen by healthy organs: from inference; as when fire is inferred from smoke: from comparison or analogy; as when a gayál is known from its likeness to a cow: and from tradition or Revelation; as when it is known on the testimony of the Vedas, that heaven may be attained by sacrifice. Wrong notions are not derived from proof, but from false perceptions; from doubt, from contradictory premises, and from errors of various kinds.

Remembrance (*smriti*), the other faculty of the understanding, has also reference both to truth and error: it may recall things correctly from within the mind; or may recall them incorrectly in confusion and disorder. In waking hours both right and wrong recollections arise: in sleep, only wrong ones.

The sixth of the objects of proof is the *Mind:* it

occurs in two places in Gautum's arrangement; first,
as one of the *Senses*, the sixth or inner sense; and here
as a distinct object of knowledge by itself. It has
already been treated under the former head.

§ 10. The remaining six of the twelve objects will
not require more than a passing notice, having already
been referred to at the outset of the subject. The
seventh, *activity* (*pravitti*), is that spirit which originates
in man the utterances of the voice, the notions of the
understanding, and the gestures of the body: all intended to secure rewards of virtue and the like, and
keeping up the condition of illusion in which men live.
The eighth, *fault* (*dosha*), is that erroneous desire in
men which produces the activity just mentioned. It
appears in three forms, of affection, aversion and in-
fatuation, or extreme delusion. The ninth is *transmigration*, the condition of the soul after death (*pretya-
bháva*), during which it wanders from one body to
another, as the result of its infatuations. The tenth,
*retribution* or *fruit* (*phala*), is the consequence of the
faults just mentioned, which in their turn spring from
activity. It is realized in connection with the mind,
body, and senses. The eleventh is *pain* (*du'kha*), which
includes pleasure also as its opposite; it denotes the condition in which men live, and from which these systems
of philosophy are intended to deliver them. The last is
the *beatitude* (*apavarga*), promised to the followers of the
system. It denotes deliverance from all the " pain,"
and the absolute prevention of all evil in the future.
This liberation differs from the temporary alleviations

of pain and of excitement that are experienced by men, in being absolute and final. This liberation is attained by the soul that has become acquainted with right notions (*tatwa*), by means of the instruction here offered. Such a soul freed from the passions which agitate mortal life will cease to desire, will cease to be active. Its previous acts being annulled, its previous body passes away; no new body is assigned to it; there is no connection with previous evils, since there is no longer cause for them. Thus pain entirely ceases, and perfect rest is secured.

§ 11. While Gautum in the Nyáya Sutras, deals chiefly with the logical mode of a sound inquiry after right objects of knowledge, KANÁDA in the Sutras of the VAISESHIKA, takes up the physical as well as mental branches of human knowledge, and enters upon them at once at the outset of his system. " Emancipation (he asserts) is to be attained through the knowledge of truth, which specially relates to the agreement and disagreements of the six categories (*padártha*). These categories or objects of knowledge are *substance, quality, action, genus, difference,* and *intimate relation.* The Bháshá Parichheda starts with a similar statement, adding, however, with many authorities, a seventh category, *non-existence,* or *negation.*

§ 12. SUBSTANCE (*dravya*) is the sole substratum; it possesses qualities and actions—(*Sutra* 15.) It should be observed here that Hindu Philosophy possesses no term exactly equivalent to the English word "matter," and comprising the class of objects which that word expresses. The Hindus never generalized so far as to reduce all objects to the two classes of matter and mind; or to distinguish the primary qualities of matter as such. The Nyáya, however, teaches that all the objects of knowledge which possess "qualities" must have a substratum in which those qualities inhere; and that such "substances" are nine in number; the five elements, time and space, "mind" and soul. Before discussing the individual substances, Kanáda compares substances, qualities, and actions together, and shows in what respects they have similar modes of action or properties, and in what points they differ. He says, substances and qualities each produce their like; but an action does not produce another action. Neither cause nor effect destroys substance; but they do destroy qualities. Substance is the cause of substances, qualities, and actions. In a jar there may be the jar itself, its colour, and its motion when floating down the Ganges. A quality also may indirectly produce all three, either from being in the mediate cause of a product (as colour in the threads of a cloth)—or as coming out only in the product itself. Action does not produce substance: it is the cause of conjunction, disjunction and momentum: and so on.

(a.) *Earth* (*prithivi*) occupies the first place among the substances. Like all other substances, it possesses substantiality and qualities. In particular it possesses form, action, and velocity. It has feel, colour, gravity, odour, and taste. Odour is its distinguishing quality: it is also the site of the various colours. It has three kinds of feel: hot, cold, and temperate. It is

eternal as atoms: non-eternal in respect to its parts.
All objects are compounds of it, from the smallest, consisting of two atoms, to the largest, the universe, " the
egg of Brahmá." Its aggregates are of three kinds,
organisms, organs, and inorganic objects. The organized
bodies are of four kinds, viviparous, &c. The inorganic are stones and the like: the organ originating
from earth is that of smell.

(*b.*) *Water* (*ap*) has fourteen qualities: touch; number, quantity, individuality; conjunction, disjunction;
priority, posteriority; velocity, gravity; fluidity, colour,
savour and viscidity. Odour does not belong to it,
except accidentally. Its colour is said to be white: its
taste and feel are sweet and cold. As atoms, it is
eternal: its aggregates and various forms are transient.
Its organisms are not born; they are beings abiding in
the realm of Varuna. Its inorganic objects are the sea,
rivers, snow, rain and the like. The organ is the
tongue: wherein saliva is produced.

(*c.*) *Light* (*tejas*) and heat are the same. Light has
eleven qualities: the first eight ascribed to water,
together with colour, fluidity, and viscidity: but possesses neither smell, taste, nor gravity. Its distinguishing quality is heat; it has white colour: its fluidity
is not innate, but accidental. Eternity and non-eternity
are attributed to it as to the earth and water. Its
organ is the eye: the visual ray, which is the organ of
sight, is lucid. Organic lucid bodies are lightning, fire
and gold. Sometimes it is both seen and felt, as with
fire; sometimes only one; sometimes, neither. There

are earthy light, celestial light, alvine light, and mineral light.

(*d.*) *Air* (*váyu*) has the same qualities as light, excepting colour and fluidity. It has no colour: it is sensible to touch. Its temperature is its distinctive quality: it is neither cold nor hot: its motion is crooked: the feel in the air is natural to it, and from this its existence is inferred. As atoms, it is eternal: its aggregates are transient. Its organisms are aërial bodies: its objects are all substances intermediate between the vital air and the great element. Besides the air upon the earth's surface, the breath and the vital airs, *i. e.*, the vital functions, are reckoned separately.

(*e.*) *Ether* (*ákása*) has for its distinguishing quality, sound. Its organ is the ear. It has many titles: it is infinite, eternal, and one. It appears white by its connection with some lucid orb. The blue colour of the sky is not derived from it, but from the southern peak of Mount Sumeru, which is all sapphire. Others say that that colour is in the eye itself, and makes the sky seem blue, as jaundice makes all things yellow. The existence of the ether is inferred in this way. Sound is learned by the ear. It cannot be a quality of earth, water, light, or air: nor can it be a quality of time, space, or mind. It must have some other substratum: this is ether. The organ of hearing is ethereal: it consists of a portion of ether, confined in the cavity of the ear: endued with the particular virtue. That virtue is wanting in the deaf.

(*f.*) *Time* (*kála*) has the qualities of number, quantity, severalty, conjunction and disjunction. It has also the attributes of ubiquity and infinity. It is inferred from priority, sequence, and the like: from quickness and slowness in motion: from the contrast between young and old. It is called past, present, and future. It has many names, moment, hour, day, year. "Time is thought to be the producer of all that is produced; and the substrate of all worlds:" that is, that they can only exist in time, and under the conditions of its progress. Upon it as a basis, the notions of priority and sequence rest.

(*g.*) *Space* (*dig*) is one and eternal, ubiquitous and infinite. It is the substrate of the notions of here and there, proximity and distance. It is known by many names, as east and west, high and low. Its qualities are those of time.

(*h, i.*) The *soul* is ubiquitous and infinite; it has the qualities of number, quantity, and the like, which are possessed by space and time. Its existence is shown from the fact that there is an agent who controls the senses, as a knife cuts: without it the senses would be useless, for they are instruments of an unseen ruler. The *mind* and the *soul* have been already examined in the system of Gautum, and need no further remark.

It is important to notice the frequent references made in connection with the earlier substances to the distinction between their atoms and aggregates. It is here arises one of the most important doctrines of the Vaiseshika philosophy, recognized also by the Nyay, the doctrine of the eternity of matter in the form of ATOMS, and also the similar atomic and eternal origin of souls. This theory will be examined at length in a future chapter.

§ 13. QUALITY (*guna*) forms the second category in Kanáda's list. It is closely connected with substance, but cannot produce either substance or quality. It is inherent in substance, cannot produce conjunction or disjunction (as action does), and has no qualities in itself. The qualities are reckoned twenty-four in number; though Kanáda only mentions the names of seventeen. The commentator supplies the remainder, and says they are implied by the great sage though not specified. They are as follows: colour, savour, odour, and feel or tangibility; number, magnitude, individuality; conjunction and disjunction; distance and proximity; thought; pleasure and pain; desire and aversion, and effort. The seven added are gravity, fluidity, viscidity, momentum, virtue and vice, and sound. In modern science they would fall into two great classes; the qualities of matter, and the immaterial qualities of the soul. The former are sixteen, the latter eight.

In the *Bhásha Parichheda* they are generally compared before their distinctive characteristics are pointed out; they are classified as general and special; as apprehended by one or more senses; as produced or effected by particular actions.

(1.) " *Colour (rúpa)* is perceived by the eye; it manifests substances, qualities, and classes: it is the cause of the perceptions of the eye." It exists as essential in three substances, earth, water, and light. In light it is the principal quality; there it is white and resplendent.

In water it is white, but not lustrous. In earth it is variable. In the primary atoms of light and water it is perpetual; in products it is not so. In earth it can be changed, as when a jar is burned red by fire. Seven colours are enumerated. White, yellow, green, red, black, orange, and variegated. Of these there are many varieties. Six simple colours occur in the primary atoms: all seven are found in the double atoms.

(2.) *Savour* (*rasa*) is apprehended by the tongue: it is of various kinds, as sweet, bitter, pungent, astringent, acid, and saline. It exists in earth and water; it is the distinctive quality of the latter. It is perpetual in the atoms of water; not so in the accidental aqueous products; it is variable in the earth.

(3.) *Odour* (*gandha*) is perceived by the nose, and is of only two kinds, good and bad. It is the special quality of earth, and of earth alone; in water it is accidentally produced by earthy particles (just as the crystal appears red when a red flower is placed behind it). In air it is the same, and is produced from the particles of flowers carried about by the wind. Flowers do not waste away; but camphor and like substances do.

(4.) *Feel* or tangibility (*sparsa*), by which is meant temperature, is apprehended by the skin. It exists in four substances, earth, water, light, and air; it is the proper quality of air. It is threefold, hot, cold, and temperate. In water it is cold; in light and heat it is hot; in earth and air it is temperate. In respect to earthy substances it is also hard and soft, and the like. It is eternal in the atoms of air; in atoms and double

atoms it is latent; but is perceptible in large products.

(5.) By *number* (*sankhya*) objects are recognized as
one, two, three, and so on *ad infinitum*. It is deduced
from comparison, as by comparing things together and
in groups, we say they are one, two, and so on. It is a
universal quality, and like others is either essential or
accidental. In eternal substances unity is eternal; it
is transient in products, and may be destroyed. Number is of two sorts, unity and multitude; or else of
three kinds, monads, duads, and multitude. All numbers from two upwards are produced by comprehending
intellect: and they are collectively apprehended in their
dependence upon more than one object.

(6.) *Dimension* (*parimána*) is the cause of the perception and use of measure. It is universal and common to all substances. It is fourfold; and is divided
into great and small, long and short. It is eternal in
eternal substances; large, as in the ether: it is also
eternal in the smallest things, as atoms and the mind.
Between these extremes of size are all the uneternal or
transient magnitudes. Transient and finite quantities
are produced from number, measure, and the aggregation of units into heaps. In two and more atoms it
arises from number; in a jar and similarly extended
things it is from measure: the conjunction of loose
things, as pieces of cotton, makes heaps.

(7.) *Individuality* or separateness (*prithaktwa*) is also
common to all substances. It is of two sorts: (*a*) of
one, or a single pair; or (*b*) it is manifold, as of a triad.

It is the cause of the knowledge of separate things. It is eternal in eternal things: and transient in transient things.

(8, 9.) *Conjunction* (*sanyoga*) is transient connection: it is also a universal quality. There are three kinds of it:—(1.) The first is simple, and results from the action of one out of two agents, as " a falcon sitting on a rock;" the action being only on the part of the bird. (2.) The second kind is when the action is mutual, as the fighting of two rams. (3.) The third is mediate; as when the contact of a finger with a tree produces indirectly a conjunction between one's body generally and that tree. Again, conjunction is produced in two ways, by violent motion or by soft motion: the former is the cause of sound. *Disjunction* (*vibhága*) is the reverse of the last; and is preceded by it: it is also a universal quality. It has the same three divisions: being simple, mutual, and mediate as before. The last is of two kinds; being produced either by the disjunction of the cause, or by that of both cause and non-cause. The former is illustrated by the destruction of that half of a jar which is only immediately connected with a tree by the other half. The commentator illustrates the other by saying that where the hand is disconnected from a tree (the cause), the body (the non-cause) is also separated; and a belief arises that the tree is also separated from the body.

(10, 11.) *Priority* and *posteriority* (*paratwa, apa-ratwa*) are correlative qualities, belonging to *place* and *time*. As belonging to place, they are called proximity

and distance: as attached to time, they are termed
youth and antiquity. The one concerns bodies which
have circumscribed quantity; the other relates to
generated substances that have had beginning. The
knowledge of these qualities is obtained by comparison;
as by the perception of greater or less distance between
places, as Muttra and Allahabad: or of the periods
which have elapsed between the revolutions of the sun.

(12.) *Weight (gurutwa)* is that which produces falling: it abides in earth and water. Gold has it (though
derived from fire) because of the particles of earth which
have become mixed with light. It is imperceptible to
the senses; but is inferred from the falling of bodies,
when opposing causes, like adhesion, are removed. Its
opposite and negative is lightness. It is eternal in eternal substances; but in transient products is transient.

(13.) *Fluidity (dravatwa)* is the cause of trickling.
It is of two kinds, innate and derived from a cause: it
is innate in water, but in earth and light is accidental,
being produced from the action of heat, as in butter
and other substances. It is perceptible by two senses,
sight and touch. It really exists in hail and ice; but
is obstructed by some unseen quality which makes the
water solid. In the eternal atoms of water it is of
course eternal.

(14.) *Viscidity (sneha)* is the cause of agglutination. It
abides in water. Oil has it in abundance, derived from
watery particles, and from this combustion is favoured.

(15.) *Sound (sabda)* is a quality which abides in the
ether: it is apprehended by hearing owing to the ether

H

which abides in the organ, the ear. There are two
kinds of sound, musical, as of a drum; articulate, as in
the pronunciation of *ka*, *kha*. Articulate sounds are
produced by the contact of the tongue with the palate.
It is propagated by undulation (according to some):
wave after wave coming from a centre; only the last
wave is heard. It originates in conjunction, disjunction, or from sound itself. The drumstick beating
the drum is an example of the first: the rustling of
leaves, of the second: these are instrumental causes:
ether is always the material cause. The Mimansa has
discussed and advocated at great length the eternity
of sound. The Nyáya, however, rejects the doctrine.

The next eight qualities are perceived by the mental
organ. (16, 17, 18.)—*Understanding, Pleasure,* and *Pain,*
have already been discussed in the arrangement by Gautum, being reckoned among his objects of knowledge.

(19, 20.) *Desire* and *Aversion* (*ichchha, dwesha*).
Desire is the wish of pleasure and of the absence of
pain. It is threefold: (1.) That which has for its
object the last end, the *summum bonum*. (2.) That
whose object is the means for obtaining something
else, the instrument of accomplishing another object;
(3.) The desire for action. Passion is extreme desire.
Aversion is the opposite of desire, and denotes disgust.
It produces cessation from activity.

(21.) *Volition* (*prayatna*) is a determination to produce
gratification. Its occasion is desire; its reason is perception. Hence it has three kinds: (1.) Active effort.
(2.) Cessation from activity (owing to aversion), and

(3) the natural efforts of the animal functions. The last are beyond the perceptions of the senses.

(22, 23.) *Virtue* and *Vice* (*dharma, adharma*), "merit and demerit," are the causes of pleasure and pain. The former arises from doing what is enjoined; the latter from doing what is forbidden. They both abide in living creatures. By works of merit, bathing in the Ganges, sacrifices, and the like, heaven is obtained. Demerit or vice is the cause of hell: it may be destroyed by expiations.

(24.) *Faculty* (*sanskár*) is the last quality. It has three kinds: (1.) *Velocity*, which is a cause of action; it abides only in material bodies. (2.) *Elasticity* is by some considered to belong only to terrene objects; by others it is attributed to the first four elements. It is imperceptible to the senses, and is sometimes the cause of vibratory motion. (3.) *Memory* (*bhávaná*): it is the cause of recollection, and is regulated and aided by association, as by the sight of objects. It is only found in sentient beings. This concludes the consideration of quality, the second of Kanáda's categories.

§ 14. The third category is ACTION (*karma*). It consists in motion; it abides only in substances; it is the cause of conjunction and disjunction; it has no qualities, and is transient. We have already mentioned that five kinds of it are enumerated.

The fourth category is GENUS (*sámánya*). By this is understood the condition of similar things. It causes us to perceive conformity. It is eternal, single, concerns many things, and abides in substances, qualities, and

actions. It has two degrees: (1.) Existence is the
highest, and regards numerous objects; (2.) Abstraction of the individual is the lower. There is a third,
intermediate. These greatly resemble genus, species,
and individual. In another view, they are only two,
genus (*játi*) and species (*upádhi*). The next category
is DIFFERENCE (*visesha*). It causes us to perceive exclusion; it abides in eternal substances,—mind, soul,
time, place, ether, and atoms, all of which are originally and eternally different in some respects from one
another. The last is INTIMATE RELATION, or có-inherence,
already stated. It is illustrated in the relation between
a web and the threads of which it is formed; between
a body and the parts of which it is made up.

§ 15. A seventh category is usually added to these,
that of NON-EXISTENCE, or negation (*abháva*). It is of
four kinds. *Mutual* non-existence, or difference, is the
reciprocal negation of identity, essence, or respective
peculiarity. " A jar is not a web of cloth." *Antecedent*
non-existence is a present negation of what will be—a
negation in the material cause previous to the effect.
In yarn, for instance, until the cloth is fabricated, there
is antecedent negation of the cloth to be worn. A jar
is not produced until its previous non-existence is put
an end to by its formation from clay. It is without
beginning and end. *Emergent* non-existence is destruction; it is negation in the cause after the effect is produced. In a broken jar, the negation of the *jar* is the
heap of pieces which remain. This has beginning, but
no end. *Absolute* non-existence is negation through

all "the three times;" as fire in a lake—a thing that can never be.

Those who have sufficient patience to wade through the details of the Nyáya system must acknowledge that, in spite of its dryly formal character, the system is one which exhibits a great advance in the analysis by the human intellect of the objects of thought presented for its consideration. It is not, like the system yet to be examined, vitiated by errors which destroy its whole value from beginning to end. In spite of its imperfect analysis and generalization, it has found a great deal of solid truth. In its method of inquiry, and in the laws which it prescribes to the instruments of investigation, it reached the truth which modern science employs in our more enlightened days. Even its physical science, un-aided by chemical analysis, by mathematical exactness and broad astronomical knowledge, exhibits a very exten-sive examination and patient research into the elements and objects of the universe. One cannot, therefore, but hope that the effort now being made in the Benares College, to render its method the means of presenting the pundit world with a view of the correct results of modern science, may prove successful, and may lead native scholars from the errors of their religious books to seek for the religion as well as the science of those from whom such correctness has proceeded. The fear, however, is natural, that with the Hindu narrowness of mind, which can receive at once as true opposite and contradictory dogmas, the partial acknowledgment of the truth of their shastres will lead them pertinaciously to reverence the whole.

# CHAPTER III.

## THE VEDÁNTA.

THE Vedantic system appears before the European scholar in three stages of development. The germs of its philosophy, and even its principal doctrines, are contained in the Bráhmanas of the Vedas; but they are not there arranged in due order, nor are they taught with that completeness and elaboration which are employed in works of later date. It is from this circumstance that the system derives its name; its special design being to exhibit the " end " and scope of the Vedas in a duly classified form. The completed system is first seen in the Sutras of Veda Vyása; wherein its peculiar aim, the reasons which have necessitated its appearance, the doctrines it teaches, and the results to which its study leads, are all laid down in proper order. Subsequently to this great authority and its cotemporaries, the philosophy is recorded in the great commentaries which eminent scholars have written upon the original authorities, as well as in works composed with a view to exhibit its truths in a succinct and comprehensive form. In all its stages, the system is substantially the same; and, therefore, the student will find little difficulty in ascertaining what its dogmas are. In all the works which expound it, the topics discussed, the doctrines laid down, and the illustrations employed, are to a great extent identical. The last stage of the system differs from the earlier two only in showing a more complete deduction of all the consequences to which its principles lead. Just as the schoolmen of the middle ages cared not to discuss the truth or falsehood of the principles of the Aristotelian philosophy, but taking those principles for granted, sought only to exhibit them in a clearer light, and to develope them to their utmost extent; so the commentators on the Vedánta, adopting without question the original truths presented for their acceptance by the earliest authority, endeavour to describe it more clearly, explain it, paraphrase it, find reasons for it, and draw out the ultimate conclusions, which that truth essentially involves. Varieties in the interpretation of the original works, led to varieties of opinion on some points, and to the founding of different schools of philosophers who adopted them. In the main, however, the grand doctrines have been taught from the same great authority, through a long succession of ages down to the present day.

The unanimous voice of Hindu antiquity ascribes to the great sage Bádáráyan, otherwise called VEDÁ-VYÁSA, the origin of the Vedantic system. Little is known concerning his personal history, and that little is of a very doubtful and legendary character. The manner of his birth is thus described in one of the works attributed to him, the *Mahábhárat.* His father, PARÁSARA MUNI, struck with the beauty of a fisherman's daughter on the banks of the Yamuná, conveyed her to an island in the river which he produced for her residence; and there a

son was born to them. From his birth-place and his dark
complexion, he was called Krishna-Dwaipáyana, "the
dark islander." From the time of his birth he became,
like Yájnawalkya and other great scholars, an ascetic in
the woods. All his time was spent in the practice of religious austerities, and in meditation on religious subjects.
With the affairs of common life he busied himself but
little: only occasionally appearing at some celebrated
sacrifice; or visiting his relations to advise them in their
quarrels. He quitted his retirement, however, on one
occasion for a special object, which illustrates the difference
between ancient and modern Hindu society. Through
the blessing of Parásara, his mother, Satyabati, had
become the wife of Sántanu, the king of Hastinápur, and
had borne him two sons. Both died without children; the
younger leaving two widows, who were sisters. Anxious
to save the royal race of Kúrú from extinction, his
mother resolved to recall Vyása from his meditations;
and besought him to raise up issue from his brother's
widows. He complied with her request: from Ambá
was born Dhritarashtra; from Ambalika, Pándu. From
the former sprang a hundred sons: from the latter came
Yudhishthir, Bhim, and Arjun. Thus the three great
heroes of the Mahábhárat were Vyása's own grandsons.

By the force of his meditations, Vyása attained
astounding wisdom, and prepared within his mind an
immense array of Hindu learning. As he was reflecting
on the proper person to aid him in writing it down,
Brahmá appeared and advised Ganesa to be sent for.
The god of wisdom, therefore, became his secretary;

and amongst the works which he dictated, forth came
the Mahábhárat. Such is the legend which the poem
itself contains. Scholars doubt whether the Mahábhárat be the work of Vyása; and the mention of Ganesa
in this very passage is itself suggestive of the gravest
doubts on the point. The greatest work ascribed to
him, and ascribed to him universally, is the compilation
and arrangement of the Vedas: from whence he derives
his celebrated name of VEDÁ VYÁSA, "arranger of the
Vedas." These various works, the collection of the
Vedic hymns, the formation of the Vedánta system,
and the composition of the Mahábhárat, are separated
from each other by hundreds of years. They cannot
all claim him as their author; and it is exceedingly
doubtful if he ever lived at all.

The book of Sutras, he is said to have compiled, is
reckoned the most direct and important authority on
the Vedánta system. It is called by the various names
of Brahma Sutras, Sarírik Sutras, and Uttara Mimánsá. It is complete in itself, delivers the system in
a clear, compact form, and, like the Sutras of other
systems, is divided into sections, which may be readily
committed to memory. Like them, also, it requires the
elucidation of a commentary.

In addition to this excellent compendium, the Vedánta has an advantage over the other systems in being
able to appeal for its authority to another class of
works, more ancient than the Sutras, and forming a
portion of the Vedas. It was mentioned in the sketch
presented of the Vedic age, that as the philosophic spirit

grew among the brahmins, various treatises were composed by the learned among them, embodying their
speculations, not only as to the meaning of ancient
Vedic rites, but respecting the constitution of their own
nature and of the universe around them. These treatises had relation to all kinds of subjects; they expressed
the notions of their authors freely; they were guesses
at truth rather than the results of well-weighed
thought; they spread over a long period; and when,
at length, such as survived were gathered as works of
authority into the Bráhmanas of the Vedas, it was only
to be expected that they would contain a strange med-
ley of opinions, would express different views upon the
same subject, and not unfrequently contradict each
other. So various are their opinions that all orthodox
systems are able to appeal to them in confirmation of
their views, and are glad to do so because of the weight
attached to the Vedas of which they form a part. The
philosophical chapters and tracts are called Upanishads,
and, though belonging to different parts of the Bráhmanas, have been selected from them, so as to occupy a
kind of independent position. More than a hundred
of them are known, and the greater part are numbered
among the treatises of the Atharbba Veda. The
authors of the most ancient and authoritative are not
known; they are all *Sruti, i.e.* inspired, and are
believed to be communications from the great Brahmá
himself. One special set of the Bráhmanas are termed
Áranyakas, because they were to be read in the forests
by those ascetics and devotees who quietly withdrew

from household life to meditate in retirement upon the Supreme. These works were composed later than the Bráhmanas in general: they contain a great number of Upanishads, and, in after days, were declared by their brahmin commentators to be "the essence of the Veda."

Eleven of these Upanishads are considered by the brahmin world to expound Vedantic doctrines, and their authority is appealed to as of the highest kind. We may well doubt whether their original authors, who lived before the Vedantic system was formed, really intended them to bear simply and solely the Vedantic interpretation which is now put upon them; but they have undergone the same fate as all the early Aryan legends and literature, in being thoroughly brahminized. By the English scholar they may be regarded in two lights. On the one hand, he cannot fail to regard these treatises with great interest, as the earliest forms of philosophic investigation produced among a great people thinking for themselves; and he will readily make allowances for their various imperfections. When, however, he comes into controversy with brahmin priests, because they assert that these tracts contain the veritable utterances of Brahmá, he may justly use every contradiction, absurdity, and folly the books contain, to prove their human origin.

The eleven Upanishads of the Vedantic school are the following: the Aitareyá, Brihad Áranyaka, and Vája-saneyi: the Taittiriyá, the Chhandogya, and Talavakár: the Mundaka, Katha, Prasna, and Mándukya; and

lastly, the Swetáswatara. The AITAREYÁ Upanishad
is taken from the Bráhmanas of the Rig Veda, and
forms four chapters in Book 2 of the Aitareyá Áranyaka. It has been translated by Colebrooke in his
Essay on the Vedas, and contains a curious description
of the process of creation. The BRIHAD ÁRANYAKA is
a very voluminous Upanishad, the last book of the
*Satapatha Bráhmana;* the Bráhmana of the Vájasaneyi
school, which under the teaching of Yajnawalkya,
formed the White Yajur Veda. The Upanishad contains an immense amount of interesting matter, including several dialogues between Yajnawalkya and his
rivals and scholars. The CHHANDOGYA is a very important and extensive Upanishad of the Sáma Veda,
full of theological disquisitions and dialogues. Several
of the others named are exceedingly brief. They are
all, however, so valuable that it will not be inappropriate to describe the character and contents of two or
three of the most popular.

The *Taittiriyá* Upanishad is found among the Bráhmanas of the Black Yajur Veda, and stands high in
the estimation of Vedantic scholars. It is clear in its
doctrine, but shows the system in quite an early stage.
It is divided into three chapters: the first of which
describes the preparation a student must undergo,
before the system is communicated to him: the second
conveys the doctrines themselves: and the third shows
how the knowledge sought is only to be acquired by
degrees, by those who patiently study all its parts, as it
was by Bhrigu, the son of Varuná.

The *Mundaka* Upanishad professes to be a discourse, containing a series of instructions delivered by Angíras to Sounaka in answer to his inquiry: "Tell me, oh illustrious sage, what is that science, by the knowledge of which this universe is understood." The treatise is divided into three chapters, each of which has two sections. It is entirely didactic, and describes with varied illustrations the nature and attributes of the supreme; the connection between the universe and him; the way by which men may acquire a knowledge of him; the fruits of that knowledge, and so on.

The *Katha* Upanishad is divided into six sections (*valli*). It describes a dialogue between Yama and Nachiketá, the son of Vájasravasa. Nachiketá had been devoted by his father to Yama, and arrived at the house of that deity during his absence. On his return, the servants informed him that a brahmin had been waiting for him for three days, and begged him speedily to offer the usual attentions in order to prevent harm. He hastened to do so, and promised Nachiketá three favours. Nachiketá asked first, tranquillity for his father's mind: secondly, an account of the sacred fire by which men ascend to heaven: and thirdly, a full explanation of the nature and attributes of the absolute and supreme Brahm. Yama consents to grant all the requests: though the last is given with great reluctance. The description of the fire is contained in the first section: that of the supreme occupies the other five. From the frequent ellipses in its language, the Upanishad is rather difficult to understand.

The *Swetáswatara* Upanishad consists of a number of oracular sayings concerning the Supreme, the Universe, and Brahm, delivered by Swetáswatara to his disciples. They are divided into six sections, but are strung together without any logical order, the same topic occurring again and again at different intervals. This Upanishad is of very late date: it was prepared long after the rise of the great systems; and is interesting as exhibiting an early attempt to fuse the Sánkhya and Vedánta into one system; and show that all their apparent contradictions may be explained away.

A similar attempt, perhaps of the same age, is found in the celebrated and highly honoured poem, the BHAGAVAT GÍTA. This beautiful production is treated by the Vedantists as one of their authorities, and is explained in accordance with their views. But it is by no means an exclusively Vedantist work. It is divided into three principal sections, each containing six lectures. The first of these dwells on the ascetic practices of the Yoga; describes them and their fruits; but also points out that every one who faithfully fulfils the duties of his own caste in his own sphere will receive the highest reward. To enforce this brahminical doctrine was one of the great aims which the poem had in view. The second section goes over the principles of the Vedánta, teaching pantheism in the plainest way; and the last accepts the scientific and general doctrines of the Sánkhya. A single system is woven out of the doctrines of all. While intended to teach a theological system, the poem is cast into a dramatic form, and so

far may be compared with the Book of Job. It professes to describe a conversation which took place
between Krishna and Arjuna immediately before the
battle of Kurukhetra. Arjuna was in the deepest grief
at the slaughter which had already taken place, and
was about to be renewed, inasmuch as all the great
warriors on both sides, and numbers of their depen-
dents, were relations fighting against each other. In
order to remove his grief and nerve his arm for battle,
Krishna argues with him, that from the nature of
things it was useless to mourn or to rejoice : that he
was bound as a Kshatriya to fulfil the duties of his
position, without regard to consequences : and enters
into a theological discussion in order to defend so strong
a conclusion. Krishna declares himself the author of
the doctrines, and in proof of his authority exhibits himself to Arjuna in his divine form. The estimation in
which this dialogue is held amongst not only native
scholars, but the people generally, is of the highest
kind. The beauty of its language ; the regularity of its
structure ; its noble descriptions of the Supreme ; and the
clearness of its explanations give it literary excellence
of a high order. It is a work of merit to hear its
exposition ; much more so to learn it in the original
Sanskrit tongue.

The works of authority which follow next in order,
and which exhibit the system in its latest stages, are the
various *Commentaries* which have been written upon
the inspired works, and compendiums of the doctrine
compiled by celebrated scholars. These commentaries

are very numerous, as the Vedant has been a favourite
system for many centuries. The greatest of all the
commentators is SANKAR ACHÁRYA. This learned
Hindu bears among his philosophical countrymen a
name and reputation for scholarship scarcely inferior
to that of Veda Vyása himself. He is perhaps the most
illustrious disciple the Vedantic system ever produced.
In an age when other philosophies were popular, he
travelled so extensively, fought so hard, and obtained
so many victories by his lectures, discussions, and
writings, as to secure for the Vedánta ever after the
foremost place in the schools of Hindu philosophy.
Various data show that he lived between 650 and 740
A. D., and that his life was protracted to a great age.
He travelled all over India, and amongst other places,
visited Cashmere during the reign of Lálitadya, where
he joined in a learned discussion, and obtained the victory.  He is better known in Southern India than in
the northern provinces.  There he appeared as the
great restorer of the Siva-ite worship.  To the impulse
given to that worship by his advocacy and example are
attributed the building of the great temples at Madura,
Chillumbrum, and Tanjore, with their mighty goprams;
and also the bitter persecution which destroyed the
Jains, subjecting them to cruel tortures, which the
Madura temple has preserved in pictures down to the
present day.  The great works of Sankar Acharjya are
his Commentaries on the Upanishads, on the Sarírik
Sutras, and on the Bhagavat Gíta.

One of the latest, most popular, and most important

authorities of the system is the VEDÁNTA SÁR. This
little work, which expounds the views of the later
Vedantists, gives a most compact and systematic outline of the chief doctrines of the Vedant with arguments in their favour. It contains comparatively few
of the more descriptive portions of the science which
will be found in other authorities, and dwells chiefly on
those points which describe the method of learning it,
the reasons for its formation, and the difficulties which
its disciples meet.

The Vedánta Sár starts with a brief statement that
four things are to be considered in the study of the
system: the student, the object, the authority, the
means by which the end is attained. To the student
and his process of learning we shall refer again. It
will be necessary here merely to consider the theory
given by this little work, of the Vedantic system. In
spite of appearances there is in the universe but one
real existence (*vastu*): the being who is existence,
knowledge, and joy, the Supreme Brahm. The various
objects of the universe, especially the individual finite
souls, are unreal (*avastu*). The unreal has been based
upon the real by an improper process of "imputation;"
just as there is sometimes imputed to a rope the unreal
notion that it is a snake. This is caused by ignorance
(*agyána*). The definition given of this ignorance brings
out a most interesting feature of the later Vedánt.
"Ignorance is a kind of thing different both from
existence and non-existence, in the shape of an entity,
consisting of the three 'qualities,' the opponent of know-

ledge." In modern language it is understood to mean
the phenomenal as distinguished from the substance
which underlies it, as we have seen all "nature" is
recognized as the aggregate of the three "qualities,"
which include all that renders it cognizable by sense.
By this ignorance has the universe been produced.
Portions of the supreme soul have been individualized :
there are separate souls (*prágya*) in which has arisen
the notion of self and the like. "There is no distinction between the supreme ruler and the individual intelligences . . . .; as there is none between the sky
which covers the forest and the trees, and the sky
which is reflected by the ocean and by many waters."
This ignorance in separate souls has two powers, a
covering power and a producing power. By obstruct-
ing the mind of the observer (as a small cloud obscures
the sun), the covering power hides the infinite soul and
makes it appear limited. The producing power gives
rise to notions of happiness, misery, possession, and
dominion: and as it educes an unreal snake from a
real rope, so in the soul it produces the expanses of
the universe, and projects them as phantasms before
the mind's eye. Nevertheless the soul which is covered
by it is ONE SOUL. It is by abstraction (*apabád*) that
the supreme is to be discerned as the only reality. By
its means all the great objects in the universe will be
seen to resolve themselves into him. The student,
purified by religious ceremonies, detaching his thoughts
from outward objects, and giving intensest attention to
his teacher's instruction, meditates on the great sen-

tence "That art thou," "thou art the one sole being." He gets to perceive that all duality is illusion, that all the varied objects in the universe are all Brahma; that he is himself Brahma. "I am he." Passing beyond this judgment, which still shadows forth duality, he ceases to assert even that as a separate thought. Subject, object, and the relation between them disappear; his "wisdom" is perfect; nothing is left but the ONE, who is existence, knowledge, bliss.

It should be added that the explanation adopted by the later Vedant appears in the mythology of the Hindus in a very debased form. The ignorance which "produces" the "egg of Brahmá" is termed *pra-kriti.* As production is the result of energy, this pra-kriti must be the energy (*sakti*) of the Supreme. Popularized for the vulgar, this *sakti* becomes a goddess, Máyá, the wife of Brahmá, the Creator in the Hindu triad.

### THE VEDÁNTA SYSTEM.

It is impossible in this brief sketch to give more than a meagre outline of the general Vedánt doctrine. The varieties of opinion held by different schools, and the differences in the truths maintained at the various stages of its progress, must all be omitted. The student who would understand the whole thoroughly, must apply to the original authorities and examine them himself. In carefully analyzing them, he will soon detect the truth which one teaches and not another; and note the shades of meaning which the same language seems to bear in different works. He will observe

how the tone of the Gita differs greatly from that of the
Sutras: how the Upanishads seem to contain the system
distributed among them: how one Upanishad, for instance, the Katha, is much more pure in its doctrine
than others: or how another, like the Swetáswatara,
endeavours to effect a compromise between the Sánkhya
and Vedánt, and on eclectic principles, suggest a system which shall embrace the concurring elements of
both. All such refinements of Vedantic inquiry we
must here pass by. The general principles of the system are few and simple; they necessarily involve the
minor details by which they are accompanied: are stated
in the earliest authorities, and described in terms not a
whit clearer in the very last. It is these general principles which we shall endeavour to lay before the reader.

§ 1. DEFINITION OF VEDÁNTISM: scope of the system; its ultimate basis: conditions and mode of studying it.

"The name VEDÁNTA," says the Vedánta Sár,
"applies to the arguments of the Upanishads, also to the
Sarírik Sutras, and other shastres auxiliary thereto."
It is also defined as the system by which may be obtained the knowledge of Brahma. That knowledge is
the chief end of man; the knowledge by which he
will be delivered from all evils, especially the great evil
of repeated birth. "They who, by their nature and
firm faith in a teacher, attain to the knowledge of
Brahma, are by that knowledge removed from a multitude of evils; as being begotten, born, growing old,

affected with diseases, and the like; or it brings them to the supreme Brahma, or removes and destroys the ignorance which is the cause of worldliness in them: on this account the science is called Upanishad." The aim of the system is to show the unity between the sentient souls of individual men and Brahma, the great soul in its pure state. Every treatise therefore endeavours to describe truly the nature, existence, attributes and works of the Supreme: in order that men, by a proper study of these important subjects, may comprehend the identity which exists between themselves and him; and may thereby attain that superior happiness which springs from such knowledge alone.

The *sources* of such knowledge are distinctly defined. The schools of Hindu philosophy generally recognize three ways of obtaining knowledge; the perceptions of the senses; the deductions of reason; and tradition or revelation. By the Vedantic authorities six methods are enumerated; and the logical system adopted is that of Jaymini. The principal authority however is the authority of the VEDA; of truth derived originally from the Deity himself and handed down from one generation of teachers to another. Hence it is named *pramán, ágama,* or *sruti.* He, then, who would acquire the science, must apply to the authoritative shastres; and lest he should err in seeking to know their meaning, he must study under the great masters and teachers, who have themselves attained it, and who have received that traditional explanation which has been handed down from the earliest time. In the Upanishads we have many

examples of such teachers communicating divine knowledge to their numerous students.   In the *Chhandogya*,
Gautam teaches Satyakáma, and he teaches Upakósál.
Yájnawalkya taught the White Yajur and its two Upanishads.   Angiras taught the Mundaka to the son of
Sunaka.   Still the series of teachers is acknowledged
to be human, however great the names or celebrated
the erudition of those whom it includes.   But the doctrine claims to be regarded as superhuman, and to be
derived in several ways from BRAHMA himself.   The
*Mundaka* Upanishad declares " Brahmá, the Lord of
the Universe, came into existence before all the gods.
He revealed the doctrine of Brahma, the most excellent
of all knowledge, to his eldest son Atharbba.   Atharbba
communicated it to Angirá : he revealed it to Satyabáha,
of the race of Bharadwáj : he made it known to Angirás."   He taught it in the Mundaka to Saunaka.   In
the *Chhandogya* it is said : " This doctrine Brahma
spake to Prajápati : Prajápati to Menu : Menu to created
men."   In the *Katha*, Yama himself instructs Nachiketá.
The Sun instructs Yájnyawalkya : " the Sun is Brahma :
this is a certain truth."   " He, the all-resplendent, who
formerly created Brahmá and placed the Vedas in him,
is the displayer of divine knowledge."   (*Swet.*)

The *classes* to whom the knowledge of Brahm is to be
communicated are also pointed out.   The dry and abstruse character of the study prevents its application to
men of various ranks in society : and a lower branch of
the system, containing only ritual ceremonies, worship
and prayers, is open for the unintelligent and those

engaged in the pursuits of ordinary life. Beyond
this, even in the early days of the Upanishads, learning
was reserved for the "twice born," especially for the
brahmins, whose authority in Bhárat, though not complete, was very extensive. In the Sutras (i. 3. 34-38)
it is plainly declared, that "the purification of the *Upa-
nayana* (the investiture of the sacred thread) is the
ground of instruction : none but brahmins, Kshatryas
and Vaisyas have authority to study the Vedas." Even
amongst the privileged classes, all will not attain it:
deficiency of natural ability, or a blinded mind, like that
of Virochan, king of the Asurs, may entirely prevent its
attainment.

The *manner* in which the study is to be prosecuted,
and the *ceremonial preparation* that should precede its
commencement, occupy considerable attention. The
study being of the highest kind, can only be undertaken
in the most serious way. Sankar Acharjya has fully
described the *adhikári*, the person " qualified " to undertake it. The Vedánta Sár describes the same. He
must first find out the sense of the Vedas, as books of
language, by the study, according to rule, of the Vedán-
gas. He must either in his present birth or a previous one, renounce all the objects of desire, such as
sacrifices which obtain heaven, and works which are
forbidden, as brahmin murder and the like. By the
performance of the *Sandhyá bandhana* and other appointed ceremonies; by offering expiations ; and en-
gaging in acts of internal worship, he must purify his
mind from errors and fix it upon Brahm. He has then

to perform "the *four* means" (*sádhan chatúshtay*).
(1.) He must distinguish between the *real* and *unreal*
thing: *i.e.*, he must regard everything unreal except
Brahm. (2.) He must free himself from all *desire* of
enjoying the fruits of merit, whether in this life or a
future one. (3.) He must exclude from his mind and
from sense everything which does not refer to Brahma.
He must endure cold and heat, pleasure and pain, without recognizing a difference between them. (4.) He
must have an intense desire after *liberation* from self,
and absorption into Brahm. These exercises duly completed, he will be qualified to learn more. With earnestness of soul, let him now hasten to a teacher, with
offerings in his hand, and becoming his disciple, beg
him to impart that knowledge which is the highest that
can be attained. Of a complete victory over the ordinary love of wealth, Nachiketa, as mentioned in the
*Katha*, furnishes an illustrious example. "O Yama,
said he, the age of this universe is short: wherefore let
these equipages remain thine; be thine the dance and
the song.· . . . Confer on me, then, the favour of a
solution of my doubts respecting the nature of God."
Nárad again shows how the most extensive knowledge
of the letter of the shastres, without a perception of their
hidden spiritual meaning, does not convey to its pos-
sessor the knowledge of the Supreme. "I have learned,
he says, the Rik, the Yajur and Sáma Veda, the Atharba,
the Itihása and Puráns: grammar and the like: yet
do I only know the text, and have no knowledge of
the SOUL (*Chhand*)." Frequent meditation, abstraction

of the thoughts from all external objects continued for a long time, must be employed during the whole process of instruction and after its completion, in order to secure a complete conviction of the great truth which the science teaches.    Amongst other things, a long and most devout contemplation of the sacred syllable OM, in each of its three letters and their meaning; as well as the combined meaning of the whole, occupies a prominent place in these pursuits : and it is only men who are prepared to undergo these toils, both tedious and painful, that can hope to attain the great reward to which they infallibly lead.    " Curbing the senses and appetites, and breathing gently through the nostrils, while meditating, the scholar should concentrate his thoughts. On a clean, smooth spot, free from pebbles, from gravel or from scorching sand : where the mind is tranquillized by pleasant sounds, by running water and grateful shade, with nought to offend his eye, let him apply himself to his task."    (*Swet.*)

With such a process, how can it be wondered at that, after all, few ever attain the knowledge offered : and even they who do attain it, have been destined to their reward by the Supreme.    " He who regulates both knowledge and ignorance is God."    (*Swet.*)    " He makes him to do good deeds, whom he wishes to bring out of this world : and him he makes to do evil deeds, whom he wishes to bring into the world again, in a future birth."    (*Kaushitaki Up.*)    Thus aided by divine choice ; thus prepared by ritual services, by self-subjugation, and by the desire of obtaining the knowledge of the Supreme: and thus provided with a competent teacher, the student must place himself at his master's feet, to receive with undoubting faith whatever that master may choose to teach: ready, if need be, like Indra (*Chhand*, vii.), to wait patiently a hundred years before that wisdom be imparted, but determined to get it in the end.

### § 2.—OF THE SUPREME BRAHMA.

The Upanishads being treatises which have for their end the teaching of the knowledge of Brahm, are of course crowded with passages descriptive of his existence, attributes and deeds.    Some of them contain sublime conceptions, expressed in the highest forms of poetical language, and illustrated by striking metaphors. Other parts are puerile; and the constant repetition of the same descriptions, confined to a narrow range of topics, wearies the reader without instructing him. All the authorities dwell profusely on the same subject, and in the same manner.    The *Bhagavat Gita*, in its tenth and eleventh lectures, contains some noble passages on the majesty and splendour of the Supreme.

The *existence* of Brahma is a point which the Vedantic authorities take not the slightest trouble to prove: even although the Sánkhya had already made its heretical assertion that no evidence can be offered of such existence.    All are employed rather in enumerating his *attributes ;* which are numerous, and described both in negative and positive terms.    " Brahma is eternal, omniscient, pervader of all things, ever satisfied in nature, ever pure, intelligent and free; wisdom and delight." "That being is the true, unchanging, eternal one. Like ether he penetrates all things: he is free from all change, ever satisfied, without limbs, in nature light itself. He, in whom right and wrong, with their effects, and the three times, have no place, he is without body, and is freedom itself." "That Supreme Lord pervades all things, and is independent and one: there is no one like him, no one superior to him; the whole world obeys his will. He is the internal spirit of everything that is: he, by means of an impure delusion in names and forms, makes himself, the ONE GOD, multiform." "He is without hearing, touch, form, taste, or smell. He is without beginning or end, mighty and supreme." "He is OM. This OM is Brahma." "He is Supreme among the Gods: the Great God: the Supreme debta of the debtas; the Lord of lords, supreme over all." "Brahma is supreme: supreme and all excellent: and pervading the body of each, dwells deep in all existences. He alone encompasses and regulates the universe." "To him there is none high nor low, nor great nor small." "He is the mighty Lord, perfect, the inciter to all good. Without hands or feet he runs and handles: without eyes he sees: without ears he hears. He knows all, but they know him not. He is without decay, ancient, universal spirit, all-pervading. He is without birth, eternal." "He is without tribe or race: without eyes or ears; without hands or feet . . . . the producer of everything that is."

With respect to his essential *nature*, Brahma is declared to be Supreme *Intelligence.* " On account of the eternal essence of intellect in Brahma (as light is the essence of the sun), no regard can be allowed to other supports of intelligence." Again, this intelligence is not only compared to light, as in the passage just quoted, but is said to *be* light. " Though Brahm is in his very nature intellect, yet the word *light* describes him, as it does the cause of the illumination of the whole world." (Sankara.) " As a mass of salt is, not internally, not externally, but entirely, a mass of savour, so that spirit is, not internally, not externally, but entirely, a mass of intelligence." His *size* is thus described : " He is less than the least atom : he is greater than the greatest."

According to some views of the Hindu mythology, Brahma is not always invested with these attributes. In the intervals between the Great Ages, or *Kalpas,* he is said to be altogether *nirgúna,* " without qualities," and to recline upon the leaves of the banyan-tree in a state of profound repose (*batpatrasáyí*). The Sutras declare that the latter is the true description of him ; not the former, nor the two together. It is only in relation to the creation that these " qualities " of various kinds are attributed to him. Really, " he is unaffected by the modifications of the world : as the clear crystal, seemingly coloured by the red blossom of the hibiscus, is not the less really pellucid." " He changes not : all change is expressly denied him by the texts in the Vedas."

The *Universe,* on the Vedant theory, as we shall

presently see, is not a *real* universe, it is only an apparent one. Yet the relation of Brahma to that unreal world, is fully and frequently mentioned in the Vedantic authorities. He is declared to be its *creator*. " When there was neither day nor night, HE was, who is without darkness and is pure goodness alone." But when the time arrived he made all. " One God produced the heavens and the earth." " He is the almighty creator of the world and the all-wise author of the Shastres." " His will alone is a sufficient cause of the universe: and he has made it for sport." The Sutras say, that he first conceived the desire to create, and employed special words in the process. " From Vedic words, the universe beginning with the gods, has sprung." " Uttering the word *bhúr* he created the earth." The *Aitareyá* Upanishad (ii. 4.) enters fully into the subject of the creation, and describes the formation of the great objects of the universe with minute detail; especially the structure of man. The passage is too long to quote here.* The *Brihad Aranyaka* also describes the formation of the animated creation, and the mode in which the male and female of each kind were produced.

Brahma is the *sustainer* also of the creation which he has produced. The Upanishads give numerous illustrations. " All things in the world proceeded from the Supreme, and in him they move. Through fear of him fire flames: through fear of him the sun shines; through fear of him Indra, Váyu and Death keep in motion."

* Colebrooke's *Essay on the Vedas* gives it in full.

" If God leave the system of man which he pervades,
then what of it can remain! Not through their vital
powers do mortals remain alive: they live through him,
by whom those powers are themselves sustained." In a
dialogue between Yájnyawalkya and his wife Gargì,
the former declares that the ether, on which the heavens
and earth rest, is woven and sewn upon the supreme
Brahm. Brahma is also the *destroyer* of this creation.
" The one destroyer, the being without a second, who
dwells in every one and who regulates these worlds by
his regulating power, after creating all worlds and sustaining them, destroys them in the end." So say other
passages. The time of destruction is defined as arising
periodically at the end of the various *Kalpas* which
mark out the progress of time: when Brahma, according
to the necessity of his nature, absorbs all his works into
himself, to produce them again when another appointed
period shall arrive. This is a matter rather discussed in
the Puráns than in the Vedánt, except in general terms.

The connection between the Supreme and his created
works is declared by all the authorities to be even more
intimate than that which has been now described.
Hitherto we have seen him as the efficient and ultimate
cause of the universe; and of the myriads of objects
which it contains. But the greater number of passages which speak on the subject show the relation
between him and them to be more direct and simple,
declaring him to be their *internal ruler,* their *substantial,*
or as we usually express it, their *material* cause: that
is, in other words, the very substance of which they are

composed.　This is the prime doctrine of the Vedant
system: whose influence has moulded all the other portions of the science, and has produced all the difficulty
which students and scholars have found in explaining
both its dogmas and the necessity which produced them.
It is also the prime *error* of the system, immensely important in itself, and also producing other errors which
naturally cluster round it as its legitimate companions.
We shall therefore defer a more particular statement of
the doctrine, of the arguments by which it is defended,
and the illustrations by which it is elucidated, to a
future chapter, and merely state briefly for the present
the evidence of its existence in the system.

There are three classes of passages contained in the
various Vedantic authorities, which teach the perfect
identity between Brahma and the universe; that is, the
doctrine of Pantheism : numerous expressions and passages most strongly imply it: it is openly and forcibly
asserted in distinct terms; and numerous illustrations
are employed to explain it.　(1.) The Upanishads, the
Sutras and Gita, frequently speak of Brahma as pervading the universe, and apply to him numerous epithets expressive of that idea.　And in order to put the
fact in a clearer light, the assertion is made, not only
concerning the universe in general, but also its individuated parts.　The term *sarvabhútantarátmá*, " the
internal spirit of all things," frequently occurs in the
Mundaka and Katha Upanishads.

(2.) The doctrine is directly taught in passages like
the following : " Brahma is the substance of the uni-

verse : for so the propositions (in the Vedas) and their illustrations require " (Sutras i. 4. 23). " Nothing exists but he" (iii. 2. 29). " I am the sacrifice : I am the worship : I am the drug ; I am the incantation : I am the fire ; I am the incense " (Gita, ix.). " Fire is that original cause : the sun is that ; so is air : so is the moon : such is that pure Brahma : and those waters ; and Prajápati. . . . . It is he who is in the womb : he who is born : and he who will be produced."

(3.) The *illustrations* employed also teach it. The universe is compared to sparks proceeding from him, the fire : to the spider's web, which is of the same animal substance with the creature which spins it : and the like. Many of these figures are drawn out at great length, and are beautifully expressed.

By far the most copious details of this dogma are taught in the earliest authorities, the Upanishads : and from thence they have been reproduced in the Sutras, the Gita and their commentaries. Nothing then appears more clear than that it was cotemporaneous with the earliest philosophy which sprang up among the Hindus, and was considered to furnish a proper explanation of the essence of their religion so far as it had been then developed. Of its great age and immense influence at the present time, no proof can be more plain than that every Hindu knows it, that every Hindu occasionally appeals to it ; and makes it the ground of all his stolid submission to the fate which seems to rule his existence from the cradle to the funeral pyre.

## § 3.—THE UNIVERSE AND ITS ELEMENTS.

In the preceding section, it has been shown that the universe has for its substance and material the Supreme Brahma himself: that it was created from his desire, and called forth by special words. In this section may be noticed the *divisions* into which it is separated; its *primary elements;* and the various classes of *beings* by which it is occupied.

According to many authorities, the universe is *divided* into three worlds (*Tri-lóka*)—viz. heaven, earth, and hades. By others a division into only two is sanctioned, of which one includes the earth. In this division the worlds are classified as the upper and lower. In the upper worlds are included, first, *Bhúr-lok,* the earth: then, *Bhuvar-lok,* the residence of the Munis, the region between the earth and sun: *Swar-lok* is the heaven of Indra: next comes *Maha-lok,* the abode of Bhrigu and other saints: *Jana-lok,* the residence of the sons of Brahmá: *Tapa-lok,* the residence of the "Vairágis:" and lastly, *Satya-lok* or *Brahma-lok,* the dwelling-place of Brahma himself. The lower worlds are beneath the earth: they are also seven in number, are placed one beneath the other, and constitute the residence of various evil beings. Their names are *Atala, Vitala, Sutala, Rasátala, Talátal, Mahátal,* and *Pátál.* These reappear also in Puranic theology. In various texts, other regions are spoken of which must be considered subdivisions of those now enumerated. Thus in ascending to the heaven of Indra, the soul of the devout worshipper passes first to the realm of *fire:*

K

thence to the *regents of the day* : thence to the *abode of the gods;* thence, through the region of air, to the *moon;* thence to the realm of *lightning.* Above this is the realm of Varuná: and finally, follows the region of *Indra.* In the Upanishads but few references are made to this subject; yet the same classification seems to have prevailed in their day. Allusions are made to the " seven retributive worlds of happiness :" and Brahma Loka is several times named: as also Pitri Lóka.

The *original elements* of the universe are always in Hindu philosophy set down as *five :* the Upanishads having started the doctrine, and no chemist among them attempting to set it aside as untrue. " From him have sprung ether, air, light (or fire), water, and the all-containing earth." The *order* in which they were created is not the same in all the passages which enumerate them; sometimes one element precedes and sometimes another: the confusion passed onwards into the Sutras and commentaries, and though they endeavour to settle the fact, they agree in arguing that in the Vedas, the order was considered immaterial. These five elements have been compounded one with another, in various proportions, arbitrarily fixed by the philosophers; and from these combinations have sprung the myriads of varieties which the actual objects of the world exhibit. The *Swetáswatara* Upanishad says: " He, by his power, at the time of creation, combined element with element, in the proportion of one, two, four, and eight." The Sutras say that ether and air are from Brahma: and that fire, water, and earth proceed mediately from him; but that they are evolved successively from one another: fire is from air, air is from ether. They are evolved in this way, by his will, not from any chemical properties of their own. At the destruction of all things they merge into one another in the reverse order, and are all reabsorbed into his essence. The Vedánta Sár gives a later view of the question; developed still farther and on a different principle. "The gross elements are composed of the subtle ones according to the combination of five (*panchikritam*). This combination of five is—to divide each of the five elements into two parts: then equally to divide each of the five former of the ten parts into four parts: to separate these four of the one half from their own parts, and to join them with the parts of the other elements, &c." From the five elements so compounded were produced all the great Lokas or worlds.

The various classes into which *organized* bodies are distributed are not spoken of frequently. In the Aitareyá they are enumerated under four heads: (1) the *oviparous*; (2) those born in *the womb*; (3) those springing spontaneously from *hot moisture* (the minute insects); and (4) those springing from *plants*. The same classification is made in the latest authority, the Vedánta Sár; physical science having made little progress since the days of the Upanishads. They are enumerated among the other objects contained in the universe, which the illusive power of ignorance has produced from the *Brahmándo*—"the egg of Brahmá."

It is important to notice among other objects of crea-

tion, the creation and existence of various DEITIES. In
the Vedas and Upanishads Indra, Váyu, Agni, Varuná,
and Mitra appear in the most conspicuous places. The
*Nirukta*, however (the passage has no Vedic authority), declares that the deities are only *three;* namely,
Agni, Váyu, and Indra; of whom collectively Prajápati is Lord : " In fact, however, there is only deity,
the great soul." In other passages, however, inferior
deities are mentioned, the Vasus, Rudras, and Adityas,
the gods of the Vedic age. These gods are not purely
imaginary beings. They are "produced;" they " boast;"
they " worship;" they "doubt" about religious questions. They were *worshipped* with sacrifices and offerings; and the Upanishads teach that such worship is
beneficial to the devotee. In the Chhandogya Upanishad (ch. v.) a number of sages go to Aswapati to
inquire about Brahma. He asks them individually
whom they worship. One worships Indra; another,
the Sun; another, Heaven, " as the soul;" another,
Váyu; another, ether, and so on. The kingly sage
acknowledges to each the benefits of his worship;
though in the end he points them all to the higher
worship of Brahma by contemplation. Not only in
the Gita, where numerous passages speak of it, but in
the Vájsaneyi Upanishad, the benefits of this lower kind
of religion are distinctly asserted as true. In the Vedánta Sár, the worship of the usual deities, included in
other ceremonies of the brahmins, is noted as a part of
the preparation essential to the man who would become
qualified to study the system. The *Gita* speaks most

fully both of the existence of the deities, and of the fruits of their worship: and that worship is frequently declared to be beneficial. " Remember the gods: they will grant you the enjoyment of your wishes." " Those who worship the gods, go unto them."

### § 4.—OF MAN.

Man is but one among the numerous classes of created things : but from the importance of his position, in fact, as well of that which he occupies in the Vedantic system, a separate section of this chapter must be devoted to an examination of his origin. He is regarded by the Vedánt as made up of two elements, the individual soul, and the vehicle constructed for its use. We will consider the latter first.

The *vehicle* or abode of the individual soul is said to consist of two bodies, one more refined, the other more gross in its constitution. The former, called the *sukhma sarira*, or subtle body, is the internal vehicle. The latter, called the *sthul sarira*, or gross body, is made up of the limbs and organs visible to us. The body in general is styled in the Upanishads, the " city of Brahma," and is frequently said to have nine gates, in allusion to the various openings into its interior. But its structure is very little described in those treatises. The five senses, the five vital airs, and the five organs of action had all been recognized even in their day: but for the particular details of the body's structure we must turn to the Sutras, and to the Vedánta Sár, in which they are fully described. The inner, or subtle

body, is said by the latter authority, to contain seventeen organs: the five organs of intelligence, the five
vital airs, the five organs of action, understanding, and
reason.   The five organs of intelligence are the five
senses: the eye, the ear, the tongue, touch, and smell.
They are derived from parts of the first quality (the
Satwa guna) of the five original elements respectively.
The understanding and the reason are both enumerated
among the "organs" of the soul's vehicle, and it is
difficult to conceive the exact shade of meaning in
respect to our constitution which they are intended to
bear.   The former is said to be that action of the mind
which asserts: the latter, that action by which it weighs
arguments.   Thinking and consciousness are two actions
included in them.   Understanding and reason both
spring from the united first qualities of the ether and
other elements.   The subtle body again is made up of
three cases, included one within the other, and made up
of the seventeen organs mentioned.   The "understanding," joined with the five organs of intelligence, is
called the "intelligent case" of the soul (vigyánmaya
kosh).   It possesses the consciousness of power, enjoyment, pleasure and pain, and constitutes the sentient
soul.   The "reason" joined with the five organs of
action is the mental case (manamaya kosh).   These
organs of action are, the hand, the foot, speech, evacua-
tion, and generation.   They spring from parts of the
five elements, of the second quality (the Raja guna).
The five vital airs joined with the organs of action form
with them the vital case of the soul (pránmay kosh).

They include the vital functions of respiration, inspiration, circulation, the guttural air, and the "equalizing air" of digestion. Of these cases, the intelligent case, having the faculty of knowledge, is the originator: the mental case, having the faculty of desire, is the causal: and the vital case, having the faculty of action, is the performer of works.

It is difficult to determine the exact application of each portion of this singular theory of our constitution. Though descriptive properly of the body, it contains much that is purely mental. Professing to account for our physical structure, it really includes a great deal that is immaterial. The description of the three cases of the soul, and of their separate functions, seems to refer to certain facts in the phenomena of human actions of this kind. We resolve mentally to lift the hand; an act of volition follows, which influences the nervous system, particularly the nerves of motion: the muscular action of lifting the hand concludes the series. It would appear that phenomena of the first kind are attributed to the intelligent case of the soul: those of the second, to the mental case: and the muscular actions to the vital case. It is scarcely to be wondered at, that while the connection between the soul and the body is so intimate and so close, philosophers of an age so early should fail to discriminate thoroughly the purely mental from the purely physical elements employed in the proceedings of human life. The Sutras differ somewhat from the Vedánta Sár in their account. They enumerate only eleven organs in the body: the five organs of sense or intelligence; the five organs of action; and the " inner sense."

The *mode* in which the body is sustained is curiously stated in the Sutras. The Supreme Ruler, as constituting the material of the universe, has transformed himself into all the objects of which it is composed; he has transformed himself into various combinations and shapes, deemed terrene, aqueous or igneous, according as one or other element predominates: it is by him therefore, in the form of these edible substances, that the body is nourished and matured. The process of digestion and assimilation is thus described. When nourishment enters the body it undergoes a threefold distribution according to its fineness or coarseness. Corn and other terrene food become flesh: but the coarser portions are rejected; the finer nourish the mental organ. Water is converted into blood: the coarser particles are rejected as urine: the finer support the breath. Oil and other combustible substances become marrow: the coarser parts enter into bone; the finer supply the faculty of speech.

When the body is *dissolved* at death, a process takes place, the reverse of the development which has been now described. The speech of a dying man, followen by the ten exterior faculties, is absorbed into the mind. The mind (or consciousness) retires into the breath, with all the other vital functions. The breath, attended by them, is withdrawn into the living soul, as the attendants of a king assemble round him when he departs on a journey. The living soul, attended with all its faculties, retires within a rudimental body composed of light. This rudimental frame remains in all its transmigrations, and during all its period of separate existence, till the dissolution of all things, when it merges into the Supreme. Here again we seem to have merely a description of the ordinary course of death : in which first a patient becomes speechless ; then his limbs begin to grow cold, and his sensations dull. He then becomes unconscious ; but still breathes. The breath ceases, and then life departs. It is important to notice that " these vital acts do not take effect of themselves : they are directed and influenced by a divinity who presides over them : the living spirit is, however, only conscious of the enjoyment, and not of the presiding power."

During life, the body is considered ever to occupy one or other of *three states :* those of waking, dreaming, and profound sleep. That of coma or fainting has been reckoned as a fourth ; and the state of death added as fifth. Sankar Acharya thus describes them :—" When awake a living man, owing to the illusions of *máyá,* perceives an inherent distinction between the objects of sense : in dreams the mind retires into itself, and from its own imaginings creates new worlds : in profound sleep both these illusions are wanting, and the mind reverts to its true union with the Supreme." " When a man sleeps, speech goes into the mind ; the eye into the mind ; the intellect into the mind ; the ear into the mind ; when he wakes, from the mind they again return." " In profound sleep the soul retires to the

bosom of the Supreme by the way of the pericardial
arteries, and obtains its own form "—(Sutr. iii. 2, 1-10.)
Similar views of sleep and dreams are propounded in
the Upanishads.

The *origin* and *nature* of the human SOUL form a
prominent topic in the Vedánt, and few things can be
more clear than the view which its authorities take of
the subject. In § 2. it was shown that all matter is
only BRAHMA, and that he is the substance and material
of which the universe is composed. We shall naturally
expect, therefore, when we inquire into the nature of
the individual souls of men, that we shall be referred
also to the Supreme. And thus we find it. While the
Nyáyá and Sánkhya find an original matter for the
physical universe, and original " souls " for its human
minds, the Vedánt ascribes their origin at once to the
Supreme, and declares them to consist of individuated
portions of his essential substance. The soul is said to
be a spark of the Supreme soul, shining by its own
light. It resides in a cavern of the heart as a diminutive " ether " in the centre of a small water-lily. Its
size is said to be that of a thumb, a mere expression, we
presume, to denote its smallness. Eternal in its nature,
it never grows old; and whatever be its history, it at
last is reabsorbed into the divine essence from which it
was originally withdrawn. This doctrine, as containing
one of the fundamental and most pernicious errors of
the Vedánt system, will be stated separately in a future
chapter.

We must not omit to notice, that in spite of the

community of origin thus attributed to all human souls, and of their perfect consubstantiality with the Supreme, the Vedánt from its earliest stages recognizes amongst them the important division of CASTES. The *Mánava Shastre*, a work of authority on the science, contains the fullest statement of its numerous details: of the origin and uses of the division; the classes into which men are distributed; and the peculiar duties incumbent on each caste. The *Gíta*, though it says comparatively little, attributes clearly the origin of the system to the Supreme himself. " The institution of the four castes was created by me, according to the distribution of the natural qualities and actions "—(ch. iv.) The particular duties of each are specified in Lect. xviii., and it is declared that the natural duty of a sudra is servitude. The Upanishads speak of it but little; and seem to point to different stages in the development of the caste system: but the allusions are unmistakeable, and the theory is maintained to the present hour. In a hymn of the Yajur Veda, of very early date, occurs the following passage: " Into how many portions did they divide this person whom they immolated? . . . . His mouth became a priest; his arm was made a soldier; his thigh was transformed into a husbandman; from his feet sprang the servile man." According to the *Brihad Aranyaka* the process was a gradual one. " The bráhmins alone existed in the beginning." But, " all being one, he did not enjoy it; he therefore largely created the Kshetriyas of excellent nature." Next he created the Vaisyas: but as there was a want of slaves,

" he therefore made the order of Sudras." Of these
four races, thus distinct from their very formation, the
conditions are very different: the first three are widely
separated from the last. " Those who do well in this
world attain to excellent races hereafter, according to
their works, whether it be the race of brahmins, Kshetriyas, or Vaisyas " (*Chhand.* v. 6). The mixed castes,
so numerous in the present age, and some of them so
honourable, are seldom referred to in the Upanishads.
The *Chandála* and *Paulkasa* are mentioned: of which
the former is one of the lowest castes in modern times.
These few extracts show that the division into four
castes is reckoned a divine institution, and to owe its
origin to the very circumstances of the creation itself.

### § 5.—The State of Man.

However noble the origin of man, however intimate
the connection between him and the Supreme, he is
acknowledged on all hands to be ignorant of his true
character. He knows nothing of his real nature, of
the reason of his existence, and of his future destiny.
He therefore yields himself to the dictates of passion;
finds his enjoyment in the fleeting pleasures of sense;
and is too happy to inquire into the sufferings which
will be the result of his worldliness.

1. The first thing, then, that is taught concerning the
condition of man is, that he is in a state of the greatest
*ignorance.* Of this ignorance, however, he is not the
original cause. When Brahma evolved from himself
the various objects of which the universe is apparently

composed, he placed them all under the influence of an *illusion* (máya) which prevented their knowing what was their real character. The illusion is specially developed in man, who looks on himself as quite distinct from the Supreme. The Upanishads upon this subject are decided and clear. "Living in the midst of ignorance, and believing themselves to be wise, fools frequently are led astray through crooked paths, like a blind man led by a blind man." They are also very decided in ascribing the origin of this ignorance (as the Vedanta theory consistently requires) to the Supreme Creator. "Knowledge and ignorance are both hidden in him who is the imperishable Brahm. He who governs both ignorance and knowledge is God" (*Swet*). "He makes him to do good deeds, whom he wishes to bring out of this world; and him he makes to do evil deeds, whom he wishes to bring again into the world." (*Kaushitaki*). "He is the cause both of our bondage in the world, and of our liberation from it." This alleged fact, the ignorance which all men possess of their true relation to the Supreme, is the first necessary conclusion from the fundamental tenet of the Vedant system: the identity between the universe and its maker. It is therefore dwelt upon strongly by the later authorities, who felt that, if this ignorance of man cannot be established, that first tenet will at once be overthrown by an appeal to human consciousness, to human reason, and especially to their sense of right and wrong. Recognizing it as such, the notion of this ignorance, produced by an illusion (or *máyá*) from the

Supreme, is strongly defended by those authorities, and
illustrated more largely than any other topic of their
philosophy. Mr. Colebrooke considers that the doctrine
of *máyá* is an excrescence of the system, added on in
later times. But it seems only a fair deduction from
the principles of an earlier age. If man be identical
with Brahm, he certainly is ignorant of the fact.
Indeed his own consciousness of independence, his moral
affections, his sense of responsibility, the duality of
nature taught by every thought and every act of life,
deny the fact and prove the contrary. The only mode
of getting rid of this great difficulty is—to deny the
validity of an appeal to consciousness, by an assertion
that its view of things is distorted and false: that it is
under the influence of illusion, gives false evidence concerning the nature and existence of things around us,
and therefore leads men thoroughly astray. This is
máyá. Without it, the original pantheistic dogma may
soon be overturned: by its aid, the court of appeal
has its character destroyed, and is pronounced unworthy of confidence. Either pantheism is false, or
man's consciousness is a delusion. The Vedánt accepts
the latter alternative.

The explanation of this illusion, as drawn out in the
*Vedánta Sár* and in the *Bhagavat Gita* is very subtle:
and is made to turn upon one of the most mystic
dogmas of ancient Hindu philosophy (xiv. 92). Every
portion of the universe has been invested by the Supreme
with one or more of the THREE GUNAS or qualities.
These so enter into their very essence and constitution

as to necessitate from them certain conclusions which must infallibly be developed. The first of these qualities is goodness (*satwa*). It is alleviating, enlightening, leading to happiness: virtue predominates in it. It is prevalent in fire, whence the flame ascends, and sparks fly upward. When present in man, as it is in those of a superior order, it is the cause of virtue. The second and middle quality is foulness, passion, or activity (*raja* or *teja guna*). It is active, urgent, variable, attended with evil and misery. Present in the air, it causes wind to move along the ground. In living beings it is the cause of vice. The third quality is darkness (*tamah*). It is heavy and obstructive; attended with sorrow, dulness, and illusion. Because it predominates in earth and water, they have a tendency to fall. In living beings it causes ignorance, sloth, and gloom. The *Gita* enlarges on the influence and natural results of these qualities, and shows the different forms in which they appear, especially in human conduct and the states of human happiness or misery. Following the Sánkhya philosophy, the Gíta declares that these qualities belong to the very essence of nature, and employs the very same term, *Prakriti*, the root-matter of the universe, to denote the substance from which they come forth. These qualities affect men in everything according to their natural tendencies: and according as they possess the higher or the lower, will they contrive to rise or to fall, to improve in virtue and in an approach to the great object of their birth; or to wander farther and farther from Brahm at each successive stage of their

existence, to be absorbed once more into his essence,
only when the mighty universe returns to him at the
final destruction of all things.   Thus it is that in their
desires, propensities, temper, mode of worship, objects
of worship, actions, aims, and enjoyments, men are and
can be only what the quality they have been endowed
with permits them to be.

It is in consequence of the great prevalence of the
Raja and Tama Gunas that men lie in such intense
ignorance of what they are.   Though Brahma is everything, and everything is Brahma, men draw "distinctions" between themselves and him, and between him
and the universe in general.   This ignorance, which
vitiates all their opinions, leads them continually into
the error of " improper attribution " (*adhyáröpa*), that
is, of falsely ascribing to things and persons qualities
which they do not possess.   "Just as a man may, from
gloom or distance, attribute to a piece of rope the quality of being a snake, so has the individual soul, under
the influence of the glooms of ignorance, created for
itself an outward world.   From this cause it has erroneously considered that the gross body in which it
resides, with all its various organs—the place which
supports that body, the ether and other worlds—in fact,
the whole ' egg of Brahmá,' are REAL things (*vastu*),
instead of unreal (*avastu*), and have their origin in
the gross elements.   From the same cause it believes
that these elements, with their three qualities, are separate existences, instead of being identical with the
' fourth Brahma,' the uninherent Soul, who is their

support." The Supreme, in all these errors, still controls and governs it. "Blind in the darkness of ignorance, the soul is guided in its actions and fruition, in its attainment of knowledge and consequent liberation and bliss, by the Supreme Ruler of the Universe, who causes it to act conformably with its previous resolves; now, according to former purposes; as *then*, consonantly to its yet earlier predispositions, accruing from preceding forms with no retrospective limit, for the world had no beginning. The Supreme Ruler makes individuals to act relatively to their virtuous or vicious propensities. As the same fertilizing rain-cloud causes various seeds to sprout multifariously, producing diversity of plants according to their kinds." (*Sutras.*)

The most important and practical result of this state is, that until the soul gets free from its delusions, it is compelled to undergo a series of *transmigrations*, ever reaping the rewards of its acts, either in punishment or in pleasure; and then returning to another body to undergo the same round. In time all its pollutions may be purified, if the tendency of its "qualities" be upward; and it may be reunited once more to its original essence, and absorbed in the glorious fulness of the Creator of all. This doctrine of transmigration is taught not by the Vedánt only, but by all the schools of Hindu philosophy: it lies at the root of all their speculations, is the basis of all their purposes and aims: it deserves therefore special attention, and will be discussed in a future chapter.

L

## § 6.—HUMAN DELIVERANCE AND ITS FINAL REWARDS.

Transmigration from one body into another, during a succession of ages, is represented as a great misfortune. The Vedánt therefore lays before its followers the system revealed by the Vedas, according to which, the misfortune may be obviated, the series of changes reduced in number, and the individuality of the soul destroyed by its absorption into the Supreme. This system contains a course of instruction that shall enlighten the mind and purify it from all the errors and illusions by which its misfortunes are caused. The student will be shown what he is, that he may be delivered from the erroneous conviction that he is something entirely different. All persons however, even among the favoured brahmins, will not be able to undergo the same arduous course of study. The science, therefore, has been divided into two branches.

1. The *inferior* doctrine is no other than that of the *Purbba Mimánsá*, viz., that liberation may ultimately be attained by religious merit; by the fruit of sacrifices, and other ceremonies of the Hindu ritual. All the authorities refer to them and acknowledge them as a distinct though preparatory part of the Vedanta system. " All this effort and knowledge of which we have spoken, rightly observed, aid the man who desires liberation and is free from worldly longings, in purifying his nature: . . . all the works enjoined in the Vedas and other shastres, are efficacious only in the acquirement of salvation by the southern road." In the Katha

Upanishad, Yama describes the mode of worship by the Nachiketic fire. In the Mundaka, ritual ceremonies are in some texts praised as elevating the soul, and preparing it for enjoyment in the next world: though in others they are declared worthless and deceptive as compared with the higher mode of securing the same end. The *Gita* is most profuse in its praise of this lower mode of obtaining celestial bliss, and the benefits of idol worship are affirmed in the strongest terms. In point of fact, however, the performance of such ceremonies and the effort to secure high rewards in the next world, are external to the Vedant as a system. All rigid Hindus in their daily worship are engaged in performing them, whether Vedantists or not. The texts serve to show that while the system as such points out the shortest and most efficacious mode of securing liberation, it allows that all those inferior ceremonies tend to increase and promote a religious spirit, and therefore to lead a man towards the high end which all religious worship is calculated to secure.

Another mode of deliverance, of the same inferior kind, is taught almost exclusively by the *Bhagavat Gita.* It is the mode of FAITH which is again and again declared to be supremely efficacious. " He who performs his actions for me, intent on me, devoted to me, free from interest and from enmity towards any being, comes to me." (ch. xi.)

2. The *superior* mode of obtaining liberation from the ignorance in which men have been born is that which the Vedánta system is specially intended to teach. We

have already seen that as 'ignorance' of Brahma is the
disease, so 'wisdom' in relation to Brahma (*Brah-
magyán*) constitutes the cure, a cure which may be
made perfect and eternal. By this '*wisdom*' is meant
the true and complete understanding of what Brahma
is, and of man's relation to him. The soul has been
accustomed to consider itself independent, a separate
being, a voluntary agent; living in a body prepared for
its own use from material substances; and residing upon
a world in the midst of a universe, external to itself
and formed also from matter. These views have
sprung from the habit of improperly attributing to
these varied objects qualities which they do not possess.
The Vedánt assumes as its special task the removal of
this ignorance by a faithful exhibition of the real character of the universe and its elements. It teaches
that all is Brahma; that the scholar is himself Brahma;
that his body is but a form of Brahma; that the
universe is Brahma, and does not exist apart from
Brahma; that his passions, pleasures, and pains are all
unreal; his relations in life unreal; and that there is
but one REAL thing in the universe—"the immortal,
fearless Brahma." All this doctrine is communicated
to the scholar by his learned teacher; but a process is
required, which the student must most steadily pursue,
before he can receive it thoroughly and make it his own.
It is not the mere communication of the doctrine, or
general assent to it, which makes a man a real Vedantist,
but the weaving of it into his very nature, so that he
embraces it in his inmost soul.

The process to be adopted, in order to secure so great a result, a result so opposed to the usual convictions of his daily life, is that of deep and continuous MEDITATION on the character of the Supreme. "MEDITATION is the root of the knowledge of the SPIRIT." (*Swet.*) "They who know the Vedánt and observe its meaning well, who exercise devout contemplation, and who are pure, at last in Brahma-loka are altogether liberated and cease to die." This meditation or mental contemplation is called by different names, and is carried on under various circumstances. The position of the devotee, the place of his retirement, and other exterior conditions of the student, are all pointed out, that he may be aided in every step to direct his thoughts, and secure the desired end. In the Upanishads, little is said of them: though one passage already quoted from the *Swet,* shows the process systematized. The different modes and degrees of religious meditation are also named and distinguished. The general application of the mind to all the details and degrees of contemplation; the retirement, the bodily mortifications, the subjugation of the passions, the direction of the mind to any individual truth, are all noticed. In the *Bhagavat Gita,* numerous descriptions of the "wise man" (*gyáni*), who applies himself to this devotion, occur: and the superiority of his worship and study to those of the sacrificer and seeker of merit are frequently dwelt upon. "The sacrifice of spiritual knowledge is better than a material sacrifice." "The *Yogi* places his couch firmly on a spot that is undefiled. Then seated on his couch, fixing his heart on the one object: restraining his thoughts, senses, and actions, he should practise devotion for the purification of his soul. Holding his body, head, and neck all even and immoveable, and firmly seated, his eyes fixed upon the tip of his nose, not looking in different directions, let him meditate intent on me." (vi. p. 45.) The *Vedánta Sár* contains the most complete and systematized view of all the processes attendant on the Vedánta study. They are called especially "*the four means,*" and include both what is needful to the study, when attending on the teacher, and what is efficient for its absorption into the mind, when privately meditating upon his precepts. They are as follow: (1.) *Hearing:* that is, fixing in the mind the opinion of the Vedánt concerning Brahma; by regarding the commencement and end of the passages which speak of him; by constant practice and repetition; by excluding other arguments than those advanced; by regarding the fruit of knowledge; by praising the subject explained; and by demonstration of it. (2.) *Attention* to Brahma by the demonstrations offered concerning him. (3.) *Contemplation* of him in the way taught. (4.) *Meditation,* especially meditation which regards no difference between him who knows the object of knowledge, and the knowledge itself. This process includes *refraining* from injury, from lying, from stealing, and from disobedience to the teacher: it includes also *sitting in a particular posture,* as in the form of a lotus, and *suppression of the breath.* It excludes listlessness, absence of mind, passion and propensity to pleasure. When these are really attended to, the student becomes immoveable in mind, "like a lamp protected from the wind." The effect of such processes on his mental constitution must be practically to pervert in an extreme degree the natural judgment, instead of developing its powers and widening its range of view. We can scarcely wonder then that the sense of duality, which is one of the prominent fundamental facts of the mind, should be so blunted, and the whole mind so distorted, as to permit a student to adopt the conviction that he and all things are Brahm.

It must not be forgotten that amongst the distinct objects of special and careful meditation, the sacred syllable OM occupies a distinguished place. The student must devoutly repeat it again and again, and fix his mind in the intensest degree upon its several meanings. The Mándukya Upanishad declares these to be four in number. The A included in it denotes Brahma, in the form of Vaishwanar, the human soul in its waking state. The U refers to him as Taijasa, in the state of dreaming: the M represents him as Prájna in the state of deep sleep: the combined syllable OM, *i.e.* AUM, denotes him at once as the Supreme, invisible, blissful, without a second. The Sutras attribute to the syllable three elements of meaning, and declare the efficacy of its repetition to depend upon the sense in which it is viewed by the devotee. He who meditates on all three, like a serpent which casts its skin, ascends at once to Brahma. "After sharpening thy arrow by devotion, fix it to that great weapon, the bow found in the Upa-

nishad, and after drawing it and carefully aiming at thy
mark, pierce him, oh beloved, who is the imperishable.
It is said that Om is the bow, the soul is the arrow, and
Brahma is the mark, . . . . As an arrow penetrates its mark, so do thou penetrate him." (*Mund.* ii.
2, 3, 4.)

It only remains to describe the various EFFECTS of
these processes, and our outline of the system will be
complete. The fourth book of the Sutras is specially
occupied with this topic, and clearly defines the separate
degrees of reward which devotees will obtain. The
Upanishads also describe them. We find that all who
give their mind to the study of the Vedánt, with the
desire to obtain its fruit of absorption, enjoy reward:
nor are those precluded who have adopted only the inferior path of ceremonies and works of merit. Three
degrees of this reward are specified: bestowed according to the amount of merit or knowledge acquired by
the worshipper.

(*a.*) The *lowest* degree is that assigned to the followers of the inferior method. They go after death to
the heaven of Indra, where they remain till their merit
is expended, when they are born into the world again.
(*Gita,* ix. p. 65.)

(*b.*) The second degree is obtained by those who have
by meditation, sacrifice, and worship, served Brahma
greatly, but have not attained perfect wisdom or the
highest rank in excellence. Their souls are conveyed
at death across the regions of the universe to the heaven
of Prajápati. They are endowed with very great power,

a power analogous to that of Brahmá, but which serves for enjoyment only and not for action. They can summon the *pitris* at pleasure, and exercise other super-human faculties. (*Chhand.* viii. 2.) Whatever they wish for, whatever they desire, they at once obtain. They are independent and can assume many bodies or one, " as a lamp can nourish more than one wick."

Both these classes have to pass through life again : though the number of migrations differs with the degree of knowledge and merit obtained. The lowest will be born again speedily : the highest may not leave the heaven of Brahmá till another Kalpa returns. The course of their journey; the steps by which they rise; the regions they cross; the place they reside in; the course of their return, and the mode in which their human birth is again accomplished, are all clearly yet concisely stated in a valuable passage in that section of the *Chhand.* Upanishad, which is called *Panchágnibidyá*. One special consolation is reserved for them all, whatever be their grade. It is that though they may enjoy and expend the fruits of their merits, the good influence of those merits will still remain, and thus from birth to birth they will rise higher in the scale of holiness, until they attain the final reward. " As the arrow which is launched stops not until it finishes its course ; and as the potter's wheel stays not till the speed imparted to it has passed away," so the good works which have begun to take effect are not annulled. The son succeeds to the good works of his father, and their good fruit is continued until absorption is secured.

(c.) The *highest* degree of reward is secured by those
who obtain by their meditations a perfect knowledge of
the Supreme. They reach the goal of "wisdom" and
they enjoy the *summum bonum* of all human effort.
Three things have to be noticed concerning the *Brahmagyáni.* (1.) His condition *during life.* He becomes
entitled to absorption the moment he obtains "wisdom,"
but he may still remain in the body for several years :
he is called during that time "*jivanamukta*," "freed in
life." His condition while he continues on earth is fully
described in the last passage of the Vedánta Sár : and it
is asserted that though he appears, like an ordinary
man, to exercise his senses, to suffer hunger, thirst, and
pain; to be a subject of grief and of error; to perform
deeds which result from his former desires and to enjoy
their fruits; still he is not really so affected. He is
like one who seeing does not see ; and hearing, does
not hear. (2.) A second thing to be noticed in reference to him, is his relation to good and evil. Par-
taking of the nature and worthy to be reabsorbed into
the essence of Brahma, it naturally follows that good
and evil are to him only what they are to the Supreme,
viz., nonentities. He can sin no more : the penalty of
the greatest crimes is blotted out: and even the merit
of good works is despised and valueless. "The knot
of the heart is divided : all doubts are dissolved; and
his works both good and evil vanish, when that Supreme
one is seen." "He can do neither good nor evil." "He
does not become greater by good deeds ; nor less by
evil ones." (*Kaushit.*) Two celebrated passages state

this dogma in the strongest terms; and one of them employs expressions and puts it in a light which, except on Vedantic principles, must be regarded with horror. "As water wets not the leaves of the water-lily, so sin touches not him who knows this: as the combings of a comb, when cast into the fire, are consumed, so are sins consumed." (*Chh.* iv. 14.) "He who steals gold; who drinks spirits; who ascends his guru's bed; and who slays a brahman; all four fall into hell: and the fifth is he who has communion with them. But he who knows this doctrine, *though he have communion with them, is not contaminated by sin, is holy, is pure, and is fit for the pure worlds.*" (v. 10.) (3.) His state *after* death. On leaving the body, the Brahmagyáni proceeds immediately to a reunion with the Supreme, in whom he is entirely absorbed. The independent existence which he had received, under the influence of máyá, is destroyed: he has recognized his true nature, and relation to Brahma: the máyá is dissipated, and he returns to his original essence once more. The passages and texts in which this consummation is promised to the true and successful devotee are endless. Some of them are more complete, and decided; others are more general. A few have become celebrated from the clear and undeniable manner in which the doctrine is laid down. *No more transmigration* remains to such. "The man who knows him obtains liberation (*moksha*) and dies no more." "He who knows the Supreme is free from all bonds, from all miseries, and is free from birth and death." Their souls are *absorbed into* the

essence of Brahma. "They who know him as present
in all things, and are acquainted with the science of
Brahma (*Brahmabidyá*), are ABSORBED (*lína*) into
Brahma, and are freed from transmigration." (*Swet.*
i. 7.) "The soul having retired to its proper place, the
heart, the summit of that organ sparkles and illuminates
the passage (the *Susamna nári*) by which it will pass
away," to the crown of the head, and the suture (*vidriti*)
in the plates of the skull. Here the solar rays meet
it, night or day, summer or winter. By these rays it
reaches the sun. Being entirely in a rudimental form,
and destitute of faculties and organs, it is like a blind
man ; and is conducted across the different regions of
the universe by their presiding divinities, to the highest
heaven, the residence of the Supreme Brahma. "The
soul of him who gets liberation, goes to the Supreme
light, and is identical with him ; as pure water, absorbed in a limpid lake, is exactly in everything con-
formed to it." The identity becomes complete and
final. "That soul, having arrived at the Supreme light,
POSSESSES HIS FORM." (*Chh.* viii. 12.) "As rivers flowing
go into the sea, and lose their name and form, so the
wise, freed from name and form, gain him who is Supreme, perfect and splendid. He who knows that
Supreme Brahma, BECOMES even Brahma." (*Mund.* iii.
2, 8, 9.) "No egress from the body or migration
can fall to him, who knows Brahma and BECOMES
BRAHMA." Such is the final reward of all the austerities and contemplations of the Vedánta—annihilation of
self: identity with Brahm.

Such is a brief outline of the ancient and still received Vedantic system, according to its well-known authorities, the *Upanishads*, the *Sáririk Sutras*, and *Bhagavat Gita*. Utterly wrong as are its fundamental assertions and the doctrinal system based upon them, no one will deny to it the merit of consistency, or that the final conclusions follow by fair logical sequence from the point whence the start is made. It holds that, there is but one Being in the universe, the Supreme Creator; that all forms and products of matter are but emanations from him, are but forms of him; that man also is both in body and soul a product or form of the sole entity; that whatever therefore implies or seems to prove him an independent being is the offspring of illusion and ignorance; that every object in the universe is endowed with that ignorance, and with the " qualities" in which it is exhibited; that these " qualities " were placed there by Brahma when he evolved the universe from himself; that on man, the effect of the illusion is to fill him with doubt, to lead him into " error;" that by peculiar processes, divinely revealed, these doubts and errors may be removed; that he will then recognize his true nature and origin; and that as a result, he will lose the individuality which seems a prime element in his being; and return by absorption into the essence and being of the Creator whence he sprang. The chief of these dogmas will be specially examined hereafter.

# CHAPTER IV.

## COMPARISON OF THE SYSTEMS.

A CURSORY glance at these great systems of Hindu philosophy will show that while they differ on most important points, they have numerous elements in common; and that while they advocate great and dangerous errors, their limited observation has yet discovered some truths which to the present day are universally acknowledged. Two of them especially exhibit the Hindu mind in a very active condition : well appreciating the advantages of clear arrangement, and able to employ sound logical principles in scientific discussion. Doubtless the presence of followers of rival schools at the same seats of learning, and the numerous controversies to which their meetings gave rise, exerted a powerful influence upon the development of their theories, and in the correction of their earlier errors. It is evident that the systems were rivals, and that hard battles have been fought at times for victory by their different adherents, followed by varied success. The Sánkhya seems at one time to have been popular. But in the seventh century of the Christian era the Vedant, under the able advocacy of Sankara Acharjya, is said to have overpowered other systems. The Nyáya, from its internal worth as a system of reasoning, has always been a favourite subject

of study, even with those who did not adopt its philosophical views.

1. The first thing observable in respect to these systems is that to a considerable extent *they are based upon
the Upanishads.* The notions current among the learned,
which became embodied in those detached tracts, have
greatly influenced all subsequent inquiries, and many
have been received without question among the tenets
of later systems. The doctrine of transmigration, with
the causes by which it is necessitated; the various
classes of character among the good and evil, with the
destinies assigned to them in consequence, are evidently
traceable to that source. The divisions of the universe;
the regions above; the regions below; the classification
of all organic and inorganic structures; the five elements to which their origin was attributed; the description of the human body; its five senses, five organs of
action, and the five vital "airs;" the separation between
soul, as a distinct entity, and the other objects of creation; the system of meditation, the submission to
authority, which were to be adopted by all inquirers
after knowledge; and the relation between human
beings and the practice of morality, are all derived
from those ancient works. Many of their notions,
expressions, and illustrations are current among native
scholars to the present day. The Vedánta in its teaching lies of course nearest to them, being professedly
their mere expounder: but the Nyáya and the Sánkhya both bear marks of that origin, or at least of the
great influence which the Upanishads exerted among

all the learned in the days when the systems were
founded.

2. Of the three systems, the Vedánta, in its *general
character*, bears the most religious tone : the others are
more scientific. The science of the Vedánta is comparatively incomplete ; it forms an inferior part of the
system, and merely repeats what was already universally believed. The Sánkhya is distinguished by its
admirable arrangement, and by the clear, logical development of the various truths and theories which it advocates. They are made to spring necessarily from the
points at which the system starts, and are shown to
follow fairly from the principles there laid down. But
even in arrangement the Nyáya is not inferior to the
Sánkhya; while its researches are all pushed deeper
into the world of phenomena, and it draws forth conclusions about physics, and about the philosophy of
soul, far beyond what its rivals had been able to secure.
Its range of topics is much wider, its classification more
complete, its principles of inquiry more sound. It has
already been noticed that the text-books of both systems,
barely as they state their object-matter, are most systematically arranged.

3. All the systems profess the *same religious end*.
All assume the fact of man's continued transmigration,
and explain its causes in a similar manner. The various migrations arise from the follies and sins of men,
which have sprung from their errors; and each system
proposes to define clearly what the error is, to show
how it may be avoided; to secure for its followers com-

plete immunity for the future; and thus to bestow upon them true beatitude. They differ, it is true, both in the account of the error, its causes and its cure: but a similar current of thought runs through them all in relation to it: and all agree that transmigration is its most dreaded fruit and consequence.

4. In their *principles of inquiry,* and in describing the sources of true knowledge, they somewhat differ. The Nyáya directs its students to four sources of information: perception, inference, analogy, and verbal communication (*i.e.* inspired authority). Of course, analogy may be readily regarded as an indirect mode of inference, and be classed with it, leaving the sources of knowledge three: perception of the senses, inferences of reason, and authority. In this form they are accepted and employed by the Sánkhya and Yóga. The Vaiseshika again admits only the first two. The Vedánta recognizes six sources of knowledge: these three, and three others reducible to them. While, however, reason and argument are extensively employed in the Sutras and all the commentaries, special stress is laid upon the texts of the Vedas.

In the application of these principles to the objects of knowledge, the Nyáya, as we have seen, far excels all the rest: its logical system being more complete, and more correctly drawn out than theirs. The difficulties in the way of an inquirer, the various classes of fallacies, the sources of wrong notions, the sound method of deducing right ones, all find a fair place in its scheme: which has exhibited the art of reasoning and the system of syllogisms in a wonderfully clear and correct manner.

5. The treatment of *causation* is an important topic in connection with these systems. The Vedánta says little about it: the subject of inferior causes being without interest to a system which holds that the qualities of bodies act not from an imparted power, but by the direct agency of the Supreme. The Nyáya and Sánkhya have examined the matter well; and both classify causes into instrumental and material. Both also lay down the law that " from nothing, nothing comes:" *i.e.* material effects must spring from some material cause; and " causes must be adequate to produce effects." Kopila, however, seems to go farther in asserting the identity between a cause and its effect; holding that effects are only the same as their causes. The Nyáya again allows the fact so often shown in modern chemistry, that the operation of two causes may result in a third kind of product, different in form and qualities from both, though actually produced by their mutual action.

6. In their notion of *substance*, the systems decidedly differ. The Vedánta clearly asserts the common origin of all objects, material and mental, in the nature and essence of the Supreme Brahm. In spite of phenomena, of appearances which may seem altogether to oppose the theory, it teaches pantheism in the fullest manner, by asserting it in relation not only to things in general, but to various objects individually. Whatever, then, be the essence of the Supreme, and whatever be its inhe-

rent qualities, the world and all its products, the universe
and its regions, must all have been fundamentally the
same. The Sánkhya, as we have seen, attributes an
ideal existence to the universe so far as its forms and
developments are concerned : declaring that the " five
subtle particles," the germs of the whole, spring from
Consciousness. At the same time it advocates the eternal existence of primeval " nature " and of souls. The
Nyáya comes nearer to modern philosophy, in tracing all
things to " substances," which are the unknown substrata of known qualities and actions. These substances
have not been produced by God or in thought alone,
but are real independent existences. Even here, however, the generalization of the system does not go deep
enough to divide the " substrata " into matter and soul,
with space as the sphere of existence, and time as the
succession of moments during which it exists. We
have already noticed that " matter" as such was unknown in the systems.

7. All the systems give to this substance an *eternal
origin*. The Vedánta does so implicitly, in identifying
it with Brahm, the sole entity, and therefore an entity
uncaused and eternal. The Sánkhya also asserts it of
that primal " nature " whence all material forms have
been derived. The Nyáya makes it not a product of
creative power, but cognate in its origin with the
Supreme Soul, and merely moulded by him into its
numerous forms. The substance when first educed or
wrought is by all declared to have been of the finest
texture. It is finer than the five original elements,

M 2

they being derived from it. The *prakriti* of the Sánkhya
has none of those properties by which visible matter is
known. The atoms of the Nyáya also are like mathematical points, without parts or magnitude. They
are imperceptible by sense, and are learned only from
their effects. By the aggregation of atoms, by the development of nature, from the essence of Brahma,
the five gross elements are first formed: and from
them all material products in the universe are compounded.

8. Only the Nyáya has gone with any depth or correctness into the question of the *qualities* of substance.
Without at all reaching the modern view of the primary
qualities of matter, it has yet discovered some of them,
adopted several of the secondary qualities, and made a
decided distinction between the properties of matter and
the attributes of the soul. Thus colour, savour, odour,
dimension, weight, conjunction and disjunction, with
others, are referred to material substances. Understanding, volition or effort, merit and demerit, desire
and aversion, pleasure and pain, are ascribed to soul.
This great advance upon other Hindu systems is the
work of Kanáda.

It has also gone into the singular question, How are
the qualities of a substance connected with that substance?—a futile attempt; for even though one single
cause be established, the question returns, How is that
cause connected with both the substance and the quality,
so as to unite the two? The difficulty is removed only
a step back, and is insuperable. The Nyáya, however,

has invented a relation between them, called Intimate relation. This intimate relation is something real, and is included neither in substances, qualities, nor actions. Again, all substances are united actually with the general notion of substance. This union is not merely the offspring of human reason, but a union real and independent of human thought. The general notion, too, is an entity. It is singular that the Vaiseshika should have hit upon the doctrine held by the Realists of Europe, which for so many centuries divided the scientific world of the schoolmen with its rival, the doctrine of the Nominalists. Finally, the Nyáyists held that the special qualities of substance are effects, and do not belong to the essence of the substance.

9. In regard to *Soul*, the Vedánta teaches the same pantheist doctrine as it holds respecting matter. The soul is an entity, separated from other objects of the universe, but in its origin identical with the original of matter, the essence of the Supreme. The Sánkhya also gives it a separate existence, and attributes a separate soul to each individual animated thing. This soul has an eternal origin, and will never cease to be. Very little is ascribed to it by the Sánkhya. It does not join with nature of its own accord. Nature does everything: forms a creation for its use, a vehicle for its residence: and a system of knowledge for its liberation. The Nyáya, like the Sánkhya, makes souls eternal and multitudinous; but ascribes much more action and thought to the soul when united to "*mind*," and clothed with a body. In all the systems souls are divided into classes.

Some are higher in rank, others lower. Hence have originated the Gods, the Gandharvas, the Yakshas and other beings, as well as men: beings whose existence is quite unproved, but is probably received on the testimony of the Upanishads, which all good Hindus were bound to believe.

10. It is important to notice the place ascribed to the SUPREME. By the Nyáya, ISWARA or God is reckoned as of the same class as other souls, there being a general as well as individual souls. Soul has a real *substratum*, in which abide its knowledge, and the various qualities attributed to souls. Soul has existence and causality. Its qualities are happiness, unhappiness, intellect, volition, &c. It has the attributes of ubiquity and infinity as general qualities: it has also special qualities, that is, it is limited in space and of momentary duration. Souls are thus divided into two classes, the Supreme Soul, and animal souls.* The Supreme Soul is God: He is one only. He is omniscient. The "mind" is the organ in which takes place the perception of pleasure, pain, and the like. It is in the form of an atom and eternal. Number, quantity, severalty, conjunction, disjunction (qualities of all substance), with intellect, desire, and volition, are sited in GOD; but He has none of the other qualities of soul—merit, demerit, and happiness—as these imply imperfection. Of the place which God occupies in creation, little is said by the Nyáya authorities. But considering the attributes ascribed to him, the material provided, and the work ascribed to

* *Tarka Sangraha*, p. 15.

Brahmá by the shastres generally, it is not difficult to infer what their opinion must be. Before the universe began to exist in its present form, there existed the eternal atoms of the nine substances, which include the "mind," soul, time, space, and ether. The atoms were solitary and unconnected, without mutual action: souls were unconscious and perfectly passive. The work of the Supreme was, to unite the atomic "minds" to souls, thereby rendering them conscious; and to unite the atoms of other substances, and develop them into the material universe. He thus became the Great Artisan of the universe. Colebrooke says: "He is demonstrated as the maker of all things." In one respect the ISWARA of the Nyáya occupies a position similar to that of the Supreme in Christian philosophy: but in the source of creation, in his personal moral attributes, in the magnificent ends and purposes of the creation, he is utterly different and inferior.

By the Vedánta, again, Brahma is reckoned everything; he is knowledge, he is bliss: all distinction between him and the universe is delusion. Duality is denied entirely. Yet to the emanations of himself he has imparted that ignorance, which leads them to consider themselves independent beings. The Sánkhya of Kopila denies the existence of God: "Nature" alone having, on her union with soul, spontaneously developed her refined original substance into the universe Brahmá and the Gods are only the highest order of created beings. The Yóga of Pátanjali, however, advocates the existence of a GOD, in whom knowledge

reaches its extreme limit.  Knowledge exists: knowledge must find its perfect limit in some being: that
being is God.*  Omniscience therefore is an essential
attribute.  As LORD he upholds all things by his mere
will, power being also natural to him.  In opposition to
Kopil's argument against the existence of God, derived
from the consideration that such a being must be affected by "troubles," &c., Pátanjali states † that the
Lord is a particular spirit, different from all other
spirits, and is untouched by troubles, such as ignorance;
by actions that involve merit or demerit; by the fruits
of action, such as birth and death; and by the tendencies which impel other souls on their particular
courses of existence.  This Lord is pre-eminent above
all others.  He is without beginning, not being limited
by time.  He is thus superior to Brahmá and all other
created beings that have had beginning, and is their
preceptor and guide.  While thus advocating pre-
eminence in existence, power, and wisdom to the Lord,
Pátanjali says nothing about his connection with the
creation; and if he adopt the views of the Sánkhya, no
connection at all is needed, NATURE developing itself.
In such a case He would have existed apart from the creation, and watched its development as an unconcerned
spectator.  Yet it is by profound meditation upon Him
that the scholar of the Yóga may soonest attain complete deliverance from his mundane existence and toil.

* So Dr. Mosheim in Cudworth: "Whence did we get our notion
of perfection?  There must be an Archetype of it: that Archetype is
God."

† *Yóga Sutras*, part i. pp. 29-32.

11. Souls are placed for residence in the *bodies* of animated beings. All the systems teach that the soul has at least two bodies: the exterior is the gross body, visible and tangible; which is born, lives, suffers disease, and dies. The interior is a subtile body: small in size, but of great power. To this the soul is joined on its first union with matter, and from it it never parts, till its own emancipation or the dissolution of all worlds takes place. The subtile body never decays. To the body are ascribed five senses, five organs of action and " the mind." The Upanishads and Vedánta speak also of the five vital " airs," the vital functions of breathing, circulation, and digestion. They also add three " cases " to the soul: making out a compound constitution for the soul as invested with body. Over the rudiment of soul is the " intellectual case;" above that, the " mental case; " then the " vital case," external to the rest.

12. Of the *operations* of mind little analysis has been made, except by the Nyáya. That system has enumerated several with considerable accuracy. Two perations especially are attributed to intellect, apprehension and memory. Under apprehension are included perception and inference. In connection with these we find also the beginning of a reference to the laws of association by which remembered facts are recalled into consciousness. It is in discussing inference that the Nyáya educes the laws of sound reasoning. The Sánkhya does not go so far: though it allows both the perceptions of sense and the deductions of reason. In respect to the mode in which perceptions are ac-

quired both systems hold curious theories.  The Nyáya considers that objects arc beheld by means of rays of light which proceed to them *from* the eye.  The Sánkhya or Yóga* holds that in perception the "mind" moulds itself to the shape of the object perceived : just as water, pouring from a reservoir, takes the shape of the vessels into which it runs.  In the case of wrong notions, the shape is taken incorrectly or partially.

We have already noticed the Sánkhya description of the first rise of intelligence and consciousness, and observed how it attributes the production of intelligence to primeval "nature ;" not to soul on its junction with nature.  When the occasion arises, one or the other must produce it: and as Kopila wished to show that nature was the great agent, he attributed the result to that cause.

13. The peculiar meaning attached by all the systems to the term "mind" (*manas*) must be specially observed.  It is quite distinct from soul.  Both the Nyáya and Sánkhya ascribe to it a distinct origin; in the former it has an atomic origin.  According to the Nyáya, it is this "mind" which perceives by means of the senses.  Judging from its acts and operations, it is evident that we must understand by the term, that portion of the mind which is the sphere of all our conscious acts.  The soul is of immense capacity, receiving and retaining immense stores of knowledge.  This knowledge is within the soul, out of consciousness : and may be recalled and employed for use.  All things again are perceived

* *Yóga Sutras*, p. 8.

originally in consciousness. This *sphere of consciousness,*
then, in which alone the mind knows what it is doing,
is what is denoted by the term "mind" or *manas.* The
ancients were of course struck by the fact that with all
its immense knowledge and power of thought, the soul
at any one time knows very little. This sphere of consciousness they seem to have regarded, not as a kind
of portico to the soul, but as a special instrument for
its use, a special faculty of internal perception.

14. The *moral feelings* are entirely omitted from all
the systems. None of them enter into our notions of justice, compassion, veracity, love, and gratitude. They say
nothing of the domestic affections, nor of anger and
jealousy, the defensive affections by which our interests
are protected. *Conscience* is never referred to as a ruling
moral power, probably from the reason, that good and
evil are ascribed to the Supreme rather than to the fault
and folly of men. Nor are the various classes of moral
duties among men, as members of society, or of a family,
or as men in general, discussed. All feeling and desire
are by the various systems reckoned imperfections.

15. The system of *caste* is decidedly taught in the
Upanishads, the Brahma Sutras, and the Gita: it is implied by all the systems, and referred to in their commentaries. It is said to have originated with the Creator
himself: and each caste is exhorted submissively to perform the duties which He has assigned to it.

It must not be forgotten that *deities* of an inferior
kind, from Brahma downward, are recognized by all
the systems, even by the Sánkhya: but they are chiefly

referred to in the Vedantic authorities, and can plead
Vedic authority for their existence, influence, and power.

16. All the systems agree in assigning to man in
the world a *condition of defect and misery*. Man is the
victim of desires he cannot accomplish, of efforts by
which he gains nothing, and of illusions by which he is
led astray. All agree that transmigration, which we
have mentioned above, is the result of these illusions,
and in many cases is the means of securing purification
and progress in the path of improvement. The systems
differ as to the character of the greater errors. The
Sánkhya and Nyáya consider it to be error respecting
the nature and relations of soul and matter: the Vedánta,
error respecting the identity of the soul and universe
with Brahma. All are confused as to the real nature
of sin: making it rather an intellectual fault, than a
moral one, and, naturally, defining right and wrong
actions by the notions and practices prevalent in Hindu
society, and in connection with the Hindu religion.
Sacrifices and idolatrous worship are reckoned among
the minor works by which the soul is raised from its
illusions, gloom and misery.

Finally here, the source of these errors and of the evil
dispositions by which they are produced is traced up by
the Sánkhya and Vedánt to the Supreme or to Nature;
and the germ of all the evil is said to have originated and
to have been imparted to individual souls and minds, at
the time when they were produced or developed. This is
the way in which almost all Eastern philosophy accounts
for the origin of evil: exhibited though it be in various

forms, physical and moral. In the same way all the material of the universe is by both systems said to be endowed, if not composed of, elements which cause it to rise or fall, to lead to happiness, to passion, or to brutal misery, according to the prevalence of these elements in their numerous varied proportions.

17. With these views, all the systems agree in declaring it to be the *chief end of man*, that is, of the birth with which souls are most frequently endowed, to seek freedom from his errors and delusions; thereby to avoid transmigrations, and to secure perfect immunity from them, by obtaining liberation. In the Sánkhya and Nyáya, this liberation is merely the separation of soul from matter, which has occasioned its varied troubles. In the case of the Vedant, it means utter annihilation of independent existence by absorption into the Supreme Brahma.

Such are the general views of the great systems of Hindu philosophy on the chief subjects connected with the universe, its elements and its aims. Such are their theories concerning the origin of man, the causes of his misery, and the course he must adopt to secure emancipation. Such too are their views of the worlds to which he is going, and of the lot which awaits him there. In comparing them together, we have merely indicated the views of each in very few words, leaving the reader to complete the comparison by examining each point in the chapters already laid before him, descriptive of each system in detail. The comparison shows how much similarity there exists between the systems in the facts received; how much they allow in common; and how they differ rather in the ultimate reasons of things, than in the intermediate details. While the Vedánta makes all Brahma; the Sánkhya, Nature without God; and the Nyáya gives us an omnipotent God, with souls and atoms as his original materials; the systems formed comprise very much the same elements and take the same Hindu shape. It would have been interesting here to trace out the great similarity between many of the tenets of Greek philosophy and those of the Hindu systems: and to show also the relation which these systems bear to the theories of the universe which have been formed in modern Europe; but we must hasten on to the principal object of this essay, a statement of their chief errors, and a discussion respecting them.

# PART II.

## The Chief Religious Errors of these Systems.

———◆◆———

FROM the earliest dawn of philosophy to the present time the inquiries of philosophers have been naturally directed to the circumstances of the sphere in which they live. The world on which we stand, the sky above our heads, the animal and vegetable products which so much contribute to our preservation and our enjoyment, in respect to their classes, their uses, and their origin, have furnished abundant materials for the consideration of the most thoughtful mind. Had the method of inquiry been as broad as the principles of inquiry were sometimes sound, the truth of these things would have been reached at a much earlier period in the world's history than it was in fact discovered: but theories, hypotheses, and speculations, too often drew off the attention of philosophers from the true sphere of science, the knowledge of existing facts, and led them away into the regions of imagination, while their contradictory conclusions served only to bring their systems generally into contempt with the vulgar. In numberless cases did they turn aside to study the nature of matter, the constitution of the universe, the primary elements of things; and forming but narrow and hasty generalizations, deduced conclusions which experience has falsified. Both in Greece and India the same classes of objects have been examined, and in numerous instances similar results have been attained : the same continue to occupy the attention of modern science; and as the boundaries of human knowledge have been more clearly defined, it has become evident that while we may hope to attain a complete knowledge of the phenomena of the universe, there are points connected with its substance which we never can know; and topics of research into which the mind can never hope to enter. We have already seen that the Hindu philosophy in its results has in some cases attained to truth, which experience has subsequently confirmed: while in other, most important, instances, it has gone into manifest error. The errors however are not all of one kind or character. Some are more vital than others; some are positively trivial. It must be noticed however that they are not introduced incidentally, as expressive of the notions of their day; but are all taught with AUTHORITY; and that such as are advocated in the Upanishads, appear to the Hindu mind invested with the solemn and unanswerable authority of the ancient and venerable Vedas themselves. All the systems are declared to be true; all profess to lead their students to that great object of human life, the attainment of final beatitude. Though some of these errors therefore are trivial, others important; though some are in their nature scientific, and others are purely religious, they all derive strength from the authority ascribed to their standard text-books: and therefore may all be referred to in controversy with the Hindus, as furnishing important illustrations of the emptiness of their claim to be considered the productions and instructions of inspired men. If the Vedas teach directly that all material products have sprung from the five elements, which are no elements at all, can those Vedas be the inspired word of Him who created all things? A few of the minor errors may be enumerated and at once dismissed.

---

### MINOR ERRORS.

1. The *Divisions of the Universe.*—The Vedánt authorities distinctly advocate the existence of fourteen worlds, seven upper, and seven lower worlds. The upper include the dwellings of Brahmá; of Bhrigu and other Munis; of the sons of Brahmá; of the Pitris; of Indra; and of the Supreme himself. Amongst the subdivisions, the sun is declared to lie much nearer to the earth than the moon: while the region of lightning is placed beyond both. The same theory is taught by the Chhandogya and Mundaka Upanishads. Lightning comes from a place more distant than the moon: the moon lies farther from the earth than the sun. Rain comes from the moon: and after falling and being evaporated, returns to the moon again. The moon at the conjunc-

N

tion disappears within the sun, and from him is produced again.

2. *The five elements.*—Chemical analysis was as thoroughly unknown to the Hindus as it was to the Greeks: and considering the importance of the most prominent objects in the universe, they (like the Greeks) attributed the origin of all substances to *five primary elements;* earth, air, light or heat, water, and ether: ether being added, to account for the origin of sound. This is the doctrine of the Upanishads,[*] and has been received without suspicion by all the schools of philosophy. The Sánkhya teaches that the five gross elements are derived from five more subtle elements of the same kind: and the Nyáya refers four out of the same elements to their original atomic forms. In respect to the qualities of these elements, it may be observed that fluidity is ascribed to earth: and the organ which cognizes it is not touch but smell. Water is declared to have colour, taste, and viscidity: although the purest water has neither colour, taste, nor smell. Light is reckoned only of a white colour: its fluidity is not innate, but derived from some unknown cause. Gold is one of its products. In the perception of objects rays go from the eye, not towards it. Ether is the cause of sound; a portion of it abides in the ear itself, without which no sound would be perceptible.

3. In regard to the *constitution of man* several singular theories are taught. One contained in the Katha

---

[*] *Aitareyá Upanishad:* Dr. Roer's, p. 33. *Colebrooke on the Vedas,* p. 29.

Upanishad is that respecting the *susamnà artery.* "A hundred and one arteries issue from the heart, and the chief among them proceeds through the brain." This is the artery by which the soul passes from the heart at death, to the joint in the skull, whence it leaves the body and travels to the upper worlds.

The theory of *sleep* and *dreaming* contains the strange notion that in deep sleep the soul of man becomes for a time reunited to Brahma. "When a sleeper sees no dreams; speech goes into the mind: the eye also, with all its forms, and the ear with all its sounds: when he wakes, they return again, as sparks come forth from blazing fire." This is the doctrine of the Chhandogya and of the Brahma Sutras.

The *theory* of *digestion* advocated in the Sutras is equally curious. "When nourishment is received into the corporeal frame it undergoes a threefold distribution according to its fineness or coarseness. Corn and other terrene food become flesh: their finer portions nourish the mental organ. Water is converted into blood, the coarser particles are rejected; the finer support the breath. Oil and butter become marrow: their finer portions supply the faculty of speech: their coarser parts become bone."

Other errors might be pointed out: but these will suffice to show in how many ways, and in connection with how many topics, objections may be brought against the sufficiency, excellence and inspiration of the Upanishads and other authorities of these systems as teachers of religious truth.

## CHIEF RELIGIOUS ERRORS.

We now proceed to consider the more important religious errors of these systems. Some appear, perhaps, to be more scientific than religious in their character: but it will ultimately be found that every one has a thoroughly religious bearing. We shall state them in the following order:—

1. The Sánkhya denial of the existence of God.
2. God is identical with matter. Vedánta.
3. God is identical with the human soul. Vedánta.
4. Matter is eternal in man. Sánkhya.
5. Matter is eternal as atoms. Nyáya and Vaiseshika.
6. Soul is eternal. Nyáya and Sánkhya: Vedant also.
7. The doctrine of transmigration. All the systems.
8. The doctrine of fate: that the dispositions of men are decreed. Vedánta and Sánkhya.
9. The nature of virtue and vice.
10. The chief end of man.

In giving a clear account of these great errors, it will be well to exhibit, as fully as possible, the evidence of their existence, with the arguments and illustrations by which they are defended; to quote the most important texts, and exhibit the doctrines in the very words in which they have been long taught.

§ 1.—THE SÁNKHYA DENIAL OF THE EXISTENCE OF GOD.

The important dogma of the Sánkhya philosophy that there is no God, self-existent from eternity, is found most clearly stated in the Sutras of Kopila. It is laid down not as a separate and distinct dogma arising independently out of the scheme of the philosophy, but is introduced indirectly whilst the sage is treating of another subject. After discussing the means by which liberation may be secured, and showing that the Vedic scripture concurs in the doctrine which he has just deduced from reason;—viz., that liberation is obtained not by ritual observances, but by discriminating soul from nature (the great doctrine of the system); Kopila proceeds to examine the means of proof. (Sutr. 88.) After defining perception as that discernment which, being in conjunction with the thing perceived, portrays the form thereof, he meets various objections. Among them appears the following:—"Your definition does not extend to the perceptions of God, Iswara;" because as these are from everlasting, they cannot result from conjunction with objects subsequently created. He answers the objection by the bold statement:—

Sutra 93. *Iswarásiddhoh.* "The existence of Iswara is a thing unproved."

In this Sutra, he does not directly deny such an existence. He might have urged that the perceptions of Iswara are beyond the sphere of human explanation: or questioned whether Iswara had perceptions at all, instead of intuitions; or argued that though they are

not included in the definition, they may still be similar
in kind : but instead of proffering any such reply, he
rather questions the existence of such a person at all,
and begins by saying that his existence has not been
proved.* But he does not leave the matter here. An
objector will naturally say that the Vedas prove that
existence, and assert it with divine authority. He then
offers in reply the following dilemma, and expounds
it :—

Sutra 94. "Of free and bound, He cannot be either,
and therefore cannot exist."

He can neither be free from trouble † (such as mundane
creatures suffer), nor bound through troubles. For :—

Sutra 95. " Either way he would be inefficient."

If he were free from such troubles, he would have no
desires which could instigate him to create : desires
being reckoned a class of those troubles. If he were
bound, he would be under illusion. In either case he
would be ineffective : he could not create. The present
universe could not therefore have sprung from *him*, and
there is no proof of his existence.

The objector then urges against this reasoning the
question : If there be no God, what is the meaning of
the texts in the Vedas which speak of the Lord or God ?
He answers :—

* The modern system of *Secularism* professes to occupy just this
position of Kapila's. It does not dogmatically assert that there is no
God, and then advance arguments to prove the negative; but it takes
up the sceptical position of doubting the sufficiency of that evidence
which is offered in proof of His existence.

† See *Yóga Sutras*, part i. p. 29. Sutra 24.

Sutra 96. " *Muktátmanah prasansá, upásá siddhasya bá.*"

These texts are either " glorifications of the liberated soul, or are homages of the recognized deities." He allows the three great deities a secondary immortality, since soul is eternal. In respect to this attribute, it is glorified under the title of Lord.

His own explanation of the work of first producing the present forms of things from the original matter and from original soul is the following :—

Sutra 97. " Soul governs nature, not from a resolution to create, but from its proximity ; as the loadstone acts on iron."

There is a kind of chemical affinity between them. Just as the loadstone acts on iron, when lying near it, so when soul is brought into proximity to nature, nature becomes *mahat*, or intelligence. In this way alone can we talk of its "creating." One of the Puránas says the same thing in the same words. Soul therefore, though apparently an agent, is really not an agent. It has no will to be such: it exerts its power only through attraction. A last objection is then offered: If there be no eternal Lord, will not the Vedas cease to be of any authority? He replies:

Sutra 99. " The declaration of the texts of the Vedas by Brahmá, is sufficient authority ; since he knows the truth."

The *Sánkhya Kárika* gives another argument based on their theory of causation. It is contained in the commentary on the 61st sutra, and is as follows : " How

can beings endowed with 'qualities' proceed from
Iswara, who is devoid of qualities? In nature it is seen
that like produces like. From white threads is produced white cloth: from black threads, black cloth.
The various objects contained in the three worlds are
endowed with qualities, the three *gúnas*, in various proportions." How can they have sprung from Iswara,
who does not possess them? On the other hand, Nature
does possess these qualities, and from nature have the
three worlds, endowed with these qualities, been derived. Iswara therefore is rejected.

The explanation which Kopila gives of the mode
and cause of creation will be described in the next
chapter, in the dialogue on the subject.

§ 2.—" The whole Universe is Brahma."—*Vedánta.*

In describing the Vedantic system, it was observed
that the texts which exhibit the relation of Brahma to
the universe are very numerous, and that to an unprejudiced mind their doctrine on the subject must appear
perfectly clear. Brahma is in several passages declared
to be the creator and sustainer of the universe: upon
whom " are woven and sewn the heavens, the earth
and the transparent region between them." But the
connection between them is far closer than this. All
the authorities from the Upanishads to the *Vedánta
Sár* exhibit him as the substantial, as well as the efficient cause of all things; in other words they teach
that their base and substance are identical with his own.

This doctrine appears in three classes of passages : first, those which very strongly imply it; secondly, those which directly assert it; and thirdly, those which illustrate it by numerous examples and defend it in answer to objections.

1. Numerous texts imply that Brahma is the substance of all things, by asserting that he *pervades* them : and in order to avoid all doubt, they assert the fact not only concerning the universe in general, but in respect to its individual parts, both great and small. The epithets most commonly used are *sarvvagatam, sarvvabyápi, bibhúmá,* and *antarátmá : i. e.* " moving in all ;" " all-pervading," " internal," " internal spirit." In the *Mundaka* and *Katha,* he is several times described as *sarvvabhútantarátmá,* " the internal spirit of all that is." " This spirit is everywhere. He is in the heavens; he is in the wind: he is Agni; he is in the earth; he is the soma-juice; he is in the pitcher of the sacrifice; he is in men; he is in the gods; he is in the ether; he is the productions of water; he is the productions of earth; he is OM; he is the productions of mountains (the rivers); he is unchangeable and vast." (*Katha,* v. 2.) " He is the ear of the ear; the mind of the mind; the speech of speech; the life of life; the eye of the eye." (*Tal.* 2.) " As the spokes of a carriage wheel are to its nave; and as the arteries are to the heart; so are all the operations of mind to him who dwells within. . . . He dwells in all space. He pervades the mind, and rules over life and body; he is in the body close to the heart." (*Mund.*) " This

divine being is on all sides. He was in beings of
former times. He is in beings now in the womb. He
was in beings that have been produced. He is in
things that are being produced. He dwells in every
living thing: he has all things for his face. . . . .
The perfect one with a thousand heads, a thousand eyes,
and a thousand feet, pervades the earth and the illimitable universe." (*Swet.* ii. 16, iii. 14.) "On me is
the universe suspended, like pearls upon a string."
(*Gita*, vii.)

2. A more important class of passages state the doctrine in direct terms. The most celebrated text is in
the *Chhandogya* Upanishad, and is as follows: "All the
universe is Brahma; from him it springs; into him it
is dissolved; in him it breathes: so meditate thou with
a calm mind." (iii. 14.) Others are of the same character; and exhibit the doctrine in its application to the
particular objects of the universe. "This divinity is
fire; he is the sun; he is the wind; he is the moon.
This divinity is the brilliant (stars): he is Brahma; he
is water; he is the Lord of all creatures. Thou art
woman; thou art man; thou art the youth; thou art
the maiden; thou art the old man with his staff; thou
art all things born; thou hast the universe for thy
face. The bee with dark plumage art thou: the green
bird with ruby eye; the cloud, the womb of the lightning; the seasons; the sea. Thou art the universe
and all things produced in it." (*Swet.* iv. 2, 3, 4.)
When Bhrigu, the offspring of Varuná, approached his
father, saying: "Venerable father, make known to me

Brahma;" Varuná in reply enumerated several objects, and instructed him to meditate upon each one: giving for his guidance the following principle applicable to them all. " That whence all beings are produced; that by which, when born, they live; that towards which they tend; and that into which they pass; do thou seek for: that is BRAHMA." He meditated accordingly in devout contemplation; and having thought profoundly, recognized food or body to be Brahm. Again he discovered breath, intellect, and felicity to be Brahm. Such is the science taught by Varuná. (*Taitt.*) Another important extract from the oldest authorities, the Upanishads, is the following from the *Aitareyá*: " This soul is Brahmá: he is Indra; he is Prajápati; these gods are he; and so are the five primary elements: . . . . whatever lives, or walks, or flies, or what is immoveable; ALL THAT is the eye of intelligence . . . . Intelligence is Brahma, the great one."

All the Vedantic authorities concur in these views, and contain numerous statements, expressed in noble language, to enforce the doctrine. It will be sufficient to select only one or two from each. The *Sutras* say (i. 4. 23): " Brahma is also the substance (prakriti) of the universe; for so the propositions in the Vedas, and their illustrations, require. The reference to his desire* to create, leads to the same conclusion." " Nothing exists, except him; although different texts of the Vedás seem to imply the contrary " (iii. 2. 29). The *Bhagavat*

* Mentioned, at length, in the *Brihad Aranyaka*.

*Gita* contains many verses of the same kind. " Brahma is the offering : Brahma is the sacrificial butter : Brahma is the fire of the altar ; by Brahma is the sacrifice performed " (iv.)　" There is nothing, says Krishna, greater than I.　I am savour in the water : light in the sun and moon : Oм in the Vedás : sound in the ether : sweet smell in the earth : I am brightness in the flame : in all beings I am life " (vii.)　Amongst other things, the *Vedánta Sár* speaks thus : " There is no difference between the Supreme Ruler and individual intelligences : as there is none between a forest and the trees ; and between water as one thing, and water as many waters."

The various passages which teach the *absorption* into Brahma of either the human soul or the elements of the universe are based upon the same doctrine of identity in the nature of the two.　" In him this world is absorbed : from him it issues ; in creatures he is twined and woven with various forms of existence."　" Recognizing heaven, earth, and sky to be him : knowing the worlds, discovering space and the solar orb to be the same : he views that being ; he вeComes that being ; and is identified with him, on completing the broad web of the solemn sacrifice."　(*Yajur Veda.*)

To these might be added a long extract from the *Brihad Aranyaka*, in which the process of creation is described fully, and in particular terms.　It is there shown that he himself became each separate class of beings ; and that for the purpose of increasing their numbers, he divided himself into male and female.

Thus did he create from himself " every living pair whatsoever, *down to the ants!*"

3. The third class of passages which teach this pantheistic doctrine, contain illustrations by which the method of production is exhibited. In other cases, the doctrine is taught dogmatically and on authority. These illustrations show the arguments and reasonings by which it is defended against those who impugn it. For greater distinctness the illustrations are numbered.

(1. 2. 3.) The process of creation and destruction is compared to the work of the spider; to vegetation; and the economy of the human body. " (1) As the spider spins and gathers back its thread; (2) as plants sprout on the earth; (3) and as hairs grow on a living person; so is this universe produced from the imperishable Brahma." (*Mund.* i. 7.)

(4.) A similar example is shown in the silkworm. " Like the silkworm, the one God has, from his own nature, encased himself in the universe with many threads, sprung from primeval ' nature.'" (*Swet.* vi. 10.)

(5.) The sparks of fire show the same. " As a thousand sparks are emitted from blazing fire; so, beloved, all kinds of beings proceed from that Supreme, and to him again they return."

(6.) He is again compared to the banyan-tree. " This universe is like an eternal banyan-tree, whose root is on high and whose branches are below. He is Brahma." (*Katha*, vi. 1.)

4. The doctrine is further exhibited, especially in the Sutras and in Sankara Acharjyá's commentary, by the

attempts to answer the objections brought against it.
The Sutras themselves notice the Sánkhya doctrine of
the " plastic nature," from which everything has been
formed ; and endeavour to disprove it by showing that
the Deity himself is the Substantial cause, and that no
other material is required.   Sankar also discusses other
objections.

a. " How can this universe (it is asked), which is
manifold, void of life, impure and irrational, proceed
from him who is one, living, pure, and rational?"   He
answers : " The lifeless world can proceed from Brahma,
just as lifeless hair can spring from a living man."

b. " But in the universe we find him who enjoys and
him who is enjoyed : how can he be both?"   Answer
(Illustration 7) : " Such are the changes of the sea.
Foam, waves, billows, bubbles, are not different from
the sea which is in its native waters.   Still a difference
is perceived in them by turns, and an activity which
agrees with their mutual union.   Nor, though they are
identical with the sea, do they obtain the condition of
each other : nor does the difference follow from the
nature of the sea, if they do not obtain these conditions
by turns.   In the same way, he who enjoys and he
who is enjoyed do not by turns gain each other's
conditions, nor are they different from the Supreme
Brahma."

c. Again he says : " There is no difference between
the universe and Brahma.   The effect is not different
from its cause.   He is the soul : the soul is he.
(Illust. 8.)   The same earth produces diamonds, rock-

crystal, and vermillion. (9.) The same sun produces many kinds of plants. (10.) The same nourishment is converted into hair, nails, and so on. (11.) As milk is changed into curds, and water to ice, so is Brahma variously transformed without external aids. (1.) So the spider spins its web from its own substance: (12) spirits assume various shapes: (13) cranes propagate without males: (14) the lotus grows from swamp to swamp without organs of locomotion."

Now all these illustrations, whether given to teach or to defend the doctrine, point to a single fact, that the creation is of the same substance and material as its divine author. They show not merely that the universe has an author, and that he is Brahma, but that the nature of the one is identical with that of the other; and that the sole difference is one of form. This is Pantheism.

It is a fair deduction from the doctrine to ask, whether by this creation, the amount of substance in Brahma is diminished: it appears to be taken from him and, it is said, will return and be absorbed into him again. How much of Brahma's substance then is contained in the whole creation: a part only; or the whole? The usual authorities seem to have avoided this subject; but the Vedas acknowledge the justice of the question, and one or two of the later texts furnish an answer. "All creatures are ONE-FOURTH of him: three-fourths are immortal in the divine abode." This one-fourth is again broken up into four: and each of these into four again: (just as a rupee is broken up into sixpences;

each sixpence into four separate annas; and each anna
into four pice.)  The different portions are specified in
the Chhandogya Upanishad, and it is declared that
Brahma is divided into sixteen minor parts.  In the
Yajúr Veda occurs the following passage, in which the
whole doctrine is briefly stated; and with it, therefore,
this account of it may be concluded: " The embodied
spirit which hath a thousand heads, a thousand eyes,
a thousand feet, stands in the human breast, while he
totally pervades the earth.  That being IS this universe,
and all that has been or will be.  .  .  .  .  The elements of the universe are one portion of him, and three-
fourths of him are immortality in heaven."  (*Yajúr
Veda*.  As. Res. vii. 251.)

In the western world it is acknowledged that most of
the ancient philosophers, both Greek and Roman, held
in some measure to the notion that the universe had
sprung from Jupiter: the general indefinite notion receiving particular applications by different teachers, in
different schools.  Amongst all their writings, the Orphic
hymns seem to come nearest in the doctrines they lay
down to the theory just developed from the texts of the
Upanishads.  These hymns assert, like the Upanishads,
a clear identity between Zeus, the Supreme Ruler, and
the universe at large.  They employ, singularly enough,
in some cases the same expressions as the Upanishads;
and illustrate the doctrine by applying it in the same
way to the details of the creation and the objects of
which it is composed.  The following passages will
show this: "Together with the universe were made,

within Zeus, the height of the ethereal heaven; the breadth of the earth and sea; the great ocean, the profound Tartarus; the rivers and fountains, and all other things; all the happy immortal gods and goddesses: whatsoever hath been or shall be, was at once produced in the womb of Zeus." The resemblance of the following passage to texts in the Gíta, and in the Mundaka, and Aitareya will be self-evident: "Zeus was the first, and Zeus the last, the mighty thunderer: Zeus is the head; Zeus, the centre: from Zeus have all things been made. Zeus was a man; and Zeus, an immortal maid: Zeus is the profundity of the earth and of the starry sky: Zeus is the breath of all things: Zeus is the force of the untameable fire: Zeus is the bed of the ocean: Zeus is the sun and moon: Zeus is King: Zeus himself is the originator of all things. There is one power, and one God, and one mighty ruler of all." Timotheus represents the Orphic doctrine thus: "All things were made by God, and he himself is all things." "There is none other beside the mighty King," say the hymns again. "Heaven is his head; the sun his eyes: the regions of air his arms, shoulders and breast; the earth and mountains his belly." "God passes through and pervades all things." "In the mighty body of Zeus do all things lie." Virgil describes the same doctrine, in the celebrated passage of the sixth Æneid; and the system was revived in great force in the schools of Alexandria by Ammonius and Plotinus under the name of Neo-Platonism.

Pantheism may be believed and advocated under

many forms. There is the poetic pantheism, which fires the imagination with highly-strained descriptions of the divine origin of the universe and the soul. Akin to this is the indefinite pantheism, which grandiloquently worships heroes as divine, descants on the greatness of the soul, the divine harmony of its powers, calls on it to awake to its divine destiny, and display its godlike internal light. " Standing on the ground, my head bathed with the blithe air, and uplifted into infinite space, all mean egotism* vanishes; the currents of the universal being circulate through me; I am part or particle of God." (Emerson.)    There is again the philosophical pantheism which in modern times has been developed in various systems of metaphysics on the Continent of Europe. These systems are by no means identical with the Vedánta, nor do they render us much assistance in comprehending all its different consequences. Spinoza identifies God with the substratum of the universe; which is the only real, eternal self-existent Being : possessing the attributes of extension and thought; and developed in the two modes of body and soul.    Schelling makes God the sole subject in the universe.    Hegel goes farther, and not merely identifies God with the universe; but makes him the law and process of creation.    God, nature, man, are three forms of the development: only in man does the self-developing entity attain consciousness.    Cousin declares that God is everything, and almost in the words of the *Vedánta Sár*, denies any difference between the per-

* In Sanskrit, *Ahangkára.*

sonality of each part of the universe, and the general personality of the whole: the individual waves of the universe being essentially one and the same with Him, the illimitable sea. All the modern systems, however, are more or less hampered by the notions and terminology of sound science and true religion : and nowhere do we find pantheism so clear, so consistent, so complete, and so fairly drawn out to all its legitimate consequences, as in the VEDÁNTA, the earliest system of the kind.

---

### § 3.—THE HUMAN SOUL IS BRAHMA.—*Vedánta.*

It is only a consistent part of the doctrine just stated, that the human soul, if selected from the various objects of creation in the world, should, like the rest, be declared identical with the Supreme. The importance of the dogma, however, is so great, and it may be so fully examined on independent grounds that it will be found useful to make a separate statement of the passages in which it is taught.

One of the most striking modes in which it has been laid down is in the following illustration in the *Brihad Aranyaka.* Yájnyawalkya, discussing with a number of pundits to whom he proves himself superior, utters these striking words: " Man is indeed like to a lofty tree: his hairs are the leaves : and his skin the bark. From his skin flows blood, like juice from the bark: it issues from his wounded person as juice from a stricken tree. His flesh is the inner bark, and the membrane, near the bones, is the white substance of the wood. . . . If, then, a felled tree spring anew from the root, from what root does mortal man grow again, when hewn down by death?" He points out that that ROOT is Brahma.

"The soul," say the Brahma Sutras, "is a portion of the Supreme Ruler, as a spark is of fire. The relation between them is not that of master and servant, ruler and subject, but that of whole and part." (ii. 3, 43.) "The distinction between the living soul and the Supreme Ruler arises from illusion, not from the thing itself." In the *Aitareyá*, a description is given of the mode in which Brahma entered the human body, in order to make it his abode. After showing why he could not have entered by any of the natural openings of the body, it is said that he entered by the join in the plates of the skull, descended the susomna artery, and took up his abode in the heart to which it leads. There he ever remains; his size, suitable to his dwelling, being only that of a man's thumb. "The perfect one, of the size of a thumb only, abides in the centre of the soul!" Owing to this high honour conferred upon the body, it is regarded not as a mere receptacle for a common soul. It is styled "the city of Brahma" (*Brahmapúr*): and its various openings are compared to city-gates. "In the city of Brahma abides a small water-lily, and in the centre of the flower is a diminutive ether. As great as is the external ether; so great is the ether in the midst of the heart: both are placed there: the sky and the earth both: . . . all that belongs to him and all that is not his, everything is placed in it."

It will naturally follow, that having such an origin, the soul must partake of the divine attributes of the Being, of whom it is a portion. "That soul (says the *Chhandogya*) is without faults; without old age: without death; without sorrow; without hunger and thirst; true in its desires, true in its will." (viii.) "This soul of mine in my heart existed before the earth, before the atmosphere, before the sky, before the worlds." It is of course indestructible. "It is not born, neither does it die: it has not proceeded from any: nor has it been changed into any: nor does it perish when the body dies." (*Mund.*) Of the same character is the celebrated passage in the *Bhagavat Gita:* "It is not born; it never dies. It has had no beginning; beginning it will never have. Unborn, changeless, eternal, it is not to be slain when its mortal frame is killed. The sword cannot cleave it. Fire burns it not. Water cannot wet it: the wind drieth it not away. For it is indivisible, inconsumable, incapable of moisture, and is not to be dried away. It is constant, capable of going anywhere, immovable, eternal; it is invisible, inconceivable, unalterable." (ii.)

Little is stated in these extracts beyond the fact of the identity between the human soul and the divine; and of its possessing some attributes to which only a divine being can lay claim. No proofs, and almost no illustrations are offered, and consistently enough, all acknowledgment of the existence of duties from man to God, or from man to his fellows, is entirely omitted.

Pythagoras appears to have held a doctrine very

similar to that of the Upanishads.  Plato also taught
that human souls are emanations from God through the
soul of the world.   The stoics held that both body and
soul were portions of the one existence: and Aristotle
seems to have believed something not very different.
Indeed the belief of a divine origin in one mode or other
for human souls seems to have been in Greek philosophy
almost universal.

----

## § 4.—Original Matter is Eternal in Mass.—*Sánkhya.*

The Sánkhya sets out with the assertion that all reali-
ties are included within its TWENTY-FIVE PRINCIPLES.  Of
these, soul stands quite apart from the rest, and plays
an independent part.   The remaining twenty-four are
reducible to one.   Among these twenty-four, sixteen
include the gross elements from which all the various
objects in the three worlds are formed; which are
cognized by the senses of men, and constitute the instruments employed and acted on in their daily experience.
They include the five senses, the five organs of action,
and the *manas* of man, which are also objects of our
direct personal knowledge.   The existence, then, of
these sixteen principles cannot be disputed.  The Sánkhya
next asserts that the existence of the gross elements
must be derived from elements of a similar character,
but of a finer description; for everything which is gross
is formed of something less gross—that is, of something
more subtile.   Hence are acquired by inference the
five subtile elements, preceding and producing the five

elements which the senses perceive. Such elements, again, and organs, can only be produced from self-consciousness; for if that self-consciousness did not cognize them, how could they be known to exist at all. Another principle, therefore, is discovered, the producer of those elements. But self-consciousness cannot stand alone: it requires a basis, and its basis is intellect. The assurance felt in self is a function of self-consciousness; but the function of the effect must result from a function of the cause. Hence intellect is discovered. But intellect has for its affections, pleasure, pain, and dulness; and these must be produced from something which, in itself and from its own constitution, possesses these qualities. That something Kopila accepts as the final cause and basis of all that has preceded, and he terms it PRAKRITI or NATURE. Immediately the cause of intellect, it is mediately the cause of all products. Kopila adds that his theory is confirmed by the Vedas; which declare that the world arises from nature; and that it is superior to the atomic theory, because limited things, like atoms, cannot be the cause of all things: and he therefore assumes one grand cause.

Soul also, he declares, is uncaused, being neither producer nor product: both soul and nature, therefore, are before everything else, and are therefore eternal: for both are uncaused. Have both then been engaged in producing? No. For soul is never modified: while nature has the capacity of modification, and hence gives rise to all visible forms of matter in the three worlds. It is their sole cause. (Sutras, 62–67.)

The description of nature and its various qualities occupies considerable space in the Káriká and its commentaries; but the doctrine may be exhibited in a small compass. The name *Pra-kriti*, usually termed NATURE, denotes " that which precedes a thing made." It is therefore doubly applied: first, and chiefly, to the *Múl-prakriti*, the root-matter, which was not created, and from which other things have mediately sprung; secondarily, to the material causes of a lower kind, from which other things are derived. The effects which follow those causes are termed *vi-kriti*. Hence intellect is the *vi-kriti* of Nature, and the *pra-kriti* of self-consciousness; the latter is the vikriti of intellect and the prakriti of the five subtile elements. These elements are the vikriti of self-consciousness and the prakriti of the gross elements. The gross elements are merely the *vikriti* of the subtile ones. Hence the truth of the verse that of the twenty-five principles sixteen are only products (*vikriti*); seven are both producers and products (*prakriti* and *vikriti*). Soul is neither, and nature is producer alone. From its relation to things universally, it is also termed *pradhána*, the chief. Amongst all things that exist, it occupies the highest place.

The qualities of nature are readily observable when it is contrasted with its effects. These effects, separated from their causes, and having an independent existence, are all products; their present form is but temporary; they are unpervading, their special inherent properties being not universally visible, but divided in separate objects; they are moveable, and change from one body to another; they are multitudinous, being repeated in various objects and persons; they are supported, resting on their cause; they are mergent, and become lost in their original elements; they are combined, and are governed by the influence of nature which compels them to produce certain effects and not others. In contrast with these things, nature possesses properties of an opposite kind. It has no cause; it has no end; it pervades all things; it is immutable; it is single; it is self-sustained; it is the subject, not the predicate; it is one whole; it is supreme. While they are visible and tangible, nature is imperceptible, owing to its subtlety; but though perception cannot reach it, it is inferred from its effects.*

The constitution of this primeval cause has also been described as well as its qualities. "Nature," says Kopila (Sutr. 62), "is the state of equipoise of goodness, passion, and darkness," the three *qualities*. Nature is the triad of *qualities*, distinct from the products to which they give rise. These qualities, however, are not "qualities," in the sense of "properties" of matter; for they themselves possess such qualities; they have the qualities of conjunction, disjunction, lightness, force, and might. "They form 'cords' (*gúna*) by which," says the commentator, "the brute-beast (*púrusha-pasu*), the soul, is bound." They are things and substances of which nature is constituted: just as the trees are the constituent elements of which a forest is made. The forest is not different from the trees of which it is

---

* *Kárika*, x. xi. viii. pp. 40—48.

made : so nature is not different from the three 'qualities,' but is the aggregate of them.   While in equipoise,
they constitute the original cause of all.   As seen in
the various individual objects of the three worlds, they
vary in their proportions; sometimes one predominating, sometimes another.   In the gods, the quality of
goodness predominates : passion in men, in animals,
darkness.   It undergoes modification entirely through
its own energy, and for a special reason, in connection
with soul.   In this respect, it is like the 'plastic
nature' of the Greek philosophers.   The Pythagoreans,
Platonists, and Aristotle, all advocated a primeval
matter, having neither parts nor form, yet the one
universal, incorporeal substance from which all others
were derived.   It must be allowed that this composition
of the one original cause is a very weak point in the
Sánkhya system.

The Sánkhya in discovering this principle, traces
back all existing things to it as their origin: in declaring it to be uncaused, the system of course implies it to
be eternal: for otherwise, at any period when it began,
the law of causation would have been broken through,
and the things which now are would have sprung from
nothing.   The dogma, however, is directly laid down
by Kopila in the Sutras.   Having traced all things to
intellect, and intellect to Prakriti, or Nature, he now
asserts that nature is eternal.

Sutra 68.  *Múle muládbhávát, amúlam múlam.*

" From the want of a root in a root, the root (of all)

is rootless." Here the system stops. That root, from whence spring other things, is rootless. Anticipating the objection: " Why do you stay there: why not trace the origin of nature to another cause; and that to a farther one"—he says:

> Sutra 69. " Even if there be a succession of causes, there is a halt at some one point; and so it is merely a name " (given to the final cause).

Whatever be its name, some one thing must at last be reached which is eternal: that at which we stop is the Primal-agency, *pra-kriti*, which, in order to prevent a *regressus ad infinitum*, is declared to be the root of all. Such is the course of Kopilá's argument for the eternity of matter.

In view of other objections he takes up the subject again at a later period. He first teaches that the existence of nature is learned from beholding her products: and it then being objected, Why trace all to this Prakriti, and not to atoms,—he replies:

> Sutra 114. " Any other cause contradicts the three-fold aspect of things."

In other words, all things exhibit the influence of the three great qualities : and the source from whence they sprang must possess them too. Pleasure and pain are not properties of atoms: the atomic theory, therefore, fails to explain them.

## § 5.—Original Matter is Eternal as Atoms.—
### *Nyáya.*

The eternity of matter is plainly and directly asserted by the Nyáya and Vaiseshika systems : which divide all substances into two classes, eternal, and non-eternal respectively. All objects and products are traced back to nine substances ;* time, space, soul and mind : ether, air, earth, fire and water. All the non-eternal substances included within these are declared to be compounds, and are divided into various classes, objects, organisms and organs, which are the direct objects of our perception, whose existence is therefore beyond doubt, and which we must fully explain. Of the nine substances, the soul is immaterial, one and eternal. Time and space are also eternal: they have the properties of ubiquity and infinity. Space is declared to be one and eternal. Mind, the sphere of consciousness, is a thing quite separate from soul. Apart from these, the remaining substances are five in number, ether, air, earth, light and water. Of these the ether is described in terms which all but identify it with space. It fills space, and must therefore differ from it only in density. It might have been attributed to an atomic origin, most consistently with the general theory of the system, but has not been so : on the contrary, it is declared one, and undivided. It would appear that the authors of the Nyáya had attained a more correct knowledge than

---

\* The term is used in Hindu Philosophy, like *substantia* among the schoolmen, the unknown substratum of known properties.

others of what the ether was, had noticed the weakness
of the arguments by which its existence is proved, and
only did not omit it altogether from their system,
because of its Vedic origin and the fact that it was
received by all other philosophies. Were it omitted
altogether, its place would scarcely be noticed.*

The remaining four substances are distinctly described in detail. (*Bhasha Parichh.* 28–43. *Tarka
Sangraha*, 10–16.) The properties of each; the organic
bodies compounded from each; their different classes;
and the organ of the human body by which they are
apprehended; are all systematically, though briefly
stated: and in each case it is declared, that the substance is twofold, eternal and non-eternal: non-eternal
in its various parts and compounds: eternal in the
atoms to which its objects are ultimately traced. For
instance, respecting earth it is said: " Earth is the [ma-
terial] cause of odours, and is the site of various
colours. It has three kinds of feel: hot, cold and
temperate. It is twofold: eternal and non-eternal:
eternal as considered in its atoms; non-eternal, as
being composed of parts. The latter is threefold, organism, organ, and object (inorganic matter). Organic
substances are [classed as] viviparous [mammalia], oviparous, engendered in filth, and vegetative. Its organ
is the sense of smell. Its (inorganic) objects are all
compound substances from the smallest, made of two
atoms, to the largest, " the egg of Brahmá," the world.
(35–38.) The same formula is repeated in reference to

* *Bhásha Parichheda*, 26, 27.

the qualities and compounds of the other substances.
All aqueous compounds, snow, hail, and rivers; all
compounds of light, fires and gold; are all said to have
an atomic origin: and their atoms to be eternal.

The definition of an ATOM is thus given by KANÁDA,
in his Sutras:

*Sadakáranabannityam*
*Ato biparitádandah.*

An atom is "something existing, without a cause,
without beginning and end. It is contrary to what has
a measure."

This is explained and applied by the commentator in
the following way: dealing first with the formation of
compounds, and afterwards showing why atoms, con-
fessedly invisible, are believed in at all. The non-eternal
compounds are those which consist of two, three, or
more atoms. Are these atoms visible either separately
or in conjunction? An objector says: "Each may be
invisible, yet their totality may be visible; as from a
certain distance the hairs of the head together are
visible, although none of them individually is visible."
He replies: "We maintain that each hair is perceived,
because it is more clearly perceived when brought
nearer. You cannot say that from a totality of invisible atoms a totality of visible atoms is produced:
visible things are not produced from invisible things.
If one atom is no object of the senses, a totality of atoms
is also beyond their perception." The objector then
suggests that, from the invisible compound of two atoms,
the production of a (visible) compound of three atoms

is impossible (the difference being but a single invisible atom)." He replies : " This cannot be said : we do not assert that the visibility or invisibility of a thing arises from its own nature, but from its necessary causes, greatness, form, and the like. A compound of three atoms is visible on account of its greatness, while a compound of two is not."

The earthy substances, as a jar, are composed of parts, each part being a compound of at least two atoms ; and they are non-eternal, for they have had beginning in their form, and can be destroyed. There is no difference, except one of degree, between Mount Meru and a mustard seed, both being compounds of parts after parts. There is necessarily a retrogression from compounds to more simple elements. We must, in this division of parts, come somewhere to an end. The point where the end is obtained is eternal ; otherwise, that point must have sprung from nothing ; and we must admit the production of an effect from something which is not its material cause. The continual progress from one great thing to another still greater finds its end in the assumption of a sky and other infinite substances : so must there be ultimately a cessation of the reverse process, the regression from a small thing to one still smaller. Hence the necessity of atoms. A compound of three atoms is not the end ; for that has parts, on account of its size : we must go back to ONE ATOM.

This argument, he adds, does not prove the necessity of a continuation of parts after parts ; because thereby the *regressus ad infinitum* (as in the same line of argument in the Sánkhya) would become necessary.

According to Mr. Colebrooke, the argument of Kanáda is as follows. The mote in a sunbeam is the smallest perceptible quantity. It is a substance—an effect; and is therefore made from something less than itself. This something is also an effect, and is a substance. It is composed of something smaller, and that smaller thing is an atom. It is simple, else the series would be endless. If so, everything great and small would contain an infinity of particles; and all would, therefore, be alike. The first compound consists of two atoms. One cannot form a compound, and there is no argument to prove more than two. The next consists of three double-atoms. If only two were conjoined, magnitude would not result; since that can consist only from the number or size of the particles. It cannot be size, since they are atoms: it must be number. There is no argument for four, because three such double-atoms are sufficient. The atom, then, is equal to one-sixth of the mote of a sunbeam. Two earthy atoms, brought together by some cause (the will of God, time, and the like), make one double-atom. Three double-atoms equal one tertiary atom. Four tertiary atoms make one quaternary; and so on. Thus it is by aggregation that the gross earth is produced. In like manner, from aqueous atoms come forth, by aggregation, all watery substances, organs, and organisms. So, also, from the atoms of light and air, the compounds classed among them. Pressure and velocity produce a union of the integrant elements. Disjunction separates them; and as by aggregation substances are formed, so by disjunction they are broken up, and return inversely to the original atoms. The qualities of the original atoms attend them in the compound substances, and it is from them that the compounds derive the qualities which they possess.

The atomic theory of the Nyáya resembles much the theory of Empedocles, who from ultimate atoms first formed the four elements, and from them constructed the sun, moon, stars and earth in general. Under various phases it had many advocates among the ancient Greeks, as Democritus and Leucippus; but with them and others it became the ground of an atheistical philosophy, very different from that which the Nyáya has advocated in connection with a God, whose agency moulded these atoms into their numerous compound forms.

----

§ 6.—THE SOUL IS ETERNAL.—*Sánkhya and Nyáya.*

All the systems of Hindu philosophy speak of the soul as something different from the body. Even the Vedánta, which teaches that, in common with all other objects in the universe, it is derived from Brahma, mentions it as a distinct thing, bearing a peculiar burden, and undergoing the labours of a peculiar history in order to get free. The Sánkhya and Nyáya are equally explicit, and each place it amongst the original and eternal substances which their systems allow. The

P

Sánkhya makes it cognate with the uncaused Prakriti; and the Nyáya enumerates it among the nine substances that have had no beginning.

(*a.*) The *existence* of soul as something distinct from nature or matter, is discussed by both systems, and both prefer arguments to illustrate it.

1. The Sánkhya lays down as its chief argument: that an assemblage of things is for another's use (Sutr. 67): as a house is for a tenant; a couch for a person to lie on; a seat, to sit upon. Now Nature, Intellect and Self-consciousness, are a combination, developing subtile elements, and thence producing worlds and a body: all are intended for the mundane experiences and the eventual liberation of something different from themselves. That something, for whose use they are thus intended, and which is different from them all, is Purusha or Soul. Here the Sánkhya employs the argument from design.

2. Again soul is distinct from body and from nature, for it does not possess the three qualities, by which they are marked in all their forms. (Sutra 142.)

3. Besides, it superintends nature. (143.)

4. It is also the enjoyer of everything. (144.)

5. It is only for soul that all this system which is to secure liberation is intended. It cannot be for nature: for soul then it must be.

The Nyáya in illustrating the same subject adduces additional arguments, which are considerably more to the point than some of Kopila's.

1. It is the soul which governs body. For an organ

must have an agent as its master. (*Bhásha Parichh.* Sutra 47.) Now body itself is not the agent. For consciousness, which an agent possesses, is not in the body. This is known from the fact that consciousness disappears at death: also that in old age the body cannot (from being frequently changed) remember (as a man does) things which occurred in childhood. Again the "*mind*" is not the agent: for it is an atom: and no perception could take place in it, if knowledge and the like were placed within it: its power being limited to the immediate object of thought.

2. The soul is again distinguished by its peculiar qualities. (Sutra 49.) It enjoys happiness and suffers misery: they are not in the body: else would one body experience the fruit of works which were done in another (in a former birth).

3. It is known also from its activity, and from the exertions it makes in respect to knowledge and desire: just as a charioteer is implied by a carriage in motion.

4. It is the site of intellect; and of perception and remembrance, which intellect includes.

(*b.*) In respect to the *nature* of soul, the Sánkhya (Sutra 146) states: " Since light does not pertain to the unintelligent, it must pertain to the essence of soul: which while self-manifesting, manifests also whatever else is perceptible." The Sánkhya adds in respect to its attributes, that the soul is without qualities, otherwise it could not be liberated. "There cannot be liberation where there is alteration: and alteration must take place where there are qualities and susceptibilities."

Hence intelligence is considered, not one of its qualities or products, but is set down as an effect of nature. The soul is ever free : it is a witness by means of its senses and is inactive with respect to pleasure and pain. This theory is very unsatisfactory; being greatly hampered by the notion of " Qualities " peculiar to Hindus. The Nyáya says little about the qualities of soul: but it teaches more than either of the other systems about its operations. Intellect is one of its qualities : in this are included apprehension and remembrance. Apprehension again includes, perception of the senses and inferences of the judgment. It has also merit and demerit: desire and aversion: volition and imagination: pleasure and pain.

(c.) It is important to notice that both the Nyáya and Sánkhya advocate the important doctrine of the *multitudinousness* of souls; thereby separating them entirely from the Deity and from the Vedánt doctrine of their unity with him. The Sánkhya advocates it on this ground. At the same moment, a variety of accidents is happening to different persons : birth to some: death to others: and that without affecting *all*. It is absurd then, argues Kopil, to think that souls can be one: and that these contradictory affections can be happening at the same time to a monad. He therefore teaches that souls are multitudinous : each person of those living contemporaneously in the world having a different soul. (Sutra 150.) " From the several allotments of birth and death, a multiplicity of souls is to be inferred." He tries also to show that this is the doctrine of the Vedas, but of course fails.

(*d.*) Both systems finally assert that the soul is eternal. The Nyáya attributes to soul the qualities of ubiquity and infinity: and from its being infinite deduces the fact that it is eternal. The Sánkhya reckons it equally with nature, an undiscrete principle, invisible: and ascribes to it the attributes of being uncaused, all-pervading, self-supporting, and the like. Only these two principles really exist: and it is for the purpose of securing liberation for soul that nature undergoes all the modifications to which it is now subject.

## § 7.—The Transmigration of Souls.

The doctrine of the transmigration of souls is not merely taught directly and indirectly by these systems of Hindu philosophy: it is the very basis upon which they all rest. Its evils are at once assumed to be real; they are acknowledged without question; the necessity of getting free is allowed; means are pointed out for securing that liberation; each system propounds its own plan, and promises all faithful followers that special blessing as the result of their studies; the systems are constructed so as to meet it; and all scholars and disciples are exhorted to employ with vigour the means of liberation placed at their command. The systems are not, however, all alike in their treatment of the subject. The Vedánta often mentions it, implies it throughout, and repeatedly assures its followers that those who embrace its doctrine in the highest form, will at death escape all transmigration, by absorption into the Supreme. The Nyáya does little more than allude to it, and state its own purpose to free men from the evil. The Sánkhya, however, enters much more into detail, and provides materials for a complete discussion of the interesting question.

(*a.*) The fact of transmigration none dispute : it is unanimously allowed, though the mode in which it becomes an essential element in man's lot is differently explained. The Vedánta furnishes numberless texts in all its authorities. "Man is like a blade of corn : he rots away : but like the corn sprouts forth again." (Katha.) "He who is without knowledge, who is of fickle mind, and ever impure, obtains not the Supreme glory, but goes again into the world." "If before death, the soul obtains a knowledge of Brahma, it is freed from worldly bonds ; but if not, it assumes a body again in these created worlds." (Katha.) "As a man casts off his old garments and puts on new ones, so the soul, having quitted its old mortal frame, enters into another which is new." (*Gita.*) "By knowing the truth," says Gautum, "in regard to the sixteen objects of knowledge, beatitude (*nisreyasa*) is attained. This beatitude is secured by the successive annihilation of men's false notions, evil desires, and the births to which they give rise." (Sutr. 1 and 2.) "Transmigration," he says, "is the being born again and again : " the same soul entering into different bodies. (Sutr. 19.)

Sutra 22.—*Tadatyantabimokshoparargah.*

"Complete deliverance from that is emancipation."

The first sixty Sutras in Kopilá's First Book are occu-

pied with developing the fact of these migrations of the
soul; of the bondage in which it is held, and the causes
which have produced it.   Then taking up other causes
which are falsely alleged as true ones, he refutes them
and sets them aside.   (Sutra 1.)

*Atha tribidhadukhátyantanibrittiratyantapurushártha.*

"Well! the complete cessation of pain which is of
three kinds is the complete end of man."   He then
shows that this cessation is not to be secured by visible
means, because the evil comes back.   Nor can it be
done by the repeated use of ordinary means; for they
are not always attainable, nor are they perfect in their
kind.   Besides the Vedas speak of liberation, not as a
trifling matter, but as one of the highest importance.

Is this bondage essential or is it accidental?   It is
accidental.   If it were essential, there would be no fitness in enjoining means for liberation.   It is not essential as heat is to fire.   What is then the real cause?
Kopila supposes and refutes several in succession.   Time
does not cause bondage: for it is eternal: and would involve every soul, even the emancipated.   Neither does
it arise from place, for the same reason.   Nor do the
circumstances of our condition produce it, for they belong to the body, and the soul remains solitary.   Nor
do the works performed by any one cause bondage, for
they belong to the mind, not the soul.   Neither does
nature cause it; for though bondage is occasioned by
the conjunction between soul and nature, that conjunction must first take place.   Neither is the bondage produced *by* that conjunction (just as a black jar becomes

red by heating): for the colour remains when the heat
is gone, and so would the bondage remain, after nature
had separated from soul. The bondage is occasioned
by it: but it is really only verbal: it is only reflected
in the soul; as the red colour of the hibiscus is reflected in pure crystal: and ceases to colour the crystal
when the flower is removed.

(b.) In entering upon the details of transmigration
the Kárika states clearly (pp. 48, 49) two important
principles, which the theory implies, and which are
essential to its completeness. First: that it is the *same
individual soul* which undergoes many changes of body,
and enters one body after another in the course of its
history.

*Ekah purusho jáyate náparah.*

" ONE soul, and not another is born " (in a regene-
rated body). " There may be various unions of one
soul, according to difference of receptacle: as the ether
may be confined in a variety of vessels."

Secondly: The SOUL itself is not subject to birth or
death. These arise from its connection with body, and
are felt in body: " Life is the combination of soul with
the pains incident to body, not any modification of the
soul itself. Death is the abandonment of those bodies,
not the destruction of soul." The soul is unchanged,
through all its migrations into various forms, until its
final liberation. It is the disguise which is changed, not
the agent who wears it. (*Kar.* pp. 69, 70.)

(c.) The Sánkhya thus explains the way in which
soul and nature, the two original and independent prin-

ciples, come to be joined and act together. Nature is
devoid of sensibility and reflection : it can neither enjoy
nor observe : its existence, therefore, would be without
an object, unless there were some one who could do
both. That other is soul. For the purpose, therefore,
both of contemplation and enjoyment, soul is united to
nature. But then, pain is inseparable from nature :
and soul becomes cognizant of that pain in all its
numerous varieties, by its continued union with nature.
After a time, therefore, it wishes to be freed from the
union : from nature only it can be freed. In this way
they are both employed. The union here resulting is
curiously compared to the association of a lame man
and a blind one, for the accomplishment of a journey.
The lame man can see, while the blind one cannot see,
but can walk. The blind man, therefore, carries the
lame : and the lame guides the blind. The soul sees,
but cannot act : the body acts but cannot see, feel, or
enjoy. Each, therefore, requires the other. When
final liberation is secured, they both separate ; just as
the two associates, the lame and blind, part from each
other when their journey is completed. This is the
argument. There is of course a fallacy in it : for nature
is after all without feeling or enjoyment : in this respect
it is like pure matter, an instrument of something
superior : even though on the Sánkhya theory, it includes intellect and self-consciousness. The advantage
is all on one side. In the illustration it is on both sides :
and is arranged by two intelligent agents. For the
purpose of this contemplation and enjoyment, nature

must be developed in products: a world is formed: for it is only in such circumstances that the enjoyment can take place. Thus soul is involved with nature. Thus it gets into all its pains and gloom. Through this service, however, soul can get to understand nature: to discriminate between itself and nature: then it can detach itself from nature, and reacquire its original solitude, independence and repose.

(d.) While for this end nature develops the world in general, it also provides a special vehicle for the soul's use, by means of which it becomes connected with nature at large: and from which it is never separated during its entire wanderings. This vehicle in which the soul takes up its residence, is called the subtile body, or rudimental body (*sukhma saríra*, or *linga saríra*). The subtile body is small in size, no bigger than a thumb, and to men's eyes is invisible. It is composed of intellect, self-consciousness, the five elements, mind, and the organs of sense and action. If self-consciousness be reckoned in intellect, the body appears composed of seventeen elements. This body in the case of each individual soul is formed at the time of the creation. Brahmá * seems to have been the first for whom it was made. This body is very strong: and is therefore permanent: it lasts till the period of universal dissolution:

---

* It may be well to notice distinctly the difference between Brahma and Brahmá. Brahma (pronounced Brum-há) is the One Supreme, the Iswara, from whom the Hindu triad—Brahmá (pronounced Brum-há), Vishnu and Siva—have sprung. Singularly enough, in South India, Isuren does not denote the Supreme, but is Siva alone.

or at least never changes till knowledge causes its wanderings to cease.   It is also unconfined: it does not mix
with animals, men or gods: it can go through rocks
without obstruction.   It is also invested with peculiar
dispositions and tendencies.   Of its final history, the
commentator says: "Subtile body is that which at the
period of universal dissolution, possessed of intelligence
and other subtile principles, merges into the chief one
(*pradhán* or nature): and exempted from further revolution, remains extant here until creation is renewed,
being bound in the bondage of the stolidity of nature,
and thereby incompetent to the acts of migrating and
the like.   At the season of re-creation it again revolves." (p. 128.)

This subtile body does not enjoy or suffer.   Hence a
connection with generated body, the gross body, is
necessary.   But gross body cannot last long: and as
the "dispositions" with which the subtile body is invested by Intellect, render it susceptible of reward or
punishment, more bodies are necessary.   Here it is the
necessity of new bodies is seen, and the *modus operandi*
of transmigration is rendered complete.   The subtile
body "migrates" (*sansarati*) from one to another, and
the worldly system through which it travels is entitled
"migration" or *sansára*.   The migrations are compared
to the different disguises and dresses assumed by an
actor, which he puts on for the amusement of others.
By means of these gross bodies, the subtile body exhibits before the soul.   The Vedánt uses also the simile
of old and new dresses.

In this view of the Sánkhya respecting the residence
of the soul in a subtile body, which provides it a permanent home during its separate history, all the systems of philosophy agree.   In fact its existence is essential to the theory of transmigration, as the Greeks also
felt.   All concur in describing it as an exceedingly fine
and subtile rudiment, which passes through gross bodies
in a long series ; and through them experiences the
worldly history of which living beings are conscious.
The Vedánt especially notes the two bodies, and their
structure, and shows how the dispositions of the soul lead
to its lot in gross bodies of a higher and lower kind.
The Upanishads are more explicit about the history of
individual migrations than any of the later authorities.
There is a passage (referred to in the chapter on the
Vedánt) in the Chhandogya Upanishad, in that section
of Chapter V. called the *Panchágnibidyá*, which details
with great minuteness the history of those who die
without obtaining complete emancipation and beatitude.
The passage is as follows : " They who in villages perform works of merit and benevolence go to smoke : from
smoke to night : from night to the time of the moon's
waning : from that to the six months of the year when
the sun goes southward : from the months they obtain
the world of the *pitris* : from the world of the *pitris*, the
ether : from the ether, the moon.   He is the Soma
King : that is the food of the gods, and they feed on it.
After they have lived there a suitable time, they return
by the same road as that they came by : they go to the
ether : from ether to the wind : the wind becomes

smoke: the smoke, cloud: the cloud pours down rain: hence they become a grain of rice or barley, or plants or trees: hence their progress is more difficult: from that nourishment they pass into men; thence into an animal embryo. They who here do works of merit obtain a womb in high rank: as that of a brahmin, Kshatriya or Vaisya mother." Of the course of punishment endured by the souls that descend into the seven hells, but little is said: it is added that on their return they enter the womb of a dog or a boar; of beasts, deer, birds, reptiles, and even immoveable substances.

The doctrine of metempsychosis appears to have been universal in ancient philosophy among those who accepted the immateriality of the soul. A few exceptions, like Leucippus and Democritus, seem to have taught that it was destroyed at death. But the ancient Egyptians, the Pythagoreans, Platonists, and others, all held its migration among various bodies: with intervals of happiness and misery between the different births, passed in the unseen world, according to their merits and demerits in the present one. Empedocles even pretended that he knew he had been at different times a boy, a girl, a plant, and a fish. Pythagoras also asserted that he had previously existed as Œthalides, the son of Mercury, Euphorbus, and others. Dr. Cudworth and his commentator Mosheim find a difficulty in the Egyptians believing both that the souls of men ascended to the councils of the gods and descended into the bodies of impure animals. But there is no difficulty in applying the two statements to different classes. The

Hindu philosophers have taught precisely the same doctrine: noting that it is the virtuous that ascend, the wicked who are thus degraded. Buddha in his teaching dwelt very largely on the doctrine, and allowed his imagination to run riot respecting it in the most extraordinary manner. He would trace back the history of previous Buddhas; and would speak without hesitation of what had happened in previous births to himself and others, for a long series of ages. Respecting his theory of transmigration, the Ceylonese Buddhist authorities teach a doctrine that differs very decidedly from that of Kopila. Kopila says, " One soul is born not another." The Ceylon books however teach as Buddha's doctrine, that the merit of a good man at his death causes the birth of another soul that is the representative and equivalent of the soul by which that merit was acquired: the man himself disappears.

The doctrine also in Europe, as in India, was accompanied by the other, that the soul resides in a subtile or refined vehicle which furnishes it with a species of dress that it always wears. Dr. Cudworth has shown that people, poets and philosophers, all held the notion. He has examined it at great length, and given numerous extracts. The philosophers termed it ὄχημα " vehicle." " The ancient assertors of the soul's immortality did not suppose human souls, after death, to be quite stripped, stark naked, from all body: but that the generality of souls had then a certain spirituous, vaporous, or airy body accompanying them, though in different degrees of purity or impurity respectively to themselves. As also that they conceived this spirituous body, or at least something of it, to hang about the soul also here in this life . . . as its interior vestment, which also then sticks to it when that other earthly and gross part of the body is put off as an outer garment." He shows also that this body was preserved to the soul, in order that it might experience in the next world the pleasures or pains which fall to its lot: and by them become purified from its evils and vices. The purifications of the soul directly by self-subjugation, and the restraint of the passions were taught in connection with the doctrine by the Greek philosophers. Dr. Cudworth's annotator says: " The whole of the Platonists were agreed that the soul always possesses a certain celestial body, and that it is invested with such a body when it descends into this concrete body, which it again takes away on its departure from it." (Vol. iii. p. 260, note, 1845.) Cudworth also shows that some philosophers, especially among the Chaldeans, taught that the soul had a third body or tunicle investing it, a luciform body, of higher rank than either of the former (p. 266). While the Sánkhya teaches that the subtile body always remains, some Pythagoreans and Platonists seem to have held that this body is changed for a better one, as the soul rises higher in virtue. The parallel between the belief of the eastern and western worlds is exceedingly interesting.

## § 8.—The Grounds of Transmigration : Fatalism.

The doctrine of transmigration, we have already seen, finds its basis and its explanation in another doctrine, universally accepted among the Hindus, both philosophers and unlearned. It is that there exists in this world an immense amount of misery, of wrong of various kinds. There exists in the heart an incessant desire that can never be gratified: wrong notions and " faults " that lead it astray ; desire for the fruits of works ; activities which nothing can subdue ; and courses of action from which merit and demerit necessarily spring. Masses of men are foolish, sunk in passion, enslaved to passion ; are miserable and spend their lives in gloom. All this is acknowledged as fact: all is traced up to a virtue and vice of some kind or other. Present evils in those now living are traced back to the lives and history of the same beings living at a nearer or more remote period of the world: they having enjoyed the immediate fruit of their actions in the unseen world ; and having now returned to enjoy other more remote fruits and enter upon actions which, according to their nature, will carry them higher or lower, in virtue and happiness, than the position which they held before. This line of argument will trace the grounds of transmigration and of the present tendencies of men a few steps back: and that is sufficient for common minds. The philosophers, however, have justly perceived that the argument begins again there as fresh as ever, and must go back more and more till an ultimate explanation be reached. These explanations are given confidently by two of the three schools, whose tenets we are examining; and the conclusion they have adopted has become a dogma held universally by the Orientals at large.

The *Nyáya* (as we have seen) attributes the present pains of men to " wrong notions " which they have formed, of themselves and of the system in which they live. These wrong notions lead them to the fault of desire or stupidity; from this springs an " activity," which looks for the reward of their merits (always mentioned as an evil). In consequence of this men have birth again and again, with all the pains and evils attendant upon mortal life. Here it will be seen that the original difficulty is avoided. The system does not state whence the " wrong notions " were originally derived. They are connected with the nature of soul and its relation to the universe: but their source and origin are not determined.

The Sánkhya, on the other hand, tells us the whole story. It attributes all the pain, the causeless, unsatisfied desire, the gloom, and misery of human life, to the connection of soul with nature. Soul has been joined to nature to contemplate and enjoy it: but numerous pains have been necessarily developed from their connection. All the results now seen, and all the special evils suffered by individuals, are the natural offspring of the tendencies of things, of the " DISPOSITIONS " with which they have been endowed. These dispositions originated with the creation, that is, with the first struc-

Q

ture of the subtile bodies from nature: it was then that particular tendencies were communicated to each individual of the multitudinous souls existing; according to those dispositions has been the subsequent history of each soul, and will continue to be. All the conduct, the misery or happiness of individuals has resulted naturally and from necessity from those dispositions. This is of course fatalism: but it is fatalism in the present instance without an overruling power: a God being denied to the Sánkhya system; excepting Brahmá and other inferior deities, who are themselves subject to the necessity which compels all other creatures. The text for this important doctrine is as follows.

"Subtile body," says *Sloka* 40 of the Kárika, "migrates, invested with dispositions." These dispositions are various: some are superhuman, belonging only to saints and sages. In character they are of two kinds as affecting men, viz., intellectual and corporeal: the two are connected as cause and effect, the intellectual being always attended by a corresponding corporeal condition. Of the intellectual conditions or dispositions, there are eight kinds: four good and their four contraries: they are virtue, knowledge, dispassion, power; and the contraries, vice, ignorance, passion, weakness. They all abide in intellect, the first product of nature: that being the instrument to which they belong. (Sutra 44.) By virtue, both religious and moral merit are intended. The effects of these dispositions correspond to their internal character. By virtue, there is ascent to the regions above: the regions of Brahmá, Indra, the Gandharvas and the like, eight in all. By vice, descent into the regions below, the seven hells. By knowledge, *i.e.* a disposition communicated to those who have studied, do study, or will study, the Sánkhya system successfully, comes deliverance; the entire separation of soul and nature, and a return to their primal condition. By ignorance again is produced bondage. This bondage denotes three different classes of errors respecting soul and nature, the prevalence of which precludes the hope of final emancipation. These are, (1.) *Prákritika*, the error of the materialists, who assert soul in nature and identify them as one. (2.) *Vaikritika*, the error of other materialists, who confound soul with products of nature: such as the elements, the senses, and so on. (3.) *Dákshina*, the error of those who, ignorant of soul, engage in moral and religious rites. These errors confine the soul to its subtile body for different periods. The second class, for instance, who confound soul with sense, are confined to it for ten *manwantaras*, a period equal to 3,084,480,000 years (p. 145). By dispassion, a third kind of excellence, an inferior kind of reward, is produced. The subtile body becomes absorbed into nature: the soul is immediately invested with another subtile body; and enters on a new period of migration till KNOWLEDGE is attained. By passion, the soul becomes subject to a repeated round of migrations, through bodies of various kinds, beasts, birds, and reptiles. By power arises unimpediment: by weakness, obstruction, to the course of the soul's improvement and elevation. These eight dispositions and their effects are thus clearly tabulated by Dr. Wilson:

| CAUSE. | EFFECT. |
|---|---|
| 1. Virtue | 1. Elevation in the scale of being. |
| 2. Vice | 2. Degradation in that scale. |
| 3. Knowledge | 3. Liberation. |
| 4. Ignorance | 4. Bondage in error. |
| 5. Dispassion | 5. Dissolution of the then existing subtile body. |
| 6. Passion | 6. Migration. |
| 7. Power | 7. Unimpediments. |
| 8. Weakness | 8. Obstruction. |

This whole system is carried on for the purposes of soul : and is enforced by the authority of Nature : who here (in the place of God) exercises a kingly supremacy. While special causes, the instrumental means of virtue and vice, affect individual souls, and take them upward or downward towards a higher or more degraded condition, it is by Nature, acting independently, that the general scheme is supervised and regulated. It is by Nature that the subtile body is "invested with these dispositions," and undergoes its varied and chequered history. The classification of the different characters and dispositions among men is well arranged : the essence of the whole is that these characters are the result of their dispositions, apart from any exercise of their own will : and that primarily Nature invested the soul with them, when her creation was first developed. Fatalism is thus traced up to its highest source.

The VEDÁNTA doctrine on the same subject does not practically differ from that of the Sánkhya. Teaching fundamentally as the basis of all its system that human souls are portions of Brahma, it also lays down in connection with this doctrine, that men are full of gloom, doubt, desire, and misery from their ignorance of it.

All nature we have seen is influenced by the three *gunas* or "qualities;" and it is from their many admixtures in various proportions that all the varieties of human character and of human condition arise. These qualities invest all *prakriti*, according to the Gíta, and thus it follows that "there is nothing in heaven or earth, or amongst the hosts of heaven, which is free from their influence." Who then is the source of the illusions in which men are involved, and of the qualities of the material of all things from which they arise? The Vedánt, consistently with its Pantheism, ascribes all to the Supreme. "Blind in the darkness of ignorance, the soul is guided in its actions and its fruition, in its attainment of knowledge and consequent liberation and bliss, by the Supreme Ruler of the universe, who causes it to act conformably with its previous resolves: now, according to former purposes; as then, according to its yet earlier predispositions; which accrued from preceding forms with no retrospective limit; for the world had no beginning. The Supreme Ruler makes individuals to act according to their virtuous or vicious propensities. As the same fertilizing rain-cloud causes various seeds to sprout multifariously, producing diversity of plants according to their kinds." Colebrooke says (Vedánta, pp. 188–9): "The Supreme Being is designated in the Vedas, as the cause of virtue and vice, as of everything else." The sixteenth lecture of the Gíta, "Of Divine and Evil Destiny" (*Prakriti-bhed*), repeats the same theory with a variety of details. Nor are the Upanishads silent on a topic so momentous: if anything, they are more explicit than the other authorities, overleaping intermediate causes and influences, and throwing the origin of all the good and evil directly back upon the Supreme. " He who governs both knowledge and ignorance is God." " He is the cause both of our bondage in the world, and of our liberation from it." Still more strongly are both the instrumental and efficient causes both of good and evil ascribed in repulsive terms to his direct agency, by the *Kaushitaki* Upanishad, as quoted in the Brahma Sutras : " For he makes him to do good deeds, whom he wishes to bring out of this world : and him he makes to do evil deeds whom he wishes to bring again into the world," by other transmigrations.

Amongst Vedic doctrines, next to that of Pantheism, few have spread more extensively or had a more potent influence for evil than that of the divine fatalism now under discussion. It has descended deep among the common people, has existed among them for centuries, influences their conduct in all their troubles, produces apathy in seasons when personal effort is demanded to avert calamity; leads them to ward off from themselves the sense of guilt arising from wrong committed, and to advocate in all its bare deformity the blasphemous dogma that *God is the Author of Sin.*

<hr/>

## § 9.—The Nature of Virtue and Vice.

Moral questions, it has already been noticed, are but little discussed in the systems of philosophy : the moral law as a rule from without, the conscience as a monitor

within man, are quite passed over. We find desire and
aversion enumerated among the qualities of mind, and
volition too: but the laws to which the will should
be subjected have not been developed, and no system of
ethics, even such as Aristotle's, has been advanced and
defended. The nature of virtue and vice has then
rather to be deduced indirectly from the works now
examined, since they have not been directly treated.

In spite of all erroneous theories respecting the basis
of virtue, it is evident that the voice of nature within
man has not been entirely silenced among these brahminical men of learning, and that many actions, which
from the nature of things must be evil, are reckoned
so even by them. In the *Gita*, for instance, purity of
heart, self-restraint, mildness, patience, chastity, are
reckoned among the virtues; while pride, presumption,
hypocrisy, and anger, are reckoned among the vices.
"There are three passages to hell: lust, anger, and
avarice: wherefore, a man should avoid them." It is
only to be expected, however, that right and wrong
should be understood to a large extent in connection
with Hindu habits, and should derive their complexion
greatly from the customs of the country, running very
far back into antiquity. Thus bodily penance, mortifi-
cation, and study, are reckoned virtues. Ignorance is
counted among the vices. The fulfilment of their special
duties by the people of the different castes is right and
meritorious: the neglect of them is the opposite. The
Hindu Yogi, stoical in relation to heat and cold, poverty
and wealth, is highly esteemed: the man of pleasure

the man immersed in business, are regarded as slaves
to illusion. The man who kills a brahmin is the greatest
of criminals: the man who defiles the bed of his guru,
is scarcely less guilty; but the way in which these
actions are spoken of, seems to imply that it is the distinguishing features of the murder and the defilement
which make them criminal, not the general quality of
those actions.

The chief point to be noticed here is the origin to
which both virtue and vice are ascribed. In the very
passages of the Gita above quoted, it is distinctly said
that the good and the evil destiny are from Brahma,
the Krishna of the poem. The last section gave
abundance of evidence that this is the real doctrine held
by the schools. Whatever be the qualities of actions,
whether they be correctly classed among the virtues
and vices or not, one thing is certain, the original
tendencies from whence both spring are given by the
Supreme, and their fruits must inevitably be worked
out, without reference to human will. If both courses
of conduct come from Him, any real moral distinction
in character must be denied to them. They must be
viewed rather as chemical powers in nature, leading
necessarily to certain ultimate consequences. Thus are
they represented by the Vedánt in their influence upon
the *jivanmukta*, the man who has attained the knowledge
of Brahma, but is not yet dead. "He can do neither
good nor evil." "As water wets not the leaves of the
water-lily, so sin touches not him who knows this."
"He who steals gold; who drinks spirits; who ascends

his guru's bed, and who slays a brahmin, these four fall into hell, and the fifth is he who has communion with these: but he who knows this doctrine, though he have communion with them, is not contaminated by sin; is holy, is pure, and is fit for the pure worlds." (*Chh.**)

---

## § 10.—THE CHIEF END OF MAN.

This important topic is closely allied with the two points recently examined. Each system starts with it: and all their followers are as familiar with both the notion and the expression itself (*purushártha*) as those brought up in Christian households. The primary evil by which men in this life are enslaved, and which is declared to be the most burdensome of all, is the liability to transmigration: the chief end, therefore, which the students of all these systems are exhorted to adopt, is their deliverance from its bonds, and from all the evils directly and indirectly connected with it. LIBERATION is thus the beginning, middle, and end of each and all these philosophies, from the Upanishads downwards. LIBERATION from these wanderings is the *summum bonum* of them all: in that consists BEATI-TUDE. "Complete deliverance from pain is beatitude." The Upanishads repeat the dogma every few sentences, and weary the reader with the endless modes in which they recur to it.

---

\* " And I will hallow him to the ends of Heaven,
    That though he plunge his soul in sin like a sword
    In water, it shall no wise cling to him."
                                         *Festus*, p. 4.

But each system puts, as we have seen, its own interpretation on the final reason, and each system offers
itself as the only competent means for securing it.
Each starts with this profession; and each expounds its
peculiar view of the evil from which liberation is to
be sought; as well as of the benefits which a study of
its precepts will secure. Thus, the Vedánta declares
the evil to be ignorance, on the part of the soul, of its
identity with Brahma, and urges its followers to strive
to attain a firm belief in that identity. By the Vedant
system will they learn to know him as he is, and
liberation be thereby secured. Hence Sankara Acharjya,
in commenting on the first of the Brahma Sutras, says:
*Brahmábagatirhi purushártha:* " The knowledge of
Brahma is the chief end of man." Hence, also, the
profuse professions of the benefits of the system, absorption into Brahma. " He who knows that Supreme
Brahma, becomes even Brahma. (*Mund.*) *Sa yoha bai
tat paramam brahma veda, brahmaiba bhavati.*

The Nyáya Sutras thus announce their remedy
for the same evils, and as loudly promise the desired
cure :

" Proof : the object of right notion, doubt, motive,
    &c. ; from knowing the truth in regard to these
    (sixteen things) there is the attainment of (*nisreyasa*)
    the *summum bonum.*" (Sutra 1.)

" Pain, birth, activity, fault, wrong notions; since on
    the successive annihilation of these by turns, there
    is the annihilation of the one preceding it; on the

annihilation of the last, there is attained Beatitude (*apavarga*)."

The Vaiseshika's scheme is as follows:

"Emancipation is to be attained through the knowledge of truth, produced by a particular kind of duty; which knowledge specially relates to the agreements and disagreements of the six categories: viz., substance, quality, action, community, disjunction, and concretion." In other words, it is to be attained by those who acquire that knowledge which the Vaiseshika system teaches. Thereby, as by the Nyáya, they will understand the real nature and mutual relations of soul and matter; about which they are now profoundly ignorant.

The Sánkhya of Kopila states the difficulty in the first Sutra already quoted, and shows that escape from it is the great end for which men obtain a human birth. "The complete riddance of pain, which is of three kinds, is the complete end of man." As the pain arises from connection with nature, so a right comprehension of nature will separate the soul from it, and liberation and beatitude be enjoyed. The Sánkhya teaches how this may be done; the study of the system, therefore, will secure that desirable end.

# PART III.

## Discussion of the Chief Errors.

———————

It may appear to some, that any attempt to refute these errors, and to discuss the subtile reasoning by which they are upheld, is only labour in vain, and that, as with similar errors in ancient Europe, the best course is to let them die out, or be replaced by the growth of a sounder and more complete philosophy. If, however, any dealings are to be maintained with the class of men among whom they prevail in India, it is impossible to leave those errors alone. They are sustained and taught by the most learned priests of the Hindu community; they exert a powerful influence on the whole system of worship, and many of the most important dogmas are current among the lowest and most ignorant of the people, from one end of the land to the other. All Hindus have heard, and have received the doctrines, that God is the author of sin; that God is everything, and that everything is God; that sin consists in violating the rules of caste, and the like; and that other births in the future are reserved for all men. The errors then must be met: by popular arguments for the vulgar, in which appeals to common sense and to conscience will hold a conspicuous place; and by arguments for the learned, placed on a basis similar to that from whence they themselves start. The latter task, the work of this essay, is by no means an easy one. On the one hand, little help is to be obtained from English philosophical works; they discuss errors that have arisen in Europe, taking them up under the peculiar phase which they have exhibited there, and either omit altogether, or dismiss with the epithet of absurd, some of the dogmas tenaciously held to this hour by millions of our Hindu fellow subjects. On the other hand, the Hindu mind is moulded in a peculiar form. In arguing with Hindus, whether learned or rude, we deal with men, not brought up from their youth, like the English and Americans, under the philosophy of common sense, and hence possessing a reason, trained by experience on sound principles to judge fitly and simply of facts before them: but we deal with men of perverted principles, of judgments warped by absurd dogmas, men who have received the Vedas as true, and are perfectly willing to forswear the evidence of their own senses, wherever the Vedas contradict them; men who know little of the physical world, who have read little even of the world within them, and have received concerning things in general the theories which they have been taught. In Indian philosophy, therefore, we leave the sphere and age of Baconian inquiry, and are transported back to the age and schools of the philosophers of Greece. The Pla-

tonists and Epicureans, the Atomists and Stoics, are
living and studying before our eyes. We behold the
same select circle of students, the same system of verbal
instruction, the same deference to authority. The same
antique principles, the same deficiency of physical research exist amongst them, as amongst the sages of
ancient Greece. The groves of Academus, and the
many schools of young philosophers, still exist at
Nuddea and Benares. Gorgias still displays his subtle
rhetoric in paradox and sophistry, Platos and Aristotles
still lecture to their disciples on the origin of the
universe, the *summum bonum,* and the future of the
soul. The defenders of pantheism still sit in conclave,
discussing the illusions of Máyá and the real nature of
existing entities; and when they have proved to their
satisfaction that everything is BRAHMA, they break up
their lecture, and proceeding to the Ganges, spend two
hours, sitting on its muddy bank, repeating mantras,
reciting prayers, throwing in flowers, sprinkling the appointed water, and bathing in proper rule, in honour of
those very gods, whose separate existence as real beings
they had just before disproved! Such examples of contradiction between belief and practice are witnessed
every day. Thousands upon thousands of men believe
that both sides of a contradictory argument are true.
In thousands upon thousands the divorce between principle and practice is all but complete. Discussion, therefore, has great difficulties before it; but we need not
on that account deem it utterly useless. There are
many sound principles to be found in the Hindu sys-

tems, of which the chief, the law of cause and effect, is more generally acknowledged, perhaps, than any other: these may be well employed as the basis of a courteous discussion of the errors which they teach: especially when the deductions of those systems are shown to be inconsistent with the very principles which they themselves allow. This process has been attempted in the following series of dialogues. It will at once appear that they are constructed principally for native readers.

---

### SCHEME OF THE FOLLOWING DIALOGUES.

Several years ago there lived in the city of KASI, that is, Benares, an English gentleman, connected with the Indian Government. He was one of the few, who take a real and hearty interest in the welfare of the people of Hindustán; and during the time he resided in the country, he aimed to promote that welfare. Sometimes he sought it in the administration of justice, in the punishment of the criminal, and the protection of the weak against the strong: at others by devising measures for enlightening the ignorant and promoting true learning and true morality among all classes. Amongst various studies, he had diligently applied himself to the languages of North India, and from time to time employed his leisure in reading the shastres of the Hindus, including their best authorities in science and philosophy. After serving the Government in various offices for many years, he went to live in Kási. He soon began to visit the various schools of learning with which that famous city abounds, and became acquainted with a large number of its celebrated pundits. Treating them with respect, and taking an interest in their pursuits, they learned to regard him as a friend, and readily conversed with him respecting the objects of their study. Numerous were the discussions which he held with them, and numerous the arguments which he advanced, to convince them of the true character of their great systems, and to induce them to study also for themselves the great book of the Christian religion, the Bible. This he reverenced as the true light for man's darkness; and often did he utter on their behalf the fervent prayer that the glorious God of heaven, who had sent that Divine Book, would Himself explain its meaning, change their corrupted nature, and teach them to love Him as their own Redeemer. Some of these discussions are now recorded in the following pages for the instruction of all who are interested in such pursuits: with the hope that they may obtain true light from Him, who is the source of all real wisdom.

One morning the judge walked down to the bank of the river at an early hour. The sun had just risen and was gilding with glory the thousand minarets and temple towers which stand out so prominently above the city. Passing through the narrow streets, amidst a mingled crowd of traders, bathers, pilgrims, and bulls of Siva, he reached one of the great ghauts, built of stone, and forming a noble flight of steps from the top of the high bank down into the honoured stream. Here

a most striking picture was presented to his view.
Along the river, for nearly five miles, the ghauts were
crowded by people of all ranks and all castes, who had
come to offer gifts at the various shrines, or to perform
their customary ablutions in what they consider the
holiest spot on earth.   In some parts were seen groups
from the neighbouring suburbs: in others the poorer
people of the city: at others the more respectable classes
of the community, the merchants and traders.   A few
ghauts were appropriated exclusively to Mahomedans,
and others were occupied solely by the brahmins who
resided in their immediate neighbourhood.   Everywhere
were to be seen crowds of fakeers, sannyasis, bairágis,
and gosáins, vociferating the names of their gods and
asking money: with the "Gunga-pútras," instructing
pilgrims in the due performance of Hindu ceremonies.
Some of the crowd were bathing; others were being
shaved on little stages raised above the stream; others
were engaged in various ceremonies in the shrines near
the water's edge; others were reciting their prayers,
though looking at the same time on the scenes trans-
acting around them; so that the prayers became mingled with conversation, jokes, laughter, and even abuse.
Some were pouring out water to the Sun: others were
observed applying the water in due order to their
various limbs, muttering a prayer or mantra as each
successively was touched.

Standing on one side, he observed his friend GÚRÚDÁS,
a well-known pundit, and having joined him, and presented the usual salutations, he proceeded to converse

R

with him upon the singular scene before them. "Thou seest," he observed, "O pundit, how the people of this city are given to idolatry; and what a multitude of worshippers has come forth this morning to pay their honours to the Sun, the Gunga, to Mahádeo, and a thousand other divinities. Is it right, O friend, that the learned men of this city should take a share in the follies of idolatry? Do they really approve of these various ceremonies in which they daily take a part?"

*Gurudás.* They do not approve of these things, O friend, as the best things: they understand these ceremonies to be of a comparatively low kind; they are classed among works of merit, which men ought not to desire, and are only fit for the vulgar. The wise only perform them for the sake of example, as says the Gita (iii. 20. 25): "Whatever the most excellent practise, other men practise likewise. Whatever example they set, the world follows. . . . . As the ignorant act, who are devoted to works, so let the wise man act, without any devotion thereto, seeking to benefit mankind." They of course believe that these ceremonies are efficacious in purifying and elevating the mind. Do not the shástres themselves say so? Thus speaks the Sruti: "By ritual observances is gained one kind of fruit: and by the worship of the deities another." Again: "They who here do works of merit obtain a womb in high rank, as that of a Brahmin, Kshtriya, or Vaisya mother." But the wise do not trust to these works; they rather despise them, consider them undesirable, and turn to other and more sure methods of deliverance. They apply their minds to the sciences, to one or more of the Darsanas, and by the study of them, endeavour to attain the *purushártha.*

*Englishman.* We have sometimes spoken of these systems of learning; but I have often wished to discuss them thoroughly with you and others. For I cannot help doubting about their efficacy in securing the purushártha for which men should live. The question involved in such discussions is of the highest importance. It is connected with the happiness of the soul for ever. I cannot but mourn when I see so many lakhs of people wandering in ignorance and error; and find that error encouraged by those who profess to know better. I feel obliged to doubt therefore about the systems which they hold: and the more I study them, the stronger these doubts appear. In doubting however about their truth, I do not despise these systems. I allow them to be very ancient; in many respects very ingenious; and to be the work of men who possessed great ability. But it appears to me that the strong trust reposed in them is misplaced; and that the consequences are most fearful. What evil can be greater than for a man to be deceived all his life, and to find at last that his precious time has been wasted, and his " day of salvation " been spent in vain? It becomes us, O pundit, to inquire seriously about these things, and to endeavour from all quarters to obtain true wisdom. Were the pundits of Benares to study other systems and to read other books of religion than their own, they would find abundant reason for changing many of their present opinions.

*Gurudás.* But why should they study other systems?
Their own systems require so much time: they are the
older systems: they were given by inspired men and
Rishis: and surely they are superior.

*Eng.* Our fathers may have been wise in some
things; but they did not possess all knowledge. Their
descendants have made discoveries which are quite
new. The knowledge they did possess forms only a
foundation for us to build upon. The Hindus of former
days asserted that the world was flat, and was surrounded by the seven seas of milk, and treacle, and the
like. No one denied it. But Bháskar at length proved
that the earth was a globe, and all who have examined
the evidence of that doctrine, and receive it in prefer-
ence to the mere authority of antiquity, accept it as
the true one. Travellers have gone over all the world,
but nowhere have the seas of milk and butter been
discovered. Besides the doctrines of the Hindu systems are not new nor confined exclusively to them.
Other people have taught doctrines very similar, which
have been long known to the scholars of Europe. In
former days there lived to the west of Persia a wise
people, called Greeks; some of whom subsequently con-
quered Persia and Cabul, and have been known in
Hindustan as the Yavanas.* Among them many
schools of learning were established; and many of
their great pundits taught opinions which are to this
day advocated in Kási and in the *tólas* of Nuddea.
Some of them advocated the origin of all things from

* The term " Yavana," however, now is applied to Musalmáns.

atoms (like the Nyáya): one ancient pundit, named
Pythagoras, taught openly the transmigration of souls:
another, the eternity of the world; others, the eternity
of matter.   Others, like the Vedantists, taught that all
is God and God is all: and one wise teacher, a prodigy
of learning, named Aristotle, expounded a system of
reasoning like that of the Nyáya.   Now none of these
learned men call their doctrines inspired.   None say,
like the Vedantists, that those opinions of theirs came
from the mouth of God.

*Gurudás.* That may be true; but does a similarity between our doctrines and the opinions of those
sages deprive the Hindu systems of their authority?
They assert over and over again that they have come
from a divine source; the names of their authors are
widely known as those of the greatest sages and Rishis,
who knew the truth.   Hence it is that we prefer them
to the systems of this age and of other lands; for they
are certain.

*Eng.* How can we reckon them to be certain, when
they mutually differ?   The three great systems, the
Sánkhya, Vedánta, and Nyáya, do agree on some subjects, but they disagree on many others.   Even the
chief points of these three systems not only differ, but
they are positively contradictory of one another.   What
can we, O pundit, under such circumstances, do?   We
cannot believe all?   Every one knows that of two contradictories one must be false.   A fish must either be
in the water or out of the water.   Either it does rain or
it does not.   If it does not rain, then it is incorrect to

say that it does rain: and if a fish is out of the
water, it is wrong to say that it is in it.   It cannot both
rain and not rain at the same time in the same place.
Now the Sánkhya teaches that there is not an Eternal
and Supreme Lord: the Nyáya, that there is such a
Lord, existing from everlasting, the Supreme Soul.
Now, which of these two is correct: both cannot be
true.   One must be positively untrue.   If so, how can
we say that all are certain?   The Vedánta again declares all matter and spirit to be identical with Brahma:
the Nyáya, that they are distinct from Him and from
each other.   Where is the certainty here?   Of the two
theories, so mutually contradictory, one must be incorrect.   Yet both say they are true.

It seems to me, O pundit, that the differences between the opinions of men on these important subjects,
at least show them to be exceedingly difficult.   They
ought therefore to be studied by thinking men.   They
ought also to be studied calmly and with patience.
Men ought carefully to examine the reasons of everything: they ought to doubt their own wisdom, listen to
others, and not dogmatize.   In this way we shall all
learn something: and the contributions of all will tend
to exhibit pure truth.   How needful it is that men of
different countries should learn from each other, and
should not be self-sufficient.   True knowledge is the
food of the soul: it adds to man's dignity; it increases
his happiness; it increases his usefulness.   The man
who possesses much knowledge can go and teach the
ignorant: and alas! how few wise men there are in

the world, able and willing to do so. However, as the sun is now rising high and the air becomes warm, let us adjourn to a more convenient spot, and, if you please, continue our discussion.

*Gurudás* invited his friend to his house which stood in the immediate neighbourhood. It was pleasantly situated on the bank of the river, and enjoyed both a large prospect and the cool breeze blowing from the water. They accordingly left the ghaut, and proceeded thither. Having ascended to the third story, they sat down in the verandah which overlooked the broad river. Several pundits gathered around them, and the Judge having courteously saluted them, they prepared to listen to the discussion which was at once renewed.

## Dialogue First.

### PRINCIPLES OF INQUIRY—CAUSATION.

### PRELIMINARY NOTE.

IN commencing an inquiry into Hindu Philosophy, it is essentially necessary that both parties should start from common ground. Happily such ground can be easily discovered, in those simple principles of common-sense inquiry which God has planted in every intellect. These principles are not numerous, and at the same time they are so simple, that the most untutored mind will at once acknowledge their truth. The Baconian method of in-

quiry, which exhibits them in full force, was not a new
thing in the world.  The principles themselves are as
old as mankind: Bacon and others taught the necessity
of applying them more rigidly, more justly and on a
wider scale than philosophers had been accustomed to
do.  Even right principles applied in a contracted sphere
may appear to lead to results which contradict almost
universal experience.  It is only a wide analysis and
generalization which will attain universal truth.  The
object of this Dialogue is merely to show, that in sound
inquiry, regard must be had both to the spirit and the
method of inquiry.  Men must possess faculties for inquiry ; must conduct the inquiry honestly, intelligently,
searchingly: and a proper method must be adopted as well
as a right intention.  Three rules are provided for philosophy:  a, Every fact must be an ultimate or simple
one: b, The whole facts of a case must be taken : c, No
foreign facts must be interpolated.  It was by making
only partial examination and by introducing extraneous
elements that almost all ancient philosophy went astray.
If these rules are completely observed, sound science
MUST come out of the inquiry : if they are not observed,
such science is impossible.  The views of the native
systems respecting causation give us great help in carrying through this method.  They allow three rules
which answer in some respects to the three just stated.
1. Every effect must have some cause.  2. That cause
must be adequate.  3. No cause must be sought un-
suitable to the effect.  If their own rules are rigidly
applied, with other principles which they well under-

stand, the disciples of these systems can be led on to see that many parts of their system are indefensible. It will be found however extremely difficult to wean them from making those erroneous applications of the rules to which they have been accustomed.

---

*Englishman.* We were just speaking of some of the mutual contradictions in most important matters, of the Hindu systems of philosophy. These systems were taught by great men and learned men: yet they advocate dogmas which are entirely opposed to each other. I am aware that you have devised schemes for reconciling them; still some great differences do exist, as your own controversies respecting them show. Are we then to believe that it is impossible to discover truth; are we to doubt about everything; is there certainty in nothing?

*Gurudas.* Not so. We all allow that sound knowledge can be attained by men, and hence prepare courses of study by which it may be attained. Man is able to get knowledge by his various senses, his eyes, his ears; and by the exercise of his reason. By these he can examine all the knowledge presented for his acceptance, and having tested the evidence for and against it, can decide on what is and what is not.

*Eng.* There are indeed means and instruments given to man for this very purpose, and there are principles of inquiry contained within his constitution by which his researches ought to be regulated. But before we look at these, let us consider the circumstances which often

hinder their proper application. A traveller going from
Kási to Brindávan has a straight road before him. But
if fogs and deep darkness, or false guides meet him, he
will lose the road, although he may be in perfect health,
possess a willing mind and be able to walk many miles
a day. So the fogs of prejudice, of ignorance, of passion, of self-interest cloud the mind. Some men find
the results of inquiry opposed to their dearest interests,
to the notions which they have indulged for years, and
therefore will not accept them. Others are led astray
by false teachers, who are themselves deceived. Others
again are indolent, and will not take the labour required
for the discovery of truth; others again are of limited
capacity, and cannot comprehend what is taught. The
Sánkhya allows this, and reckons three classes of scholars, the dull, the mediocre and the best : of whom only
the best attain completely the knowledge to which all
applied.

*Gurudás.* Many are the causes which will hinder
sound inquiry. Of these the Nyáya has spoken much.
It shows that the spirit in which it is conducted must be
honest as well as wise. Thus the Nyáya Sutras say
(p. 37): " Those who are desirous to know the truth
are the persons who are competent for discussion."

*Eng.* Quite true. Let us take as an illustration the
process adopted in a court of justice. In examining
into a case of murder, there are required honest witnesses, competent to give evidence of what they have
seen; complete evidence of all the facts; and an honest
judge, to weigh them all. Ignorance in the witnesses, or

falschood; and partiality in the judge will lead only to false conclusions, as the courts of different countries often show. So in examining philosophy, we must examine honestly and completely all the sources of knowledge open to us, and then will our conclusions be sound. If we reject any, either through carelessness or unwillingness, those conclusions must be erroneous. Remembering this important fact, let me ask you, O pundit, what are the *sources of knowledge* commonly allowed in the Hindu systems?

*Gurudás.* Our authorities, O friend, on this point somewhat differ; but may be considered substantially alike. Thus the Sánkhya enumerates three: Perception, Inference, and Testimony. The Nyáya adds to these Comparison: and the Mimánsa, Conjecture: but it is generally considered that the first three include the others: the authority of Revelation being embraced by Testimony. The Vedánta allows six sources of knowledge, which are also reducible to the three first named.

*Eng.* It seems to me, O pundit, that this arrangement is clear and correct; if we add to it the intuitions with which the intellect of man begins its work. All the philosophers of Europe agree with those of the East in looking to these as the ordinary sources of the knowledge we acquire. And indeed it is not difficult to assent to their opinion. Beyond his own intuitions man either learns knowledge which he is able of himself to attain; or which by himself he could not obtain. If he attains the latter at all, the information must be conveyed to him in common matters by his fellow men;

and in extraordinary cases by some higher authority, as
God, to whom it is familiar.   In ordinary matters this
is called Testimony.   All knowledge coming from a
supernatural origin, and relating to super-human matters, men call Revelation.   When a man turns to things
which lie within the range of his own powers, he observes them by means of his senses, and pronounces
decisions upon them by his Reason.   How wonderfully,
O pundit, has man been endowed with instruments of
knowledge.   Reason is the master, and the five senses,
like five slaves, together with the *manas,* convey to
him information about the world without or the mind
within, which the master analyzes and weighs and compares, and which often he combines into new and beautiful
forms of truth.   The eye tells him of the thousand objects
it sees: the ear relates all that it hears; and the touch tells
him how things are shaped and feel.   All these items of
knowledge the reason analyzes, and putting them together in new combinations infers great conclusions and
wonderful principles, unknown to all except the intelligent beings in the three worlds.   Thus it is we see clearly
how the perception of his senses, the inferences of reason,
the testimony of his fellows, and the supernatural revelations of God, furnish him with the materials of which his
knowledge is composed.

But the same facts, O pundit, show also the sphere
to which his attention should be confined.   The senses
of men can examine the earth in which they dwell and
the heavens which are visible; but how can they penetrate into the upper or lower worlds, which are in-

visible? Even if we infer their existence, how can we learn their condition? If God should condescend to inform us of them, then we can learn so much as he pleases to reveal, and no more. We can find out nothing by ourselves. Is it not then foolish, O friend, to speculate about bhúts and prets (goblins), and pretend to describe the habitations of superior beings, which no mortal eye has seen? Ought we not to confine our researches to the sphere to which our senses are confined? Therein we have the wonderful earth, and all that it contains: and long, long will it be before we exhaust the facts which it reveals concerning its constitution and structure; its physical history; the great divisions into which it is mapped out; its vegetable, mineral, and animal products: and above all, the history and constitution of men; the history of their societies and the laws which govern them; together with the study of the right means by which all nations may live in peace and unity, helping each other, and doing all they can to secure each other's endless happiness. These are objects of inquiry open to every right-hearted philosopher; and are worthy of the powers with which the great Creator has endowed him.

There is another great object of philosophical pursuit, O pundit, closely connected with that which I have described. Men not only ask continually, What has happened; but also, Why it has happened: and spend a large amount both of time and effort in seeking for the reasons of things which they do not know. This naturally leads us to consider the LAWS OF CAUSA-

TION, because they are the rules by which such examinations are conducted.  May I ask you kindly to say what are the opinions of Hindu philosophers generally upon the subject?

*Gurudás.*  All our philosophers are not entirely agreed as to the fact of causation.  The honoured Váchespati* enumerates four kinds of opinions: (1) some say that that which is, may proceed from that which is not.  (2) Others say that that which now is, is only the revolution of an existing thing.  (3) Others again say that that which is not may be produced from that which is.  (4) The ancients assert that that which is comes from that which is.  The majority of Hindu philosophers accept the last principle.  The Vedantists do not regard the subject as important; owing to their Pantheistic theory, which declares the existence of only one Being in the three worlds.  The Nyáya and Sánkhya, however, classify the different kinds of causes, and announce the rules on which they act.

*Eng.*  It is singular that any men, like some Bauddhas, can even seem to deny the existence of causation; or, what is the same, can lay down as a principle that a thing which now is can have come from that which is not.†  All men see causes in operation around them every day: even common people, who are ignorant, confess that some things produce others; that movements lead to changes of place; and that actions pro-

---

* *Sánkhya Káriká*, p. 30.

† The statement *may* denote a thing can come from something not homogeneous.

duce results. All men know that to get milk, one must milk the cow; that to make cloth we must weave yarn; and that to make pots we must employ a wheel and mud. All languages are filled with terms expressive of causality; with such terms as *cause, effect, produce, production, do, generate,* and *create.* To speak, to write, to run, to strike, to cut, all denote actions performed by an agent with the express purpose of producing certain results, which experience shows to follow from such actions. Thus the common words of every-day life show that we live under the complete control of this principle. You said just now that the Nyáya and Sánkhya classify the different kinds of causes: will you kindly state them?

*Gurudás.* The Nyáya teaches that there are both special and general causes: meaning by general causes the active agents by whom effects are occasioned. The special causes include the instrumental (as the weaver's loom), the intimate cause (the threads of a cloth), and the non-intimate, the conjunction of the intimate causes. The latter notion is peculiar to the Nyáya, and arises from its doctrine of intimate relations. The Sánkhya again refers especially to three causes: the active or efficient cause; the instrumental; and the material cause: as the potter, the wheel, and the mud are three causes of a jar. If we take away the non-intimate cause of the Nyáya, the three latter causes are identical with the former, and differ only in name. All effects have immediately these three causes. Thus oil is produced by the bullock, the beam and mortar, and the

sesamum seeds.    A statue requires the sculptor, the
iron chisels and hammer, and the solid stone.    Milk is
pressed from the cow's udder, by the hand of the gwálá.
Cloth is woven, by the weaver, working his loom, with
numerous threads.

*Eng.* This description is clear, and the opinions of the
two great schools are the same as those of philosophers
in Europe.  Other classes of causes, especially of a more
remote kind, might be mentioned, but these are the
chief.    Will you now kindly mention the principles
upon which causes are sought for, and applied?

*Gurudás.* The first great principle is, that *every effect
must have some cause.*    This has been stated in two or
three different forms.    Thus Kanáda plainly says: " If
there is no cause, there is no effect; if there is no effect,
there is no cause."    The great Kopila states (Sutra 79)*
" a thing is not made from nothing."    " The product of
something is something, and of nothing, nothing." (81.)
Again he declares, "a nonentity cannot be developed
into an entity;" as a man's horn; it is an impossibility.
" There must be a material from which the new product
comes."    He also points out the reason of this.    If
entities could be produced from nonentities, or products without materials, there would be no certainty

---

* Sutra 79, taken literally, expresses the law of causation here
advocated, and such a meaning may fairly be drawn from the terms
which it employs.    It is a fact, however, that all the Hindu and
Greek philosophers have made a special application of the rule,
which is not necessarily true; viz., that " a material thing is not
made from a non-material thing."    Here we may allow the former
application of the words: the latter will be specially disallowed in a
future dialogue.

in anything; anything might occur anywhere at any time.

*Eng.* This is certainly an admirable principle and clearly stated. Among the wise Greeks whom I mentioned to you, the same doctrine was taught in almost the same words, and their principle has been universally recognized as true. Men know of no existence being produced, nor even of change produced, even in the commonest things, without a cause. If we want something, we must get it from something: and out of a nonentity, nothing can be produced. In all your systems, however, an erroneous application has been made of this principle, which will be discussed hereafter.

*Gurudás.* Another great rule of causality is thus expressed by Kopila: "A thing possible is made from that which is competent to produce it." (118.) And this rule also is expressed and illustrated in different ways. "Fit materials must be selected." A man who wishes for curds, takes milk, not water, for the purpose. "Everything is not possible from everything else." Gold is not produced from silver, nor from the fruits of trees. Cloth is not produced from the mud of the potter. "What is capable, does that to which it is competent." The potter, the wheel, the mud and water are capable of producing a jar: from these the jar is produced. The potter cannot make bracelets, or cloth, or brass vessels; and no one goes to him for them. Milk does not come from stone, nor does rice grow on the stalks of sugar-cane. Hence again, "Like produces like." Rice comes from rice, barley from barley, milk

S

from cows,.jars from clay, and cloth from threads. This
is the rule.

*Eng.* This law is also of the highest importance, and
ought to be observed in all our examinations of the
world and what it contains. Effects must be attributed
to adequate causes. Causes set in motion must produce
corresponding effects. The two must suit each other.
The causes of effects must be adequate in time, and
adequate in power. If a cannon-ball is fired now, I
attribute its flight not to the effort of a little boy who
tried to throw it yesterday. I must find a powerful
cause which produced that rapid motion now, and drove
it that immense distance. The melting of the immense
snows of the great Himalaya, can produce nothing less
than the mighty Ganges as it flows in the month of
Srávan in its full stream. A great city like this is
built by none less than the intellect, and wealth, and
hands of man: and so it is, in my opinion,* that the
production of the universe we can attribute to no cause
less than that of the omnipotent and eternal God.

*Gurudás.* There are other principles of causation
laid down both by the Sánkhya and Vaiseshika. The
Sánkhya for instance, lays it down, that a product is
nothing else than the cause in another form: that production is therefore only manifestation, and that destruction is only the resolution of a product into its

---

* Of course, Kopila does not make this application of the law, or
allow it: but it is a perfectly just application. One of the objects
here kept in view is to show Hindus how much truth is involved in
their own principles of philosophy, which they themselves have not
deduced.

causes. The Nyáya again describes a number of superfluous causes, and warns the student against recognizing
them.

*Eng.* In tracing back effects to causes, it is not easy
to say exactly what those causes were, owing to the
want of a correct knowledge of the secret nature of
things. We therefore meet with difficulties. However,
the general laws of causation are quite clear, and there
can be no mistake, either about the laws themselves, or
their use. It is plain that every effect must have a
cause; that out of nothing, nothing can spring; and
that effects can be produced only by adequate causes,
even supposing those causes actually unknown. We
need only add, that too many causes ought not to be
sought for an effect, nor causes too great for its production. We require to know the true cause, the whole
cause, and nothing beyond the cause of the product
examined.

*Gurudás.* The principle just named was laid down
of old; when sufficient proofs for a thing are found, "no
addition to them is to be sought; because of the cum-
brousness" of such a proceeding. (Sánk. Sutras, p. 96, *b.*)

*Eng.* These then are the few, but important principles upon which all our inquiries into philosophy are to
be based. By the aid of our perceptions, guided and
examined by Reason, we can study the facts of all this
universe laid before us, and endeavour to understand
its constitution and history. If we look to its many
changes, we have two great laws of causality to guide
us, and so long as we keep within them, we cannot go

wrong. If too the Omnipotent God reveals to us any supernatural intelligence concerning the worlds invisible, or the ages yet future, or his designs unknown, we are able also to receive it, and can make that knowledge our own. I shall be very happy now by the aid of these principles to accompany you into a careful examination of the great systems of Hindu learning. I have looked over their authorities, studied the doctrines they teach, and weighed the arguments by which they defend them. I find many good things there; the very principles of inquiry we are speaking of are correctly stated, and if the great teachers, the founders and scholars, of these systems had never broken through their own rules, they would have arrived at a greater number of correct conclusions than they have found. I think that while they teach some correct things, they also advocate some things which are most erroneous: errors indeed of great magnitude: and if you are willing, I shall be most happy to discuss these doctrines with you; and having done so, to state what I think to be the chief outlines of the truth which men can learn from the sources of information opened for our use.

To this proposal *Gurudás* and the assembled pundits readily agreed, expressing the hope that much pleasure might be derived from such a discussion. They wished to hear what fault their English friend could find with their various shastres: but felt little curiosity as to the ultimate effect it might have upon themselves. Their English friend accordingly having fixed to meet them another day, then left them and returned to his own home.

## Dialogue Second.

### IS THERE A GOD?

——◆——

### PRELIMINARY NOTE.

In treating this important subject, two things have to be done. First, to examine Kopila's own reasoning in defence of his views; and secondly, to bring forward a few cogent arguments in proof of the being of a God. In examining Kopila's reasoning an endeavour has been made to state it fairly and completely: and to show that it may be most justly turned against himself. He has himself employed the argument from design; and made use of some very happy illustrations, in the course of his discussion, which, however, he does not fully apply. His own illustrations prove that the Framer of the Universe was an Intelligent Being. While Pátanjali, the head of the Yóga school, shows that his single argument against the existence of God will not apply to such a Being.

There are three branches of the argument of Natural Theology usually employed by English writers to prove the existence of God. First: the argument from existence and causation. Second: the argument from mind. And thirdly: the argument from design exhibited both in mind and matter.

In selecting a few reasonings on the subject, the second of these branches has been omitted; because from the peculiar views held by the Nyáya and Sán-

khya respecting the eternity of souls, any argument
from their existence in favour of a CREATOR would
necessarily lead us away from the main question into
topics which must be hereafter treated separately. The
discussion must therefore mainly depend on the other
two branches, and can be made cogent and convincing
enough by their means alone. Only a few specimens
of design have been considered necessary. The most
happy as well as most complete treatment of the entire
argument, in a form suited for English readers, that I
have seen, will be found in the recent work of the Rev.
Dr. Buchanan of Edinburgh—*Faith in God and Modern
Atheism compared.* Vol. i. § 1 and 2.

———

Some days after, at the invitation of their English
friend, several pundits who followed the Sánkhya doctrine, met together at the house of the pundit Gurudás,
who had himself made a complete study of that philosophy. Having taken his seat among them he thus
addressed the assembly : I have recently been reading
the Sutras written by Kopila respecting the existence of
an ISWARA, as well as the Slokas of the Sánkhya
Kárika upon the same subject. These books contain
much that is good, and advocate many admirable principles, which the wisest men of this age allow : but in
respect to our present subject, the reasoning appears to
me decidedly defective ; and if you please I should like
to talk it over with you. I observe first that Kopila
does not treat the subject specially, as for instance the

Yoga does; but only speaks of it incidentally, and in quite an indirect manner. Now it seems to me that this was not giving to it the importance which it naturally claims. If such a Being exist, then in every way the truth concerning that God must be of importance to every man: God is the Ruler of his life, to him he looks for all things: Kopila, therefore, could scarcely have had an adequate conception of the greatness of the doctrine, and of the Being to whom it refers, when he treated the matter so briefly and so indirectly as he does. I see that, when speaking of perception, and examining whether his definition applies to such a being as Iswara, he boldly declares that in his opinion the *existence of God is not proved.*

*Gurudás.* True, sir, he does assert this; but he also gives arguments against that existence. The chief argument he propounds in the form of a dilemma; thus: " Of free and bound, he cannot be either, and therefore he cannot exist: either way he would be inefficient." (Sutra 94, 95.)

Kopila's meaning as explained by Patanjali, is; If God were " free" from all the ignorance, error, conceit, desire, and the like, which come on the " soul" when connected with nature, he would be indifferent: he would not wish to create. If he were " bound" by those desires and troubles, through being united to nature and fettered by it, then he could not create. Either way he would be ineffective to produce anything. There can be no such being.

*Eng.* This argument of Kopil's seems to me to be

quite insufficient, and that for two reasons.  *a.* He assumes that a being, bound by desires and other troubles,
incident to mundane existence, troubles such as men
and the gods experience, cannot effect anything.  But
this is untrue.  The potter, the weaver, the farmer,
though numbered among men, who are "bound" by
desires, troubles and activity, do engage continually in
new labours, and produce new things, in many new
forms.  Desire does not prevent action in inferior beings,
who work according to their inferior capacity: Why
should it prevent him?  Even then if God were bound
by desires, what should hinder him from forming matter
into new combinations so far as his great power ex-
tends; just as the potter makes new vessels according to the inferior skill which he possesses?  The sage
actually allows this, and thus contradicts and over-
turns one horn of his own dilemma.   Thus in the Káriká
(Sutra 58), it is written : " As people engage in acts to
relieve desires, so does the undiscrete engage in acts to
liberate the soul."  Supposing then that Iswara were
like other souls, united to nature, bound by mundane
troubles, why should he be unable to engage in acts for
the liberation of souls?  I offer this only as a minor
objection to Kopil's reasoning, though I think it quite a
sound one.  But the argument is insufficient for another
reason.  *b.* Kopila here argues that Iswara must either
be " bound," or be " free," whether originally or by
liberation.  He assumes, therefore, that ALL intelligent
beings from the highest to the lowest must be either the
one or the other.  But Iswara, as commonly received,

is neither.  He is not subject to the laws or the conditions of mundane existence like other beings.  He is their author and therefore in a condition above theirs.  Kopila himself allows that Iswara is not endued with the three *gunas*, from which all delusions are said to arise: and therefore he is not bound by the troubles to which they are subject.  He has never become free by liberation.  He is, however, always free: God is not like other souls: and Kopil must prove that he is like them before his argument be accepted.  This dilemma, therefore, is quite unsound: the sage elsewhere answers his own arguments.  I would ask you, has Kopila's reasoning satisfied all the disciples of the Sánkhya school?

*Gurudás.*  No.  The Yóga of Pátanjali, which is reckoned a branch of the Sánkhya school, and is termed the *Seswara Sánkhya*, differs entirely from Kopila on this subject.

*Eng.*  Would you kindly tell us what Pátanjali says when he discusses it?

*Gurudás.*  Having referred to one method of attaining abstract meditation by profound devotedness towards Iswara, the Lord, the sage in the next Sutra describes Iswara thus: " God is a particular spirit (*Purusha*), untouched by troubles, works, fruits, or deserts."  He thus declares Him to be of the nature of souls, but calls him a " particular " spirit, unlike the other multitudinous souls with which the universe in its several regions abounds.  Alluding to the statement of Kopil, that Iswar must be " bound " or " free," after declaring him to be unlike all other souls, he describes him as

" untouched* by the troubles, works, fruits, and deserts"
which a connection with nature has brought upon
them.   He adds that He is possessed of power, able
to uphold all things by His mere will.†   He is also
omniscient; because knowledge finds only in Him that
extreme limit and perfection which it must find somewhere.   Possessing this Supreme Wisdom, He has been
the teacher even of the earliest beings, the gods, having
existed long before them, and being, in fact, from everlasting.   This is Pátanjali's reply to Kopila.

*Eng.* His reply we cannot but deem excellent and
sound.   With good reason does he assert that the God
above us is in a condition very different to ours.   Accepting Pátanjali's reasoning, we may regard the argument of Kopila as quite insufficient to establish the
important dogma which he advocated, that there is no
Iswar: and to get rid of that which all men believe,
that there is such a God, their Preserver and King.
The Yógists, therefore, have done well.   Nor are they
the only Hindu philosophers who have maintained this
truth.   The Nyáyists also defend it, and describe the
existence and attributes of God in clearer terms than
even the Yoga.‡   They hold that God is not mere knowledge, but He is a substance of which perfect knowledge,
intellect and volition are attributes.   He is altogether
different from nature and different from spirits.   It was
He who formed the universe by developing its original

---

* *Yóga Sutras*, pp. 29–32.
† This statement is from his commentator.
‡ *Bhásha Parichheda*, pp. 17–20.

atoms, and uniting "mind" to its many souls. In pressing upon you, therefore, the unsatisfactory nature of the argument of Kopila, I am not introducing reasons formed by strangers, who follow a foreign philosophy. I bring forward objections which have been felt by a branch of his own system, and by the wise teachers of other systems that are equally old and renowned with his. Nothing can be clearer than that Pátanjali felt the objection to that argument which I have expressed; and that Kopila, in making Iswara the subject of troubles and illusion, assumed the very point to be proved. I have shown, too, that Kopila has contradicted himself in arguing that an intelligent being, though under illusion, is unable to effectuate anything. But there are other objections to his argument which may be drawn even from his own system. He is quite inconsistent in three things: first, in his reference to the Vedas; secondly, in not applying to this subject the same reasoning as that which he employs to prove the existence of soul; and thirdly, in arguing that all things originate from an unintelligent source.

*First:* he is inconsistent in rejecting the existence of God, while he acknowledges the authority of the Vedas and of Brahmá. Has he not asserted the authority of the Vedas?

*Gurudás.* Certainly. In the 150th Sutra, he says: " Scripture is of higher authority than intuitions."

*Eng.* Has he not also allowed the authority of Brahmá?

*Gurudás.* Yes. An objector to his doctrine asks: If

there be no Eternal Lord, will not the Vedas cease to be of any authority? He replies (Sutra 99): "The declaration of the texts of the Vedas by Brahmá is sufficient authority, since he knows the truth."

*Eng.* That is the passage I refer to. Kopila allows that Brahmá knows the truth, and yet contradicts the very thing which Brahmá declares. In the Upanishads, especially in the *Mundaka*, which is said to contain the doctrine he taught to his son, *Atharbba*, Brahmá is represented as everywhere teaching the doctrine of the Supreme Brahma; affirming his existence again and again, and also enumerating his attributes. If Kopila received his authority and that of the Vedas, why does he reject the existence of the Supreme altogether, of whom they speak so much?

*Secondly :* he is inconsistent in not applying to this subject the same argument which he elsewhere employs for a similar one. Will you kindly say how he proves the existence of unseen soul?

*Gurudás.* In Sutra 67, he argues that the combination of the principles of nature is for the sake of another. A couch, a bed, and the like, are made not for their own use, but for the use of another. All their various parts conduce to the effect they are intended to produce, and they have evidently been made for a purpose.* Now there must be a being for whom they are made; and that Being is Soul.

*Eng.* Well; may not the same argument be applied

---

* It is extremely interesting to find in the Sánkhya such an early application of the doctrine of "final causes."

to show the existence of a Superior Being who is above
souls? Each body is indeed fitted to be the residence
of a soul: the organs and senses are all intended. to
convey to it information from the outer world, and most
admirably serve their purpose. The world, too, is
fitted up for the same end. Its vast seas, its great
mountains, its broad fertile plains, its flowing rivers, its
mines of gold, silver, and iron, its endless forests, are
all fitted to serve the purposes of man, to sustain his
life, to add to his comforts, to increase his wealth, to
employ his thoughts, and in a thousand ways advance
his happiness both of body and of mind. Intelligence
and happiness do arise in his soul, and all the souls
of men enjoy these numerous sources of pleasure and
convenience. But for whom are all souls made, with
all these stores of happiness? When they are happy,
who is the sharer of that happiness? Who is the chief
enjoyer, not only of this world, but of other worlds?
Whose glory is shown in all these things: whom do
they all praise: to whom do men look as the giver of
all good? They all acknowledge God. All nations
look up to him as the Great Soul: all people adore a
Being whom they consider the giver of this good; as
the maker of themselves; as the Being whom they
ought to please. The glory of God is promoted by it
all: and therefore he made it all: he made the unintelligent for the use of the intelligent: and he made
the intelligent for his own honour. He delights in their
happiness, the happiness for which he has made such
abundant provision. The jeweller makes ornaments for

the child to wear: and the father of the boy rejoices
in the delight which the wearing of them produces.
The Great God rejoices in the happiness of his intelligent creatures, for which He himself has provided.
In this way it seems to me, that Kopila ought to have
proved the existence and greatness of God, in the same
way as that by which he argues the existence of soul.

*Thirdly :* I have said that Kopila contradicts himself
in rejecting a God, and attributing the origin of all
things to unintelligent nature, while his own argument
shows that the real agent must be intelligent.

*Gurudás.* How, O friend, can this be? He distinctly
declares that all things, except soul, come from nature,
the aggregate of the Three Gunas.

*Eng.* By the illustrations he employs. Will you
kindly quote those which are mentioned at the end of
the Kárika?

*Gurudás.* They are these. (Sloka 58.) "As people
engage in acts to relieve desires, so does undiscrete
nature engage in acts to liberate the soul." Again, "As
a dancer, having exhibited herself to the spectators,
desists from the dance, so does nature desist, having
manifested herself to soul." "Generous nature accom-
plishes the wish of ungrateful soul."

*Eng.* Exactly, those are the illustrations I mean.
Now, what has the author of the Káriká said here?
Nature engages in acts to relieve the desires of soul,
just as people commonly do. The potter having formed
the desire of making a jar, engages in efforts to produce
it; the jeweller, having desired to form a bracelet, en-

deavours to make one; the weaver wishes to make a
beautiful *sári*, and applies his skill to its production.
Nature, having finished her work, desists from it; as a
dancing girl, having danced and completed the character she has been acting, desists from the efforts she
has made. Again, nature is generous to soul—shows
kindness to soul, though ungrateful; just as a benevolent man endeavours to relieve the distress of the poor.
All these illustrations apply to intelligent persons. The
potter, weaver, and jeweller, are intelligent, and act
according to reasons, in what they do. The dancing
girl is intelligent; she knows when her work is completed, and therefore desists. The benefactor of the
poor is intelligent; he understands their wants, knows
how to relieve them; and continues his kindness,
although some prove ungrateful. The argument, therefore, requires that, in the same manner, the agent who
has acted to relieve the desires of the soul, who has
desisted when the work was done, and has exercised
benevolence to ungrateful soul, should be reckoned an
intelligent agent. Only by intelligence could the work
be accomplished; only intelligence can learn when it is
completed; and only intelligence can understand what
benevolence is. Kopila, however, makes his agent unintelligent nature! In this he is inconsistent. After
employing these excellent illustrations, he deduces a
conclusion which the illustrations do not allow. An
intelligent agent is what they prove; an intelligent
agent is accepted by all nations: to an intelligent agent
no valid objection can be made. Such an agent is

God, who is Supreme Intelligence as well as Almighty Power. Have none of the followers of the other schools distinctly noted this position of Kopila's?

*Vedántist.* It has been specially referred to by Veda Vyása in the *Brahma Sutras.* Without saying anything about Kopila's inconsistencies, he takes up the doctrine that the origin of all things is unintelligent nature. In the Sutras (B. i., ch. ii., Sut. 5), he argues that the first cause must be an intelligent one, and that in the Vedas he is always spoken of as such. The Nyáyists also argue in the same way.

*Gurudás.* It should be said, however, that in practice there are few learned men who reject the doctrine of a Supreme Iswara; and the difficulty we have been discussing has long since been satisfactorily explained. It is understood that the great Kopila here does not intend to teach that there is no Iswara, but that he merely asserts against an objector that his existence has not been sufficiently proved.

*Eng.* I am quite aware, O pundit, that few learned scholars in Upper India are really atheists, though they study the Sánkhya system; and that, as orthodox Hindus, you all believe in the Supreme Brahma. But the explanation given can scarcely be called satisfactory. Kopila not only asserts, for the sake of argument, that the doctrine is unproved, but he treats it as unproved: he treats the existence of Iswara as entirely unnecessary, and, in his scheme of creation, does entirely without such a being. In ancient days, his contemporaries and successors regarded his views as unsound. They called this system *nireswara;* they held long controversies with his disciples. The Yogists and Vedantists argued specially against him ; and when schools like those of the Swetaswatara Upanishad and Bhagavat Gita were formed, while they adopted his philosophy in some cases, they distinctly recognized a Supreme. Besides, the Buddhists, whom you all reckon unorthodox, because of Kopila's doctrine, which they received, rejected not only an Iswara, but Brahmá and the authority of the Vedas. All this shows that his errors were regarded as important; it tells against his authority as a teacher, and proves that he is not to be regarded as a safe guide.

Leaving the arguments of Kopila, let us examine this great subject for ourselves. Some men have rejected the existence of a God in Europe as well as in India. But the proofs of that existence are numerous, and, in my opinion, most satisfactory. Let us briefly review one or two of them. (*a.*) Let us take first the argument from *causation,* the principles of which we noticed a few days ago. Will you kindly state those principles?

*Gurudás.* We noticed that every effect must have a cause, and that an adequate cause. On these points nearly all philosophers are agreed.

*Eng.* Will you kindly state also the classes of causes engaged in producing effects?

*Gurudás.* We noticed three, generally employed among men : the material cause, the instrumental, and the efficient cause. Sometimes, however, no instrument is employed. But two causes are always needed ; the

T

agent, who is the efficient cause, and the material from which the effect is produced.

*Eng.* Well then look at the world in which we live: its surface is formed into mountains and valleys, rivers and seas: it is clothed with forests: it is inhabited by beasts, birds and men. All these things are effects: they have sprung from causes which have preceded them. Trees have sprung from the trees of former ages: animals have been produced from others now dead. We can trace back existing effects to their causes: those causes have sprung from previous causes: and so we go farther and farther back to some beginning. Do not all your systems allow this process to be a sound one?

*Gurudás.* Certainly they do. And all the systems trace up the present forms of existence in the world to the five elements; which are considered to be the primitive material of all.

*Nyáyist.* There is, however, this difference. The Vaiseshika traces all things to ether, soul and the original atoms of the other four elements and of "mind:" the Vedánta also recognizes these five elements: but the Sánkhya adopts finer forms even of those elements; then reduces them back to one origin, Nature.

*Eng.* That is the point to which I wish our attention to be turned. Supposing that we reduce all the material causes of the world to two, the union of which will produce another effect, from which again other effects may be multiplied: the question properly arises, how are those two material causes to be brought into union?

*Nyáyist.* Of course by an agent, who will be the efficient cause. Without the efficient cause the two material causes can never join. Allowing the wheel and the clay, how can the pot be produced without the potter?

*Eng.* Just so. Whatever be the system of philosophy we each adopt, it seems clear that all must allow the necessity of an effective agent who shall be the prime mover in the creation of this world. Without such an agent, possessed of power to do, and of intelligence which knows what to do, how can two unintelligent materials come together to produce an effect? In order to unite to produce an effect, they must be moved near to one another. But they have no power to move themselves. If they move, their motion must come from nothing, which cannot be: out of nothing, something cannot arise. An agent, however, can originate motion; can originate action; and can be governed by motives. An agent, therefore, was absolutely necessary to produce the first effects of matter in the great universe. Such an agent is God: able to do what was needful; and wise to understand its results. It seems to me, therefore, that the Laws of Causation, which all men believe, prove beyond doubt the existence of GOD, who is the FIRST CAUSE. We shall see further the truth of this if we consider the contrivance Kopila has adopted for bringing his causes together. What, O pundit, does he consider to be the original causes?

*Gurudás.* He reduces all products to two, Soul and Pradhán, "nature," which are from eternity.

*Eng.* Does soul then become the Creator, and employ pradhán for its purposes?

*Gurudás.* No. Soul is inactive: free from desire. But the sage teaches that for the purpose of giving pleasure to soul, nature joined herself to soul.

*Eng.* How could that be; how could the unintelligent act in this way?

*Gurudás.* He explains it in the following illustration: " Soul governs nature not from a resolution to act, but from its proximity: as the loadstone acts on iron." When soul came near to nature, the latter (as by the power of attraction) became Mahat, and its system of development began. Again, in the Karika it is said: " As grass and water . . . become milk and nourish the calf, and as the secretion stops when the calf is grown, so nature acts spontaneously for the liberation of soul."

*Eng.* But these illustrations are childish; and cannot account for all the grand effects which are visible in the universe. The first one also directly sins against the Law of Causation. " Soul attracted nature when they were brought near to each other: " we therefore ask: Who brought them near? Were they eternally near: then according to the illustration nature must have been attracted from eternity; and its creation been produced eternally: an impossibility: for there was a beginning at a distinct time. This must have been effected by the moving power of some agent; and

thus again we see Kopila's argument leading us to an
intelligent agent possessed of knowledge and power.
The other illustration implies that nature is already
organized, like the udder of a cow, and is organized for
a suitable end: whereas the very argument itself is
based on the idea that nature is then unformed and only
begins to act for the liberation of soul.   Both the illustrations however are trifling, and are utterly insufficient
to account for the origin and plan of this stupendous
universe.   Are we not right, O pundit, in rejecting
such an explanation, which at most is analogy, but
contains no proof?   And are we not right in considering that the Laws of Causation imperatively call upon
us to believe in an Intelligent First Cause, who first
put together and set in motion the various material
causes at work in the world?   Without him, how could
those causes have begun to work?   Kopila has given
his account of their original impulse, but nothing can be
more unsatisfactory.

(b.) Let us next take up the argument from design.
The necessities of causation show that in creation there
must have existed an efficient intelligent cause to put
material causes at work: much more is this shown by
the argument from design.   Let me now describe it
to you.

The universe in which we dwell is full of contrivances
of all kinds, great and small.   Men continually apply
to them the resources of their minds: and animals also
exhibit in them their skill.   The nest of a bird, the
hole of a field-rat, the nest of a wasp, are all made, and

made for use: they are not natural, do not grow like
vegetation, but are artificial, and are just adapted for
the use which they are intended to serve.   The contrivances produced amongst men are seen most frequently
in the work of the artisans.   The houses we live in;
tables; desks; brass pots; mud pottery; the hookah;
paper and ink; books; carriages; boats; are all works
of art, and are intended for certain specific uses.

Now, are these things the mere work of unsentient
matter?  No.  Every one knows they are the product
of intelligence applied to matter; and that only by
intelligence can they be contrived.  We see again that
the amount of contrivance varies with the amount of
intelligence, and of the resources which that intelligence can command.  A man whose contrivances and
products are unusually skilful and useful is called very
clever; while another whose works are clumsy is called
stupid.  We have all heard of the celebrated engravers
at Delhi, who cut such beautiful Persian inscriptions
upon precious stones, and can cordially join in the
praise which their skill receives.  These are common
facts, but they teach us great principles, upon which we
always act in ordinary life, and which we ought not
lightly to set aside in more important matters.  Contrivances spring from intelligence.  Their skilfulness
varies with the amount of intelligence displayed.

. The universe is filled with an immense multitude of
objects, exhibiting these signs of contrivance.  The inorganic masses possess various qualities (I use the term
in the Vaiseshika sense), which admirably fit them for

the use of men: coal burns; mud is made into pots and jars; water washes; metal melts with heat. The organic again are distinguished by a wonderful structure designed to promote their growth and their multiplication: and are also wonderfully adapted for the use of man. Thus trees grow through the supply of sap in their myriads of vessels: the bud and the flower prepare the way for fruit. The horse, the cow, the elephant, and the camel by their strength and activity are fitted for the various labours to which men assign them. What do we then fairly deduce from these facts? We see that they must have been made by some intelligent Being. Could unintelligent nature, merely drawn as by a loadstone, or influenced like the udder of a cow in secreting milk, have made all these things? It is impossible. Why has every man five fingers on each hand? Why has every man two eyes placed in his head and not in his feet: why has he two ears at the sides of his head and not on the top: why do fruit trees always bear the same fruit after their kind: why do mango trees give only mangoes: and plantains, plantains: why, if rice is sown, does rice spring up: why, when black threads are woven, does black cloth result: why is there order, regularity, and exactness in the world: why does the sun rise in the east day after day, giving light and warmth: why does the moon show her bright face at night: why, in a word, is the world full of order, full of beauty, full of contrivances for the wealth, the support, and the comfort of men? It is because it was made by a Being possessed of intelligence and wisdom.

We see also in the extent of these contrivances and works the greatness of this intelligent Agent. The views which the Nyáya, Vaiseshika, and Yóga have taken up concerning the Creator of the universe, while true to a certain extent, seem to me to be defective, in not giving an idea of him sufficiently glorious and great. Will you kindly give us, O pundit, the opinion which Pátanjali has expressed upon this subject?

*Gurudás.* He declares that Iswara is possessed of power; for so his name implies: and that in him the germ of the Omniscient becomes infinite: knowledge in him reaches its utmost limit: but he gives no particulars concerning his agency in creation.

*Eng.* But if we do descend to particulars, and examine the extent to which design and skill are displayed by him in the universe, we shall obtain the most exalted notions of his nature, power, wisdom, and goodness. We see the proofs everywhere. There is not a single object in nature that does not exhibit them: while presented upon the most stupendous scale in the sky above, they appear in the most minute forms of animal and vegetable life in this world. An enumeration of individual cases would add nothing new to the argument. They would merely increase the number and breadth of the instances in which the attributes of the Creator are exhibited.

We are compelled to believe in the existence and agency of a First Great Cause, an efficient cause, by whom the material causes of the universe were first set in motion. We are compelled, by the system of design in the universe, to believe that this Great Cause is possessed of the highest possible intelligence, power, and goodness. Such a Being is He, whom we call God: and whom we ought to honour as the most exalted and glorious of Beings. As the first Being, the cause of other beings, he is himself uncaused. He must therefore possess within himself the power of existence: he MUST exist; he cannot but exist; nothing can destroy his existence. He is therefore pre-eminently self-dependent. The immense extent of the universe; the vast resources it contains; the greatness of the bodies of which it is composed; the might, the speed, the tremendous effects of the natural agents which it contains: all exhibit the immensity of his power. The nature, variety, and multitude of the contrivances exhibited throughout the universe, illustrate his boundless wisdom: and their wonderful effects in securing the comfort, the health, and the welfare of all living creatures, of securing their safety and ministering to their enjoyment, show forth his goodness. Such is the Being whom the great universe presents to men as its creator, its daily preserver, its daily benefactor, its tender father. By the side of proofs like these, how insufficient do the arguments of Kopila, of the Bauddhas, and the Jains appear, when they wish us to believe that all things came by chance and sprang from nothing! Let us reject such a faith: let us hear the voice of Reason, and accept the conviction that He is, and that He is the rewarder of them that seek Him. With these words the dialogue on this subject closed.

## Dialogue Third.

### PANTHEISM.

———◆———

### PRELIMINARY NOTE.

THE subject of this dialogue is one which has but little engaged the attention of modern Christian writers in Europe. Very little has been written against it in English even in India. As a specimen of the mode in which discussions intended for England fail to help us in India, attention may be called to the following arguments against Pantheism, occurring in a popular essay on Infidelity:—"(1.) If true, creation is not a free act, but a necessity: it is therefore fatalistic. (2.) Pantheism inevitably destroys all moral distinctions. (3.) It shuts out prayer. (4.) It destroys the immortality of the soul." To all this a Vedantist would reply that the writer understood Pantheism to a certain extent, and had stated some of its consequences: but that there are other consequences, even of a stronger kind, which he had quite overlooked. So far, however, from being shocked by these consequences, and hence rejecting the system as unsound, the Vedantist would accept the whole as true, and as perfectly legitimate elements in the system, which thus proves itself so consistent! To people trained amid the influences of European society, the statement of such consequences may perhaps be left to imply the falsity of any system which teaches them. But with the Vedantist the argument against his system

at that point is not even begun : it must take up those
consequences, and show why they are wrong, and why
they pull down the system with them. We are left,
therefore, to go much deeper into the very first principles of common sense and common morality; the very
foundations of both must be reached before we attain
that firm ground on which the thorough-going Pantheist finds he cannot set his foot. Few processes of
reasoning are more difficult than this. Happy is he
who can carry it through successfully.

---

The next subject which engaged the attention of the
English judge and his friends, was the important doctrine of the Vedánta respecting the nature of God and
of the universe. The discussion was conducted chiefly
with Vedantic pundits, although Gurudás was well
acquainted with the tenet and the objections made to
it by Hindu philosophers. Their friend opened it by
asking one of the pundits who were the first teachers of
the Vedantic doctrine.

*Vedántin.* The Vedánta system was formed by Veda
Vyása; but he is said to have compiled the Brahma
Sutras from the Upanishads of the Vedas. These
Upanishads were communicated by most celebrated
sages of former days: as Angirás, who taught the Mundaka, Swetaswatara, Yájnavalkya, and others. They
expounded the doctrine to their disciples; and from
them it has descended to the present time.

*Englishman.* The most important part of the system
seems to me, the doctrine concerning Brahma: we

have already examined the proofs that there is a God
Supreme, ruling over all.    Let us now consider the
question, whether God is everything and everything is
God: and first let us hear, O pundit! how the doctrine is stated by the authorities.

*Vedántin.* It is said in the Sruti, " All the universe
is Brahm." This statement is repeated again and again
through all the Vedánt Upanishads in many forms.
Many illustrations also are given of the way in which
the universe sprang from him.   As the threads from
the spider, plants from the earth, hair from animals,
sparks from fire, silk from the silkworm, and trees from
the ground, so the universe sprang from the imperishable Brahm.

*Eng.* But is this asserted of the whole?  Is nothing
excepted from the general doctrine?

*Vedántin.* Nothing is excepted.   On the contrary, in
many passages, individual objects of various classes are
pointed out as exhibitions of him.   Thus: " He is fire;
he is the sun and moon; he is wind; he is water.
Thou art woman; thou art man; thou art the youth
and the maiden; thou art all things born: birds of
various plumage; the seasons; the sea, art thou.  Thou
hast the universe for thy face."  Many a similar passage is found in the Katha Upanishad and other authorities.

*Eng.* Is it plainly declared that the soul of man also
is a product of Brahm's?  Are there more passages than
the one you just quoted?

*Vedántin.* Vyása distinctly states : The soul is a por

tion of the Supreme Ruler, as a spark is of fire: the relation between them is that of whole and part. It is said in the Upanishads, that on the formation of the body, Brahma penetrated into it and took up his dwelling in the heart, on the water-lily that is placed there. Hence the body is called the city of Brahma, with its nine gates.

*Eng.* But if the universe is formed from Brahma and returns to him again, how much of the whole of his substance is reckoned as contained in these various objects?

*Vedántin.* The Yajur Veda declares that one-fourth is so employed.

*Eng.* Are any special arguments advanced in favour of this doctrine, or does it rest upon the authority of the Upanishads and other shastres alone?

*Vedántin.* No special arguments are used: but Sankar Acharjya, in commenting on the Brahma Sutras, considers several objections against the doctrine, and thus confirms its truth. Otherwise it is taught on the direct authority of the Vedas.

*Eng.* Very good. Such is the doctrine and the evidence in its favour. One thing, however, strikes us at the outset; the followers of the Nyáya, who are most numerous, as well as those of the Sánkhya philosophy, entirely reject the doctrine: though they do not at any length argue against it: this they do, though Vedic authority carries weight with all Hindus.—Looking at the doctrine, however, on its own merits, it seems to me quite erroneous. Its very nature and effects are so contrary to reason, that it cannot be sustained by sound argument: I will endeavour to state clearly several proofs against it.

*First.* The great God of the universe ought to be reckoned a glorious being: but the Vedánt makes him appear *very contemptible.* You say, God is everything: all animals; whatever the universe contains. He is, therefore, the sun, the moon, the stars; he is mountains; he is rivers; he is the sea. He is trees and plants: he is the flowers, fruits and vegetables. He is all men. He is not only brahmins and Vaisyas; he is the lowest caste, the Chandál, the Hári, the Dóm. He is the man of wisdom; but he is also the thief, the liar, the lowest, the most degraded of men or women. Can we believe that? He is all animals:* not only the elephant, the tiger, the horse; but he is the ravening wolf: he is the buffalo, the deer: he is the lizard, the scorpion, the crocodile, the centipede: he is the crow that eats everything, the kite and the hawk: he is the very ants. Does this give us a proper idea of God? If again Brahm is everything, then he is the food we eat, the water we drink; we write with him, we walk on him; we touch him wherever we go. Does not this present him in a very insulting and contemptible light? Can any one really believe that the lizards and flies and centipedes, our food, our water, our air, are all God? It cannot be. If again Brahm is everything, it is he who does everything, whether performed by animated or inanimate things. Can we believe that it is God who is eating,

---

* This is the argument of Origen against Pantheism.

drinking, sleeping? Is it God who follows all the sensual habits, and performs the sensual acts, which daily
disgust even men? It is most revolting to the mind
even to speak of such things: but if the Vedánt theory
be true, Brahma, and none but Brahma, does all this
and infinitely more. The honour, therefore, which we
pay to God, and which the Upanishads so often assert
concerning Brahma, prevents us from considering that
he himself actually holds such a degrading position or
performs such degrading acts.

2. I find a *second* argument against it in this: it confounds entirely *matter* and *soul*. Though they differ
entirely in properties, it ascribes to them a common substance; and that is the substance of the divine nature.
It puts all things, as to their origin and nature, on one
level. The intelligent and the unintelligent are alike;
they are Brahm. The potter and his vessels are the
same; the brazier is of the same substance and occupies
no higher rank than his brass pots: the blacksmith is
not better than his frying-pans, anvil and hammer: the
weaver is of the same origin as his loom and thread:
the hunter and his gun; the boatman and his boat;
the builder and his stone, are all alike. Brahma is alike
the substance and material of which all are composed.
Is this true? Are all things in this world on such a
level? Are there no things superior in their nature, as
well as their uses, to others? Are there no things common; while others are superior? We know that there
are: and especially do we acknowledge that the souls
of men, by their reasoning powers and their ability to

acquire knowledge, are greatly superior to the earth on which we tread.

But this theory does more than level them: it actually confounds the substance of things; and thereby sins against the law, that like produces like. I mean this. God, as we have seen, must be a Being full of intelligence, possessed of the highest power in himself, and of the highest wisdom. Now intelligence, wisdom, and self-acting power, are attributes of soul. Such attributes he has given also to the soul of man. We shall see hereafter, how correctly both the Sánkhya and Nyáya discriminate between soul and matter on these very grounds. The substance therefore, of God (so to speak) must be a substance of which intelligence is an attribute. He is a spirit, the Great Soul. Now matter, as we call it, is quite different. Soul thinks, loves, is angry, rejoices, hopes, sins, does good. Matter cannot do *one* of these operations: it can only be known as long or short, hard or soft, possessed of shape, incompressible, and the like. The two substances differ entirely in their phenomena, their capabilities, their uses: and men are compelled, therefore, to believe that they possess substances of entirely different kinds. They feel compelled to believe that iron, which is a hard metal, is a thing entirely different in its very nature from the thinking soul of the blacksmith who shapes it. But the Vedánt teaches us they are the same; and it teaches not that there is no soul, but that all is soul, all has emanated from the Supreme Soul. It teaches us that the iron and the smith's soul have the same substratum, although they differ

entirely in their properties and acts. Now we cannot
believe that. If like produces like, then the substance
of the all-wise, all-powerful God, which must be a
spiritual substance, is not the substance of iron, wood,
and water, which have a material substratum. The
Vedánt dogma, therefore, must be erroneous. Take
now a third árgument : you allow, O pundits ! that
there are many defects in matter, do you not? You
allow that the actions of animals are in many respects
degrading, and that the conduct of men is distinguished
by faults and sins of various kinds.

*Vedantin.* Certainly. All the authorities show that
the whole universe is enveloped by the three gunas ;
and that, according to the nature of the guna in each
part, and the amount of it, will be the peculiar character which it exhibits. There is nothing in the
universe free from the influence of the three gunas,
except the Supreme in his own nature.

*Eng.* Well. But if the universe is Brahm, then all
these gunas influence him, and the different forms which
a portion of his substance has assumed. Not only does
the Satya Guna influence him, but the Raja Guna, with
all its varieties of passion, and the Tama Guna, with its
numerous degrees of vileness (according to your doctrine), rule him, and exhibit their fruits in him. You
have yourselves pointed in strong terms to the corrup-
tion and decay of the world around us, as well as to
the follies and vices of men. Can such things occur to
emanations and forms of the incorruptible God? The
Vedantic world itself has endeavoured to avoid this

consequence of their doctrine, by applying the theory of
the three qualities to those forms. Still it must be from
Brahma that they are derived: the Sánkhya tells us
that they belong to Prakriti; but the Vedanta can find
no other origin for them than him, from whom all
things spring. If men are forms of God, then in their
thefts, adulteries, and murders, it is Brahma who steals,
Brahma who murders, Brahma who is the adulterer.
He is guilty of covetousness, anger, lying, ingratitude to
parents, and impurity of heart. Every fault we find with
men or with each other, all the disorder of human
societies, all the destruction produced by wickedness of
all kinds, we throw entirely and without exception upon
him. Is not this a fair deduction?

*Vedantin.* Yes, it is fair; even the Shastres attribute
these evils to him: the Sutras and Gita say so distinctly. The words of Vyása are: "The Supreme
Being is designated in the Vedas as the cause of virtue
and vice, as of everything else." (Colebr. Ved. p. 231.)
He must be, therefore, the author of their results, of
the sorrow, trouble, and misery which follow vice, as
well as of the joy which springs from virtue.

*Eng.* But who can believe that this is right? Who
can charge upon the great Benefactor and Father of
men all the misery which the world contains?

There is a *fourth* argument, cognate with the last one,
which we may next consider. I asked just now, How
can all the defects, decay, and wickedness of the universe spring from the pure, wise, and happy God? Now
I ask, If the universe be an emanation from Brahm, and

all its various objects be so many forms of him, *why do they not possess his excellences?* His substance is the same throughout. If he can be divided into parts, then every part is endowed with all the divine excellences which belong to his nature : every part must have these excellences, for it is essentially divine. If then, you and I, and all men, and animals, and things, are forms emanating from his divine substance, how is it that the one-fourth of Brahma contained in the universe does not exhibit those excellences at all? Everything here is just the opposite. It ought to be incorruptible : it is full of decay. It ought to be happy, it is full of misery. It ought to possess divine power, it is all weakness. It ought to be wise, the densest ignorance and degradation rule over all. How, then, can this universe be God?

*Nyayist.* This same argument is offered by the followers of the Nyáya. "True knowledge, that is, the Supreme Brahma, is not found in individual souls, because they are clearly distinguished from it by knowledge and ignorance, happiness and unhappiness, and similar qualities; and in consequence, the difference between them and Iswara is established. Otherwise servitude and liberation were names without meaning." (*Bhásh. Parichh.* comment. p. 21.)

*Eng.* Let me present to you, O pundits! a *fifth* argument, which more directly relates to the souls of men. Is not Brahma declared to be " without a second ?"

*Vedantist.* He is so declared in many passages. "He is one, and without a second." The meaning of these statements is thus given by Veda Vyása:* "Nothing exists but he, though different texts of the Vedas seem to imply the contrary."

*Eng.* If nothing exists but he, the universe contains but one substance. Whence then, O pundits! is the *sense of duality* derived? With one intelligent substance, and no more, there can be no duality.† Yet the soul of man possesses the sense of duality and acts upon it at every moment of our waking existence. Thus speaks Kopila on this point (Sutra, 42):— "Not thought alone exists, because there is the intuition of the external." Every thought of the human

---

* Sutras, iii. 2. 29.

† The wonderful doctrine of the Trinity relieves Christianity altogether of several of those difficulties which the acute Hindu sages detected as necessarily attaching to any doctrine—that God is absolutely *one* and without a second. It would seem to follow that if God be absolutely and solely *one*, if his knowledge be always perfect, and his nature unchangeable, his ideas would everlastingly be the same ; one notion or one state only would be experienced; that state would be without contrasts, and would seem to be equivalent to insensibility. The Sánkhya philosophers felt this when they say: " The cause of the world cannot be a God who is fixed in one monotonous state; because there is neither the possibility of action or of knowledge in such a Being."—(Dr. Ballantyne's Vedanta Sutras, p. 16.) We cannot wonder, then, at the Hindu doctrine of Brahma sleeping alternately with waking. The cause of any awakening under such circumstance they have not explained: they can only, with M. Cousin, assume the thing to be proved, and say that he wakes from a necessity of his own nature, and begins to create, because his "distinguishing character is an absolute creative force, which cannot but pass into activity." Consistently they ought to hold that awakening is impossible; *but* the fact of a creation upsets the doctrine. The Bible clears all this away. With perfect unity of essence, knowledge, and purpose in the Divine nature, there is plurality: a plurality which becomes the source of eternal activity, eternal bliss; which can contemplate for ages a mighty purpose, and realize it only when the fulness of time is come.

soul, every notion of which we are conscious, and every
act which we perform, implies to us that we differ
both from other persons and other things.   Myriads of
objects exist around us, which we call by different
names, and employ for different purposes: every
thought and every affirmation concerning them implies
a mental affirmation that they are different from us,
and from each other.   We also have different states
of mind, at different periods, in relation to different
objects.   We act for various reasons: possessed of
limited knowledge, we examine the consequences of
actions; and, determine, therefore, what course to
pursue.   Here is duality at every step: a conviction
of differences between beings, differences between
things, differences between rights, differences between
opinions and states of mind.   This duality is felt by all
men, in all places, and has been so felt during all ages.
What do men mean by "mine," "yours," if there is
no duality?   Under the theory that everything is
Brahm, and there is no duality, such a universal conviction of duality, and such universal acting upon it,
would be impossible.

Closely allied to this argument, O pundits! is another.
I have spoken of the conviction of duality in the soul,
which the soul is every moment asserting: let us now
consider *the actual differences* between things.   These
actual differences entirely refute the pantheistic doctrine which the Vedánta advocates.   That doctrine
says there is no real difference, no real duality: those
which we observe are only apparent.   I think, however,

it can be shown that these differences are real, and therefore overturn the doctrine. These differences are shown in two ways:—(*a.*) In the universe there is a multitude of contrarieties in respect to *condition.* Some beings are happy, others are miserable; some are rich, others are very poor; some rule, others serve. Some, again, are virtuous; others are loaded with crime; others are partly good and partly evil. All grades of character lie between. How can this be, if all be equally parts of Brahm, one and indivisible? They should be all perfectly alike. In the same way, how can *rights* exist, if all be Brahm? One individual has not different rights over the same thing. Yet such rights exist in the world, and are protected by law. Your land is yours; my house is mine: but if all be Brahm, my right is your right; yours is identical with mine. Or, rather, all right ceases; for the property we hold is on a level with ourselves. Will men listen to such a doctrine? They acknowledge duality; and they defend it by force, by laws, by police and punishments. Will they believe that there are no such things as rights, and that "mine" and "yours" are mere names?

Again. (*b.*) Not only do these conditions differ, but some are directly the *contradictory* of others. Your Shastres declare how the gods even quarrelled with each other; how, at the feast of Daksha, Mahádeo fought with other gods, and, amongst other deeds, deprived Surjya of his teeth. So do men quarrel; so do rebels disobey their king's commands; so do foreign

enemies make war. Some men punish, others are
punished; some reward, others receive the rewards;
some love, others hate. These are perfectly contradictory of each other. But, according to the Vedánta,
God does all this to himself. He sins against himself;
he takes himself prisoner, tries himself in court, con-
demns himself to prison, and punishes himself by fasten-
ing himself in gaol. The existence of these contrarieties
is a complete answer to the doctrine that all is Brahm,
and that there is no duality.

*Vedantin.* But there is a special answer, O friend!
furnished to this argument by Sankar Acharjya. An
objector tells him, as you have done, that in the world
there exists the enjoyer and the enjoyed; and asks,
How can Brahma be both? Sankar replies: " Such are
the changes of the sea. Foam, waves, bubbles, are not
different from the sea itself, though a difference is perceived in them by turns. Nor do these changes obtain
each other's condition. So the enjoyer and enjoyed do
not obtain the condition of each other; they remain
separate."

*Eng.* This argument of Sankar does not, O pundit!
meet the difficulty. As to the illustration, it must first
be noticed that the foam, waves, billows, and bubbles.
of the sea are only different forms of the same substance, viz. salt water. They differ in appearance, but
they are water still, and possess all the essential properties of water. They are produced from the water
by certain causes, as the winds, and subside into water
again. They do not differ in character and qualities

from one another, as the other objects of the universe
do.   The same sea cannot be both land and water at
once: it cannot be foam and mountains, billows and trees,
bubbles and grass, at one and the same time.   But that
is what the Vedánta asserts of Brahm.   Part of his
substance quarrels with another part; part is vicious,
part is virtuous ; part is matter, part is soul ; though
the essence of all ought really to be identical.   The
difference is not merely one of form, it is a difference
between characters, which are not only distinct but
contradictory.

I might add a seventh argument here, showing
especially the inconsistency of the Vedas, and of the
disciples of the *Vedánt,* in teaching the worship of different gods and the observance of distinctions in caste.
If Brahm be one great being, without a second, there
cannot be separate gods at all.   One limb of a living
being is not a separate animal or a separate life by
itself; it cannot have a separate consciousness of its
own, and especially it cannot exercise by itself the
rights of the complete being from which it is taken.
There can, therefore, on the pantheist theory, be no
Mahádeva, no Indra, no Ráma, and no Káli: not one
of them can possibly possess the right of acting as a
separate god.   How inconsistent it is, then, O pundits !
to honour them as such, and to allow the common
people to honour them as real living beings, when, after
all, they are nonentities !   How inconsistent, moreover,
it is for the Upanishads and the Gita to recommend
the worship of these gods to the common people as

beneficial, when, on the Vedantic argument alone, these deities must at once cease to be gods and to exercise influence as such.* Besides, if it be true that all is Brahm, the worshippers are Brahm as well as the deities; and what service, what reverence do they owe to them? Again, if all be Brahm, how can the distinctions of caste be maintained?—for all men have one origin, and all possess the substance of Brahm. Why should you, then, reckon some high and some low, some as pure and others impure? The consistent Vedantist ought to give up both the worship of the gods and the observance of caste, but the disciples of the system do neither.

*Vedántin.* But the Shastres approve of both: the Vedas say that both gods and castes were ordained by Brahm: and encourage the worship of the former, as well as commend the observance of the latter.

*Eng.* But if, O pundit, the Veda teaches doctrines which are opposed to one another, where lies the fault. Is it in us, who find it out; or in the book which so teaches? The Vedas do teach such things; and this doctrine, which we are discussing, compels a wise man to condemn them as teachers of religious error.

* Augustin, in his discussion with the Manichees, brings forward another argument against pantheism, which, however, is of no use to us. He says, if all beings are parts of God, and a course of study is good for men, in order that they may obtain " wisdom " and absorption, consistently the gods ought to undergo the same labours and by the same plan !

The Vedantists allow that the argument is sound, and show that the gods have so acted. The Chhandogya Upanishad (viii. 11.) declares that Indra was a student under Prajápati for a hundred years before he attained " true knowledge !"

*Vedántist.* We have heard, O friend, all your arguments against this great doctrine, and can acknowledge
that in appearance they do condemn it. No doubt there
seems to be in the soul of man a consciousness of
duality : a perception of good and evil. There seem to
be in the world contrariety of condition, opposite conditions and opposite courses of good and evil. Even
the Shastres speak of different classes of beings, and
describe them as acting independently. But all this is
consistent with the theory. Apparently, men and things
do differ from Brahma; but the Shastres prove that
they do not differ in reality. There is an illusion
(MÁYÁ) in men's consciousness, a Máyá enveloping the
universe, which makes these appearances; and it is from
the influence of this Máyá that so many errors have
been propagated instead of the true doctrine of the
Vedánta. All the Vedantic authorities refer to the
ignorance and delusion in which man is bound : and it
is the object of the system to free him entirely from
their influence.

*Eng.* I am quite aware, O pundit, of this explanation; and have perceived also that it is given more
especially by the later schools of the system. It is
certainly clear to my mind that if man's mind is not
filled by delusions, like those of a dreamer, it is impossible, for many reasons, to believe that the universe
is God : and that we are all parts of the Supreme.
Either pantheism is false, or the consciousness and
reason of man are bound by illusion. You accept the
latter alternative. You maintain that the doctrine is

true: and that the reason why men believe it false is because they really are deceived by their illusions of soul. Let us now examine this point: it has most suitably been reserved to the last.

Taking, then, this doctrine of Máyá, as expounded by the Gíta and the Vedánta Sár, we are taught that all which men are accustomed to look upon as real, all things of which they seem daily to be conscious, are unreal. They appear to differ from one another in name, and form, and properties; but they do not really differ. They have only been drawn, if drawn at all, from one substance. The illusion which makes them appear real to us has deceived us; and as we are parts of God, the illusion has enveloped the Supreme himself. "The illusive power of ignorance produces the universe from the egg of Brahmá." The glorious sun which enlightens the world by day, the moon which lessens its darkness by night, are unreal. The stupendous sea, the glory of our world, has no existence: the mountains, rivers, forests, and fields are illusory appearances. No beasts really roam the boundless wilds, no birds really warble their sweet songs. The mighty cities of men, that include the abodes of the wealthy, the huts of the poor, the bazars for trade, the courts of justice, the shops of artisans, are all illusive too. The very world has no existence. These things appear to exist in the eye, the ear, and the touch of him who imagines them; but they do not really exist. Reality is unknown. The different conditions of men, the different bonds by which they are associated, are unreal. The

relationships of father and son, husband and wife, ruler
and subject, master and servant, are a deception.    Men
are not really companions, fellow-subjects, or friends:
the duties which spring from these relationships are not
really obligatory; pleasure and pain do not truly exist;
real virtue and vice are unknown ; the rules of law, the
instructions of wisdom, the pleasures of piety, are only
imaginary: all that is wise, good, and holy has no absolute foundation.    The world with all its substances, its
variety of beings, its principles of pleasure, morality,
and religion, is all a LIE.    There is nothing true in our
whole life, or in the history and continued existence
of all the nations of the world.    Everything is false:
and the deceiver is the Supreme Brahm: who is thus
engaged for innumerable years in deceiving himself!
What an awful conclusion to come to !    Who can
believe that this doctrine gives a fair and true account
of the real system of the universe ?    Who can believe
that he himself is a lie ; his life, a lie ; the world, a lie !
No one.    The judgment with which we have been endowed, which reasons on such sound principles, works
on sound system, examines so wisely and builds up such
wonderful masses of knowledge, is made and constructed
too well to let us for a moment imagine that the Creator
intended, in forming us and all men in the world, only
to lead us astray.    We are formed to establish certainty.    Can the God who so formed us have planned
everything to delude?

To this explanation respecting Máyá, we reply (a)
that the doctrine greatly insults God.    It is said that he

assumes these forms, and produces these distinctions for illusive sport. He has made intelligent beings from himself, and made them so as to appear independent, only to please himself. He has enveloped them in a Máyá, which leads them into error, and which has governed millions of men for ages, yet he has done this to please himself: their errors, wanderings, doubts, and troubles give him pleasure. All the acts that are done, he does: yet it appears that it is not he that does them. Whether these acts be acts of devotion, or of wickedness, of impurity, cruelty, and blasphemy, or of benevolence and mercy, he does them all; yet he deceives men into believing that there is a difference between them, while really and truly there is not. Is not all this blasphemy against God?

(*b.*) If men are Brahm, and possess the nature of Brahm, it is impossible that they could have been deceived in this way. Men of confined knowledge are deceived in consequence of their imperfect acquaintance with things around them. But Brahma knows everything. Brahma too is really one and indivisible. How then can different portions of him be so deceived as to forget their own origin, their very nature, and the knowledge in which, so to speak, they shared. They could not forget. Neither is it possible in any way for God to deceive himself.

(*c.*) Again, if men be bound in the illusions of *Máyá*, it is impossible that they could ever have been taught that they were so. Here I may say: If my mind is deceived by Máya, how am I, while still in Máyá, to

know it.    The knowledge that I am in Máyá, is itself
Máyá.    All things around and within me are full of
deception.    That very piece of knowledge is part of the
errors by which I am involved.    How am I to distinguish between what is error and what is truth?    The
knowledge of the illusion is itself illusion; the power
which recognizes the confusion, is itself confused.    We
can understand this by reference to a class of people,
who are really under illusion, viz. the insane.    We
know that the insane lie under various delusions.    Some
call themselves kings, some reckon themselves wealthy
men with numerous attendants: and so on.    By calling
them insane, we mean that their reason is perverted,
and cannot judge of things like the reason of other men.
We cannot therefore accept their conclusions.    Can any
insane man, whose reason is thoroughly deluded, be
made to understand that he is insane; and can any such
be brought deliberately to say, "I am in all respects
insane?"    He cannot understand the difference between
insanity and sanity : how then can he pronounce himself insane?    To speak thus, requires a large amount of
sagacity and reason.    He therefore who can, deliberately and with understanding, come to the conclusion,
"I am insane," shows by that act that he is not insane
at all.    In the same way, if all men are deluded by
Máyá, it is impossible that in their delusion they should
be able to understand that they are so.    It is impossible
that they could sit down, as we are doing, and discuss
the various arguments to prove that they are.    Such
conduct implies that their power of judging is free from

Máyá, and is thereby enabled to contrast Máyá with
certainty and with truth. It proves that amidst universal
illusion their own judgment is a thing fixed and free
from doubt. If we can see the uncertainty of all things,
and pronounce that everything is illusion, we must in
respect to that judgment be ourselves certain.

(d.) Still more clear also is it, that men involved in
Máyá could never undertake a long course of study to
get themselves out of their illusions. How, in such a
case, is the true knowledge of Brahma to be communicated to those whose every thought and every judgment
is led astray by error? No one can expect the insane
to do any such thing, and the attempt is never made
by insane persons themselves. Yet those deluded by
Máyá are invited to undergo a long course of severe
Vedantic study, in order to cure them of illusions and
set their judgment of the universe right. This only
proves that in respect to its followers, the Vedánt does
not apply its own doctrine.

*Vedantin.* The meaning which you have attached to
some of the Vedantic authorities does not, however,
express the views of all. The system taught in the
*Vedánta Sár* does not hold that all material substances
and all souls are in all respects identical with the
Supreme; but teaches that so far as we know these
things we know only their appearances or phenomena:
and that the only real and existing substance which
underlies them is the Supreme: without him they cannot be.

*Eng.* I am quite aware of this doctrine of the recent

Vedant schools: and can easily believe that thinking men must give up the gross pantheism against which I have been speaking. Even that doctrine, however, is by no means a sound one: and the system of the Vedánta Sár, which contains the explanation of Maya or Illusion is open to several of the objections I have raised. But I have referred to the doctrines taught in the oldest and most honoured authorities of the system. The refined doctrine taught by the Vedánta Sár is very different from that of the Sutras, the Upanishads, and the Gita, where the identity between the Supreme and all objects in the universe is asserted in plainest terms, objections are answered, the system is rendered complete, and its great consequence, the making God the author of sin, is set forth in clear and direct terms. Philosophers may refine such a doctrine: but the common people of Hindustan have made the grossest use of it. It has blinded them to the real nature of sin; and made them fatalists in the hour of calamity. And were not men often better than their creed, did they not listen to the conscience within them, the evil effects of this mighty error among the Hindus might be much greater than they now are.

---

## Dialogue Fourth.

### THE ETERNITY OF MATTER.

—◆◇◆—

#### PRELIMINARY NOTE.

In the next two dialogues we have the most difficult subjects of all to treat of. I have no hope whatever that the discussion will be considered satisfactory. The more deeply the subject of creation is studied, the more clearly does it appear to my own mind that bare reasoning upon the phenomena of the universe is insufficient to settle the question: and that any course of argument, which is drawn out on principles that Greek and Hindu philosophers will allow, must of necessity be incomplete and inconclusive. To show this, let us briefly examine the capabilities of the argument and consider how far it is possible for proof to go.

Supposing the entire creation to be a pyramid, induction and analysis inquiring into its origin, and tracing its progress, according to the strictest application of the Laws of Causation, bring us, without question, to its apex. There we find seated an Intelligent Being, who is the First Cause, endowed with power and wisdom, sufficient to have developed that universe from the earliest causes in the series. Since two causes are required to produce one new effect, we are certain that at the commencement of that series there must have been at least two material atoms to begin with. The Framer of the Universe must be an Intelligent Being,

X

seeing how greatly thought, design and foresight have been exhibited in the universe. He must have existed before the work of development began; He must therefore have been uncaused; that is, He must have been self-existent: and judging from what He has done, His power, wisdom, skill and goodness must be of the most surpassing kind.

Can we go higher in this process, and seek for something earlier? Were those two original atoms produced from one by the Supreme Intelligence? Were they produced from no material at all in some way that only His superior wisdom knows? Does He now occupy by His presence any part of that space which lies beyond the limits of the universe, and which the very weakness of our intellect compels us to believe to be unbounded on every side? Are His power and skill, which are proved to be immensely great, even greater than what is proved, and in reality perfect and unlimited? Has He power to create matter? Has He power to create souls? Did He at first exist alone in the vast ether? And did He at some special time or times cause matter and soul to begin their existence; and people one portion of space with substances and living creatures?

It seems to me that creation itself does not give a complete reply to these questions. We, who are a part of creation, produced after it began, can never learn from nature itself, when, how, and from whom it first began to be. Vast as we see the universe to be, it is still limited: vast as are the designs, the power, the wisdom displayed in its structure, they too are limited. We know that they must be great enough to produce what now exists and has existed: they may be somewhat greater: but we can by no means prove them all to be unlimited. All around us is finite: the infinite is unproved. Probable it may be: the Architect of the Universe may possess perfect attributes; but the limited universe does not prove them perfect.

Dr. Buchanan, in his excellent lectures, suggests that, as the mind of man has the power to pass from concretes to generals, from particulars to universals, and does so in a thousand things connected with the facts and phenomena around us, so we can pass from the limited universe to the perfect God. I feel hesitation however in accepting on such a subject the testimony of Christian writers, who have already got the notion from another source. I fear that, like those who saw Columbus make the egg stand firm on its broken end, they argue from reason, in favour of a doctrine which reason would not have discovered for itself. It is a striking fact, that while the ancients did rise in thousands of cases from particulars to generals in common things; and while they used the terms " Almighty Power " and " Omniscient," no Hindu or Greek philosopher ever rose to the idea of a creation properly so called. They never got to a higher stage than that of placing God in relation to the universe where the potter stands in reference to his vessels. That eternal matter, either in mass or atoms, is conceivable, we learn from the fact that hundreds of the learned and

acute both in Greece and India have believed in it:
and they accepted that explanation in reference to the
universe, without imagining the far nobler theory laid
down in the Word of God. So much for the capabilities of the argument. Let us consider the best mode of
treating the discussion.

*a.* The Hindu systems assert the eternity of matter:
is it fair to throw upon us the burden of disproving
it? Have we not the right of insisting that they shall
prove what they assert? Otherwise we are called upon
to prove a negative: and to prove it by simply pointing
to the defects of matter, or its uses, or the obvious purpose of its constitution. Even if we can show that
there is a Power sufficient to create it, we do not prove
that it was so created. It may possibly have been eternal
after all.

*b.* On the other hand, it is clear that they do not
directly prove that matter is eternal. All they can say
is that matter in its present form can be and must be
traced back to the fewest primal causes. Then, because
they do not know whence those causes came, they boldly
declare their material is eternal. That however is
merely a theory to explain a fact. Undoubtedly some
explanation is necessary: the primal causes must come
from somewhere: but it by no means follows that
theirs is the right one: and in point of fact it is impossible to prove that it is the right one. Another explanation, another theory may be suggested. The Supreme
Intelligence, whose eternal existence is certain, and whose
power and skill are proved to be immensely great, may

possibly possess sufficient power to provide these materials by creation, in some way above the comprehension of our minds. To assert in answer to this suggestion, that a material cause for such primal agencies is necessary, is to assume the very point to be proved. We may not understand either the nature or process of creation; it is impossible that we should do so. Yet he may really create these original substances. Nay more, we must allow it to be perfectly possible for such a Being to produce many other kinds of *substrata* besides mind and matter; and many other qualities of which we are totally ignorant. Had we seventy-two senses instead of five, we should probably find out hundreds of properties in the substratum of matter, which hitherto we have never conceived. All this is possible. If we can suggest an origin of matter as sufficient as that of its eternity, our theory has as much right to be accepted as theirs.

c. In this difficulty I think it perfectly fair to avail ourselves of the admissions made by the systems, that God is omnipotent and knows all things. However they got the idea (and I think it is not difficult to show that it is a remnant of patriarchal teaching, the full force of which is not perhaps understood), there it is: and we have a right to use it and show what it involves. Perfect power on the part of God is quite sufficient to account for the origin both of matter and of human souls.

d. With these views, it appears to me that the strongest argument against the eternity of matter is found in the fact that it has been made for a grand purpose ; that every property and attribute it possesses has been interwoven into the system of the universe ; and that it is subordinated and controlled entirely by him who rules that universe. Believing him omnipotent, it is far more reasonable to suppose that he produced it for himself, than that he found it accidentally possessing the very properties which he required.

*e.* It is wearisome to plod one's way through these courses of argument, when one single word of authority carries us straight to the truth. " In the beginning God created the heavens and the earth." But all shows us the truth of the assertion that we really learn the fact not from the works of God but from his word. " Through FAITH we understand that the worlds were framed by the word of God, so that things which are seen were not made of things which do appear."

———

Having shown that it is impossible on numerous grounds for men of wisdom to regard the universe as identical in substance with the Supreme God, the judge, on his next visit to his pundit friends, took up another theory advocated among them as to the origin of matter. This was the theory advocated by the Sánkhya and Nyáya, in two separate forms, that matter is eternal. In discussing this subject, he addressed himself to his friend Gurudás, and to some Vaiseshika pundits, who had come to meet him for that object. On opening the discussion, he proceeded to say :—

*Eng.* We have seen by numerous proofs that all intelligent men must acknowledge the existence of an Eternal God, supreme in wisdom, almighty in power, and full of goodness, a Being of intelligence, who has had supreme control in the formation and preservation of the universe. We now turn to that universe itself, and ask, what is its origin? whence did it come? We have seen that we cannot regard it as a form of Brahma himself, for it is material while he is spiritual. There were different theories advocated in Europe respecting these questions among ancient philosophers: some thought that the world itself was eternal; others, merely that its material had existed from eternity.

*Gurudás.* No Hindu pundit says that the world is eternal. On the contrary, every system among us, including the Vedant, traces the present constitution of the three worlds to original elements: it is these elements that are regarded as eternal.

*Eng.* Very true, O friend. I am aware that the opinion is not a Hindu one: and I merely mentioned it, in order to show that other philosophers besides those of Hindustan have speculated on the subject. The opinion again is easily disproved. All the causes now at work in the world are but the effects of previous causes: and those causes again spring from causes preceding them. Active causes produce changes: how then, with these causes ever in operation from age to age, can the world which now is, have existed as it is, unchanged from everlasting? It is a contradiction in terms to say so. Besides, the great sciences of chemistry

and geology prove beyond all doubt that the most numerous and important changes have taken place upon the
surface of the earth.   Seas once stood over what is now
dry land: mountains have given place to valleys, and
valleys to mountains.   Mountains have been worn down
by the washing of water, as the Himálaya are being
worn now: and their particles have gone to form fertile
plains far distant from them, like the rich plain of the
Ganges.   Thus a long succession of ages gives the earth
a different appearance from that which it once bore.
These sciences show that the earth in its present form
had a beginning: they teach what was the lowest stratum
of its surface, as the eye now sees the uppermost, and
they show how these successive strata were formed and
deposited in the course of many ages.   But we need not
trouble ourselves with this theory.   Let us turn at once
to the theories of the Sánkhya and Nyáya systems.   The
Vaiseshika traces all substances to atoms, and declares
these atoms to be from everlasting: while the Sánkhya
traces all things up to a final nature to which the same
eternal origin is ascribed.   Will you, O friend, kindly
state the Sánkhya doctrine upon the subject?

*Gurudás.* The Sánkhya traces all present existences
to twenty-five principles.   Sixteen of these are again
traced to the five elements: these again to five subtle
elements.   The five subtle elements are traced to self-
consciousness: this to intellect: and intellect is traced
to nature.   Soul is represented as a separate existence
never modified.

*Eng.* Nature, then, you reckon as the last of all, and

therefore the first producer. But why is production attributed to Nature and not to Soul?

*Gurudás.* Kopila, O friend, gives the reason of this. He teaches that all the products in the universe are distinguished by the effects of the three gunas: all the thoughts of men, as well as the objects around us. Now these three gunas are not in the soul, they are in nature: hence, many of these things called intellectual, and deemed to belong to the soul, have really sprung from nature. He says (Sutra 114): "Anything else than nature involves a contradiction to the threefold aspect of the products."

*Eng.* But this does not get rid of the difficulty. To avoid the alligator behind, Kopila leaps into the mouth of the tiger in front: but he does not thereby save his life. To avoid the difficulty about the gunas, he confounds material with spiritual products. But let me ask, on what ground does he declare nature to be from eternity?

*Gurudás.* He shows by his reasoning that nature is the first producer. Soul is inactive: nature therefore produces. Now, unless something spring from nothing, nature cannot have been produced from anything before it. It is uncaused, and therefore eternal. On this the sage argues :—

" *Múle mulábhávát amúlam múlam.*"

" From the want of a root in a root, the root (of all) is rootless."

As the root is the commencement of a tree and has no root to itself: so the uncaused producer of all things has no beginning and is therefore eternal.

*Eng.* But, O pundit, while the principle is a good one, it will not in this case prove the eternity of matter: for as I have already shown you,* we must believe that the Primal Agent in the production of the universe is an intelligent agent; that He is GOD. So say Vyása, Pátanjali and Kanáda. It would appear, therefore, that Kopila gives no special argument in favour of the eternity of matter: as distinct from that which shows the original intelligent producer of the universe. But Kanáda and the Nyáyists have done so, have they not?

*Vaiseshik.* Yes, O friend: they accept the great doctrine of a God; but they also believe that in forming the universe, he had the eternal atoms of various elements to commence with: and that without them the universe could not have been formed at all.

*Eng.* How many kinds of atoms, O pundit, do you consider uncaused?

*Vaiseshik.* We reckon nine substances, of which only five are in their eternal form atomic: viz., " mind," earth, water, light, and air. The other four substances are soul, ether, time, and space, each having qualities and actions. All the substances are eternal. Time and space have the qualities of infinity and ubiquity: and ether fills all space.

*Eng.* Apart from the question of the eternity of these substances, the classification of them seems in itself deficient. Of soul and mind I need not now speak: as we shall discuss them separately hereafter. But I cannot but ask, How is it that TIME and SPACE are num-

---

* See Dialogue on the Being of a God.

bered among substances? I am aware of Kanáda's reason
for making them so; viz. from his very definition of
substance: but this is insufficient. They are not things
at all. They are merely the conditions upon which
existence is possible. If a being exists he must exist
somewhere: and if he continue to exist, the continuance
supposes time. They are thus conditions and attributes
of existence. We see the universe around us. Let us
imagine it not to exist: take away this world and all its
inhabitants; the moon, the stars, the sun: leave only
God; still the space exists: all the place which these
beings and these substances occupied is empty, but the
place itself exists still. The space does not depend
on my idea of it: or on my knowledge of it: or on
the knowledge of any one else. It existed before I
was born: before men at all were made. It existed
before the universe was formed. The space within
which our planets and comets move existed before they
were placed there: it was then empty: now it is partly
occupied. So it is with time. We mean by time succession of existence: its continuance during successive
moments. The world exists, and has existed for years:
before its production space also existed: and continued
to exist. Space must have existed from eternity, and
continued to exist in time, whether occupied or unoc-
cupied. These things, however, we can see are not
things. The Creator, the First Cause, has always
existed: and continued to exist. He must have existed
somewhere. He who exists nowhere and for no period
of time is a nonentity. That somewhere is space: that

period is time : space may be, as far as we know, infinite in extent : as time is endless in the succession of its
moments. But they are quite independent of a creation,
a universe : and are merely the conditions under which
anything exists at all. To reckon them among substances must then be regarded as a mistake. The
Nyáyists and others have made a mistake too in count-
ing ether* among the substances. From the qualities
ascribed to it, it appears to differ from space only in
density, for it is coextensive with space : but there is
no proof whatever of its existence : and we need not
believe in it till such proof is given.

Regarding the atoms of the four substances, viz.
water, light, earth, and air, it is easy to show that these
substances cannot be reduced to ultimate atoms of the
same kind as themselves : for they are themselves compounds, and their simple constituent elements are well
known. So far, therefore, the teaching of the system
must be regarded as erroneous : no such atoms exist.
But I am aware that Kanáda did not teach the doctrine
from an actual examination of these substances, and
from an actual sight of their atoms : he only considered
by reason that they must have such ultimate atoms,
especially as the Vedas referred to such. Neither did
he actually inspect the combinations of atoms, for he
himself teaches that they are invisible, and are only

---

* *Ether* was invented in the days of the Upanishads merely to
account for the origin of sound: an object being required for hearing, just as light and so on are objects of the other four senses.
The Greeks were not hampered by this theory: and therefore believed
only in the four substances.

discovered from their aggregation in compounds.   The assertions he has made concerning their size and their combination are mere assertions, of which there is no proof.   All statements concerning such things ought to be the result of direct examination and experiment. Modern chemists have made many such researches, and it is from the results of their examination that the doctrine of four elements is rejected.   They do not reject the doctrine of atoms in general.   That may be true, or it may not: they know nothing for certain. They have merely shown at present that all material substances may be traced to fifty-nine originals: and they hope to prove that these are reducible to a smaller number.   Be this as it may, what is the reason given, O pundit, for regarding atoms as ETERNAL?

*Vaiseshik.* Kanáda declares that every atom is eternal, without beginning and end *(nityam)*, and also without a measure.   He says too that atoms are uncaused, putting the case thus: There is necessarily a regressus from compounds to simples: and in this process we come somewhere to an end.   The point finally obtained is eternal.   Otherwise at the last step we must admit the production of an effect from something which is not its material cause.   This argument both shows the existence of atoms, and that they are eternal, because they are the uncaused commencements of visible material products.   The argument is illustrated by the case of the potter.   A potter requires mud for the production of his pottery: and also his wheel: if there be no mud, there will be no pots.   So when the Supreme Soul

formed the universe, how could he have done so without material to begin with?

*Eng.* It seems to me then, O pundit, that the argument offered for the eternity of atoms resembles closely
the argument offered for the eternity of nature by the
Sánkhyas.   It is said by each that products can be all
traced back and back, and that the point at which a
stoppage is made is eternal.   Both the systems do the
same thing for different purposes.   The Sánkhya does
it to find the First Cause in unintelligent nature: the
Vaiseshika, in order to find out the primeval elements
of the material world.   But it appears to me that the
argument cannot stop where it does.   You come to
eternal matter, in order to avoid the regressus *ad infinitum*.   But that regressus must be made.   All things
physical are effects, produced from causes: those causes
are the effects of previous causes: these we trace back
and back, and still back: and so long as we confine
ourselves to such causes, there is NO STOPPING.   The
reasoner must go on.   Hence the difficulty pointed out
in the case of the Sánkhya: "When did Prakriti begin
to act?"   It is impossible to find an answer.   The
infinite regressus must be made, until we reach some
adequate cause from which matter or atoms could have
been produced.   The mind compels us to make it; yet
in point of fact such regressus is absolutely impossible.
How then can the eternity of matter, whether as Prakriti or as atoms, be proved by such an argument, either
by the followers of the Sánkhya or of the Nyáya?   The
argument has no base to stand upon.   Besides, since

you feel the difficulty of accounting for the origin of matter, and fall back upon an impossible regressus of causes to explain it, may I ask you, would you not feel the difficulty disappear, if we could discover some other sufficient cause from which it could be originated?

*Gurudás.* Certainly, O friend, it would vanish away; and we might then give up all other attempts to explain the origin of matter. But such a cause must be an adequate cause: as Kopila says, "A thing possible is made from that which is competent to produce it." (Sutra 118.) Where shall we find such a competent producer? We accept the eternity of Prakriti, because we do not see how it can be anything else but eternal.

*Eng.* I think we find that competent producer in the Great God by whom the universe is ruled. And, in addition to establishing such a cause, which would render the doctrine of the eternity of matter unnecessary, I think we find substantial reasons in the very constitution of matter itself for considering that it could not have been eternal. My arguments, then, divide themselves into two classes, derived from the character of matter, and from the character of GOD. First, let us look at the character of matter. You will allow, O pundit, that whatever is uncaused, must be self-existent: and being self-existent, so far as we can judge, will be independent.

*Gurudás.* Certainly, O friend, we allow these notions. For they have been advanced several times during our discussions. It is because we reach an ultimate material, which is uncaused, that we say it is eternal. That

which is eternal must exist by itself: the power of
existence is not derived, it must therefore belong essentially to that substance, whether it be soul or nature:
this is what we mean by self-existent.* Again, if a
potter makes a jar, and a weaver some cloth, those
articles belong to them, for they have produced them.
The right of ownership belongs to all who produce
such things by their own efforts and skill. Beings and
substances which are self-existent have that right in
themselves. The *Bhásha Parichheda* says, " Dependence
is the attribute of everything save eternal substances."

*Eng.* So it seems to me, judging from the circumstances of the world around us. But look at the position of matter in the universe. Everywhere it is
passive and subject to the control of intelligent beings.
Animals employ it. Man uses it in a thousand forms.
But chiefly must we notice that it is everywhere under
the control of God. There is no single portion of it,
in any place, which seems free from His sway. Whatever portion of matter we examine, we find that,
whether organized or inorganic, it has been moulded
by wisdom and skill. All is adapted for use. So far
as we can see, the entire universe constitutes one vast
system, governed by one Soul. The heavens are constructed on a plan. They are under the influence of
fixed laws, and all the bodies in the sky obey those laws
with perfect exactness. The earth has also been constructed on a plan, and takes its proper place in the
great system. Its surface has been formed gradually

* *Swayambhúta: Swayamjivi.*

and with great skill for the use of men. The animal world in every part is constructed throughout upon fixed plans, and with a view to evident and wise designs. Thus has been devised the body of man with all its organs, its senses, and elements. Thus we see matter rendered subservient, primarily to the happiness and comfort of animated beings, and ultimately to the designs of the Supreme God, who has laid his hand on every particle of it and moulded it entirely to his purposes. We do not find a single particle of matter which has not its appointed place in this vast system.

*Vaiseshik.* But the followers of Kanáda fully allow that all the present forms of matter have been produced by God; and that He, by His wisdom and power, moulded the three worlds into their present shape.

*Eng.* Very true: but the argument is not yet complete. We will go deeper into the question. Mere control of matter, and mere system in its arrangement, will not prove that it did not at one time exist independently by itself. Let us move a step further.

Whence is it that the great system of the universe derives its character? Whence is it that all the different parts accomplish the various designs which they subserve: and how is it that these parts are applicable to so many thousand uses? We say that these things arise from the properties and qualities which the substance of matter possesses; and if we go back and back from the properties and uses of all the compounds of the universe, and trace them to the simplest elements

Y

with which we are acquainted, what do we find ?
Chemists assure us that all these wonderful properties
of which I speak are found in those simplest elements,
and that all the uses to which the many kinds of matter
are put are directly traceable to those qualities. All
the qualities of matter (so far as we have examined)
are brought out in these uses ; and if the properties
had been different, the uses of all the parts, and the
construction of the entire system, must also have been
different to what they now are. Considering, then,
that every particle of matter finds its own place in the
great system of the universe, and that the design, and
structure, and laws of the whole are directly dependent
upon the very constitution of the original elementary
forms of matter, is it not natural to believe that, instead
of matter being independent and eternal, it was actually
produced by the Architect of the universe for the purposes to which it is now completely applied, and that
HE endowed it with the many properties upon which·
those purposes depend ?

*Vaiseshik.* He might have found matter originally
existing, and possessing these properties. His work
would then be limited to wisely adapting those properties to the system which he wished to construct, or
adapting His system to them.

*Eng.* I allow that that supposition may be made. It
is, however, only a supposition, and may on that ground
be compared with my supposition as to the origin both
of the elements and the system of which they form an
essential part. But, considering that the properties of

matter are a part of its constitution, and will attend it
wherever it is found, your hypothesis really leaves
very little for the Constructor of the universe to do.
If material of a certain kind were already provided, his plans would be compelled to take a certain
shape, owing to the qualities of that material. My own
hypothesis seems the more probable, because it puts
away all such difficulties; it gives to the Great Ruler
of the universe the honour of the whole—of the plan,
the designs, the material itself, the development, the
wonderful working of all the elements and qualities
seen in every part; in a word, of the perfect unity
seen through the entire universe. Therefore, it seems
to me the most natural to believe that He whose existence, whose intelligence, whose eternity are undoubted,
both contrived the universe and provided the material
of which it is composed. This hypothesis seems to me
to be more simple, more complete, more consistent, and
more comprehensive than either of those which your
three schools respectively offer. One can at least comprehend it, but who can accept a regressus of causes
in an infinite series, which is absolutely impossible?

*Vaiseshik.* But, O learned friend! if you thus get
rid of some difficulties, there remains a greater difficulty
still in the theory which you advocate. How could God
" provide " a universe without a material? How can a
potter make a jar without mud?—a weaver, cloth without yarn?—a jeweller, bracelets without gold or silver?

*Eng.* I acknowledge, O pundit, that the difficulty is
shifted from the material to the framer. If God were

like a potter or a jeweller, He could not make a universe without something to make it of.   If He had
only the imperfect knowledge and the limited skill of a
human being, He could not make a world.   But we
should be careful how, in this subject, we compare God
with men.   Men are not infinite; they are limited in
power, limited in wisdom.   They begin from perfect
ignorance, and gradually, by experience, they attain
some measure of skill and knowledge.   According to
that measure do they effect things in the world, and
beyond it they cannot go.   Hence a potter becomes
skilled in pottery, the builder in building, and the
pundit in the pursuits of science.   It is this limit upon
their power which in all these things compels them to
seek material for any work they effect.   They can combine, they can change the forms of matter, but they
cannot create.

But this is not the case with GOD.   To Him I ascribe
a higher power than that of a mere architect.   I say
He CREATED matter from nothing.   We have already
seen, by strong arguments, that He must exist, and
must exist from eternity.   We have seen how both
causation and design in the universe compel us to believe that He, the prime cause of all things, must be
eternal, and must be intelligent.   We have seen, also,
from the vast multitude of instances in which design is
displayed, and from the greatness of that design in some
particular cases, how unspeakably grand His intelligence and wisdom must be.   We see that wisdom, also,
in His perfect knowledge of the nature and qualities of

all His materials, and in their adaptation. We look again at the amount of power now exerted in the world —the power of natural agents, earthquakes, storms, gunpowder, steam, and air; we see the gigantic results of such power in the formation of mountain chains, the elevation and depression of continents, in the control of the illimitable sea; we see the vast amount of motion existing in the universe, begun by the mightiest Power; we see everything in the universe governed, preserved, controlled by the hand of God; and what is the conclusion to which we come? That He, who has done all this—who has done it with perfect wisdom, with perfect benevolence for the good of His creatures, and who has done it for numerous ages—must be a God of Almighty Power, who is able to do whatsoever he will. Instead, therefore, of comparing God, who is perfect in wisdom and almighty in power, with an ignorant and weak man like the potter, I look up to Him with wonder and adoration, and find no difficulty in believing that He who devoted them to such uses, and applied so much power in their motions and effects, once produced the original elements from which they all sprang, endowed them with their inherent properties, and CREATED those elements in a way known only to Himself. I base this belief on the doctrine that God is ALMIGHTY. Is not that, O pundits, your own doctrine likewise?

*Gurudás.* That is the doctrine generally received by scholars. And there are several texts which lay it down. Thus in the Brahma Sutras* (i. 1, 1-4), Vyása

* Dr. Ballantyne, p. 5, para. *d*; p. 7, paras. *g* and *f*.

declares that He is the cause of the world, and is therefore omniscient and omnipotent.   In Sutra, ii. 1-30, he
is distinctly called Almighty; and the Vedas declare
him to be so.   Pátanjali specially declares him to be
Omniscient.

*Eng.* The doctrine is plainly a reasonable doctrine.
What, then, is the meaning of it?   How far can it be
applied?   By the term " Almighty " we clearly mean
that God possesses all possible power; that He is able
to do everything which power can possibly effect.
There are some things which no amount of power can
do.   No power can make two real contradictories both
true.   No power can put two distinct things in exactly
the same place at the same time.   But these are not the
things now under discussion.   How much can power
produce?   We all understand the formation of things
from materials.   The greater the materials, the greater
must be the power.   But, beyond this, if God be
ALMIGHTY, and possess all possible power, unlimited
power, why should we doubt that He can produce his
materials by creation, as well as form them into the
shapes and systems which he designs?

The same argument may be put in another form.
We have seen that all the present forms of matter are
traceable to earlier forms.   This world had a beginning.
All the great sciences show this.   The science called
Geology distinctly shows that it had a beginning, and
points out the stages through which it has passed.   The
laws now in operation are the products of a wise mind
and must have been set in motion at some definite time.

All motion implies a beginning. All causation implies a beginning. The world and the universe clearly then at some time began. Their present form is derived from the form which was first given. But consider the vast amount of wisdom and power exhibited in the development of these primary forms; look at the mighty results now apparent: the immense power required to sustain, rule, and keep in order the great systems in the animal, vegetable, and mineral worlds. Now since we allow God to be ALMIGHTY, is it difficult to imagine that He, who has so developed the original forms into the present wonderful universe, at first GAVE EXISTENCE to these original elements? I find no difficulty in attributing their creation to such a Being, after seeing the greatness of the effects which He has produced, the causes He has set in motion, the operations He has carried on, and the designs he has accomplished.

*Gurudás.* I can see, O friend, the force of the argument you advance: but at the same time, how can we imagine the universe produced without a material?

*Eng.* It is doubtless, O pundit, very difficult to imagine it: indeed it is certain that no one of us can really understand it. All our experience is connected with changes in the forms of matter, and it is within the power of man to produce these changes. But in all this there is no originating of a new material element. We are bound to what already exists; present matter we combine into new forms, compound in new proportions, and realize corresponding results. But let us never forget that God is far above us. We are but ignorant and weak beings as compared with him: and if we do not understand all He does, let us not therefore think that He has done nothing. It cannot be expected that we understand Him. We cannot understand very much even of his works. Although we are surrounded by material things all our life, no one of us can tell what the SUBSTRATUM of matter is. We see it, feel it, discern its properties, analyze it, compound it, yet no one knows what the base and substratum is: and no amount of effort and experiment has yet enabled man to find it out. How then can we comprehend the creation of a thing whose very "substance" is hidden from our eyes? On this subject let me state to you, what is declared in the Christian Bible, the Book which we regard as our authority in religion; and which for numerous reasons we believe to be really a revelation from God to man. On this subject the Bible speaks as follows: "In the beginning God created the heavens and the earth." "The worlds were framed by the word of God, so that things which are seen were not made of things which do appear." "By him were all things created, that are in heaven and that are in earth, visible and invisible; all things were created by him and for him: and he is before all things, and by him all things consist." These and numerous other passages state most distinctly that God is the creator of all things: and that they are not formed from eternal elements. As a Christian I receive this on authority, as God's own word: but reason also confirms the doctrine. The theory I have advocated at least explains the case sufficiently: and is far more consistent and complete than your views of the eternity of matter. That eternity you entirely fail to prove. Both the Sánkhya and Nyáy give for it no other argument than a presumed necessity arising out of an impossible regressus of infinite causes: a supposition quite uncalled for, if we can find a sufficient origin and commencement of causation. I think my theory provides such an origin. After showing that matter is in every way worked into the system of the universe, and that its inherent properties make the universe what it is, the theory announces that the Framer of the universe himself created this material, and caused the system of causes to begin operation. He was competent to be the originator of these materials: because He is Almighty. The explanation is thus complete.

*Vedántist.* But surely, O learned friend, the theory which you advocate confirms the Vedántic doctrine, that all things are from God, and that his substance is the only substance existing in the universe.

*Eng.* No, O pundit, we cannot receive such a doctrine. The two cannot be identical. God, a spirit, and the matter of the universe possess essential qualities, which are perfectly distinct from each other. The one therefore cannot have been formed directly out of the other. To say that God created matter is a very different thing from saying that God is matter.

*Nyayist.* But does not the theory break through that law which declares that something cannot come from nothing? If the new substance is not God, whence then does it come?

*Eng.* Not so, O pundit; in this doctrine we do not set aside this excellent rule of causation, which all wise men receive. In saying that "something cannot come from nothing" we need not imply that matter can be produced only from matter, as you all do: it is sufficient if we mean that a thing cannot be produced by itself; a thing cannot be produced without some adequate cause: its producer must possess qualities as good at least as its own. No imperfect being can produce a new thing. With this interpretation the rule is quite sound: and I make no false application of it. In advocating the *creation* of matter by God, we do not violate these laws. We do not say that matter, which was not, can exist while it is not. We do not say that this something was made from nothing. We say that the Omnipotence of God, which can do everything, can produce a new thing: a thing which did not exist before. We may not understand how it is done. Indeed we are incompetent to do so. We are ourselves portions of the very universe which has been created. But in attributing the creation of matter to the Almighty and Glorious God, we attribute it to a real cause; to an adequate cause; to a cause whose wonderful skill and power have been for ages displayed in sustaining matter, developing its forms, carrying out the laws by which those forms are governed, and especially making all things tend to secure the happiness of all the living creatures that inhabit the world. It seems to me that this argument is adequate to the conclusion derived from it: while certainly the arguments which defend the eternity of matter are insufficient.    On this account I cannot but allow a full assent to the simple and sublime declaration of the Bible, the first sentence on its holy page:

"In the beginning GOD CREATED the heavens and the earth."

---

## Dialogue Fifth.

### THE ETERNITY OF SOULS.

—◦◦—

### PRELIMINARY NOTE.

ONLY a few words need be added after the introduction prefixed to Dialogue Fourth.    In treating the present topic it is fair to keep continually in mind that the Eternity of Souls, as of matter, is not proved by the Hindu Schools; yet the burden of proof ought to be laid upon them.    It is at the utmost an hypothesis invented to explain a fact.    They find them existing: they do not see where they came from: therefore they must have existed from eternity.    We cannot prove a negative: except by establishing its contradictory.    We may therefore endeavour to show reasons for believing that souls are of late origin.    I have mentioned four reasons of this kind.    Soul does not possess the attributes of a self-existent intelligence: its knowledge is not the accumulated store of ages: but is all acquired in this its present life: it remembers nothing of another existence: even its sins are learned by experience.    I have then ad-

vanced a direct argument in favour of its being created,
similar to the chief argument in the last Dialogue, viz.,
that it seems adapted for a special purpose, in connection with the system of the universe; its character, functions, capabilities are all interwoven with the universe;
it is most natural therefore to believe that it was originally constructed for that purpose. The Omnipotence
of God furnishes a sufficient explanation of its origin.

On a subsequent day, the same parties met again at
the house of the pundit Gurudás, to examine another of
the great doctrines of the Nyáy and Sánkhya systems,
viz., the ETERNITY OF SOULS. The judge in opening the
discussion thus addressed them:

*Englishman.* We have recently, O friends, been inquiring into the origin of the universe, into its different
agencies, and the causes of its numerous products and
forms. We have asked, who created all this? and have
considered whether the Supreme God formed it by
moulding matter already existing, or created the original materials, which he subsequently developed. We
have now one agent left: we have still one particular
form or kind of existence to inquire into, namely the
HUMAN SOUL: and again we observe that each of your
systems has a distinct theory respecting it. Although
the Nyáya and Sánkhya differ in their reasons, both
agree in advocating the eternity of souls, and implicitly
deny that they were ever created. The Vedánta, as
we have seen, teaches that the soul is a portion of the
Supreme Brahm, and therefore makes it coeval and

cognate with him.  We have seen, however, that this doctrine has powerful arguments arrayed against it. To-day, let us carefully review the theory advocated by the Sánkhya and Nyáya.

At the outset, I would state that several things, in the general doctrine of the soul, defended by these two systems, deserve commendation, especially in the Nyáya. Difficult as the subject is, it is yet beyond doubt that they have discovered some most important truths concerning the nature and operations of the soul. It is a singular fact, that amongst these systems, not one makes the soul material. The Vedánta certainly makes both spirit and matter to spring from one substance, and so far its proceedings resemble those of material philosophies; but as in its theory all springs from Brahm, the system becomes one of spiritualism. The Sánkhya again has almost become a material system : since it only advocates the existence of soul for one or two reasons, and yet makes very little use of the soul throughout its various dogmas : even intellectual operations, and the " mind," are declared to spring from Nature. But the Nyáya has acted far differently, and has made the nearest approach to a correct mental philosophy amongst all the systems of learning in Hindustán. Will you kindly state, O pundit, the reasons for which the Sánkhya advocates the SEPARATE EXISTENCE of souls.

*Gurudás.* The great sage Kopila, in the first book, declares in Sutra 140, that soul is something different from body, and then assigns five reasons for the opinion.

1. The combinations and contrivances in the three worlds are for the use of some one; just as a house, a seat, a bed, are for the use of a living person. That some one is soul.

2. In soul there is the reverse of the three qualities, which distinguish all material forms. Prakriti is formed from their aggregation in equipoise; but soul has them not.

3. Soul superintends Nature.

4. Soul is the enjoyer (*bhoktri*) of all that nature has formed.

5. It is for soul that liberation is wanted. Nature possesses three qualities. Connection with nature has given the soul pain. Liberation is needed, and hence all the processes which nature carries on. If soul did not exist separately they would be aimless.

*Eng.* These reasons are very poor. Some of them are sound, but others are not so; while important reasons are omitted. The strongest reason of all, derived from the separate character of the operations of soul, the Sánkhya could not give; seeing that it has confounded those operations with the productions of Prakriti. The second reason respecting the qualities is not identical with this, for that reason is intended to refer to the faults and defects which are exhibited in the products of the gunas. Will you, O Nyáyist pundit, also state the arguments of the Vaiseshika and Nyáya.

*Nyáyist.* The reasons given by the Nyáya for the separate existence of souls are five.

1. Soul governs the body: for an organ must have

an agent as its master.   The body is not its own agent, for consciousness is not in the body; it disappears at death, and the body also, from being often changed, has no recollection in old age of the things which a man did in childhood.   The "mind" also is not the agent; its knowledge is limited, and if all perceptions were laid up there, new perceptions would be impossible.

2. Soul is known by its distinguishing qualities. These qualities prove it to be a substance, one of the nine original substances.   Amongst them are happiness, and unhappiness.   These are not in the body: else one body would not experience, as it now does by the transmigration of the soul, the fruit of the works done in a former body.

3. Soul is known from its activity.   From the regular motion of a carriage is learned the presence and activity of the charioteer.   So from the exertions of the soul to obtain knowledge and fulfil desire, its agency is also known.

4. Soul alone can be the site of intellect, perception, remembrance, and other qualities which are seen to exist, and of operations which are performed.

5. A fifth argument may be stated from Sutra 29. "The soul and the elements have special and contrary qualities; what is the property of one is the opposite of the others."   Here the perfect contrast between the qualities and actions of soul and of the elements, is plainly asserted.   Kanáda thus combines these proofs: "The vital airs, which go upwards and downwards, the closing and opening of the eyes, life, the actions of

the ' mind,' and the modifications of the other senses, happiness and unhappiness, desire and aversion, and endeavour, or will, are proofs of the soul." (Bhásh. Par. p. 25.) These are the five arguments.

*Eng.* And they are excellent arguments; although the defence of the second, by a reference to transmigration, was unnecessary. It is indeed by the peculiar operations of the soul, the exercise of its perception, its memory, its reasoning faculty : the display of its feelings, its anger, joy, and pain; the products of its will in actions and purposes : and the happiness and misery which it draws from virtue and vice; that the soul is distinguished from the body. Its operations are quite different from the qualities of matter ; it rules the body and its many organs as a master rules a house, and often it is found most active, as in dreams, while the body soundly sleeps. What are the operations attributed to soul by the Nyáya?

*Nyáyist.* In the *Bhásha Parichheda* the operations are thus classified. The immaterial qualities are demerit and merit; happiness and unhappiness; desire and aversion; intellect and memory; and the like. Intellect includes apprehension and remembrance. Under apprehension are included: perception by the senses and by internal consciousness ("mind"); inferences of reason ; comparison and verbal knowledge.

*Eng.* These are indeed a chief portion of the operations of the soul, and may be conspicuously observed in the daily life of every human being. There are others, however, which have not been referred to. It

is interesting to notice that the Nyáyists have remarked
the same things as have been noted in the philosophies
of Europe. We need not, however, dwell upon these
things: it is to the eternity of souls I wish to draw
your attention. Will you kindly state, O friend, the
argument for the multitudinousness of souls adduced by
the Sánkhya.

*Gurudás.* The argument of Kopila is; that there is
a great variety in the accidents and events occurring to
different persons at the same time. Some are being
born, others are dying. Some are enjoying pleasure;
others are in pain. Some are happy; others are
wretched; some are following virtue, others are drowned
in vice. These states of condition and character are not
only different but opposed. It is therefore impossible
to believe that all individuals possess, as the Vedánt
asserts, but *one soul.* One soul cannot be at the same
instant in these contradictory states. To this the Nyáya
also agrees.

*Eng.* The argument is identical with one which I
adduced against the Vedantic doctrine, and seems to me
unanswerable. Thus we find that all souls are really
separate from matter; and that the soul of each individual is independent of the souls of others. This
doctrine is most important: but few ancient schools of
science arrived at it. The Nyáya and Sánkhya have
the honour of advocating it, earlier in the world than
any others, except the Christian Bible. Now let us
take up the argument for the eternity of souls.

*Gurudás.* The Sánkhya, O friend, traces all products

z

that possess the three gunas up to nature. Nature, again, acts for some one else, by whom nature is governed: that being is soul. Now souls and nature exist side by side; when they join together through "proximity," they become the first causes of things. The Karika says: "Soul is united to nature in order to contemplate it, and be abstracted from it. By that union creation is effected. This creation is the development of 'intellect' and other principles." These principles are themselves uncaused. We know no cause that could have produced them. Hence both are from eternity. The argument is the same for both. Soul is undiscrete, uncaused, self-supporting. Each soul therefore that exists is from eternity.

*Eng.* And what is the reason assigned by the Nyáya?

*Nyáyist.* It is taught that time, ether, soul, and space have the qualities of infinity and ubiquity.* "*Mind*" also is eternal: it is innumerable, because one remains with each soul: it is in the form of an atom. These all exist: no producer is assigned as their origin: their eternity is inferred from their being uncaused. It is said also, "eternal unity is ascribed to eternal substances:" it has no beginning; as the text says: "it is not born."

*Eng.* It seems to me that these arguments are unworthy of the great doctrine which they are employed to prove; and that their proof is quite insufficient.

---

* In the Nyáya system, the ascribing of the quality of eternity to both "mind" and "soul," and making them two separate "substances" when their powers show them to be but one, is a special error.

The Sánkhya argument naturally follows from the peculiar dogmas of the system. The agencies in the world must have a cause, a master; and hence a superintendent, an enjoyer is felt to be necessary, a soul uncaused and eternal. If the premises were sound, this conclusion would follow; if there existed only matter and souls in the universe, and no origin can be found for them, those souls must be eternal.

But let us look at the character, constitution, and experience of these souls, and endeavour to ascertain what they indicate as to the length of time that they have endured.

*a.* In their nature we find no such elements as belong to a substance that is everlasting. An eternal, intelligent being, having the power of life in itself, must be independent and free: it must be great and noble. But the soul shows none of these characters. It is dependent upon its body for even a connection with the world at large: without its senses the soul can acquire no knowledge of external things. When the eye is asleep or injured, the soul cannot see. When the ear is asleep or diseased, it cannot hear. Instead of being *great,* it is in its knowledge, its pursuits, its enjoyments, a follower of trifles. What signs, then, does it show of an independent origin?

*b.* Look at its ignorance. The soul is continually getting knowledge during a man's life. Even the poorest man adds to his knowledge of persons and things day by day. He sees new faces, visits new places, and does new things. Much more do the very intelligent, the

z 2

learned, acquire by their studies additions to all that
they had learned before. In this way men obtain a
large stock of experience, if they live to become old.
But every man when he is born is perfectly ignorant.
Every man has to begin afresh, like all his prede-
cessors. Every pundit here had to begin his course of
learning with A, B, C. From such a beginning do we
all toil slowly on, step by step; making painful efforts
to add to our knowledge, and attain to that information which yet lies beyond our reach. And so much
is there to be learned, that no man ever yet learned
everything: no man ever yet acquired all the science,
of all the countries in the world, which other men had
separately attained. What do these facts prove? They
show the imperfection of the soul. Though intelligence
is its nature, its knowledge begins in this life: and God
to aid it has supplied it with the necessary subordinate
agents for acquiring knowledge. These things seem to
show that the soul begins to be, when a man is born:
and that the soul has a beginning as well as the body.
Instead of being eternal, its intelligence and its activity
begin with a man's birth; and every atom of knowledge it acquires it acquires between birth and death.

    *c.* Look at its memory. If the soul is from eternity,
it has lived through countless years. Even on your own
theory, since the time when it was united to "mind,"
its intelligence must have been displayed during the
years which have passed since that union took place.
It must have acquired knowledge, all these years, of the
various scenes through which it has passed, of the

persons it has seen, and the events which have happened. Now all such knowledge, acquired during human life, it lays up in memory. From memory it recalls that knowledge when it is needed. The memory retains it down to the time of death. Old men recall the faces of those whom they saw in the days of youth: they retain the knowledge of languages which they then spoke and have forgotten for many years. The body is frequently changed during a long life (as the Nyáya allows); but the memory remains the same: this shows that the memory belongs purely to the soul and not to the body at all. If then the soul has lived before this, has lived from eternity, and has seen and heard countless things before its present life and history, where is the remembrance of it all? Not a particle of such knowledge exists. All the knowledge which a man has in his waking hours relates to his experience in this world. All that rises up in his dreams can be traced, so far as its material is concerned, to the same experience; but where, whether in dreams or in waking hours, does he ever recall the memory of past experience in any life or period previous to his present existence in the world? If any such knowledge had ever existed, there ought to be a remembrance of it in every individual who has a soul. But not one has it. The inference then is surely fair, that the soul never experienced such a life at all: and that (as its ignorance implies) it began to act as an intelligent agent upon its birth into the present life.

*Gurudás.* But this argument, O friend, goes to show that there is not even a transmigration of souls, as well as that souls are not eternal. You surely do not question that doctrine which has been received by all Hindu pundits of all schools from the commencement of time?

*Eng.* The argument certainly does bear upon that celebrated doctrine, O pundit, and I must say, that I do doubt altogether about the truth of it: although it is so ancient, and has received the sanction of so many of the Hindu learned. But I do not wish to say anything more about it just now: as I propose to make it the subject of our next discussion.

*d.* Another argument against the eternity of souls arises from their sinfulness, weakness, and defects. Every human being knows that there is in his own soul a large amount of thoughts and wishes which even the Hindu shastres declare to be sinful: and that the soul leads him to do many of those acts which the shastres say ought not to be done. Some men are sunk in these evils, are quite slaves to their passions, and scarcely ever do any good thing at all. Now all the progress in evil, which leads to these mournful results, is made during the life of every human being. When he is born he is not thus depraved. When a little boy, he does not commit the same vile deeds which we afterwards see in the grown-up man. He feels ashamed of them, his mind rebukes him for even thinking of them. Evil is learned and practised by degrees, just as the knowledge of the intellect is acquired. Boys are not so clever nor so bold in sin, as men: and older men are greater adepts at wickedness than young men. This shows that even with its sins and defects, the soul runs

its course in the present life: that it has not brought experience and knowledge of evil from a former existence.
Thus the growth of the soul's sinfulness in this world
brings new evidence of the notion, that the soul has had
no existence before this present life.

*Gurudás.* But whence, O friend, does the tendency to
evil spring, if the soul knew nothing of it in a former
life? Does not its readiness to commit sin prove that it
did know it before?

*Eng.* I expected this question, O pundit: but it requires full consideration, and we will talk of it again at
some future time. A great deal must be said respecting
it, and I trust I shall be able to explain the tendency to
evil without referring it, as you do, to a former life, and
to the soul's migrations.

These four considerations, applied to the soul, without
any thought about the mode of its appearance in the
world, seem to me to show that its present existence is its
first existence: that it has not existed before its present
birth: and certainly is not from eternity. We see none
of the dignity, the power, the purity, that should belong
to an eternal being. We find that it is very ignorant:
and all its knowledge is acquired during its earthly
career. Its wonderful memory brings no information
from any previous state; while if soul were eternal we
should expect such tidings to appear both in our waking
moments and our nightly dreams. All souls too are
imperfect, and gain experience in evil during their present life. All these facts show us the soul only in a
single life: we never go beyond it: and left to consider

these things alone, no man would ever have imagined that his soul had existed from eternity.

Remembering these things, I would now lay before you a special reason for thinking that souls were produced by the Great Ruler of the Universe, and that He caused them to commence an existence. You will remember how I argued for the creation of matter from the fact of its constitution and qualities fitting it exactly for the purposes which it serves and the position which each part occupies in the vast system of the universe. I think the same reason applies with not less force to the origin of souls. I speak now only of human souls, because of their existence we are certain. Men occupy a most important place in this system. Even your systems admit that the " creation " is made for souls to control, to use and to enjoy. Now the Framer of the Universe has first of all provided for each man a most wonderful instrument for connecting the soul with the material system. The body of man, with its wonderful senses, organs, limbs and joints is this instrument. It is perfectly suited to be the residence of the soul, and to serve the purposes which soul has to accomplish. Still more is the soul itself so constructed as to be exactly fitted to occupy the place which men take up in the world, both in relation to their Creator and to each other. Its intellect, affections and will are all formed on the most wonderful principles: its sense of right and wrong; its reasoning powers, its knowledge of God, all are required and are all suitably employed in the right occupation of that place.

Men live in societies holding certain relations to each other as men, as fellow citizens, as parents and children, as relatives, as neighbours; there are certain laws which rule these relations, and the souls of all men are so constituted that these laws and duties can be easily understood, appreciated and observed. Not one faculty, not one element in the soul's constitution is useless or superfluous. The world was evidently made for the use of men, that they might live on it, be fed by it, and find comfort in it: men were made to live together in societies; to help each other and to serve God. Our constitution teaches us all this. Now shall we believe that God, in framing the universe in this manner, accidentally found souls endowed with the qualities and faculties required: or that in constructing the universe with a grand design, and creating its material with the qualities exactly required, He did the same with its souls; produced them also, and endowed them with exactly the faculties and powers which they would require, to fulfil all the purposes which He had in view in making them? I think the latter supposition by far the most natural. The supreme fitness of souls for the position which men occupy must be observed by all; and I think that such a fitness shows they were intentionally endowed with the powers which secure it.

I would point out also here, that while this argument in relation to matter is strong by itself: and in relation to mind is strong by itself also: they both become stronger when examined together. The system appears all the more vast, the more complete, the more wonderful, when we consider souls and matter acting together, and together accomplishing the great purpose of the universe. For they are both fitted, not merely each for its separate work, but to work in harmony together: the unity observable in each one, is observable also in their mutual action; and tends to bring home an irresistible conviction that both were constructed and produced for these grand purposes by the great God from whom the design of the system sprang.

The history of the world seems to me powerfully to confirm this. An examination of its rocks shows how each separate layer, as well as the mighty whole, had its beginning at a certain time. It shows that each separate class of animals, fishes, reptiles, birds, and beasts, was produced or created at a certain special time: that they did not spring from each other, and were not made at the same time; but that they began to exist at a special period; * that the scale of creation gradually rose with these successive classes of creatures, as the world became more and more fit for the dwelling of men; and it shows distinctly that human beings also began to exist only six thousand years ago. Everything serves to show that the system was thus developed, and creatures added under the most entire control of the Great God: and I cannot therefore help believing that He himself made everything just as it was wanted. Remembering that human souls in all their knowledge, memory, and even sins show that they have had but one life in the world; and that they are

* Hugh Miller's *Testimony of the Rocks.*

so wonderfully adapted for their proper place, I argue that they received a distinct beginning from the hand of God.

*Gurudás.* But still we may ask, where do these souls come from?

*Eng.* As in the case of matter, we cannot understand the process by which they are produced: we are ourselves numbered among the objects that have been created. It is sufficient to find a cause competent to produce them, and to assign them a fit place in the great scheme of the universe. Such a cause we find in the perfect wisdom and almighty power of the Supreme God. To attribute their production to Him quite satisfies all the facts of the case. It explains the origin of souls; it explains the condition in which they enter the world; and accounts fully for all absence of the remembrance of previous existence in other spheres of life. A competent power is referred to as the cause of these souls: spirit is regarded as creating souls and intelligence. What more is required?

*Gurudás.* Still, O friend, the migration of souls is not accounted for on this theory: and it is difficult to explain the conditions existing in human life except upon the belief that such migration exists.

*Eng.* I feel with you, friend, that the two doctrines cannot stand together: I feel and acknowledge, that if the soul is only introduced into human society for the first time on each human birth, that the migration is set aside. That subject we will discuss at our next meeting. At present I would only add, that if this transmigration of souls were not believed, all Hindus would have no difficulty in accepting the proofs I have now presented against the eternity of souls. It would at once be seen, that the arguments which confine the existence of the human soul to this life, and make its history begin with the birth of each individual, have great weight in themselves and quite explain all the facts which that history, so far as we know it, presents. I feel therefore that we cannot longer delay the full examination of a doctrine so powerful in its influence and so generally believed.

## Dialogue Sixth.

### THE TRANSMIGRATION OF SOULS.

On the day appointed for discussing the doctrine of TRANSMIGRATION, a large number of Hindu pundits assembled at the house of the pundit GURUDÁS. The importance of the subject was felt to be very great, because the doctrine occupies such a conspicuous position in all the schools of learning, and is so largely treated of, especially in the Sánkhya and Vedánta. The judge also was not unimpressed with the task he had undertaken, and determined, as far as he was able, to secure a complete examination of the whole subject. After the usual salutations, he took his seat, and a few preliminary remarks having been made by one and another, he opened the discussion as follows:—

*Englishman.* In our last conversation, I objected altogether to the doctrine, advocated by the Nyáya and Sánkhya, of the eternity of souls, and stated several reasons on which the objection is founded. I endeavoured also to show that all the facts with which we are directly acquainted exhibit to us the soul of each individual entering this world in perfect ignorance, but fitted with various senses and faculties intended to aid it in the acquisition of knowledge: and that nothing in its condition proves it to have existed anywhere before such entrance among the human race. To this argument it was objected that their TRANSMIGRATION shows that souls do pre-exist, and have existed for thousands of ages: and that, in your estimation, the fact of their transmigration has many arguments and reasons in its favour. I propose, therefore, that our present discussion be devoted to this doctrine alone, and that we endeavour to examine it thoroughly. First, I would ask, O Gurudás, is this doctrine accepted by all the schools of Hindu learning?

*Gurudás.* It is taught, O friend, and upheld by them all. The necessity of transmigration is, in fact, the great evil which all profess to remove: thus it forms, in one sense, the foundation of our philosophy. Our earliest authorities, the Upanishads, teach it in very distinct terms, and refer to it again and again; adding that an attainment of the knowledge of Brahma will deliver man from its evils. The Sutras of Veda-Vyása assert the same: the Bhagavat Gita repeats it again and again. The first Sutras in the works of

Gautam and Kopila, in the Yoga and Vaiseshika, the opening Slokas of the Sánkhya Káriká, assert it as the necessitating cause of their several philosophies: while the Káriká and the Sutras of Kopila give much instruction concerning the mode in which it is carried out, the reasons which have produced it, and the objects which it is intended to accomplish. The Puránas teach the doctrine also, and the Mánava Dharma Sástra. All the pundits, all the brahmins, and all castes believe it to be true.

*Eng.* Clearly have you stated, O friend, the extent to which the doctrine is believed: in order that we may make no mistake, will you kindly state what the doctrine is?

*Gurudás.* It may be stated thus. All human beings have souls. These souls now born into the world have not begun to exist for the first time. They existed before, and they have come from worlds in which they were suffering pain or enjoying reward. This pain and reward are the result of actions committed in a previous birth. Into that birth they entered from a previous one; and into that again from one earlier still. And thus we reckon them to have had existence in this world, alternated with an existence in the worlds of punishment and reward: the latter being regulated by the character they had in the former. This alternation has taken place an infinite number of times, and is to be traced back to the very beginning of the present constitution of the universe, if not to an earlier time.

*Eng.* Does this theory apply merely to human souls?

*Gurudás.* No, O friend; it applies to others: it is difficult indeed to speak of human souls: for those which have animated a human body may subsequently pass into an animal or a tree. All objects may be animated by these souls: the commentator on the Kárika describes them as animating " animals, deer, birds, reptiles, vegetables, and minerals." The Chhandogya Upanishad similarly speaks of souls entering " vile wombs; as those of a dog, a boar, or a Chandála." The multitude of souls is infinite, and they may inhabit all kinds of forms, from the highest to the lowest. The theory even applies to the gods: thus it is said in the Kárika: " Many thousand Indras have attained not merely heaven, but the sovereignty of heaven: and yet have passed away, overcome by time."

*Eng.* During this long course of ages, and under this multitude of varying circumstances, does the soul always remain the same?

*Gurudás.* Certainly it does. The doctrine of course implies that it does; but the great Kapila, to avoid all doubt, has stated two principles concerning it in very plain terms. Thus he says: " One soul is born and not another." (*Eka purusho jáyate náparah.*) " There may be various unions of one soul, according to difference of receptacle." Next he asserts that the soul itself is not subject to birth or death: these arise from its connection with the body. " Life is the combination of soul with the pains incident to body: *not any modification of soul.*"

*Eng.* Will you also state, O pundit, under what circumstances the soul thus migrates?

*Gurudás.* On its first connection with matter, there is formed for the use of the soul, a subtil body. This body is small and of an exceedingly refined nature. It envelops the soul, and is its constant habitation. This is the doctrine taught clearly both by the Vedánta and Sánkhya. The subtil body however is unable to perceive or to enjoy the gross world: in order therefore that soul may be connected with the gross world, the subtil body enters gross bodies of various kinds. As a rule the subtil body never changes: it remains constant to the soul during all its migrations; but the gross bodies are changed at each successive birth. The Sánkhya enumerates the qualities of subtil body thus: It is primeval, it is permanent, it is confined, and does not mix with animals, men, or gods: it can go through rocks and solid substances. It migrates through the three worlds; as an ant, the body of Siva.

*Eng.* According to what law are these migrations determined?

*Gurudás.* They are determined by the rule of virtue. Those souls which grow in virtue and attain higher degres of religious merit, rise to a higher kind of body and a higher rank of existence. Those who sink deeper into irreligion and folly, get lower births on successive occasions. "Virtue and vice are the efficient causes of the bodily conditions."

*Eng.* What then is the particular reason assigned for these migrations?

*Gurudás.* Soul when joined to nature becomes subject to pain, although it was connected with nature in order to contemplate and enjoy it. These continued migrations are deemed a necessary consequence of the tendencies and dispositions by which souls became affected on their union with matter: they may be employed as opportunities for breaking that union, and when soul and matter separate, they will entirely cease.

*Eng.* But your systems claim the merit of securing that liberation speedily.

*Gurudás.* Yes, each of the Hindu systems of learning professes to provide a short road to liberation and beatitude. I have just described the common lot of the majority of men, to whom this learning is unknown. Both the Sánkhya and Vedánt, in all their authorities, advocate this view of the case. Both state that by studying their doctrines men may get speedily free from the " doubts " and " activity" into which they have fallen: otherwise their migrations may not cease till the present *Kalpa* comes to an end.

*Eng.* You have well stated, O friend, the various branches of the theory of transmigration, and the subordinate principles connected with the chief and essential doctrine. Will you now kindly state what is the *authority* for the doctrine? How are we to know that it is true?

*Gurudás.* All the systems of course teach this doctrine on the authority of their teachers, such as Kopila, Gautum, and Veda-Vyása. Of these, the oldest and most revered authorities are the VEDAS, which, in the

A A

Upanishads, distinctly assert that transmigration is true. But various arguments also are drawn from reason to illustrate and confirm it.

*Eng.* You say that the Vedas teach it. Do they teach that human souls ever go into the bodies of animals or the structure of minerals and trees?

*Gurudás.* Yes; in the passage I recently quoted from the Chhandogya, the wombs of a dog and a boar are specially named. On the whole question, the Vedas are the earliest authorities, and are regarded of course with the greatest respect.

*Eng.* Let us, however, now put away for a time the Vedic authority, and the great authority of your ancient sages. Let us look at this doctrine, as it stands, by itself; and let us examine it, with the grounds on which it is advocated, by the aid of reason only. Is it considered that any parts of this doctrine are observed by direct perception?

*Gurudás.* No. It is not seen or felt by any one, that he pre-existed, that he has passed through different lives, in different places, and that he has visited the lower worlds, or the upper heavens. Reason tells us there must have been previous existence, and the authority of the mouth of Brahmá confirms it.

*Eng.* Very good. There is no direct perception in any one of this previous course or of its processes as it was going on. Do all the systems give the same reason for it?

*Gurudás.* No. There are many arguments assigned. There are popular arguments which pundits commonly employ, and there are special reasons connected with the different views of the systems.

*Eng.* Let us then take up these arguments, and examine all that can be said for such a doctrine. Let us remember that, apart from transmigration, we have shown that there is no reason for believing either matter or soul to be eternal: on the contrary, there are many reasons to show that both have been created by the almighty power of the one Great God who exists without doubt from everlasting. Let us then enter on these arguments. Will you kindly state, O pundit, the first.

*Gurudás.* First, then, we consider—that only by this doctrine of transmigration can we satisfactorily account for the present *mixture of good and evil* among intelligent beings: and *for their different degrees of happiness and misery.* Men do differ greatly in the happiness they enjoy, and in the ranks which they occupy. Why is this, if they have all received birth for the first time? If, as you advocate, there is one God, Almighty, who now produces new souls, and sends them into the world for the first time, is he not partial and unjust in distributing his favour; in placing some high, some low; and in giving to some great prosperity, and to others misery? This argument is stated in the Brahma Sutras by Vyása himself. "Injustice and unkindness ought not to be attributed to Brahma, because some (the inferior gods) are happy, others (animals) are miserable, and others (men) are both. For every one has his lot according to his merit in a former stage of the universe." (*Colebr.* p. 179, Vedánt.) Unless we admit the truth of those former stages of existence, such injustice and unkindness may be ascribed to him. "The rain-cloud distributes its rain equally; but the plants vary according to the seed whence they spring." (*Ibid.*)

*Eng.* The fact which you have described, O friend, constitutes a difficulty, and has troubled many minds. But you offer only one mode of explaining it. Are there no other explanations? Are there no better explanations? Are there no explanations freed from the difficulties which attend the one you give? Does even yours truly and completely explain it? We may ask all these questions. For it does not follow that because you give one reason for a fact that reason must be sound, or that no other can be given. I shall endeavour to show that other explanations can be given, and that your theory of transmigration, while it endeavours to avoid an imaginary evil, runs into a real one.

. (*a.*) First, let me ask—Are the inequalities of condition among men so great as men think them? It is true that some do exist; but greatness is not always attended by happiness, nor is poverty necessarily connected with misery. Sometimes they are not real, but imaginary, and people make numerous mistakes respecting them. The poor man, who deals honestly with his neighbours, and who is kind-hearted, often enjoys much happiness of mind; while his rich zemindar, possessing abundance of wealth, is afraid of robberies, is plundered by flatterers, cheated by his servants, wretched in his own vices, sick in his luxuries, and is rendered exceedingly miserable. The different conditions of life are not necessarily connected with certain conditions of joy and sorrow. Wealth, power, and fame, do not always give pleasure. Neither does sickness always make men sad. How often have we seen that great kings, like the emperors of Delhi, have been surrounded by great dangers; and, like the Emperor Humáyan, have sometimes enjoyed unbounded power, at others have been nearly starved. Happiness is the great thing men desire; where, then, is God unjust, in setting one thing against another; when he makes the poor peasant contented, and leaves the rich king miserable: for, after all, this very happiness is the fruit of a man's own doing? This brings me to a second argument.

(*b.*) The varying conditions of happiness and misery (which are the chief and the most important) can be explained in a different way. They may all be traced to two sources. (1.) Personal happiness and misery are to a great extent the result of personal conduct. The industrious man, by his very industry, secures wealth and prosperity. The idle man, by his idleness, is compelled to live in poverty. The careless rich man, who received from his dead father lands, and houses, and money, spends them on luxury, on women, on flatterers, and comes to poverty. The imprudent man continually falls into mistakes and losses; the wise man successfully preserves himself amid dangers. These things are seen in thousands of instances. The happiness and misery which result from them are not traced by men to another and previous life. They are rightly ascribed to men's own dealings, to their own

character, and to their own conduct. No one reflects
on the justice of God, because the drunkard falls sick
and poor; no one reflects on the justice of God, when
the son of a poor man honestly labours and becomes by
diligence an honoured and wealthy man. No brahmin
reflects on the justice of God, when such a prosperous
man invites him to his house, and pays him large fees,
and offers large gifts that he may celebrate some great
puja with pomp and show.

(2.) Again: this happiness and misery spring to a
very great extent from our connection with others.
Men are connected together closely in this world, and
must be so. Parents and children, relatives and friends,
fellow citizens and neighbours, are necessarily connected much together, and have a great influence upon
each other's happiness. A wicked son gives his parents
great sorrow: a profligate father renders his children
sickly and weak. A murderer brings disgrace upon all
his family, however innocent they may be. Men are
so involved together that all human independence is
destroyed. No man stands alone. He is daily influencing others by his words and acts: and others are
daily influencing him. If he does good, all will be
benefited. If he does evil, all will suffer. Every one
knows how much discomfort is produced in a large
village by one quarrelsome man. A boy, playing with
fire, perhaps sets fire to his father's house. A high
wind is blowing; the whole bazar is burned down:
much property is destroyed: a few lives are lost. Why
do so many people suffer? Not from any fault of their

own. Not from any partiality on the part of God. But because they lived near to each other: because their houses were within the influence of the same fire and the same wind. The misery and suffering have nothing to do with a past life: they are produced by the carelessness of one individual: and no injustice can for a moment be charged on God.

These two facts go very far towards explaining the differing conditions of happiness and misery in which human beings are placed. They depend far more on ourselves than on any previous life; and they are largely affected by the conduct of others. If all men were holy, honest and temperate in themselves, and were all honest, prudent, just and holy in their dealings with each other, there would be comparatively little misery in the world. All classes, from the poorest to the richest, would be happy. Where would be the argument for transmigration then? We should get rid of it by removing, not any imagined injustice on the part of God, but merely the evils which men inflict upon themselves and on each other. Many instances, in fact, of happiness, produced in this way, may even now be found.

*Gurudás.* But, supposing men to be thus upright to each other, that does not get rid of the inequalities of their condition.

*Eng.* True, O friend, it does not do so. But I have argued that it is only in respect to their happiness that men have any apparent ground for charging injustice on God. That is what all men continually seek; whether by wealth, or pleasure, or fame, or power, they wish to fill their minds with happiness.  Now, if God fills all minds with happiness, whether they be the minds of kings or fishermen, of men or women, need he do any-thing more?  Can any one find fault?  Why are men not happy, then?  I have shown you that it is their own fault.  As to the inequalities of condition, I now advance a third argument.  (*c.*) These inequalities are the appointment of God: they must exist; they are in-tended for the good of society.  So far from being a cause of fault-finding in respect to God, we must ad-mire them and accept them as beneficial.

Men live together in very large societies; they have a great variety of wants; they carry on a multitude of employments.  Now, can all men be equal?  All the Shastres say that they cannot.  All men cannot be brahmins; else how would those brahmins eat?—how would they be clothed?—where could they all live?  The Gita says that the caste of Sudras is made to serve the other castes, and that in serving them they fulfil their special duty.  You yourselves, then, allow the in-equality of castes to be an ordinance of the Supreme; this ordinance the authorities declare to be coeval with the creation, and to be quite independent of merit and demerit.  I do not believe that caste, with all its minute rules, is of divine origin; but I argue that, in the very nature of things, some inequalities must exist.  Thus, there must be male and female in the human race; the two sexes must exist side by side; and of these that of the father will be the stronger, requiring him to discharge duties abroad; while that of the mother will require her specially to act at home. There must be inequality again between parents and children. The parents must be the older, and more experienced : they will therefore rule; while the children must be younger, and will learn from their parents. There must, again, be amongst men a common submission to the law of the land; and some must administer that law as rulers, while all obey as subjects. All the various employments which are necessary to the comfort of men will be divided amongst them. Some of these are easier; others, more difficult. Some will give more profit; others, much less. These different employments, being necessary, will at once produce different classes. Some of them require more intellect; others, greater bodily strength. On these considerations, we see why it is that the Supreme God has distributed mental capacities so variously among men, and why he has endowed men with such different measures of physical strength. Hence we see also how and why it has been appointed, that there should be such differences between the different nations of the world. Some live in mountains; others, on the great fertile plains. Some live in colder climates; others, amid tropical heats. All these things influence and maintain these physical differences. All these varieties of pursuit and varieties of condition tend to promote the comfort and welfare of human society. All men are necessary to all others. None can live independently; none can get through life without the aid of thousands of others. The poor are necessary to the rich; the labourer is necessary to the landholder; the merchant only prospers by trading with a community; and the community is benefited by the skill of the merchant. These things benefit men by uniting them; all classes help each other; none can live without the others. God intended that men should depend on each other and live like brothers. Equality of condition would make every man work only for himself, even for common things; it would make all independent; it would produce disunion; it would separate all the inhabitants of the world; it would lead to their destruction; and thus the very end for which men are formed would be completely frustrated. Thus, instead of regarding the inequalities of their condition as an evil, for which we must apologize, it seems to me that wise men must regard them as a means of promoting the happiness and the prosperity of all nations. I am aware that there is great misery connected with the lower classes in society; but the misery arises from the injustice, oppression, and robbery to which the poor are often subjected. If all men were just, and honest, and holy, all such oppression would be removed. The rich would pay the poor their wages rightly, and would befriend them. The poor would work diligently and faithfully for the rich; and the inequalities of condition would then be scarcely felt at all.

*Gurudás.* But when, O friend, will such a state of society come about in this world, with all its *máyá*, its follies, and false activity?

*Eng.* The time will come, O friend. The religion,

which I believe, has produced it in some places: and
will do it at length everywhere. It is the special fruit
of this religion, that it teaches all men to do to others as
they would that others should do to them. This is the
law given by that Supreme Creator whose existence
and agency I endeavoured to prove: and who formed
human society in the condition we have just considered.

(*d*.) A fourth answer to the theory of transmigration,
as based upon the differences of happiness and of condition, I find in the fact: that while God appoints these
inequalities of condition, he does not do so from mere
caprice, but he does it with the view of trying men in
various situations, and of testing the qualities of their
character. It is not from injustice that he appears to
favour one more than another. He gives to all the
opportunity of happiness by making that happiness dependent upon the discharge of duty. Every man who
faithfully performs that duty will be happy so far as he
himself can promote his happiness. But duties are not
the same to all. The man who is rich has higher duties
than the poor. The man of learning has more to account for than the ignorant man. The king has heavier
duties to discharge than the poor people whom he rules.
All men who have power of any kind have to account
for that power. All men are stewards of God. Just as
the Great Mahájan places money in the hands of his
servants, that therewith they may trade, and rewards
them according to their fidelity: so the Great God
places wealth, or learning, or power, or fame, in the
hands of men, that they may thereby do good to their

fellow creatures. Those who have much will have to
account for much. Those who have little will be re-
sponsible for little. One day he will settle the accounts
of all, and then he will reward every man according
to his works. Are the rich then to be envied; or shall
we wish to change places with the powerful? Rather
may the poor and the ignorant be glad that they have
not to bear the same responsibilities as the rich. Living
as we do in a sinful world, and surrounded as we are
by various temptations to evil, we are very liable to do
wrong, to forget our responsibilities, and use in an evil
way the gifts of God for which we must give account.
May we not then say : Happy are they who have to
account for little? Again then we find that in this view
of men's probation we need not go back to a previous
life to find it explained. The differing responsibilities
of men explain their differences of condition and endowments, just as the differing situations of judges and
magistrates explain the difference of duty expected from
them.

In this way it seems to me that a reference solely to
our present life explains all the difficulty which this
variety of condition and happiness produces respecting
the justice of God, and entirely obviates all appeal to
some life previously enjoyed.

You invent the hypothesis of transmigration in order
to account for these inequalities of condition : I show
you that they can be satisfactorily explained without
such an hypothesis. That supposition therefore becomes superfluous : and may be rejected on that ground

alone: quite apart from any special difficulties which the hypothesis itself involves.

*Gurudás.* We acknowledge, O friend, that you have skilfully met the proposition that I advanced in favour of transmigration, but there is one fact in this inequality that you have quite overlooked: and I therefore propose it as a *second argument* to prove the necessity for a previous life: viz. *Some men are born lepers, blind, deaf and dumb, lame, idiots and diseased.*\* No explanation of this sad fact is so simple as that which ascribes these calamities to sins of which they were guilty in their previous birth. Other inequalities may perhaps be accounted for by the circumstances of this life: but how can these be so dealt with?

*Eng.* I acknowledge, O friend, that this is the real difficulty, among the inequalities which you so strongly dwell upon: but I have thought it over and do not doubt of explaining it too. The cases you refer to are comparatively few, yet we may in many instances trace them to causes connected with men's present life. Men who are born with these defects cannot have them from any

---

* I have not seen this argument stated in such plain terms in any of the authorities: it was presented to me by pundits at Nuddea, and considerable stress was laid upon it. It is only one special form of the more general argument which has been first discussed, and which is advanced by Vyása himself. It is the argument implied in the question put to our Lord (John ix.), "Who did sin; this man (in a previous birth) or his parents, that he was born blind?" It is an argument well known among the common people, and frequently referred to by them. A friend of mine was told by a lame native that he must have kicked a brahmin in a former birth. To the man himself such an explanation of his misfortune seemed natural and satisfactory!

fault of their own, that is clear. They cannot be charged with folly, like the spendthrift who wastes his ancestral property, and be told that they suffer the consequences. But I have shown you how closely individuals are connected together in this world; and how much harm is done to innocent beings by the evil conduct of those with whom they are connected. I think these cases are an illustration of that fact.

*a.* Many cases of this kind are the result of hereditary diseases. Thus, where persons marry, who are too near of kin, it frequently happens that their children are born with numerous and painful defects: and if the same thing is repeated again and again by people and communities, who are much separated from others, who marry in and in, these defects are greatly multiplied. There are places well known in Europe in which idiocy abounds that has arisen from this very cause. Leprosy again is reckoned one of the remote forms of the diseases which spring from impure connections among men. The same kind of reason is true of deaf and dumb children. Medical men find little difficulty in tracing all peculiarities of bodily health to nearer or more remote causes of constitutional disease. The actual cause may be concealed: but the nature of it is not thus unknown: Experience has shown where to look for such causes.

*b.* But even allowing the uncertainty of these actual causes, I answer again, that all diseases of the body, and all the sufferings of human life in general, are the consequences of sin. Sin has come into the world, has confused everything, has corrupted everything. What

wonder, then, that its fruits should be extensively felt
and should appear in strange and unexpected forms.
What wonder, that connected as we all are, some men
should be the victims of disease, and suffer when they
are not personally in fault.   Had not sin prevailed in
the world and produced so many evils, these things
would never have occurred.

c. A third consideration bearing upon these few cases
is, that we can explain this application of the consequences of sin to these individuals, as the act of
sovereign power on the part of God.   He rules over all.
We all acknowledge that He does appoint to men their
lot in the world : and we can believe this without saying that He controls every act and incites to every act,
whether good or evil.   Only God can appoint the place
where a man is born, the time of his birth, the day of
his death.   These things are absolutely beyond human
control.   In them He shows his sovereign prerogative.
But he does not act arbitrarily.   There are reasons at
work even in cases like these, which can produce
benefits to men, although they see only evil.   Thus in
such cases (1)—God shows his great *displeasure at sin.*
Men do not like the natural consequences of sin ; but
He will develop them, to show how evil its effects are ;
to show how guiltless persons are involved in them ;
and how widely spread these remote effects really are.
Thus he adds to the warnings which he addresses to
sinners, and by the acts of His Providence impresses
those warnings more deeply on men's minds.   Again
(2) He intends to excite gratitude in all those who

have not been visited by evils so great. They see the
consequences of sin, they know themselves to be sinners,
and then wonder why He did not visit them with such
effects of it. That He has not done so should excite
gratitude in their minds to Him for His special favour.
Besides (3), He makes these sufferings a part of the
probation of those afflicted by them. He tries all men :
some by duty, some by sorrows. For the purposes of
such trial, it is necessary that men be placed in circumstances opposite to their character and worth. Thus
good men suffer adversity : bad men are rendered prosperous. In this way the virtue of the good man shines
the brighter for his sufferings : while the vice of the
wicked is made more manifest by his abuse of good fortune. A mother's love is more tried in the sickness of
a child than by its health. If we would test gold well,
we should put it in the fire.

*d.* Another fact explanatory of such cases is—that by
them the Supreme God is teaching us to sympathize
with the afflictions of our fellow-creatures. I cannot
at all agree to the caste rules adopted among the
Hindus, by which people of different castes are rendered
incapable of giving food and water to those of other
caste than their own; of helping them in sickness and
in accidents: and thus showing to them the kindness
really due from all who possess the same nature. I
wish to see all men united, mutual friends, mutual
helps, and always ready to promote each other's welfare. On this principle the Supreme God has constructed human society; for this he has established

different ranks among men ; and it is for this also that
he permits the sicknesses, and the accidents which produce human suffering.    It is that therein men " may be
kind one to another:" " may rejoice with them that
rejoice, and weep with them that weep."

*Gurudás.* But, O friend, there is one thing frequently
referred to in these several arguments, which you have
still left unexplained.    You have spoken much of the
effects of sins and faults of various kinds, and shown
how widely their miserable effects are spread.    You
have not, however, explained why God permitted sin at
all, that sin to which you trace the misery.

*Eng.* True, O pundit, I have not distinctly indicated
an explanation of that difficulty.    I think we can find
a most satisfactory one, in the great purposes of His
moral government : but this is not the place to dwell
on it.    I am endeavouring to show that the inequalities
of rank, health, and happiness are not merely produced
capriciously by God, but are greatly dependent upon
the very sins which men have themselves committed.
And in reference to those who suffer from leprosy and
other sad defects, the explanations I have offered seem
to me suitable and proper.    They do not require to be
transferred to some previous life, in which, without any
proof, these persons are said to have existed.    At all
events let me add, even if such considerations do not
clear up the whole difficulty ; let us remember that we
are very imperfect in our knowledge of things ; and
that though we understand many things in the world,
there are many common things which we do not under-

stand : especially things connected with the work of
God, either in the material world or in human society.
His operations are the hardest to understand : for is He
not far wiser and higher than we ? I will say only
another word, and that is, allowing the difficulty in the
case of the few we have spoken of, will their cases,
so rare in number, prove transmigration to be true of
all men in all ages of the world ? Supposing they do
prove their own case, they cannot do more : and it will
be quite unfair to apply the principle to those, by whom
it is not needed. This is my reply concerning them.

*Gurudás.* You have given an elaborate reply to the
arguments advanced, and which are generally deemed
conclusive by us ; and it is very difficult to refute your
positions, especially as you draw proofs of them from
subjects about which we have thought but little. But I
cannot but think we have a strong ground for the doctrine in the fact, that it provides so well for DISTRIBUTING
REWARDS and PUNISHMENTS to the VIRTUOUS and the
WICKED. Indeed, without it, how can those rewards be distributed? This is the great argument used on its behalf.

*Eng.* I am quite aware, O pundit, that this is a common argument, and that with transmigration, the notion
of retribution is always connected. But I would ask,
first, Is no other scheme possible ? Can the Supreme
God, whose wisdom and power are so great, devise only
this one scheme for getting rid of human imperfections,
and rewarding men according to their works? This
cannot be. Your own systems of philosophy prove that
other means of avoiding the punishment have been in-

vented. Besides, this system of retribution is one that
is never adopted anywhere else. You advocate that
human souls are thus rewarded or punished by repeated
alternations of residence in the earth and in the other
worlds. You subject men to an intermittent fever; to
seasons of happiness in Vaykantha or Pitriloka, when
they are virtuous, followed by a birth among the evils
of the world again. Why may not God settle their
retribution once for all: and appoint the good to a
permanent happiness and the evil to permanent misery?
There are more reasons for such a course than for
the one which you advocate. (1) Governments in
this world always punish in this way. They give a
definite punishment: a certain fixed amount which
must be gone through. Sometimes a man is im-
prisoned for a month; sometimes for a year: in very
bad cases, like those of the Thugs or Phánsigars, they
imprison them for life: or perhaps they put them to
death. They never give a man changing periods of
pleasure and pain, making each period to depend upon
the last. Why may not the all-wise God act in the
same way? (2) In the same fixed way we deal with
everything: and we make the present qualities of things
decide on their future use. Thus good, sound pots are
sent into the bazar for sale: damaged ones are put aside.
Well-woven cloth is offered in the markets. Good corn
is preserved in *gólas* for future food; sound trees are
reserved as beams for houses: and rotten wood is sold
for fuel. Good and bad things have their future lot
decided by their present worth. You reckon the other

way, and think that the present life of men is a fruit of
past conduct. Why may not the Great God deal with
men in the way in which we deal with material things,
and with offenders against society? Why may He not
try men's characters now: and having done so, give the
wicked a place of punishment, and take the righteous to
live with him eternally in heaven? To me this seems
a far more reasonable plan than your theory of transmigration.

The great element in your argument is, that the system of transmigration is a system of justice. I have
thought this over, and intend to speak of it when I
come to the arguments which I have to offer against the
doctrine: I will only say now that so far from exhibiting
justice, it seems to be most unjust throughout, and
therefore cannot be received. I will endeavour to prove
this hereafter. At present I am only listening to your
arguments in favour of the doctrine: and endeavouring
to show that they are unsound. Will you kindly advance
any others that you have adopted?

*Gurudás.* I will present you, O friend, with one more.
You are aware that we all believe that no new production takes place in the world. Every one of our systems of learning regards the matter of the universe
and all souls, under whatever form, as being eternal:
hitherto we have thought there could be no doubt on the
subject. But you have argued with us on these subjects,
and have shown that much can be said on the other side.
Now, if transmigration be untrue, and every human
being has but one birth, then new souls must continually

be produced as new births take place. The matter of new bodies is of course older matter under new forms: that we can all understand. But we have been accustomed to think that no addition is made to the three worlds, and that what exists now, has existed always.

*Eng.* Why should not God create new spirits, if He thinks fit? He is able to do it. He may easily form the purpose of such a creation, and desire to fill this world with inhabitants; and, having tried them here, to remove them to other worlds for which they prove themselves fit. He knows all that is best for his creatures: and will do what is best. We are really ignorant of his purposes until He reveals them ; and to say He does not create new souls, or that He will not, is very presumptuous on our part. It implies such a knowledge of His doings, as we by no means possess. We have only to look to facts, to see whether He does create them or not: leaving the reason and mode of such a thing entirely to Him.

But why may not new souls be created? What difficulty is there in such a supposition? Matter is not newly created every day (so far as we know), but we see it endlessly combined and moulded into new forms. The forms are new : the combinations are new: the conceptions are new. The potter makes his pots not out of the old broken materials of former pottery, but he takes new earth, and shapes that earth as it never was before. Pundits continually form new conceptions in their mind and write new books. Poets make new poems. Artists paint new pictures. In fact all men are continually

forming new purposes; inventing new ideas, and adapting themselves to new circumstances.   Every day by
means of muscular power they produce new motion: in
this case, the force and the motion are absolutely new.
Where then is the difficulty of the Supreme God
creating new souls and new intelligent beings to people
his mighty universe?   Is he not giving us new things
daily?   His sun sends out new beams of light.   His
rain, and sun, and earth give us new trees, vegetables,
and fruit.   Every year new crops of corn cover the
ground, intended for the food of man and beast.   All
these gifts are new: and are all bestowed by him.   If
we consider these facts, and contemplate his power and
wisdom, I do not see any difficulty in our receiving
what seems to be a fact also; viz., that on each human
birth, a new soul is introduced into the world.   I say
that seems to be the fact: we have no sound reason for
believing it to be a soul come from some former birth in
a previous age, and why should we not receive the fact
as it appears?

   If we look to the history of the world, I think we
find that a new creation has actually taken place again
and again at different periods.   By careful examination
we can trace back every tribe of living creatures to its
origin: we see in all cases that each had its beginning at a
certain era.   There was a time when it was not: at a certain period it began to be.   Numerous classes of animals,
birds and reptiles have existed on the earth and become
extinct.   None of these sprang from any others.   Each
separate class was a separate creation: these creations

were effected at many different periods, distant from
each other. The souls of men, with all their peculiarities, appear for the first time only about six thousand years ago. If God has thus actually made a new
creation repeatedly at successive eras, where is the difficulty of believing that he does now create a new soul
each time a child is born into the world? I see no
difficulty in believing he does so, although the exact
period of its creation may be unknown to us.

*Gurudás.* This argument of mine is the last of the
reasons commonly urged amongst both pundits and
common people in favour of the migration of souls.
You are aware, however, O friend, that our systems of
learning have other arguments, connected with their
doctrine of the eternity of souls, which each propounds
in its own way.

*Eng.* I am aware of it, O friend; especially of the
argument given by the Sánkhya in its doctrine of the
*Dispositions*: and by the Gita,* in its notion of *Divine
destiny.* But these doctrines are so important, that I
propose to make a separate discussion respecting them.
They are closely connected with the dogma of the eternity of souls, and are intended to show why it is souls
and their history vary in their qualities and destiny, by
attributing the primary cause of all to the conditions of
their actual creation; that cause both necessitating
transmigration and determining its character in each
individual case. I doubt the whole doctrine: and have
many reasons to offer against it, derived both from the

* Bhag. Gíta, " Divine and infernal fate." *Sec.* xvi., *Prakritibheda.*

character of God and the actions of men. These doctrines, however, do not compel us to believe in transmigration. They rather serve to account for it. Perhaps
it is more correct to say that they are derived from
transmigration, than that they lead to it.

You have now offered, O pundit, four arguments for
our examination, by which it is generally believed that
the migration of souls is proved. You have based it upon
the varieties of happiness and misery in the world, and
the inequalities of human conditions; upon the fact
that some men are lepers and the like; upon its excellence as a scheme of just retribution; and upon the
objection to the creation of new souls. I have endeavoured to show that all these reasons are futile: that
their difficulties can really be explained by a reference
to the present life of men, including their probation and
preparations for a state in the future: and that, in
order to secure a satisfactory explanation, we do not
require the theory of transmigration at all. When all
the arguments for a principle are set aside, it of course
falls to the ground. Such ought to be the case with
this doctrine; and from the deficiency of reason on its
side, the scholars and common people of Hindustan,
like those of Europe, ought to cease to believe it. But
I am aware that it is taught by all the Shastres; and
first of all by the Vedas. Reason, however, has nothing
in its favour: on the contrary, I propose now to show
that reason brings forward the most powerful arguments
against it.

## PART SECOND.—DIRECT ARGUMENTS AGAINST TRANSMIGRATION.

*Eng.* Having offered my opinion with respect to the arguments in favour of this doctrine, and shown you that the hypothesis of transmigration is unnecessary, I propose now, O pundit, to point out the various arguments against it, which render it in itself objectionable.

*First.* The doctrine of transmigration *confuses the various classes of beings* existing in the world. We were told distinctly that both the Upanishads and the Sánkhya Karika assert that in the course of punishment, the worst of mankind go into the forms of dogs and boars, deer, trees, and even rocks. In other words, that animals, vegetables, trees, and even the rocks of the world, are inhabited by the souls of intelligent human beings. Now this is entirely opposed to all we know of the universe. We all see that perfectly distinct classes of things and beings exist in the world. Hindus, as well as European men of science, divide them into organic and inorganic; the viviparous and oviparous; fishes, birds, insects. Some are animate, some are inanimate. More than this, we see that all the organic beings reproduce their own kind exactly. An hibiscus (yabá) produces an hibiscus: a bilwa-tree, a bilwa-tree. Mangoes produce, not oranges, but mangoes. Horses produce horses: from elephants, only elephants spring. Kites again produce kites: hargilas lay eggs from which young hargilas come forth. In all these cases, the different genera do not mix:

whether they be oviparous or mammalia, they adhere to
this rule. If an exception occur, as in the production
of a mule, the exception stops with the individual: it
is not continued into a new species of a cross breed.
The exception doubly confirms the rule itself. Now
we know again that in multiplying their kind, all the
special characters of the class continually reappear.
The wisdom of the elephant, the fierceness of the wolf,
the patience of the ass, the rapacity of the kite, continue in each kind from generation to generation. They
retain the same properties of body, the same amount
and the same signs of intelligence. Now man is distinguished from them all by his soul: by his memory; by
his reason; by his power of speech; by his use of language; by his power to attain and to employ abstract
ideas. Men produce such men: from age to age, the
human race continue to be men. But transmigration
tells us to confuse all this beautiful order, which the
Creator has established in the world.

But this is not all. A consideration of the peculiarities which distinguish human beings from other
classes of living creatures, an examination of that which
makes them human beings, will show that such a confusion of classes as your theory contains could not
exist: at all events, it could not exist without displaying
itself. Let me ask what are the qualities of soul?

*Nyayist.* The fourteen qualities of soul, are intellect,
pleasure and pain, desire, aversion, volition, and so on.
The soul also rules the senses and the body.

*Eng.* What do you include in intellect?

*Nyayist.* We reckon in it two things: apprehension and recollection: under apprehension are ranged perception, inference, comparison, and verbal knowledge: under these also are various subdivisions.

*Eng.* Well. Without discussing minute details, we can all see how intellect, recollection, inference, perception, and the like, belong to soul: and how the soul obtains a knowledge of its own proceedings, its internal perceptions, and the like. Now it seems to me that all such faculties distinguish the human soul from all other souls or beings said to possess souls. I go beyond this, to points that your systems do not notice. I look at the whole constitution of the soul's nature, its feelings and desires, as well as its intellect; at its knowledge of good and evil, its conscience; at the power which it possesses to know God, the Ruler; to worship him, and fear him; at its power to feel its duties to others, the duties which men owe as parents to children, children to parents, and the like: and I say that in all these things a human being differs entirely from the animals, birds, and reptiles of the world. His body again is exactly suited to his soul: its five senses assist him to get knowledge; its organs help him in motion and action: and all its powers are exactly fitted in every way to help him in the various works, duties, employments, &c., which he must carry on. On the other hand, the bodies of animals are exactly suited to their position, habits, and characters: different tribes and classes each having a body suited to itself. According to your theory, these

animals, and even trees and rocks, possess the same kind
of soul as a human being, a soul united to a perceiving
" mind," and having intellect, reason, and recollection,
amongst its powers. Yet of all this we scarcely see
the slightest sign. No one would ever imagine, from
examining animals and men together, that they were all
animated by the same kind of souls.

And you cannot say here that the difference consists
in the different kinds of " mind " they possess: for all
chief qualities are qualities of the *soul:* the " mind " is
only the instrument by which the soul perceives its
internal work; and is aware of its own activity. The
animals do not show that they possess any of those
qualities except in the slightest degree. In all these
qualities men and they differ most strongly. More
than this, it is not a mere difference of body that
makes the difference between the two classes of beings.
The body is only the dwelling of the soul, and though
it does somewhat modify the soul's actions, according
to the state in which it happens to be, we nowhere find
that the mere body makes an entire change in the constitution of the " being," so that he can no longer act,
exercise his chief powers, and be the same as he was
before. All these things show that the soul of man is
something peculiar by itself, possessing special qualities
which distinguish it from other classes of beings; having a home of its own, duties of its own, responsibilities
of its own. Animals seem entirely different in their
qualities, capabilities and place in the world. How can
we then believe that the one class ever becomes the

other? Your theory asserts that they do: but you give no proof and no instance: there is no sign that they ever do so, or that they can become so. Everything points the other way. May we not then on strong grounds object to a theory exhibiting such important defects?

2. My *second* argument is that HUMAN RECOLLECTION is entirely opposed to this migration of souls. We know that the human soul by means of its faculties acquires knowledge by perception, stores that knowledge in memory, recalls it when required for use, and applies its judgment to an examination of the knowledge so acquired. The memory, we all know, is a very great faculty. It lays up carefully in store the knowledge which has passed through the mind; and if we look attentively at the interesting cases in which its phenomena have been developed, we can scarcely resist the conviction that it never loses an atom of the information which it has once acquired. Under ordinary circumstances a man attends to and keeps before him those objects which are prominently brought up by the demands of daily life. His previous knowledge is not, however, lost. It may be hidden or thrown out of view: but it is all laid up in the memory, and any effort of recollection or a peculiar suggestion may recall on a sudden any item of it which had been long forgotten. Thus it is that, though the body of man changes every seven years, the soul retains till old age what it acquired in youth. Thus it is that the old man recalls the history of a long lifetime and enumerates

the varied incidents which have happened during that period.

Such is the ordinary history of our waking and conscious life. But there are two kinds of extraordinary facts, which exhibit the contents of the soul far more fully (though not so systematically) as the common process of recollection. These extraordinary facts are *dreams* and *delirium*. Dreams are not under the control of the reason. The soul produces them at random (merely following the laws of suggestion): and in so doing mixes up times, places, persons and things which never in our experience stood side by side in fact. The contents of the mind are thrown up in great confusion. Delirium goes much farther, and tosses up the contents of the soul in a very much greater degree, and in far greater disorder. At such times the most concealed thoughts, the most secret items of knowledge have been unexpectedly revealed. In hundreds of cases the most secret crimes have been brought to light among the wicked: and the most secret thoughts and elements of knowledge among those who had nothing to conceal.

Thus it is that in severe fevers, the unconscious patient has often been heard to utter the language which he spake in youth, but in his conscious hours had forgotten for more than twenty years. Under such circumstances uneducated servants have been known to repeat passages from Greek and Roman books which their learned masters had perhaps on a single occasion been reading in their presence. Though the impression made at the time of hearing could only have been slight, yet the memory retained it, and retained it for many years; and all of a sudden in this delirium the whole wonderfully reappears. Now amidst all these revelations of the most secret, most hidden, long-forgotten objects of the soul's knowledge, we observe one most striking fact. All the items of knowledge thus thrown up from the innermost recesses of the mind to its surface, have related to the one single life of which these individuals have been conscious. The forgotten languages were those which it is known that they had learned in earlier life: the forgotten words were those which they had heard (it may be only once) many years before: the forgotten events were such as had actually happened to them. No single thing has ever been revealed from the inner soul of any one which could not be explained in this way.

Upon these facts and phenomena connected with the soul's MEMORY, I build this argument. Considering the amazing power which the soul has to lay up within itself the events of its history; and considering the numerous cases in which, without control from the reason, the most secret and forgotten events have been thrown out again, on extraordinary occasions,—if these souls had ever experienced a former life in the world, such as you say, much more if they had experienced many,—then it seems to me that in some cases, if not in all, numberless facts would and must have been revealed respecting that previous experience: and thus we should have obtained certain information respecting their transmigrations. But not a single case of the

kind has ever been known.   All knowledge revealed in
this way has invariably been knowledge acquired in
their one single life.   On this ground alone, I feel perfectly justified in rejecting the doctrine of the transmigration of souls.

Let us examine here the illustrations of migration
given by your authorities.

a. A traveller who journeys through Hindustan, and
goes from city to city, of course remembers his home,
his parents, his neighbours, and all that happened to
him among them.   He remembers, too, what he sees in
each new city, what kinds of people he meets with, and
what he says and does.   All this is quite natural, and
occurs every day.   Now the Vedantists tell us that the
body is the city of Brahma: if the soul really enters
new "cities" in the course of many ages, why does it
not carry with it the remembrance of what has happened during its residence in each?   Or if we cannot
recall such events voluntarily, why do such never come
into the mind in dreams or in times of delirium?   The
fact that such a thing never happens, proves incontes-
tably that there is no recollection in the soul of such
events: and therefore that they have never occurred.*

b. Let me take another illustration from the Sánkhya.   We are told in the Kárika, that the subtil body
assumes different gross bodies for the contemplation of
soul, just as an actor assumes different disguises for the

---

* A familiar argument, very convincing to the common people, is
derived from the illustration of a speaking parrot, removed from one
cage to another, yet retaining his knowledge of names and his power
to express them.

amusement of a crowd. The people see the changes of dress; they compare them; they trace the same man in them all, and enjoy the contrast produced by the change. Now why cannot the soul in the same way remember all the disguises which, on your supposition, the subtil body has assumed? It cannot remember one. Can we believe then that it ever put them on? *c.* A third illustration is given by Veda Vyása, when he says: "As a man casts off his old garments and puts on new ones, so the soul, having quitted its mortal frame, enters into another which is new." Now a man when he changes his dress carries with him all that makes him a man; he does not lose his memory of what he is or has. Nor should the soul lose its recollection of such things, when it forsakes one body to enter another. Thus once more the illustration given disproves transmigration. Again we ask: why does not the soul remember its former births? It does not, because they never took place. Had they taken place, the soul must have remembered them. We thus see that the illustrations employed by the great sages to prove the doctrine actually serve to disprove it. If bodies are "cities of Brahma," the traveller, soul, ought to remember them, as it journeys, age by age, through them. If the soul is spectator of the disguises assumed by subtil body, it will of course remember and compare those disguises. If soul merely puts on new bodies, as a man puts on new garments, like that man, it will not lose a remembrance of all its past history. Memory, which is so powerful in soul, is entirely deficient in all that relates to toher lives than our present one.   The inference then is, that such lives we never had.

*Gurudás.* Your argument, O friend, respecting memory would be a sound one, if the soul remained perfectly the same.   But you have forgotten that at each death the soul is divested of mind, understanding, and consciousness.   This is the view held both by the Vedánt and Sánkhya.   Only the rudiment is left.

*Eng.* I am aware, O friend, that such is the theory of soul held by Hindu pundits; but I did not refer to it, because I deem it quite incorrect.   How could such a fact be known except by memory: and yet that memory you want to get rid of.   But your own theories (even if incorrect) supply a better answer.   Supposing these faculties necessary to a perfect soul, when embodied in the form of a man, and supposing that at death and during its stay in the other world, it is deprived of them, yet on its birth into the world again, it is again invested with them, and becomes once more the perfect human soul.   Is it the same soul?   Kopila distinctly declares it is.   The Nyáya also says:[*] "Eternal unity is attributed to eternal substances: of which soul is one."   Its powers then will be in perfect action: its memory will be complete and sound; and in the new birth it will be quite able to do and to reveal all that my argument pleaded for.   I think this conclusion follows from your own theories.   The Nyáy actually shows us one instance in which recollection of the circumstances of a former birth is seen in opera-

---

[*] *Káriká*, pp. 48, 49.   *Bháshá Parichh.* p. 59.

tion. " Why does a child begin to take milk from its mother?" "The commencement of the action takes place *by the recollection* of the causes of the desires experienced in a former birth."* He acknowledges that it ought to recollect other things, but *fate* prevents! But I should not argue thus on my own principles. I have shown you that I think the theory which separates "mind" from soul is incorrect: and that the soul exhibits a unity of constitution so complete that if any part or faculty is taken away it ceases to be soul any longer. Just as the living body has its five senses and many organs, and ceases to be a complete body where they are all absent; so soul is possessed of faculties belonging to its very nature: and ceases to be soul, if they are lost. What is soul, for example, without perception, without reason, without memory, without consciousness? It is not the same being: it can learn nothing, it can do nothing. It will cease to be soul. It seems to me that it is not possible for a soul to lose its memory and yet remain the same soul, as Kopila says it is. Such is evidently the opinion of the Nyáy.† And if it cannot lose its memory, then it will be sure to remember all its past history. The argument I used respecting it, I therefore adhere to still.

3. Let me now propose to you a THIRD argument

---

* *Bháshá Parichh.*, p. 18, Commentary.

† Also *Bh. Parichh.*, p. 18, Commentary. "If consciousness belonged to the body, there could in old age be no recollection of things perceived in childhood, the body being subject to increase and decrease by acquiring and losing its particles." Recollection here is purely an attribute of soul: and that soul (see above) is always ONE.

against transmigration, which, while quite different from the others, is of itself extremely forcible. It is this: transmigration is a system of great injustice.

*Gurudás.* Injustice! It is advocated amongst us, because we think it is the only mode of defending the justice of the Supreme.

*Eng.* Yes, I think it injustice. You will remember that I spoke of this before, and I will now state the argument which I then referred to. If soul existed previously, and does not remember the least event of its history (a fact about which we all agree), then something must have happened to it, which has removed that remembrance. Allowing that such a change in its constitution is possible, some compulsory change must have occurred, which cuts off its connection with all the previous events of its history. The pleasures which it enjoyed in that former life; the pains from which it suffered; the friends with whom it held intercourse, are all forgotten. All the events which happened to it; all the good, and all the evil which it did, are entirely forgotten. It knows nothing of its former virtues: it knows nothing of former faults. The knowledge of them is lost for ever. If a man were to be told of all these things, he would not recognize them as events, or faults, or virtues connected with himself; he would listen to them as to the actions and virtues of another person. He would not feel himself worthy to be honoured for the good; nor to be punished for the evil. Now is such a man the same being that he was? No: though the rudiment of soul be the same, he is to all intents a NEW MAN.

But you say transmigration is necessary as furnishing a time of retribution.   Now the Supreme God in distributing rewards or punishments distributes them with a view to encourage virtue and to discourage vice.   He wishes both to punish and to reform a guilty soul.   But if a man who has committed faults in a previous birth, is to suffer for them here, how can he feel the benefit of such a punishment, when he is so changed in soul, as not to be the same being that he was ?   The punishment therefore of his faults falls upon another being altogether (*i.e.* himself in an entirely changed state).   He cannot remember what he did or why he is punished.   He will say of course that he is totally another man.   So will a good man say if he be rewarded for virtue : of that virtue he can know nothing.   By the destruction of memory, he too has become another being.   Here then the theory involves the great injustice of the Supreme rewarding one man for the virtues of another, and of punishing one man for the faults of another.   Can we speak thus of the Great God whom we ought to honour ? You stated at the outset that the theory was framed in order to avoid what seemed the injustice of an unequal distribution of happiness and misery.   But by the loss of memory, the theory formed to provide against an apparent injustice, involves a real one !—Let me now present you with a FOURTH argument against it.   What is the great end of this migration of souls ?

*Gurudás.* The end is explained differently by our systems, but all agree that by its means the soul works out in the course of ages the full fruit of those tendencies and innate dispositions, with which it was originally endowed. The evil work out a course of evil; the good travel to higher and higher positions, and at length attain " deliverance," even if it be delayed to a future *Kalpa* or " great period."

*Eng.* This theory is a theory of fatalism. Is there nothing by which the soul is able to rid itself of its troubled condition and by effort rise to a higher rank than that which it now occupies?

*Gurudás.* Special causes, the instrumental means of virtue and vice affect individual souls, or take them upwards or downwards towards a higher or more degraded condition. Our various systems of knowledge are all contrived with the purpose of delivering souls more speedily from this condition and ensuring liberation at once.

*Eng.* But if you are consistent, the formation of those systems and the study of them by individuals, with the adoption of any other of the special causes you have mentioned, should all be considered as merely the natural development of those " innate dispositions " of which the systems teach. Apart however from them, I turn to the great fact observed by many learned and thoughtful men, and already pointed to by me in this discussion, that our life in this world on many grounds must be considered a life of discipline and trial preparatory to another state of existence, " the worlds of reward." In reference to this fact, I find another argument against transmigration, that it introduces souls repeatedly into the world of sin, in which it is impossible, that without special help (of which your theories know nothing) they should improve and grow better.   Many who believe in transmigration have considered that one of its objects is the progressive improvement of the soul.   This is one of the ideas lately received by many Hindus in Calcutta: an artificial result of the mixture of English and Hindu ideas.   I do not see how such improvement can be secured: especially if every soul on being born again into the world, has no remembrance of its previous faults.   All punishment for crime ought to inflict suffering on the offender, and ought, from fear of its repetition, to deter both him and others, from the commission of such a fault again.   Look at the way in which the Phánsigárs (or Thugs) are treated at Jubbulpore.   There they are confined because of their crimes and made to work: but with a special view to their reformation, they are taught also the nature and wickedness of their crime, in order that such as regain liberty may never return to their former practices.   But for this end memory is again required.   If a man has no memory, how will he be able to confess, " I did that deed : I committed that crime " ? How will he know that it is a crime at all : and that he is undergoing punishment, deserved by him for such deeds ?   All association between the crime and its consequent suffering is cut off.   The two things stand separate.   How then will the moral character of the criminal be improved ?   The system of transmigration then viewed as a retribution for evil cannot in the nature of things accomplish the improvement of human souls and their complete reformation.   Let me ask you, O pundit ; you

think it has been going on for thousands of years: do
you consider that the Hindus are improving and becoming better age after age?

*Gurudás.* Alas! O friend, your question is a painful
one. Do not the Shastres say that the first age was the
age of truth: and that passing through the Treta and
Dwápár, we have entered into the Kali Yuga? Do not
all allow that this is the age of ignorance, of folly, of sin?
And do we not all look forward to the time, when all
men shall cease to fear and honour brahmins and shall
form but one single caste? Are not the shastres less
studied than they used to be? Are not brahmins turning
away from our systems of learning in order to acquire
the English language, with a view to profitable employ-
ment under the Company's Ráj? Alas, O friend, we
cannot say that the Hindus are improving or that the
Kali Yuga is becoming more pure.

*Eng.* Even on your own theory, O pundit, how can
it become so? We have just seen how, by the deficiency of memory, the effect of punishment must be
frustrated, and fear of doing evil cease to have influence. Let me add another fact that will cause the
same failure;—viz., the circumstances under which the
punishment is carried on. The Government of India,
we have seen, in trying to improve the Phánsigárs, has
placed them in a separate habitation, removed then
from the society in which they lived, and deprived
them of the opportunity of crime. It also gives them
good advice and wise instruction: and teaches them to
work in the production of useful things. But according

to the theory of transmigration, the Supreme in punishing impure souls, sends them back to the very world where they became impure, with their tendencies and dispositions unaltered; places them in the very midst of the associates with whom they carried on crimes in former days, and does this without a word of good instruction or one fact of warning from their previous history. Can this be wise? Can it possibly be a successful plan? Can any one be improved by being placed amidst his old temptations, surrounded by scenes of sin, and subjected again to the influence of the six passions in a gross body, as before? Can any man with an impure nature be drawn from his impurity by being made to inhabit the body of a cow, a dog, or a boar? No. The souls of men will become like the filthy birds and beasts they are compelled to inhabit, and cannot possibly enter from thence the path of true wisdom. Such a scheme must fail: and only increased ignorance, debasement, and sin be the result. Men well know that they cannot make their sons temperate by putting them in a spirit shop: nor their daughters chaste by associating them with dancing-women. Why should they think that the Supreme God will act in a different manner?

I have thus endeavoured, O pundits, to state clearly a few arguments which seem to me to render the theory of the migration of souls impossible. I showed first that, as believed in India, it confuses all the distinctions of classes among created objects in this world. It teaches that soul, possessing essential powers for which

a human body is required, can be united to animals,
rocks, and trees. It is utterly inconsistent with the
condition and operations of our memory. It charges
upon the Supreme the great injustice of punishing one
person for another's faults. It is rendered futile, as a
means of improvement, by destroying all recollection
of the crimes that are punished. And its end must be
defeated, owing to the circumstances by which it surrounds the guilty one who is to be improved. Where
is the use of a system, which has so few reasons in its
favour, and so many strong arguments against it? The
more it is examined by a calm, unprejudiced mind, the
more defective, the more useless, and the more unlikely
will it appear to be. Even you yourselves allow that it
has failed hitherto. Have you hope that it will succeed
better in the future?

I leave argument here, and conclude this long discussion by asking you, Does this theory give you any
hope in the prospect of death? Death is the lot of all:
and at the time appointed by God, every one must quit
this world. Does this plan make you happy? If you
have done well now, may you not fail in some future
birth; and thereby be compelled to undergo one or
more degrading births: and descend lower and lower in
the condition of your existence? You do not see any
rising: you see all society in Hindustan going back-
ward. Can you hope to fare better?

*Gurudás.* Your words, O friend, are sad words: your
reasons are strongly urged. What better belief is there
for us?

*Eng.* The system, which I believe, teaches that there is but one birth for men: that they live in this world but once: that they are accountable to God for what they do: and that they will be rewarded according to their works. It teaches that in the future world, there is a heaven for the righteous and a hell for the wicked; in which they will reside for ever: and which they will leave no more. It tells us, as we all feel, that men are very sinful: are quite unfit to dwell in heaven. But through an all-sufficient atonement, offered by a true Incarnation, it' offers pardon for all past sins: and it tells man, that while he cannot purify himself, GOD will give him a new nature, a purified soul: and will give him strength and favour, whereby he may live pure and forsake sin. That change and that purification of heart are the true " regeneration;" the true birth, is the new birth not of a second body, but of a purified soul. Here is a LIBERATION complete and worthy: a true deliverance from the pains of life and the sins from which they spring. Let us pray God to give us this divine change of nature. It is what we want. Without it we never can be reformed: we never can get to heaven. But if we possess it, we shall enter, when we die, the heaven of God, and leave it no more for ever.

## Dialogue Seventh.

### INNATE DISPOSITIONS.—FATALISM.

#### PRELIMINARY NOTE.

SEVERAL of the arguments used in this dialogue are of a popular kind: appealing to the natural feelings of the mind more than to the deliberate judgments of men who rule everything by processes of thinking. I employ these arguments now, because I have found them effectual in experience, convincing men, where more abstruse argumentation failed.

———

The next discussion in this assembly of Hindu pundits turned upon a subject closely akin to the last one, the migration of souls; and embraced that point which proves the ultimate resting-place both of the Hindu systems, and the common Hindu belief. Their English friend thus opened it for consideration.

*Eng.* In our last discussion, O pundits, there was one argument against the migration of souls, which I might have brought forward, but preferred not to employ in this assembly. It is a special argument against transmigration as received by the common people. We see a great amount of evil in this world of many kinds. How has it come here? whence did it spring? We are told: "It came from the previous lives of those now in the world." But whence did it come into those lives?

It is answered: "From earlier lives." And into those?
"From lives earlier still." This process, it is evident,
is quite incomplete. It traces evil a few steps back, and
removes the difficulty of its origin from our sight, only
to throw it upon others who lived long before us. But
the difficulty remains still. When you have repeated
the removal several times, and gone back into distant
ages, the question still arises: Where did that evil
spring from? The origin of that distant evil is as difficult to account for as that of the evil which we see in
our own day. The only consistent course for a philosopher to adopt is to go back and back, and never to
stop till he arrives at the primal origin of things, and
examines whether it is traceable there. The Sánkhya
and Vedánt do so: and furnish their ultimate explanation of the existence of evil by boldly making it an
element in the original creation of the matter of the
universe. Will you kindly tell us, O Gurudás, the
view of the Sánkhya on this subject?

*Gurudás.* Kopila asserts that intellect, the first product of Nature, exhibits as its affections, goodness, passion, and foulness (the Satwa, Raja, and Tama gunas):
that from which intellect springs must then possess these
things in its constitution. He therefore defines Nature
as " the state of equipoise of *goodness, passion,* and *darkness.*" These are not " qualities" (in the ordinary sense),
but are the actual material engaged in the service of SOUL :
just as a " cord " is used to bind an animal. There is
a triad of these " qualities;" and neither less nor more.
Hence spring the varieties of products in the universe.

*Eng.* By this statement then, Kopila teaches that all
the varieties of pain and pleasure, virtue and vice in
the three worlds, are derived originally from the creation. He teaches that all the mixtures of character, not
only in the hearts of men, but in the animal, vegetable,
and mineral worlds, result from impulses which are to
be traced back to the very origin of things. He finds
good and evil in the objects among which we dwell,
and that which partakes of the quality of both : and he
reckons that the original materials of the world contained these things, or rather, he even teaches that they
are made up of these things ; and therefore their products in every combination contain more or less of
three material or natural substances. We have already
noticed the singular theory which traces all things to
one substance (Prakriti), which is after all a compound.
of three other contrary substances in equipoise; and have
argued against the notion that such substances are
eternal. Let us look at the theory now as it bears upon
the origin and existence of evil, and ask whether it
properly accounts for what we daily see and experience.
The good, the evil, and the mixture of both, are worked
into the very constitution of things : just as we see the
colours of the sun's rays reflected in all sorts of combinations on the surfaces of material things. If we
reckon three primary colours, blue, red, and yellow ;
and say that all the colours of every shade to which their
mixtures can possibly give rise, are traceable to these,
whatever be the position, the locality, and the circumstances of such colours, we should make an argument

perfectly similar to that of the Sánkhya.   Undoubtedly
in the physical world, we see such rules being carried
out.  The very law of causation implies them in connection with material objects.   Mangoe-trees spring from
mangoe-trees, and nothing but the branch, or seed, or
root of a mangoe-tree can produce such a tree again.
Elephants produce exclusively their own kind.   Kites
produce the eggs of kites; and from these eggs only
kites are hatched.   The hilsa fish produces spawn, from
which only hilsa are produced.   Whether they be beasts
or birds, fish or insects, each kind produces only young
of its own species.   There is no confusion: one kind
does not give birth to another indiscriminately; there
is perfect regularity kept up, and even in the production of living creatures, the law which we see ruling in
material products also holds good, that like produces
like.   If we trace back each kind of living creature
now in the world, we have every right to expect that
we shall go on, until we come to a pair (or more)
created by God.  You will remember that I have argued
for a real creation of each separate species of living
creatures.  It seems to me perfectly just to conclude that
to each separate species, the Supreme Creator gave what
the Sánkhya terms a "disposition," an innate tendency
to produce only their own kind: so that it is with them a
law ; they cannot help it ; they cannot get free from it.
So long as the proper process of reproduction is employed,
the result is sure to be a product exactly resembling in
its essential elements the producer from which it sprang.
In the same way the same distinguishing qualities are

preserved to the different classes even of inorganic minerals. The same processes carried on by similar agents, under the same conditions, lead to similar results. We all see this: we look for it, we count upon it, and lay our measures accordingly.

*Gurudás.* All this, O friend, we can indeed see and entirely agree to; and this is but a fair development of the doctrine of Kopila concerning the three gunas, which make up the original element of all things, Prakriti. Hence it is that the S. Karika lays down very fully the doctrine of *innate dispositions.* By this it shows that while the dispositions communicated to men and other creatures are of various kinds, corporeal and intellectual, essential and incidental, leading upwards or urging downwards, and productive of all the numberless varieties of character, lot and history of created beings in this and other worlds, yet they are all derived from the different amounts and proportions of the three gunas, with which each individual is formed.

*Eng.* I am quite aware of this fact, O friend, and of the Karikas in which the statement is made; and allow that this doctrine is precisely similar to that of the gunas you first mentioned. But I have not finished my argument concerning it. While acknowledging its just application to the physical properties of all portions of matter, and also to the reproduction by each class of living creatures, from the ants upwards, exclusively of its species, I ask, is this the analogy by which you explain the defects and sins of men? Do you account for the virtues and the vices of men by the same rule which accounts for the production of heat in fire, and the hatching of parrots from their parents' eggs. Allowing the physical application of the rule, and allowing that there must have been such an "innate disposition" imparted to them, I object altogether to apply the theory to the virtues and vices of men. The cases in my view are thoroughly different, and the same explanation cannot serve for both. The origin of the Gunas and of Prakriti I need not again object to. Kopila gives us a system of designs, and of dispositions, originated without a producer; and acting under regular laws, established without any lawgiver: and this alone, apart from other arguments, might justly be urged as false to the whole scheme. However, let us rather look at the doctrine itself.

*Vedantist.* Besides, O learned friend, granting that the Sánkhya fails from their rejection of an Iswara, to secure a foundation for the doctrine, the Vedánta cannot be charged with a similar defect. The Vedánta allows the existence of Brahma, yet teaches the same doctrine. In the *Bhagavat Gita*, the same theory of the three Gunas is laid down: and all dispositions, all characters, all courses of conduct, are said to flow naturally and necessarily from them. It is added that there is nothing in the three worlds freed from the influence of the Gunas. The consequence is that men, amongst other beings, are born with different tendencies: some have "divine destiny:" some are subject to "infernal destiny;" according as they possess more or less of the Satwa, Raja, and Tama Gunas.

D D

To the same purpose, Veda-Vyása in his Brahma Sutras (ii. 3. 41, 42) speaks in the clearest terms: "Blind in the darkness of ignorance, the soul is guided in all its actions and fruition, . . . by the Supreme Ruler . . who causes it to act according to its previous resolves: now, according to former purposes, as then, in a manner consonant to its yet earlier predispositions, accruing from forms without limit." And he adds: "The Supreme Ruler makes the individuals act relatively to their virtuous or vicious propensities."

*Eng.* Does he not give an illustration of this very important doctrine?

*Vedantist.* Yes; he says that the Supreme Ruler makes individuals to act thus, just "as the same fertilizing rain-cloud causes various seeds to sprout multifariously, producing diversity of plants according to their kinds."

*Eng.* Exactly so. He makes them act by the same rule as that according to which vegetables, animals, and birds are produced. Virtue and vice come forth from a man's heart, as sweetness comes from the sugar-cane, and acidity from the tamarind.

*Vedantist.* Nor does Vyása alone mention this. The Upanishads teach the same doctrine. While the Sánkhya places Prakriti above all to enforce this law of innate dispositions, the Upanishads ascribe the law to Brahma himself. "He who regulates both knowledge and ignorance is God."

*Eng.* Even such things do the Vedas teach; and yet, O pundits, you can regard them as divine books! The

Vedánta, then, joins the Sánkhya in teaching this doctrine. Both teach that all the dispositions of men, their ordinary actions, their longings, their enjoyments, their virtuous conduct, their vicious practices, are all the necessary development of their nature, and of the proportion of the Gunas which they individually contain : it is said also that all this is done through the controlling power of Brahma.

We need not again refer to the Pantheistic dogma that we have already discussed, and show how this doctrine in the Vedánt is the natural offspring of that : nor will I meet the Vedánt and Sánkhya separately by showing that each bases its doctrine on an error, which we have already examined and set aside. Let us examine this doctrine by itself, a doctrine which so many millions of Hindus believe : and which is so frequently spoken of among them. 1. I ask then. FIRST : If men are compelled to act in all things as trees and animals " act " in bringing forth their natural products, how is it that men are conscious of *freedom*, and that they are seen in numberless instances to *exercise choice ?* If words mean anything, then *compulsion*, which rules in everything, is the very opposite of free choice. A tree is a tree, and produces leaves, branches, fruit, and seed, because that is the law of its nature. It cannot help it. A monkey, except in trifling things, where its instincts allow choice, is just an animal, and performs all the functions of its monkey-life, because such is it compelled to be by the law of its being. But men are not living under such a law. In respect to their animal

nature, they do follow certain laws to which their
nature is subject: but in respect to their actions and
their purposes, the products of their intelligence, they
exercise choice every hour of their waking life.

*Vedantist.* Why then do they ever declare themselves
subject to fate?

*Eng.* In countries where this doctrine is part of their
religion, men constantly use such an expression. In
Hindustan and in Persia it is very common; for both
Hindus and Musalmans believe it. But on what occasions do they talk of fate? In great events, which are
beyond a man's control; in accidents in which he is involved by others; in misfortunes which he has not expected, or which he much regrets but cannot hinder;
men are found to console themselves by such professions
of belief. Sometimes, though not often, they utter the
same on occasions of unexpected success. The expression also is often used wrongly, where events can be
plainly traced, as the fruits of a man's own prudence or
of his folly. But if fate were true, it ought to be felt
always: men ought to make no exertions to avoid coming
evil: they ought to care nothing about anything that
happens. Like the Yogi, they should sit still, exercise
no choice about anything, and do nothing all their lives.
But it is not true: and although some do profess it, we
find the voice of their real nature speaking against it,
and see them doing a thousand things without any reference at all to this doctrine; we see them acting as if
they had never heard of it. Let us look at the history
of one man through one day: and we shall see that his

whole life is a life of choice, and of effort to produce
certain desired results, by measures which experience
teaches him will lead to them.   On rising in the morning, he takes his clothes, procures flowers and vessels,
and goes away to the river to worship and to bathe. He
has chosen to do this; for he approves of it, and knows
how to accomplish the end.   Were he desirous of seeing
a sick mother in a distant village, he would not choose
it: he would omit such a work that morning, and at
daylight, would (from choice) set off for the distant
village in order to see her.   In the one case he would
choose to go to the river: in the other he would not.
After bathing, he walks home again, dresses, and takes
his food.   He uses his hands in order to feed himself:
he lifts the food and the cup to his mouth: he is not acting under compulsion, and in such things never thinks
that it is his fate to lift his hands or eat and drink.   He
walks away to the bazar: he there engages in business:
he employs not only his hands, but all the skill and
wisdom and prudence of his mind.   He wishes to be
rich: he therefore uses all his skill to buy cheap, to sell
dear, and to sell fast.   Perhaps he deals honestly; perhaps he overreaches: but he chooses to act so: for he
has an end to accomplish, and these are the means by
which it will be secured.   Clever men, by means of
their skill, obtain large profits: unskilful men subject
themselves to losses.   Observing this, he tries to avoid
the mistakes of the one and follow the prudence of the
other.   Such is his practice during all the hours of
business.   When evening comes and business closes, he

returns home; again takes food, and then voluntarily retires to rest. Throughout the day, we see nothing in his doings, of the compulsion which we allow to exist in making a tree what it is; we see him master of his own actions; he is independent; he does things and refrains from other actions because he chooses so to do. He gives reasons for what he does; and in his actions fulfils certain objects, such as pleasure, gain or fame hold out to him.

All men act in this way. They act for reasons: they are swayed by motives; they keep in view certain objects: and they adopt certain measures. Here we see ample proofs of freedom: but none of compulsion. We see freedom of thought and reason; and freedom of will. Look at the case of disease. Men are liable to sickness, sometimes from known causes, sometimes from causes unknown. They know that medicines are very useful to promote a cure: and a class of physicians therefore is found in all civilized communities who administer these medicines, to the satisfaction and for the welfare of society. If men were subject to a compulsory fate, they would not take care of their patients, or trouble themselves about the removal of diseases. They could say: This is God's doing: I am not free: this is the effect of the Tama Guna; he will do what he likes: and there they would leave the matter. But very few are so unwise. Almost all do call the doctor and use the means of cure which experience suggests as useful. Here again is freedom of choice and action clearly manifested.

2. Taking the fact of this freedom as the first argument against the theory of compulsory dispositions, let me present to you a SECOND argument in the fact that *motives* are the causes whence human actions spring. Now, motives can be acted on only when there is a freedom of choice. We mean by them the variety of reasons which influence the mind. Physical causes affect the production of objects in nature. In the soul of man changes of state are produced by what we term motives and reasons. Reasons are suited to the judgment; motives are suitable to men's will. The use of these terms in all languages—*reasons, will, choice, purpose, unwilling,* and the like—all point to the fact that men are able to do or not do, according as they incline. In most cases, the courses of action which men pursue have both advantages and disadvantages attending them. Men examine both, and choose between them. The man who is fond of drinking thinks, on the one hand, of the pleasure which that vice gives; on the other, of the disgrace to which it leads; and according to the weight which he allows, either to the one reason or the other, will be his final history. Now, what motives has a tree to act upon? It follows the laws of its being, which are indeed innate. And in its growth the human body follows the same; but the understanding, the affections, furnish reasons to the soul; and the will chooses between them, and then acts. Do you not, O pundits, on this ground lay before your disciples the advantages of following your respective systems of learning; and do you not argue with each

other to prove that your own systems are correct and those of others erroneous?

3. A third reason—a strong reason—against the doctrine of compulsion is that, according to the choice which is made between motives, men administer to each other praise or blame; declare they have acted *rightly* or *wrongly,* and that they are *virtuous* or *followers of vice.* What is the meaning of these terms? They are entirely inapplicable to a tree, to a fish, to a horse, or to a tiger. The tree follows the law of its being; the tiger does harm, in the destruction even of human life; but herein he follows the " innate dispositions " with which his nature has been invested. No one, therefore, thinks him deserving of blame and of punishment. If, now, it is true that men are placed under the same law of compulsory " dispositions," how is it that terms expressive of blame and praise are applied to them? They are not more applicable than they are to a tiger, a parrot, or a tree. We constantly apply them, however. We apply them to children, even from infancy, and they appreciate the force of the arguments which we present to them from this source. We apply them to grown-up men. We embody them in public laws, and appoint magistrates, ameens, and judges, to see those laws enforced. Why do we not seize tigers and have them publicly punished? Why do we not collect the búlbúls and Syámá birds, and publicly thank them for their sweet songs. We know that they all act from innate dispositions, without choice; we know that men have a freedom of choice,

and that no innate disposition compels them to do
things which they cannot help. We make them,
therefore, accountable ; the animals we leave alone.
In your authorities you continually speak of *merit,
demerit, reward, punishment,* and the like : these terms
always imply choice, freedom of purpose, and freedom
of action. You use them in speaking of the system
established in the universe, and of men's dealings with
God. They are quite inconsistent with your doctrine
of innate dispositions; but they agree entirely with
men's general feeling and experience. In this case, I
think your natural feelings have led you rightly where
consistent adherence to your theories would lead you
wrong.

*Vedántist.* It is hard, O friend, to deny that there
does seem a great difference between the actions of
men and the proceedings of animals and the like. But
still it may be said that this system under which they
so act is *appointed* to them, and they are *compelled* so
to live.

*Eng.* But, O pundit, if their so acting is called compulsion, then what is freedom? So long as men have
the power to choose courses of action for themselves,
we cannot help considering them free. God has truly
established in the world the system under which they
live ; but, as I showed you before, His system is intended to try men's character, and for this purpose
freedom of choice between motives is essential. The
compulsion of those innate dispositions is a very different thing. The system as such may be a fixed one :

individual action is left independent. I might add that, if there be a real compulsion, why is it not uniform? It ought to be in a wise system, and is uniform in the animal and vegetable world. In the conduct of men the same circumstances ought to produce the same results. A man, in circumstances similar to those by which he was once surrounded, ought to act in a similar manner. But this is frequently not the case; on the contrary, men often act a second time differently to what they did at first. And they do this from choice, as the result of experience, from knowing what results followed. On the theory of freedom, we can fully explain the difference: on that of dispositions it cannot be explained?

*Vedantist.* If God choose to act so, what can we say against it?

*Eng.* But we cannot charge such conduct on him. We can easily see how men differ in wisdom and prudence, and we give them these names according to their qualities. If a man say: I will swim across the Ganges in the month of Asára, who will call him prudent? If he do it and get drowned, will men blame his folly or impute the fault to God?

*Vedantist.* They will generally impute it to him; but they ought really to do so to God. Even the shastres teach us this: as says the Sruti: "He makes him to do good deeds, whom he wishes to take out of the world: and him he makes to do evil deeds, whom he wishes to introduce into the world again."

*Eng.* I allow, O pundit, that this is the consistent

result of your doctrine. According to your mode of arguing, it is clear that all evil and all defect of every kind in the three worlds is traceable up to God. He is the Author of all actions, all tendencies, all characters. He is therefore the sole Author of Virtue and He is the AUTHOR OF SIN. It is natural that we should arrive at this result of your arguments: and I now desire to express my belief, that the fact of your teaching this openly is the strongest argument against your doctrine. *God is the author of all sin!* What a blasphemous doctrine to teach! Yet, alas! there are millions of Hindus who believe him to be so. The Vedas themselves teach it: and what shall they say against the Vedas? I wish therefore to examine this assertion, and by showing sound reasons against it, add new arguments against the doctrine from which it consistently springs. Let me present to you one or two plain reasons such as the most illiterate can understand.

(1.) The *Yóga* allows that God possesses *infinite wisdom,* and that all wisdom finds its source in him.

*Gurudás.* Certainly that is the doctrine which the Yóga teaches.

*Eng.* What would you say to a man, who, after spending much money building a splendid house, furnishing it with everything his family can desire, and at length bringing them to enjoy it, should deliberately set the whole on fire?

*Gurudás.* We have never heard of such a man: if such ever existed he must have been mad: no man in his senses could commit such folly.

*Eng.* Very good: but do you not ascribe the same folly to the Supreme God, in asserting that having created this universe with all its wonderful contrivances; having created men, superior to trees and to dull animals, and given them intelligence, and the choice of right and wrong, he then compels them to sin, and thus leads them, through sorrows in this life, to punishment in hell? Is this course of folly possible on the part of the all-wise God?

(2.) God's *holiness*, again, would prevent such a course. Have we not seen in the Upanishads passages which declare him spotless and free from all impurity.

*Vedántist.* Certainly: there are numerous Srutis to that effect: in the Puráns also.

*Eng.* But if God loves holiness, and is holy, and therefore dislikes sin: if, as we read in the Gita, he so far disapproves of murder, theft, lies, and adultery as to command men not to do them, how can he possibly incite men to do such evil deeds? Would any one of you, O pundits, incite a man to murder your parents, destroy your children, and plunder the property of your relatives?

*Vedántist.* No one surely would do that: such wickedness we must abhor.

*Eng.* If we, who are imperfect, abhor such deeds, how then can we attribute them to the pure and holy God: how can we attribute them to him not once, nor ten times; but attribute all the evil that is or has been or ever will be? God hates evil, and how can he possibly himself commit it, and be the author of all men's wickedness?

(3.) God rewards men according to their merits and demerits. And he is to be reckoned *just*.

*Vedantist.* Certainly. All authorities say so: and that is the rule by which we say migrations are determined.

*Eng.* Are not the virtuous really made happy: are not the degraded and vicious made to live degraded lives in this world, and then rendered miserable in the next world in hell?

*Vedantist.* Yes, that is the doctrine we believe.

*Eng.* But if God be the author of all good dispositions, and also of all evil ones, how can he be reckoned *just* in treating these two classes so differently? The virtuous are good from no excellence of their own; but from his controlling influence. From the same cause the wicked are not wicked of themselves: they cannot help it : they are obliged to be so. Where is the justice of God in thus punishing men for doing what he obliges them to do? He does punish them indeed; because their evil acts are the offspring of their own voluntary sin. That is justice which we all approve.

(4.) Let me ask one other question: Is not God full of *benevolence?*

*Vedantist.* Yes, he is "mangal swarup," goodness personified: for he feeds men and beasts, and provides for the wants of all.

*Eng.* Well, then, I ask, what is the cause of all the

misery in this world ?   In our last discussion I showed
that it all arises from the evil conduct of men towards
God, towards themselves, and towards each other.   SIN
is the cause of all sorrow, and all misery.   Were a
man secretly to put poison in your food, and your life
were destroyed amidst the greatest pain and torture,
would you reckon him benevolent, or count him as
your enemy ?

*Vedantist.* As my enemy surely : if he did it purposely.

*Eng.* But SIN is the poison of the world : and he
who has introduced sin has been the occasion and
commencement of all the misery that is suffered.   How
can we ascribe such misery to God, the ever benevolent
and good ?   That he is kind and good, he proves by
all the care he takes of us : by the rains of heaven,
the corn harvests, the fruit, he gives : by the constant
change of day and night : by giving us medicines to
check disease, and wisdom to apply them.

Thus we see that this doctrine that God is the author
of all virtue and of all sin, opposes entirely his greatest
attributes.   If we believe the Vedas, we must allow
that he is an unwise, unholy, unjust, and unmerciful
God.   Which of us is prepared to accept this necessary conclusion from that theory ?

*Vedantist.* Still it seems strange, if he had nothing
to do with it.   We allow that he made all things : He
gave our minds, souls, bodies, and limbs : it is with
them sin is committed : how then can he be free from
all connection with it ?

*Eng.* God has certainly given us our limbs and organs: our five senses, our understanding and speech. But why has he given them? Surely that we may do good with them: and if we use them otherwise, the fault lies not with him but with ourselves. If, O brahmin, you have given to your servant to-day a rupee to make purchases for your family, and he go and waste it, or spend it in drinking or in folly, who is to be blamed, you who gave the money, or he who misspends it? He surely is guilty, and he deserves punishment.

*Vedantist.* Certainly he is guilty.

*Eng.* But supposing he pleads that that rupee which led to the folly and theft, was given by you, and that you therefore were the cause, what would you say?

*Vedantist.* I should tell him that it was given for my purpose, and not his own, and because he is my servant.

*Eng.* Thus will God reason with us, his servants, respecting sin. All our organs, and all this world, he has given that we may serve him. If then we sin and turn all these gifts to evil uses, he is not chargeable with guilt: it is we who sin. Therefore, it is he who punishes.

*Vedantist.* But we would ask, O friend, If sin is so evil; if God hates it, and will surely punish, why did he allow it to enter the world at all: why was not all made perfectly free from sin?

*Eng.* Do we not say, O pundit, that the state of man is the highest, and is much superior to that of stones, trees, and animals? If God compel men to remain sinless, whether by " innate dispositions," or otherwise, then there is no virtue in refraining from evil.　There is then no more virtue in a man than in a tree.　Real virtue arises from the willing obedience of a soul that can do wrong but prefers to do right.　Such is the obedience which God wishes to see in men.　It was for this reason that he gave them their intelligence, their freedom, their power to choose.　Thus their goodness is tried and tested.　Those who, in the presence of evil, prefer to practise what is holy, and to do what pleases God, are shown to be willingly virtuous, and therefore God rewards them.　The wicked, in the presence of what is good, prefer to sin; and therefore God punishes them as beings really evil.

*Gurudás.*　There is reason, O friend, in your words; still you have not yet touched the difficulty which the Sánkhya and Vedánt theories seek to explain.　There is evil in the world: and it can be traced to yet earlier evil: how did the first evil arise?　Was the world made evil at first?

*Eng.*　This subject, O friend, has always perplexed the minds of men: and must do so: because the ultimate reason for permitting evil lies deep in the mind of God.　You have offered your explanation: let me give you that which is contained in the Christian Bible. That Book states that God made this world perfectly pure.　Every part of the creation was good.　There was no defect.　Then he placed in it, in a garden, a pair of human beings.　He made them perfectly holy: he made them free.　Then he gave them this com-

mand: " Do not eat of the fruit of one particular tree
in this garden: all the rest is yours:" and he left
them.   This command was given in order to try their
obedience, and see whether they were above all things
anxious to please him.   They were free to obey or
disobey.   They disobeyed.   From that time sin has
been in the world.   Men are surrounded by sin, see
sin, and practise sin.   Yet do they bear marks of their
pure origin.   Sometimes they long to do good, to
oppose what is evil.   Then they fall into temptation:
and they commit the sins which they profess to dislike.   Thus it is man is in general a mixture of good
and evil: and that both are seen in his conduct, language, and thoughts.   While you explain it unsatis-
factorily by a reference to the Gunas, THIS is the
explanation of the origin of sin in this world, given
by the Christian Bible, which, for many reasons, we
honour as the WORD OF GOD.   That word has been
given to warn us against the effects of evil; to show
us how sin is pardoned, and the soul freed from its
guilt and power.   Its whole purpose is to fight against
sin: and ultimately the grace of God will restore all
things unto himself.

# PART IV.

## An Outline of Truth.

In the preceding Dialogues, the chief errors taught in
the great systems of Hindu Philosophy have been discussed: the arguments and authorities upon which they
are based have been stated; and the various considerations which reason urges against their validity, have
been expounded. So closely are the various dogmas
connected together; they are so intimately bound up
with the very structure and end of these systems; that
if the reasonings against them be sound, the systems as
such must fall to pieces. Many of their topics are
wisely chosen; and many of their individual principles
are sound; but as systems they must be reconstructed,
if they are to stand. The Nyáya alone can safely
retain any considerable portion of its original plan. The
Sánkhya, though ably constructed and singularly consistent, proves utterly deficient both in its beginning
and its end. The Vedánta disappears in like manner;
its very root being the gigantic error of pure Pantheism.
Aware that he had appeared chiefly in the invidious
position of a critic; that he had hitherto been examining the dogmas of others; had endeavoured to
destroy the credit of the systems which his pundit
friends highly valued; and though he had advocated

several important principles of truth, had not yet presented them as a system, the English judge prepared, as was just, a brief outline of the system of truth usually received by educated Christians in modern times; that his friends might know how European scholars not only destroy fallacies, but build up truth in their stead. Imitating to a small extent their own forms of text-books, he compiled this brief outline in the form of Sutras; and having requested the pundits to write them down, he dictated and expounded the Sútras in their hearing on several succeeding days.

---

## AN OUTLINE OF TRUTH.

### Victory to the Supreme God.

May the Glorious God, by whom have been created the three worlds, grant unto us the light of His wisdom; that our souls, being freed from the glooms of passion, may contemplate His works and His honoured words with attention; that we may comprehend the lessons of instruction which they teach, and accomplish those holy works, which these lessons, acting as motives, ought to produce in our souls.

### BOOK FIRST.

Sutra 1. To please God is the chief end of man: in so doing he will escape all pain; and will attain everlasting happiness.

At the outset four questions will be asked: What is the object proposed for consideration: What is the occasion

which calls it forth : What is the purpose for which attention to it is invited : and, Who are the parties to whom it is
addressed ? We have stated the object; the attainment of
the *purushártha* or chief end of man. We now proceed to
the remaining questions.

2. Concerning this chief end, and the method of its
attainment, many wrong notions are prevalent in the
minds of different learned persons, as well as among
the vulgar. All these must be laid aside, and it is
essential to the fulfilment of the end, that we acquire
right notions of both.

3. Because permanent happiness can be secured, only
by the fulfilment of duty in pleasing God; and because
in such happiness alone can the object of man's creation be accomplished, therefore all persons ought to seek
sound instruction respecting the chief end, and give to
it the most careful attention of reflecting minds.

> Most men desire immediate pleasure; which is of many
> kinds. They find it in the enjoyment of wealth ; in the in-
> dulgence of evil passions; in the praises of their fellow-men ;
> in the exercise of power; in the gratulations of self-righteous-
> ness; and the like. Our instruction is addressed to the
> reflecting, who know that all such pleasures are transient:
> and should therefore desire a happiness which is lasting.

4. This chief end is proclaimed, not to the learned
only, but to all men. Through the infinite mercy of
God, the means of securing it are provided for all classes,
and can be understood and employed even by the poor.
While therefore it is good for the wise, like the corn
and the fruits of the earth, it is beneficial also to the
unlearned; and they are invited to secure its accomplishment by their most earnest endeavours.

Having answered these four questions, we next consider the instruments of knowledge, by which right notions can be obtained.

5. The instruments by which right notions of the chief end and of its means may be secured are, the perceptions of sense; the inferences of reason; and the revealed book of God.

Each of these we consider in turn in three Sútras.

6. By the perceptions of sense, we acquire a right knowledge of the various objects which our five senses recognize.

By means of our senses, which are five in number, we come to know the multitudinous objects which are in the world; our fellow-men, animals, trees and the like. We see and hear from others what God is doing in the universe; we also receive the knowledge which is laid up in books.

7. By inferences of reason, which are of three kinds, and which are based upon its innate notions and intuitions, we deduce from the things we have perceived, the general principles and laws by which they are governed.

a. Inferences of reason are of three kinds. (1.) *A priori*: when we infer effect from cause: as when from the sight of clouds we infer rain. (2.) *A posteriori*: when from effects we infer cause: as when from a seat we infer a carpenter. (3.) *Analogical*: tracing the resemblance of relations: as when from seeing the mango blossoms in my own garden, I infer that there are blossoms on the mango-trees of others.

b. By examining, in this way, the facts and objects which our senses present, we infer general facts or laws: as the rising and setting of the sun; the causes of tides; the value of rain; and the like. We also observe design in the structure and arrangement of the universe, and hence infer the wisdom and goodness of Him who created it.

8. By Revelation we acquire knowledge of things which lie beyond the ordinary observation of men: and which our reason could never discover: such as things which only God knows; or which have been done beyond the sphere of our senses; in heaven, hell and other worlds.

> These are the instruments of knowledge: we now proceed to examine the various objects made known by their means.

9. God, human souls, sense-objects, understanding, the mind, holy and evil deeds, evil passions, mundane life, retribution, the purification of the soul from sin, and the future world: these and similar objects are brought to the knowledge of men by these instruments. These objects are divided into two classes. Some, especially numerous classes of sense-objects, are only partially connected with the chief end of man: and a knowledge of them is not necessary to his fulfilment of that end. Others are necessary to its attainment; and it is with them our inquiry is concerned. We shall mention the former for such as find a pleasure in studying them.

> The sources of our knowledge of these numerous objects will now be pointed out.

10. Knowledge connected with the chief end of man may be learned from two sources: from the works which God has made; and from the special book which he has caused to be written.

> Each of these sources is now described.

11. By the works of God we mean, all things which exist in the universe; especially the earth and its con-

tents, and the heavenly bodies. Such works teach many lessons concerning the wisdom, power and goodness of God. The relations of society also teach our duties to God and to each other: and exhibit the principles of his government, and the like.

12. The special knowledge which God has caused to be written concerning himself, concerning the chief end of man, and the mode of its attainment, is contained in a book called the Bible. This book confirms what we infer from reason, concerning the works of God and a future world, and adds to those inferences a great deal of divine knowledge, which reason and perception could not attain by themselves.

> The revelation of God (called by Hindu scholars, tradition) is not contained in the Vedas, the Darsanas, the Puranas, and other Shastres. We judge this from their many deficiencies; from their numerous important errors; and from their mutual contradictions. Books liable to such charges cannot by a wise man be regarded as books which teach sound and undeniable truth.

13. The Bible is a book, which contains many separate treatises: these were written at different periods, during successive ages, by holy men who were taught by the Spirit of God what to write. These numerous books are collected in two divisions, called* the First and Second Parts. In them is recorded a great amount of religious instruction, which men could not have discovered by their unassisted efforts, and which is essential to them in explaining and enforcing the chief end for which they have been created.

* *i. e.* in various Indian versions.

Some of these instructions could not have been discovered by men: such as the complete account of the character of God; the origin of the universe; the nature and description of the future world. All are useful. Thus Part I. of the Bible tells about the creation ; the creation of the first human pair; the beginning of sin; the gradual increase of sin and its evil effects; the separation of one nation to be the special disciples of God; the holy law which declares our duty to God and duty to men ; various hymns and prayers suitable for the worship of God; moral instructions concerning mundane life and holy conduct; the lives of good and evil men; and prophecies concerning the future. The Second Part describes the life of the divine incarnation of mercy, Jesus Christ : his holy instructions, his acts of kindness, his sufferings, his death ; his resurrection from the grave ; his atonement for sin; and the means of pardoning the wicked. It contains also the lives of his disciples; the account of the first spreading of his religion ; the moral instructions given to his followers by which they must regulate their conduct; the account of heaven, and hell ; of the great day of judgment; and similar subjects.

How this book, written by men, is yet known to be the Book of God is next declared.

14. That the Bible is the special book of God is shown by two classes of proofs, called the internal and the external evidences. Each of these is described in two Sutras.

15. By the internal proofs we mean, the internal character and contents of the book. The doctrine displays the highest wisdom; the moral instruction inculcates the purest holiness; the moral duty enjoined requires the kindest spirit of benevolence; and the effects of all exhibit nothing but justice, love, peace and happiness. No error can be found in its descriptions of God, its doctrine concerning the duties of men; or in those prophecies which have been fulfilled. Although written at different times by different men, the purpose

of the Book, its doctrine, its morality, its effects agree
with each other in every part.

16. By the external proofs we mean other circumstances which, apart from the contents of the book
and the nature of its teaching, show them to be of
divine origin. Thus its teachers and writers performed
works of wonder which only God can properly do.
They also displayed in their prophecies (many of which
have been fulfilled) a deep knowledge of future events
which only the All-wise God can of himself possess.
Since as men they could not of themselves exercise
either this divine power or divine knowledge, it is evident that (as they themselves declared) God must have
communicated it to them, in order that people might
believe in their authority.

> The object for which God condescended to publish this
> special book of divine wisdom is now to be considered. God
> has done much for the happiness of men by the regular course
> of his providence. It is not to be supposed that he will
> lightly or for a trifling reason interfere with that providence
> by sending special messengers or giving special laws. Why
> he did so is now to be stated, in one Sutra.

17. Since among men numerous errors prevail concerning the chief end and its attainment; concerning
the character of God, the evil of sin, and the existence
of another world: since also men, rendered blind and
foolish by the practice of evil deeds, are liable to forget
God, to forget the retributive worlds of punishment,
and are therefore in danger of everlasting destruction;
therefore God, in his boundless compassion, gave this
Book of Wisdom, that thereby he might communicate

to men right notions in the place of their errors, and
might warn them to flee from eternal wrath; both by
the fear of certain punishment, and the hope of pardon
to a true penitent.

We have now completed the first division of these
Sutras, which speak of the object to be accomplished,
the instruments and sources of knowledge, and the
purpose for which such knowledge is required. We
now proceed to consider the various objects of knowledge rightly made known in these several ways. First
we speak of God.

### BOOK SECOND.

SUTRA 18. There is but ONE GOD. He is the first
Great Being: a spirit; eternal; self-existent; infinite
in wisdom, in power, in holiness, in justice, in goodness,
in mercy, truth and joy.

> The great attributes of the character of the glorious God
> are frequently described in the Bible in the most exalted
> language: and the numerous texts should be studied by the
> reflecting with humility and awe. In regard to his nature
> we lay down one Sutra.

19. The Bible teaches that in the Godhead there is
a Trinity of " persons ;" the Father, the Son, and the
Holy Ghost.

> How the Godhead subsists ever must be a mystery which
> the limited soul of man cannot possibly comprehend : we
> can only receive with faith and humility such knowledge
> respecting it as God himself is pleased to reveal. We next
> speak of his works.

20. He created all things which exist; he did not
produce them from himself; or merely make them from

some eternal matter which he shaped and fashioned into
new forms; but he gave existence to the substances
themselves in some way known only to himself. Having
created them, he continues to preserve them by the
work of his superintending providence, according to
the laws which he has established.

21. The matter thus created and thus preserved, the
Great God has distributed through the universe in the
form of globes: known as the earth, the sun, moon, and
stars. Of these, the fixed stars are most distant: the
planets, including the earth, revolve round the sun;
the moon revolves round the earth.

> We nowhere find, either in nature or the Bible, anything
> concerning regions like the realm of Indra, of Prajápati,
> the Gandharvas, and the like.

22. The various created objects in the universe are
divided into two classes, the animate and the inanimate.
The inanimate are subdivided into vegetable and
mineral. The animate, into intelligent and unintelligent. The unintelligent include beasts, birds, fishes,
reptiles, and insects. All these classes of objects exhibit
the wonders of God's wisdom, power, and goodness.
The knowledge of them constitutes the different
branches of human learning: which may be examined
and studied by the intelligent, and will produce great
pleasure in their minds. It is not, however, essentially
necessary for the fulfilment of the chief end.

> For the sake of the intelligent, who may wish to know
> more about these things, a few particulars are added:—
> 1. All these objects possess the quality of existence. Con-
> nected with the modes of existence, namely, number, size,

and motion, there arise several sciences: such as Arithmetic, Geometry, Algebra, and the Calculus.

2. All these objects (excepting the intelligent) are composed of matter in numerous forms. Matter is either imponderable or ponderable. Imponderable matter gives rise to the sciences of Heat, Electricity, and Optics. Ponderable matter, viewed in relation to its essential properties, gives rise to the sciences of Mechanics and the like. If we consider solids we get Statics, when they are at rest: and Dynamics, when put in motion. If fluids, we get Hydrostatics: and if the subject of sounds, Acoustics.

3. Matter, again, in mass, according to its distribution, gives rise to other sciences. Astronomy shows the mutual relations of all the heavenly bodies, and the movements of the planets, &c. In regard to the earth, our dwelling-place, numerous branches of learning are required. Geography shows how its surface is laid out; and tells of the various appearances of the mountains, seas, rivers, islands, cities, forests, and the like.

Geology describes the structure of the body of the earth, and the mode in which the different elements of its upper part have overlaid each other. Mineralogy shows the various materials of which the upper part has been formed: and Chemistry analyses all these elements, in order to discover their essential properties, and trace out the actual number of primary materials. This science has not established the doctrine of the five elements, but has proved that most of them are compounds. These things belong to inorganic matter.

4. The organized matter is divided into vegetable and animal. The vegetable kingdom is described by Botany, in reference to the various classes of trees and plants; and by Vegetable Physiology, in relation to the manner of their structure and organization. The animal kingdom is similar. The habits of animals, birds, and the like, are described in Natural History. Their different classes and kinds in Zoology: the functions of their different organs in Animal Physiology: and their organization by Anatomy.

These are the various sciences connected with the physical matter created and distributed in the universe. Of the intelligent we shall speak hereafter.

23. Amongst the created objects of the universe, intelligent beings are the chief. So far as known, they are divided into two classes, angels and men.

> There is no proof of the existence of any beings like the gods spoken of in the shastres. There is no proof of the existence anywhere of Indra, Agní, Varuná, and the Máruts: of Brahmá, Vishnu, and Mahadeo: of Krishna, Surjya, Ganesha, and Kartik: of Lakshmí, Durgá, Káli, and Saraswati: of Sitola and Kálu Ráy. The character of these gods, the wicked deeds ascribed to many of them in the shastres, and their numerous deficiencies in respect to divine attributes, prove that no such gods exist. It is also said in the Bible, there is but one God: and that idolatry is evil.

24. The angels are intelligent beings of high rank, who were created to be servants and messengers of God in different parts of the universe. They reside near him in heaven, where he especially manifests his presence: but are his messengers everywhere. They are numerous, powerful, and holy. They are specially engaged in promoting the welfare of men. There are also bad angels, who were once holy in heaven, but were in consequence of sin cast out from it. They employ themselves in endeavouring to accomplish the injury and destruction of men.

25. Men were also created by God. They have been formed of body and soul. He created at first but one pair, and from them have sprung by ordinary birth all the human beings that have lived in the world. The body of men is not developed from consciousness, nor formed of three cases, but consists of organized matter, like that of the different classes of animals.

*a.* The sciences of Anatomy and Human Physiology explain the structure and the functions of the different organs of the body. They do not show two different bodies (as the Sthúl and Linga Sarira); nor do they exhibit the Susamna artery, as taught in the Upanishads.

*b.* Again, a comparison of the different races of men confirms the doctrine of the Bible and the inferences of history, that all races have the same origin.

26. The soul of man is not a part of God: nor is it eternal in its origin. Souls are multitudinous. Each individual possesses a soul independent of all other souls; the time when these souls is created is not known, though it is probably produced when each child is born into the world.

27. The soul of man was made "in the likeness of God." That is; man was created with intelligence, affections, a will, and a conscience. He was made perfectly holy: able to understand the designs of his Creator, and to please him by obeying his commands.

(*a.*) There are many branches of knowledge connected with the intelligence of men. The instruments of the soul are explained in Language, Grammar, and Rhetoric. The operations of the soul are described in Psychology or Mental Philosophy; which tells of perception, recollection, imagination: reason with its intuitions: the feelings, and the will. The laws which govern reason are expounded by Logic. The laws which govern the will are developed in Moral Philosophy. These laws are divided into several branches: Religion shows the laws of duty towards God: Morality, of duty towards men in general: Political Morality, of men to each other as fellow-citizens, and so on. Men viewed in relation to experience, are described in History: They are the subjects also of Laws in reference especially to their social relations and political connections.

(*b.*) The moral powers are the chief faculties of the soul. By their means, the soul judges of right and wrong; perceives the duties which arise from all our relations with others ; and incites us to perform them completely. From them spring our notions of justice, love, benevolence, forbearance, and the like.

28. All human beings are formed in like manner. Though they differ in the amount both of mental and bodily strength, in the degrees of ability, and in the depth of their feelings, they all agree in being formed with minds and bodies of the same kind. Born also from the same first parents, it is evident that they constitute but ONE CASTE or race (*játi*), the caste of MAN ; and that all are brethren.

(*a*.) Besides the chief differences above mentioned in their capacities, they differ also in colour, in manners, in dress, in habits. But many of these things are merely the result of special differences in their circumstances, as of heat and cold, and modes of living, especially when continued for many generations.

(*b*.) The Hindu notion of a creation of four castes by Brahmá is nowhere proved to be a correct one. Many reasons can be brought against it. If Kshatriyas, for instance, in former times, like Visvamitra, could become brahmins, where is the separate creation of the castes ?

29. God created men, and placed them in this world, that they might rule in it ; might exert all their faculties ; might understand his doings ; might praise him for his character and works ; might enjoy the beauties of their dwelling-place ; and be happy.

30. Besides this, he wished also, that being able to understand good and evil, and being left free to do it, they might undergo trial, in order to show whether their good or evil conduct sprang from their own will. Hence arose the chief end, of which we have spoken, that all men should please God.

How the trial was to be borne will be next explained.

31. With a view to this trial of their moral nature, God placed man in circumstances, from which spring certain relations. These moral relations involve moral obligations: and each position has its own peculiar duty. The chief relations are those of man to God as his Creator, Preserver, Benefactor, and Proprietor: and of man to his fellow-men, as father, son, mother, neighbour, fellow-citizen, and the like.

> Good and evil therefore can never be the same thing. As long as the same relations exist under the same circumstances, the same duties must arise.

32. Thus the duties of man are of two kinds: his duties to God, and his duties to his fellow-men: the former are called religion; the latter, morality. Both classes are summarily described in the Two GREAT COMMANDMENTS, " Thou shalt love the Lord thy God with all thy heart," and " Thou shalt love thy neighbour as thyself."

33. An important statement of these duties is contained also in the TEN COMMANDMENTS. Several duties of man to God are stated in four commandments: (a.) Men are to serve and honour as God the one true God alone. No other god of any kind whatsoever can be worshipped. (b.) They are to worship only in the heart, with love and faith: no image is to be made, and no image is to be honoured. (c.) God's holy name is always to be reverenced; his holy service maintained, and all profanity in words and actions be put away. (d.) God has appointed a holy day, or Sabbath, in the week, in which men must rest from labour, and occupy

themselves in his service or in seeking the good of their own souls.

34. Several most important duties of man to man are described in six commandments. They contain and enforce—(*a.*) The duties of parents to children; children to parents and the like, which arise from blood relationships; and from our relations to the government of the country. (*b.*) Respect for life and the safety of others. (*c.*) Respect for the purity of others and the maintenance of their own, by the complete control of the passions. (*d.*) A perfect regard for the property and rights of others, shown in honesty and in upright dealings in trade. (*e.*) The observance of strict truth in all their words and actions; and (*f.*) the control of the thoughts, by suppressing all unlawful desire after those things which others possess, since from covetous desires spring the beginnings of evil. All the moral duties of men are explained and enforced again and again in many parts of the Bible.

35. He who observes these rules, and performs all the duties which spring from his relations to God and man, will accomplish the END of his existence : he will please God : his trial will prove the faithfulness of his love and obedience; and, therefore, he will receive the reward of everlasting happiness.

36. He who does not observe these rules; nor perform these duties; who disobeys the command of God and the obligations which his relations impose; he will not please God. He commits sin : his trial proves that his love is defective, and, instead of being rewarded, he will be punished.

F F

37. From these things it is evident that SIN is the breaking of those obligations which God has made to arise from our relations in life, and has declared in his word that it is man's duty to observe. It is the breaking of the LAW of God, expressed both in his works and in his revelation.

> It is therefore plain that sin does not consist in breaking caste; in touching a dead body; in neglecting idol-worship; in not performing a *sráddha* for the dead. These are not sins. But ingratitude, idolatry, theft, lying, adultery, malice, revenge, murder, covetousness, and the like—these are sins. It is evident, also, that God is not the author of sin ; but sin is produced when the covetous desires of men seek for that which the law of God forbids.

38. The beginnings of sin did not arise from the internal constitution of man ; but it occurred when the first moral being first broke the command of God. In this world it began when the first woman, being tempted and deceived by a bad angel named Satan, coveted something which God had forbidden, and disobeyed his command. The first man repeated the act: and both became sinners.

> The account of this is written in the Bible.
> The effects of sin will now be declared in two Sutras.

39. The first effect of disobeying the commands of God is, that in consequence men are liable to punishment: while living they are unhappy through the dissatisfaction, reproaches, and despair produced by their conscience : and at death they are carried to that hell where the punishment of sinners has been appointed by God.

40. The second effect of sin is that it corrupts the nature and practice of all who commit it: and incites them to repeat the evil they have once done. This corrupted and depraved nature is the real cause of all the darkness (*tamah*) and the evil tendencies that exist in the world. It is the natural fruit of sin, and has not been produced either by the direct agency of God, or by the dispositions with which man was originally endowed.

### BOOK THIRD.

Having explained the real nature and origin of the sins and defects under which man is labouring, and in consequence of which the accomplishment of his chief end might naturally be destroyed, we proceed to consider the special means, which the merciful God has appointed for preventing such a calamity. These are declared in the following Book :—

SUTRA 41. All men without a single exception have broken God's commands ; have become liable to punishment in this world and in hell; have lost their present happiness and the hope of future bliss ; it would therefore only be the natural fruit of sin, if every one were destroyed, because not one has accomplished the end for which he was created : not one has pleased God.

42. The wonderful mercy of God has prevented this awful calamity : and has provided a TRUE DELIVERANCE. This blessing is not merely a deliverance from wrong notions concerning soul and nature; but from evil prac-

tices, and their just punishment; from a corrupt nature and a love of sin.

The mode of this deliverance will next be explained.

43. The deliverance of a sinner cannot be accomplished without a suitable atonement to the law he has broken, and the Lawgiver whom he has disobeyed. This atonement must be offered by one who is not a sinner: and must be equal in value to the crime committed.

> *a.* All injuries to the law of men or of God must be atoned for either by punishment or ransom: as thefts, debts, and the like.
>
> *b.* If the ransom be equal to the crime, the full debt must be paid off by some one else. Thus the blood of buffaloes and goats can never be a fit ransom for the sins of man: nor bathing in the Ganges, nor offering myriads of cowries. Nor can good works be atonements, for men's works are the works of sinners.

44. Men cannot find such atonements: for they are themselves sinners: and the life of even a pure and sinless man can only ransom the life of one man.

45. To provide a fit ransom, the SON OF GOD, JESUS CHRIST, became incarnate. He took the form of a man, bore the responsibilities of a man; and being sinless and divine, He died in the place of sinners, bore their punishment, and opened a way for their forgiveness.

> Here an account of his birth, actions, instructions, and life ought to be justly considered. The full particulars are recorded in his own Book, in the four "Lives" written by his disciples.

46. God has now appointed that all, who wish to please Him and accomplish their chief end, shall come

to Him and pray for pardon and for deliverance from their punishment in the name of Jesus Christ, the Atonement. He is thus appointed to be the Mediator through whom men come to God. None are excluded from this offer of his mercy. All classes, poor and rich, learned and unlearned, are invited to accept it. Their acceptance of his atonement, instead of their own efforts, is FAITH.

> We now describe the results of this atonement. They are of two kinds, answering to the two effects of sin.

47. The first effect of faith in the atonement of Christ is that God, for His sake, forgives all the sins of the repenting sinner: he is therefore FREED from the punishment in hell which he deserved for his sins.

48. The second effect is that by Divine grace, he is purified from his evil desires. The Spirit of God will give a new nature by removing his corrupt propensities, and giving him a love for holiness. Thus are both the effects of sin removed.

49. Being thus pardoned and purified, a man must henceforth live very holy, striving daily to please God, by loving Him supremely, by subduing all desire after sin, and by obeying His commandments.

> God has also appointed means for this: these will now be described.

50. Believers must diligently use the FOUR MEANS which are appointed for this purpose. (a.) They must study the instructions, warnings, and encouragements which are written in the Book of God. (b.) They must

continually keep watch against the temptations to which they are subject; and be careful not to sin. (c.) They must daily pray for the assistance which God has promised to give them in obeying Him. (d.) They must keep the Sabbath-day of worship, observe communion with their fellow-believers, keep the ordinance of the Lord's Supper; and listen to the instructions of religious teachers.

### Each of these means may be more fully described.

51. The extent of this work of holiness is, that it must be carried on so long as the believer lives. During all his life he is on trial, and his chief end can only be accomplished by the testing of his love and obedience.

52. Probation ends with death: all men will die, at various times appointed by God, who gave them life: but they will only die once. There will be no transmigration: having left this world, they will enter it no more, but will live in the other world for ever.

53. Their probation being completed, all men will be judged by God, as to whether they have fulfilled the chief end or not. At a time appointed, all men that have ever lived will be gathered together on one great day of judgment: their bodies will be raised again from the dead and reunited to them: and on that day their condition for ever will be fixed.

54. Those who have pleased God by accepting his mercy in Christ will be taken to heaven. There they will receive the reward of everlasting happiness. They will not be absorbed into God, nor will they be sepa-

rated from matter. They will dwell with God for ever, in perfect happiness, exercising their various powers in the highest condition, contemplating the works of God, and the character of God; and always striving to please and obey Him. From this condition they will never remove.

55. Those who have not fulfilled their chief end, will each receive a punishment due to his sins in hell. There he will be confined, and there will he live for ever, in misery and despair unutterable.

56. This is the chief end of man, and this the way of attaining it. This is the effect of fulfilling it: and this the sad result of leaving it unaccomplished. May the grace of God help us to gain the former happy lot: and DELIVER us from the misery of the latter.

THE END.

# AUTHORITIES.

ANCIENT SANSKRIT LITERATURE: an Introduction to the Literature of the Vedas, by Professor Max Müller. London, 1859.

ESSAYS ON THE RELIGION AND PHILOSOPHY OF THE HINDUS, by H. T. Colebrooke, Esq. A new edition, in one Volume. Williams and Norgate, London. 1858.

THE SÁNKHYA KÁRIKÁ, translated by Mr. Colebrooke; with the Commentary of Gaurapáda, by Prof. H. H. Wilson. Oxford, 1837.

INTRODUCTION TO THE RIG VEDÁ SANHITÁ, by Prof. Wilson.

THE SUTRAS of Kopila, Part I.: of the YOGA, Parts I. and II.: the NYÁYA SUTRAS, two parts: the VAISESHIKA, Part I.; and the BRAHMA SUTRAS of Veda Vyása, Part I.; translated by Dr. Ballantyne; Benares.

THE BHAGAVAT GITÁ; translated, with Notes and an Introduction, by J. Cockburn Thomson, Esq. Hertford, 1855.

THE KATHA, MUNDAKA, Isa, Kena, Taittiriya, Aitareya, Swetaswatara, Prasna and Mandukya Upanishads: translated by Dr. Roer, Bibliotheca Indica, Nos. 41 and 50. Calcutta, 1852-3.

THE BHÁSHA PARICHHEDA: Categories of the Nyáya Philosophy; translated by Dr. Roer. Bib. Ind., Nos. 32 and 35.

THE TARKA SANGRAHA; Lectures on the Nyáya: translated by Dr. Ballantyne; Benares. 1852.

THE VEDÁNTA SARÁ; by Dr. Roer: Calcutta, 1845.

SANKARA; Sive de Theologumenis Vedanticorum; by Prof. Fr. H. Windischmann: Bonn, 1833.

Printed by SMITH, ELDER and Co., Little Green Arbonr Court, Old Bailey, E.C.

65, *Cornhill, London,*
*February,* 1860.

# CLASSIFIED CATALOGUE

OF

# NEW AND STANDARD WORKS

PUBLISHED BY

# SMITH, ELDER AND CO.

## CONTENTS.

# The Cornhill Magazine.

## *Edited by W. M. Thackeray.*

### Price One Shilling Monthly, with Illustrations.

*\** The Second Edition of No. 2, for February,* 1860, *making* 100,000, *is just published, and a New Edition of No.* 1, *making* 100,000, *is now ready.*

" It is a long time since any event unconnected with politics or battles has been so eagerly looked for as the appearance of the first number of the *Cornhill Magazine.* . . . . We offer a cordial and respectful welcome to the new comer from Cornhill, as one well fitted to take a place in the foremost rank of the serial literature of our country. The *Cornhill Magazine* makes a capital start. . . . . Every page in this opening number tells. Every page is marked with a distinctive superiority."—*Daily News.*

" The *Cornhill Magazine* will completely satisfy the expectations of the public. . . . . It is one of the marvels of the time that so much material, and of so good a quality, can be provided at so moderate a price."—*Morning Herald.*

" The first number of the *Cornhill Magazine* enters the world as one assured of a wide welcome. . . . . We heartily congratulate both editor and publishers on the brilliant success of the first number."—*Examiner.*

" Mr. Thackeray's venture has met with great and well-earned success."—*Athenæum.*

" We can see about this periodical higher promise than we have witnessed in any other enterprise for a long time."—*Press.*

" The *Cornhill Magazine* is at last in presence, and from its cover to its last page it is a model of the 'best.' . . . . The *Cornhill Magazine* at once takes as high a place in literature as its promoters could have desired."—*Literary Gazette.*

" We came to the perusal of the *Cornhill Magazine* with great expectations: it has surpassed them all. A new and glorious light has risen on the literary horizon."—*Illustrated News of the World.*

" It is obvious from the character of the articles, the reputation of the writers, the illustrations, paper, and press-work, that Messrs. Smith, Elder, and Co. intend the *Cornhill Magazine* to be one of the permanent institutions of the country. It is a marvel of cheapness, and a model of excellence."—*Notes and Queries.*

" It is almost impossible to imagine any further development, either in quality or quantity, of the periodical literature of this country than that which is attained in the new monthly serial issued from the house of Smith, Elder, and Co."—*Sunday Times.*

" The first number of the *Cornhill Magazine* has fulfilled the high anticipations which rumour had excited. It is a marvel of excellence and cheapness."—*Illustrated Times.*

" The first number of the *Cornhill Magazine* has made its appearance, and in the record of serial literature it has perhaps no rival in success."—*Liverpool Courier.*

" The *Cornhill Magazine* possesses the elements of success in a remarkable degree."—*Dublin Daily Express.*

# A New Romance.

*By Nathaniel Hawthorne,*

Author of the " Scarlet Letter," &c.   In 3 vols.

*[Nearly ready.*

# A Mother's Trials.

*By the Author of " My Lady."*

In three volumes.   *[Just ready.*

# A New Fiction.

*By Mrs. Gaskell.*

# A New Novel of English Life.

*By Sir Arthur Hallam Elton, Bart.,*

Author of " Below the Surface."   In 3 vols.

# A New Novel.

*By Mrs. Chanter,*

Author of " Ferny Combes."   2 vols.

# Isabel Grey:

Or, " The Mistress didn't Know."

Intended for all Mistresses of Households.

*By Mrs. Sewell.*

Author of " Homely Ballads."

Price 6*d.* cloth, gilt.

# A New Series of Stories in Verse.

*By Mrs. Sewell,*

Author of " Homely Ballads."

# The Book of Job in English Verse.

*By the Right Hon. the Earl of Winchilsea.*

A 2

# Voyages and Travels.

## A Visit to the Philippine Isles
in 1858-59.

### By Sir John Bowring,
Governor of Hong Kong, and H.M.'s Plenipotentiary in China.

Demy 8vo, with numerous Illustrations, price 18s. cloth.

"The work of Sir John Bowring on the Philippine Islands is exhaustive in scope, if not in substance. It does not pretend to set forth all that is known of the islands; but, in a series of condensed chapters, connected together by the author's reminiscences, presents a brilliant view of that rich region of sun and colour."—*Athenæum.*

"Anything coming from the pen of the ex-Governor of Hong Kong is entitled to a welcome and a hearing. He has brought back a fund of information of the utmost value, ranging over the four heads of history, politics, literature, and commerce. The information it contains is of the highest value. It is profusely illustrated."—*Morning Post.*

"This book upon the Philippine Islands is very welcome, because it describes a part of the world, about which very little is really known."—*Critic.*

## Life in Spain.
### By Walter Thornbury.
Two vols. post 8vo, with Eight Tinted Illustrations, price 21s.

"Two volumes of more entertaining and instructive matter are not discoverable in the literature of the day. They unite the charms of travel and romance."—*Leader.*

"Mr. Thornbury's book will be acceptable to a very large class of readers."—*Morning Post.*

"The book is to be recommended as a wholesome body of light reading, from which plenty of substantial knowledge may be gleaned."—*Examiner.*

"The sketches of character with which this volume abounds are amusing and effective."—*Morning Herald.*

## Heathen and Holy Lands;
Or, Sunny Days on the Salween, Nile, and Jordan.

### By Captain J. P. Briggs, Bengal Army.
Post 8vo, price 12s. cloth.

"Freshly and naturally written; the landscapes are graphic, and the personal anecdotes are adventurous."—*Daily News.*

"This volume has the peculiarity that it introduces us into the Holy Land from the other side of the world. . . . The Captain's descriptions are those of an eye-witness, and of a keenly observant one. They are admirably graphic, full of genuine enthusiasm, and of fine feeling."—*Illustrated News of the World.*

"It is seldom we meet with a book of travels so original as this."—*Leader.*

"This book is extremely well written, and its descriptions have a vigorous freshness about them which would reflect no discredit upon a much more 'practised' hand.—*Morning Herald.*

## Through Norway with a Knapsack.
### By W. M. Williams.
With Six Coloured Views.

Second Edition, post 8vo, price 12s., cloth.

"Mr. Williams will be an excellent guide to all who wish to travel as he did, on foot, and with the least possible expense. They may also place thorough reliance on all he says, his good sense never allowing his enthusiasm to dazzle him and delude his followers. It is a useful and trustworthy book."—*Athenæum.*

"The book is amusing; the author saw much that was new. There is frank graphic writing, and much pleasant thinking, in his volume, which is elegantly produced, and liberally illustrated with tinted views and woodcuts."—*Examiner.*

"'Through Norway with a Knapsack' is a work of intrinsic interest, very instructive and amusing. Mr. Williams is a model pedestrian traveller, and his book is the best guide we know of for those who intend to explore Norway on foot."—*Spectator.*

"A very instructive book on Norway, and the manners and customs of its inhabitants."—*Literary Gazette.*

"Every chapter of it will be read with interest."—*Morning Post.*

# Voyage to Japan,

Kamtschatka, Siberia, Tartary, and the Coast of China, in H.M.S.
*Barracouta.*

## By J. M. Tronson, R.N.

8vo, with Charts and Views.   18s. cloth.

"The able and intelligent officer, whose work is before us, supplies the first authentic information on the present state of Japan and the neighbouring settlements. . . . An extremely interesting book."—*Athenæum.*

"The book possesses all the qualities of a book of travels, with the prominent advantage of breaking comparatively, and in some instances altogether, new ground."—*Illustrated London News.*

"Mr. Tronson writes well, and imparts a great deal of new and useful information. The clear and beautiful charts and sketches, accompanying the volume, are of great value."—*Globe.*

"It contains a great deal that all the world ought now to know."—*Morning Herald.*

"We cordially recommend it."—*British Quarterly Review.*

---

# To Cuba and Back.

## By R. H. Dana,

Author of "Two Years before the Mast," &c.

### Post 8vo.  Price 7s. cloth.

"Mr. Dana's book is so bright and luscious, so pictorial and cheerful, so essentially pleasant and refreshing, that even the rule of a Spanish capitan-general appears tolerable where the subjects are so courteous, and the strangers so gracefully petted. Mr. Dana has a pen to paint such pictures well. His voyage and residence occupied scarcely a month, yet he has written a volume not only fascinating from its warmth and glitter as a narrative, but also intelligent, instructive, and of obvious integrity."—*Athenæum.*

"Mr. Dana does not spare his faculty of description. The pictures he gives of the Cuban metropolis itself, with its tropical luxuries and laziness, its dirty and dainty ways of existence, the Spanish grandiosity of its national manner, and the pettiness of its national character, are pleasantly and forcibly drawn. A coasting voyage to Matanzas, and a railroad journey, brought him into closer contact with the essential characteristics of the country and its history."—*Saturday Review.*

---

# Life and Liberty in America.

## By Dr. C. Mackay.

Second Edition, 2 vols. post 8vo, with Ten Tinted Illustrations,
price 21s.

"A bright, fresh, and hopeful book, worthy of the author, whose songs are oftenest heard on the Atlantic. Dr. Mackay writes as healthily as he sings; describing 'Life' as he saw it, and 'Liberty' as he studied it, in the North and in the South."—*Athenæum.*

"We recommend these volumes to perusal, as the result of careful and diligent observation, assisted by personal association, well calculated to facilitate the attainment of truth."—*Leader.*

"Dr. Mackay's volumes are eminently readable and amusing."—*Press.*

---

# Life in Tuscany.

## By Mabel Sharman Crawford.

With Two Views, post 8vo.  Price 10s. 6d. cloth.

"There are many traces of quiet, genial humour, brilliant and harmless as summer lightning, which agreeably relieve the more serious portions of the work. Miss Crawford's reflections are as sound and practical as her perceptions are lively

and acute, and she has succeeded in contributing a really valuable addition to that otherwise redundant department of literature."—*Press.*

"The peasant life in Tuscany has, perhaps, not been so well photographed before."—*Athenæum.*

# Narrative of the Mission

From the Governor-General of India to the Court of Ava in 1855.
With Notices of the Country, Government, and People.

## By Captain Henry Yule, Bengal Engineers.

Imperial 8vo, with Twenty-four Plates (Twelve coloured), Fifty Woodcuts, and Four Maps. Elegantly bound in cloth, with gilt edges. Price 2l. 12s. 6d.

"Captain Yule, in the preparation of the splendid volume before us, has availed himself of the labours of those who preceded him. To all who are desirous of possessing the best and fullest account that has ever been given to the public, of a great, and hitherto little known region of the globe, the interesting, conscientious, and well-written work of Captain Yule will have a deep interest, while to the political economist, geographer, and merchant, it will be indispensable."—*Examiner.*

"A stately volume in gorgeous golden covers. Such a book is in our times a rarity. Large, massive, and beautiful in itself, it is illustrated by a sprinkling of elegant woodcuts, and by a series of admirable tinted lithographs. . . . . We have read it with curiosity and gratification, as a fresh, full, and luminous report upon the condition of one of the most interesting divisions of Asia beyond the Ganges."—*Athenæum.*

# Hong Kong to Manilla.

## By Henry T. Ellis, R.N.

Post 8vo, with Fourteen Illustrations. Price 12s. cloth.

"The narrative fulfils the object of the author, which is to present a lively account of what he saw, heard, and did during a holiday run to a rarely visited place."—*Spectator.*

"Mr. Ellis has given to the public a most valuable and interesting work upon a race and country little known to English readers."—*Illustrated News of the World.*

# Antiquities of Kertch,

And Researches in the Cimmerian Bosphorus.

## By Duncan McPherson, M.D.,

Of the Madras Army, F.R.G.S., M.A.I.

Imperial 4to, with Fourteen Plates and numerous Illustrations, including Eight Coloured Fac-Similes of Reliques of Antique Art. Price Two Guineas.

"It is a volume which deserves the careful attention of every student of classical antiquity. No one can fail to be pleased with a work which has so much to attract the eye and to gratify the love of beauty and elegance in design. . . . ."

The book is got up with great care and taste, and forms one of the handsomest works that have recently issued from the English press."—*Saturday Review.*

# Captivity of Russian Princesses in the Caucasus.

## Translated from the Russian by H. S. Edwards.

With an authentic Portrait of Shamil, a Plan of his House, and a Map.
Post 8vo. Price 10s. 6d. cloth.

"A book than which there are few novels more interesting. It is a romance of the Caucasus. The account of life in the house of Shamil is full and very entertaining; and of Shamil himself we see much."—*Examiner.*
"The story is certainly one of the most curious

we have read; it contains the best popular notice of the social polity of Shamil and the manners of his people."—*Leader.*
"The narrative is well worth reading."—*Athenæum.*

# Biography.

## The Autobiography of Leigh Hunt.

Revised by Himself, with additional Chapters by his Eldest Son.

One vol., post 8vo, with a Portrait engraved on Steel from an Original Drawing. Price 7s. 6d. cloth.

"It is perhaps the first charm of an autobiography that it should make us like the writer; and certainly this is a charm which the 'Auto- | biography of Leigh Hunt' possesses in an unusual degree."—*Saturday Review.*

---

## Life of Schleiermacher,

As unfolded in his Autobiography and Letters.

*Translated from the German by Frederica Rowan.*

Two vols., post 8vo, with Portrait. Price One Guinea, cloth.

---

## Shelley Memorials.

### Edited by Lady Shelley.

Second Edition. In one vol., post 8vo. Price 7s. 6d. cloth.

"We welcome the present biography. It presents Shelley to us as he was understood by those who knew him best."—*Athenæum.*

"Lady Shelley touches with a reverent and loving hand, the incidents of the poet's career; and the gentleness, ardour, and truthfulness of his nature reappear in her unpretending pages. . . . . We gladly welcome this interesting volume."—*Daily News.*

"The present biography presents Shelley to us, as he was understood by those who knew him best."—*Leader.*

"The beauty of style and feeling, with which this work abounds, will make it acceptable to many."—*Saturday Review.*

"Lady Shelley's work is a real acquisition to the biographical literature of the day; it will be read with profound interest for its perspicuous and truthful delineation of some hitherto neglected traits in one of the most extraordinary characters that ever lived."—*Illustrated News of the World.*

"We heartily recommend it to our readers."—*Critic.*

---

## The Life of Charlotte Brontë

(CURRER BELL).

Author of "Jane Eyre," "Shirley," "Villette," &c.

### By Mrs. Gaskell.

Author of "North and South," &c.

Fourth Edition, revised, one vol., with a Portrait of Miss Brontë and a View of Haworth Parsonage. Price 7s. 6d.; morocco elegant, 14s.

"All the secrets of the literary workmanship of the authoress of 'Jane Eyre' are unfolded in the course of this extraordinary narrative."—*Times.*

"Mrs. Gaskell's account of Charlotte Brontë and her family is one of the profoundest tragedies of modern life."—*Spectator.*

"Mrs. Gaskell has produced one of the best biographies of a woman by a woman which we can recall to mind."—*Athenæum.*

"If any one wishes to see how a woman possessed of the highest intellectual power can disregard every temptation which intellect throws in the way of women—how generously and nobly a human being can live under the pressure of accumulated misfortune—the record is at hand in 'The Life of Charlotte Brontë.'"—*Saturday Review.*

"Mrs. Gaskell has done her work well. Her narrative is simple, direct, intelligible, unaffected. No one else could have paid so tender and discerning a tribute to the memory of Charlotte Brontë.'"—*Fraser's Magazine.*

# Life of Lord Metcalfe.

## By John William Kaye.

New Edition, in Two vols., post 8vo, with Portrait. Price 12s. cloth.

"A work which occupies the highest rank among biographies of the great men of modern times."—*Observer.*

"The new edition contains new matter of the utmost value and interest."—*Critic.*

"One of the most valuable biographies of the present day. This revised edition has several fresh passages of high interest, now first inserted from among Lord Metcalfe's papers, in which his clear prescience of the dangers that threatened our Indian empire is remarkably shown."—*Economist.*

"This edition is revised with care and judgment. Mr. Kaye has judiciously set forth Lord Metcalfe's views of the insecurity of our Indian empire."—*Globe.*

"A much improved edition of one of the most interesting political biographies in English literature."—*National Review.*

---

# Life of Sir John Malcolm, G.C.B.

## By John William Kaye.

Two vols. 8vo, with Portrait. Price 36s. cloth.

" The biography is replete with interest and information, deserving to be perused by the student of Indian history, and sure to recommend itself to the general reader."—*Athenæum.*

"One of the most interesting of the recent biographies of our great Indian statesmen."—*National Review.*

"This book deserves to participate in the popularity which it was the good fortune of Sir John Malcolm to enjoy."—*Edinburgh Review.*

"Mr. Kaye's biography is at once a contribution to the history of our policy and dominion in the East, and a worthy memorial of one of those wise and large-hearted men whose energy and principle have made England great."—*British Quarterly Review.*

---

# The Life of J. Deacon Hume.

## By the Rev. Charles Badham.

Post 8vo. Price 9s. cloth.

" A masterly piece of biographical narrative. To minute and conscientious industry in searching out facts, Mr. Badham conjoins the attractions of a graceful style and a sincere liking for the task he has in hand. He has produced one of the most useful and judicious biographies extant in our literature, peculiarly full of beauties, and peculiarly free from faults."—*Atlas.*

" It is well that the world's attention should be called to such a man, and that the particulars of his character and career should be preserved in a biography."—*Spectator.*

---

# The Life of Mahomet

And History of Islam to the Era of the Hegira.

## By William Muir, Esq., Bengal Civil Service.

Volumes 1 and 2. 8vo. Price 32s. cloth.

"The most perfect life of Mahomet in the English language, or perhaps in any other. . . . The work is at once learned and interesting, and it cannot fail to be eagerly perused by all persons having any pretensions to historical knowledge."—*Observer.*

---

# The Autobiography of Lutfullah,

A Mohamedan Gentleman; with an Account of his Visit to England.

## Edited by E. B. Eastwick, Esq.

Third Edition, small post 8vo. Price 5s. cloth.

"This is the freshest and most original work that it has been our good fortune to meet with for long. It bears every trace of being a most genuine account of the feelings and doings of the author. Lutfullah is by no means an ordinary specimen of his race."—*Economist.*

"Read fifty volumes of travel, and a thousand imitations of the Oriental novel, and you will not get the flavour of Eastern life and thought, or the zest of its romance, so perfectly as in Lutfullah's book."—*Leader.*

# Art.

## WORKS OF MR. RUSKIN.

# The Elements of Perspective.

### With 80 Diagrams, crown 8vo. Price 3s. 6d. cloth.

"Mr. Ruskin, seeing the want of a clear and accurate code on the subject, has set himself to the task of arranging and explaining the necessary rules in a form as nearly approaching the ideal of a popular treatise as can be managed consistently with the object of practical completeness. No better way of blending the two purposes could, we believe, have been found than the way Mr. Ruskin ingeniously discovered and has ably worked out. A careful perusal of the work will enable the intelligent student not only to solve perspective problems of a complexity greater than the ordinary rules will reach, but to obtain a clue to many important laws of pictorial effect less than of outline."—*Daily News.*

"This book, provided by Mr. Ruskin for the use of schools, bears its recommendation on the title-page. The rules are arranged in a short mathematical form, which will be intelligible to students reasonably advanced in general knowledge."—*Leader.*

"The student will find in this little book all that is necessary to lay the foundation of a thorough scientific knowledge of perspective."—*Illustrated News of the World.*

"To the practical student it is likely to prove a most valuable manual."—*Literary Gazette.*

# The Elements of Drawing.

### Sixth Thousand, crown 8vo, with Illustrations drawn by the Author. Price 7s. 6d. cloth.

"The rules are clearly and fully laid down; and the earlier exercises always conducive to the end by simple and unembarrassing means. The whole volume is full of liveliness."—*Spectator.*

"We close this book with a feeling that, though nothing supersedes a master, yet that no student of art should launch forth without this work as a compass."—*Athenæum.*

"It will be found not only an invaluable acquisition to the student, but agreeable and instructive reading for any one who wishes to refine his perceptions of natural scenery, and of its worthiest artistic representations."—*Economist.*

"Original as this treatise is, it cannot fail to be at once instructive and suggestive."—*Literary Gazette.*

"The most useful and practical book on the subject which has ever come under our notice."—*Press.*

# Modern Painters.

**Vol. I., 6th Edition. Price 18s. cloth. Imperial 8vo.**

**Vol. II., 4th Edition. Price 10s. 6d. cloth.**

**Vol. III. OF MANY THINGS, with Eighteen Illustrations drawn by the Author, and engraved on Steel. Price 38s. cloth.**

**Vol. IV. ON MOUNTAIN BEAUTY. Imperial 8vo, with Thirty-five Illustrations engraved on Steel, and 116 Woodcuts, drawn by the Author. Price 2l. 10s. cloth.**

"A generous and impassioned review of the works of living painters. A hearty and earnest work, full of deep thought, and developing great and striking truths in art."—*British Quarterly Review.*

"Mr. Ruskin's work will send the painter more than ever to the study of nature; will train men who have always been delighted spectators of nature, to be also attentive observers. Our critics will learn to admire, and mere admirers will learn how to criticise: thus a public will be educated."—*Blackwood's Magazine.*

"Every one who cares about nature, or poetry, or the story of human development—every one who has a tinge of literature or philosophy, will find something that is for him in these volumes."—*Westminster Review.*

"Mr. Ruskin is in possession of a clear and penetrating mind; he is undeniably practical in his fundamental ideas; full of the deepest reverence for all that appears to him beautiful and holy. His style is, as usual, clear, bold, racy. Mr. Ruskin is one of the first writers of the day."—*Economist.*

"All, it is to be hoped, will read the book for themselves. They will find it well worth a careful perusal."—*Saturday Review.*

"Mr. Ruskin is the most eloquent and thought-awakening writer on nature in its relation with art, and the most potent influence by the pen, of young artists, whom this country can boast."—*National Review.*

"This work is eminently suggestive, full of new thoughts, of brilliant descriptions of scenery, and eloquent moral application of them."—*New Quarterly Review.*

"Mr. Ruskin has deservedly won for himself a place in the first rank of modern writers upon the theory of the fine arts."—*Eclectic Review.*

"The fourth volume of Mr. Ruskin's elaborate work treats chiefly of mountain scenery, and discusses at length the principles involved in the pleasure we derive from mountains and their pictorial representation. The singular beauty of his style, the hearty sympathy with all forms of natural loveliness, the profusion of his illustrations form irresistible attractions."—*Daily News.*

"Considered as an illustrated volume, the fourth is the most remarkable which Mr. Ruskin has yet issued. The plates and woodcuts are profuse, and include numerous drawings of mountain form by the author, which prove Mr. Ruskin to be essentially an artist. He is an unique man, both among artists and writers."—*Spectator.*

"Such a writer is a national possession. He adds to our store of knowledge and enjoyment."—*Leader.*

# The Two Paths :

Being Lectures on Art, and its relation to Manufactures and Decoration.

One vol., crown 8vo, with Two Steel Engravings. Price 7s. 6d. cloth.

"The meaning of the title of this book is, that there are two courses open to the artist, one of which will lead him to all that is noble in art, and will incidentally exalt his moral nature; while the other will deteriorate his work and help to throw obstacles in the way of his individual morality. . . . They all contain many useful distinctions, acute remarks, and valuable suggestions, and are everywhere lit up with that glow of fervid eloquence which has so materially contributed to the author's reputation."—*Press*.

"The 'Two Paths' contains much eloquent description, places in a clear light some forgotten or neglected truths, and, like all Mr. Ruskin's books, is eminently suggestive."—*Literary Gazette*.

"This book is well calculated to encourage the humblest worker, and stimulate him to artistic effort."—*Leader*.

# The Stones of Venice.

Complete in Three Volumes, Imperial 8vo, with Fifty-three Plates and numerous Woodcuts, drawn by the Author. Price 5l. 15s. 6d. cloth.

### EACH VOLUME MAY BE HAD SEPARATELY.

Vol. I. THE FOUNDATIONS, with 21 Plates. Price 2l. 2s. 2nd Edition.
Vol. II. THE SEA STORIES, with 20 Plates. Price 2l. 2s.
Vol. III. THE FALL, with 12 Plates. Price 1l. 11s. 6d.

"The 'Stones of Venice' is the production of an earnest, religious, progressive, and informed mind. The author of this essay on architecture has condensed it into a poetic apprehension, the fruit of awe of God, and delight in nature; a knowledge, love, and just estimate of art; a holding fast to fact and repudiation of hearsay; an historic breadth, and a fearless challenge of existing social problems, whose union we know not where to find paralleled."—*Spectator*.

"This book is one which, perhaps, no other man could have written, and one for which the world ought to be and will be thankful. It is in the highest degree eloquent, acute, stimulating to thought, and fertile in suggestion. It will, we are convinced, elevate taste and intellect, raise the tone of moral feeling, kindle benevolence towards men, and increase the love and fear of God."—*Times*.

# The Seven Lamps of Architecture.

Second Edition, with Fourteen Plates drawn by the Author. Imp. 8vo.
Price 1l. 1s. cloth.

"By 'The Seven Lamps of Architecture,' we understand Mr. Ruskin to mean the Seven fundamental and cardinal laws, the observance of and obedience to which are indispensable to the architect, who would deserve the name. The politician, the moralist, the divine, will find in it ample store of instructive matter, as well as the artist. The author of this work belongs to a class of thinkers of whom we have too few amongst us."—*Examiner*.

# Lectures on Architecture and Painting.

With Fourteen Cuts, drawn by the Author. Second Edition, crown 8vo.
Price 8s. 6d. cloth.

"Mr. Ruskin's lectures—eloquent, graphic, and impassioned—exposing and ridiculing some of the vices of our present system of building, and exciting his hearers by strong motives of duty and pleasure to attend to architecture—are very successful."—*Economist*.

"We conceive it to be impossible that any intelligent person could listen to the lectures, however they might differ from the judgments asserted and from the general propositions laid down, without an elevating influence and an aroused enthusiasm."—*Spectator*.

# The Political Economy of Art.

Price 2s. 6d. cloth.

"A most able, eloquent, and well-timed work. We hail it with satisfaction, thinking it calculated to do much practical good, and we cordially recommend it to our readers."—*Witness*.

"We never quit Mr. Ruskin without being the better for what he has told us, and therefore we recommend this little volume, like all his other works, to the perusal of our readers."—*Economist*

"This book, daring as it is, glances keenly at principles, of which some are among the articles of ancient codes, while others are evolving slowly to the light."—*Leader*.

# Religious.

---

# Expositions of St. Paul's Epistles to the Corinthians.

### By the late Rev. Fred. W. Robertson.

One thick Volume, post 8vo. Price 10s. 6d. cloth.

"These lectures were the last discourses that Mr. Robertson ever delivered from his pulpit. High as is the standard of thoughtfulness and originality which we expect in everything that comes from the pen of this preacher, these pages are not unworthy of that high standard. This single volume in itself would establish a reputation for its writer."

---

# Sermons :

### By the late Rev. Fred. W. Robertson, A.M.,

Incumbent of Trinity Chapel, Brighton.

FIRST SERIES.—Seventh Edition, post 8vo. Price 9s. cloth.
SECOND SERIES.—Seventh Edition. Price 9s. cloth.
THIRD SERIES.—Fifth Edition, post 8vo, with Portrait. Price 9s. cloth.

"There are many persons, and their number increases every year, to whom Robertson's writings are the most stable, exhaustless, and satisfactory form of religious teaching which the nineteenth century has given—the most wise, suggestive, and practical."—*Saturday Review.*
"There must be a great and true heart, where there is a great and true preacher. And in that, beyond everything else, lay the secret of Mr. Robertson's influence. We feel that a brother man is speaking to us as brother men; that we are listening, not to the measured words of a calm, cool thinker, but to the passionate deep-toned voice of an earnest human soul."—*Edinburgh Christian Magazine.*

"These sermons are full of thought and beauty. There is not a sermon in the series that does not furnish evidence of originality without extravagance, of discrimination without tediousness, and of piety without cant or conventionalism."—*British Quarterly.*
"We recommend the whole of the volumes to the perusal of our readers. They will find in them thought of a rare and beautiful description, an earnestness of mind steadfast in the search of truth, and a charity pure and all-embracing."—*Economist.*
"They are very remarkable compositions. The thoughts are often very striking, and entirely out of the track of ordinary sermonising."—*Guardian.*

---

# Quakerism, Past and Present :

Being an Inquiry into the Causes of its Decline.

### By John S. Rowntree.

Post 8vo. Price 5s. cloth.

\*\*\* This Essay gained the First Prize of One Hundred Guineas offered for the best Essay on the subject.

---

# The Peculium :

An Essay on the Causes of the Decline of the Society of Friends.

### By Thomas Hancock.

Post 8vo. Price 5s. cloth.

\*\*\* This Essay gained the Second Prize of Fifty Guineas, which was afterwards increased to One Hundred.

## Miscellaneous.

# On the Strength of Nations.

### By Andrew Bisset, M.A.

#### Post 8vo.　　Price 9s. cloth.

" We can safely recommend the perusal of this work to all who have not maturely considered the subject. It will set them thinking in the right direction."—*Daily News.*

" Frequent concurrence with him, and general sympathy with his views, even where we do not accept his principles, dispose us to recommend Mr. Bisset's book for perusal."—*Spectator.*

" Mr. Bisset has dealt with this important subject in a way that will be equally acceptable to the scholar and the true economist."—*Morning Star.*

" We commend most heartily Mr. Bisset's able volume."—*Examiner.*

" A work exhibiting considerable research; many of the author's views will be found correct, and valuable at the present moment."—*Literary Gazette.*

# Social Innovators and their Schemes.

### By William Lucas Sargant.

#### Post 8vo.　　Price 10s. 6d. cloth.

" Mr. Sargant has written a very useful sketch. His book is impartial, pleasantly written, and excellently arranged."—*Saturday Review.*

" It has the merit of going deep into the subject matter at one of its most vital points; and it is this merit that constitutes the special value of Mr. Sargant's book. His views are sensible and sound, they are brought forward clearly and dispassionately, with quiet vigour and telling illustration."—*Press.*

# Lectures and Addresses.

### By the late Rev. Fred. W. Robertson.

#### Post 8vo.　　Price 7s. 6d. cloth.

" These lectures and addresses are marked by the same qualities that made the author's sermons so justly and so widely popular. They manifest the same earnest, liberal spirit, the ardent love of truth, the lucid eloquence, the wide sympathy, and singleness of purpose."—*Lit. Gaz.*

" They throw some new light on the constitution of Robertson's mind, and on the direction in which it was unfolding itself."—*Saturday Review.*

" In these addresses we are gladdened by rare liberality of view and range of sympathy boldly expressed."—*Daily Telegraph.*

# The Education of the Human Race.

### Now first Translated from the German of Lessing.

#### Fcap. 8vo, antique cloth.　　Price 4s.

" An agreeable and flowing translation of one of Lessing's finest Essays."—*National Review.*

" The Essay makes quite a gem in its English form."—*Westminster Review.*

" This invaluable tract."—*Critic.*

" A little book on a great subject, and one which, in its day, exerted no slight influence upon European thought."—*Inquirer.*

# William Burke the Author of Junius.

### By Jelinger C. Symons.

#### Square.　　Price 3s. 6d. cloth.

" A week's reflection, and a second reading of Mr. Symons's book, have strengthened our conviction that he has proved his case."—*Spectator.*

" By diligently comparing the letters of Junius with the private correspondence of Edmund Burke, he has elicited certain parallel passages of which it is impossible to evade the significance."—*Literary Gazette.*

# The Oxford Museum.

### By Henry W. Acland, M.D., and John Ruskin, A.M.

#### Post 8vo, with Three Illustrations.　　Price 2s. 6d. cloth.

" Every one who cares for the advance of true learning, and desires to note an onward step, should buy and read this little volume."—*Morning Herald.*

" There is as much significance in the occasion of this little volume as interest in the book itself."—*Spectator.*

# India and the East.

## Christianity in India.

### By John William Kaye.

8vo. Price 16s. cloth.

"Mr. Kaye has written a history of the development of Christianity in India by all its agencies and all its manifestations. . . . His whole narrative is eloquent and informing, and he has again made a valuable use of his great opportunities and indisputable talents, so that his book will probably become a standard authority."—*Times.*

"The author traces the history of Christian Missions in India from their earliest commencement down to the present time, with a light and graceful pen, and is not wearisomely minute, but judiciously discriminative."—*Athenæum.*

"Mr. Kaye's is, in many respects, an able book and it is likely to prove a very useful one. Mr. Kaye is not only most instructive from his familiarity with all points of detail, but he sees and judges everything as it was seen and judged by the great statesmen whose wisdom has made British government possible in India."—*Saturday Review.*

---

## District Duties during the Revolt
### In the North-West Provinces of India.

### By H. Dundas Robertson, Bengal Civil Service.

Post 8vo, with a Map. Price 9s. cloth.

"To all who desire interesting information on India we commend this volume."—*Athenæum.*

"An exceedingly valuable book, of vital interest to the empire of Britain in the East."—*Illustrated News of the World.*

"Mr. Robertson has opinions of his own, and expresses them with point and clearness, on many disputed questions connected with the revolt."—*Economist.*

"Few men have such a tale of hardship, endurance, and peril to relate, and few men are better calculated to do it justice."—*Morning Post.*

---

## Narrative of the Mutinies in Oude.
### By Captain G. Hutchinson,
Military Secretary, Oude.
Published by Authority. Post 8vo. Price 10s. cloth.

---

## Campaigning Experiences
In Rajpootana and Central India during the Suppression of the Mutiny in 1857-8.

### By Mrs. Henry Duberly,
Author of a "Journal kept during the Russian War."

Post 8vo, with Map. Price 10s. 6d. cloth.

"Mrs. Duberly has produced a very readable and even amusing volume. Indeed, it is not easy to lay it aside when once opened, and there can be little doubt that it will attain a considerable circulation."—*Press.*

"Mrs. Duberly's 'Campaigning Experiences' is a pleasant, chatty, little volume."—*Critic.*

---

## Papers of the late Lord Metcalfe.

### By John William Kaye.

Demy 8vo. Price 16s. cloth.

"We commend this volume to all persons who like to study State papers, in which the practical sense of a man of the world is joined to the speculative sagacity of a philosophical statesman. No Indian library should be without it."—*Press.*

𝔍𝔫𝔡𝔦𝔞 𝔞𝔫𝔡 𝔱𝔥𝔢 𝔢𝔞𝔰𝔱—*continued.*

# The English in Western India:

Being the Early History of the Factory at Surat, of Bombay.

## By Philip Anderson, A.M.

Second Edition, 8vo. Price 14s. cloth.

" Quaint, curious, and amusing, this volume describes, from old manuscripts and obscure books, the life of English merchants in an Indian Factory. It contains fresh and amusing gossip, | all bearing on events and characters of historic importance."—*Athenæum.* "A book of permanent value."—*Guardian.*

# Life in Ancient India.

## By Mrs. Spier.

With Sixty Illustrations by G. SCHARF.

8vo. Price 15s., elegantly bound in cloth, gilt edges.

"Whoever desires to have the best, the completest, and the most popular view of what Oriental scholars have made known to us respecting Ancient India must peruse the work of Mrs. | Speir; in which he will find the story told in clear, correct, and unaffected English. The book is admirably got up."—*Examiner.*

# The Parsees :

Their History, Religion, Manners, and Customs.

## By Dosabhoy Framjee.

Post 8vo. Price 10s. cloth.

"Our author's account of the inner life of the Parsees will be read with interest."—*Daily News.* "A very curious and well-written book, by a young Parsee, on the manners and customs of his own race."—*National Review.* | "An acceptable addition to our literature. It gives information which many will be glad to have carefully gathered together, and formed into a shapely whole."—*Economist.*

# Tiger Shooting in India.

## By Lieutenant William Rice,

25th Bombay N.I.

Super-royal 8vo. With Twelve Plates in Chromo-lithography. 10s. 6d. cloth.

"These adventures, told in handsome large print, with spirited chromo-lithographs to illustrate them, make the volume before us as pleasant | reading as any record of sporting achievements we have ever taken in hand."—*Athenæum.*

# Indian Scenes and Characters

## By Prince Alexis Soltykoff.

Sixteen Plates in Tinted Lithography, with Descriptions.

Edited by E. B. EASTWICK, Esq., F.R.S.

Colombier folio. Prints, 10s.; proofs (only Fifty Copies printed), 15s.

# Naval and Military.

## England and her Soldiers.
### By Harriet Martineau.

With Three Plates of Illustrative Diagrams.   1 vol, crown 8vo,
price 9s. cloth.

"The purpose with which Miss Martineau has written about England and her soldiers is purely practical, and equally so is the manner in which she has treated the subject. There is not in her whole volume one line of invective against individuals or classes. No candid reader can deny that this effort has been made opportunely, ably, and discreetly."—*Spectator.*

"The book is remarkable for the clear, comprehensive way in which the subject is treated. Great credit is due to Miss Martineau for having so compactly, so spiritedly, with so much truth of detail, and at the same time so much force, placed the matter before the public in this interesting and well-timed volume."—*Shipping and Mercantile Gazette.*

"Miss Martineau has worked out her subject with courage, power, and conscientiousness. Faithful in fact and rich in suggestion, she has given us in this volume a very valuable addition to our present store of knowledge as the conduct and condition of the Crimean troops."—*Literary Gazette.*

## Narrative of the Siege of Delhi.
### By the Rev. J. E. W. Rotton,
Chaplain to the Delhi Field Force.

Post 8vo, with a Plan of the City and Siege Works.
Price 10s. 6d. cloth.

"A simple and touching statement, which bears the impress of truth in every word. It supplies some of those personal anecdotes and minute details which bring the events home to the understanding."—*Athenæum.*

"'The Chaplain's Narrative' is remarkable for its pictures of men in a moral and religious aspect, during the progress of a harassing siege and when suddenly stricken down by the enemy or disease."—*Spectator.*

## The Defence of Lucknow:
### By Captain Thomas F. Wilson, 13th Bengal N.I.
Assistant Adjutant-General.

Sixth Thousand.   With Plan.   Small post 8vo.   Price 2s. 6d.

"The Staff-Officer's Diary is simple and brief, and has a special interest, inasmuch as it gives a fuller account than we have elsewhere seen of those operations which were the chief human means of salvation to our friends in Lucknow.

The Staff-Officer brings home to us, by his details, the nature of that underground contest, upon the result of which the fate of the beleaguered garrison especially depended."—*Examiner.*

## Eight Months' Campaign against the Bengal Sepoys during the Mutiny,
### 1857.
### By Colonel George Bourchier, C.B.
Bengal Horse Artillery.

With Plans.   Post 8vo.   Price 7s. 6d. cloth.

"Col. Bourchier describes the various operations with a modest forgetfulness of self, as pleasing and as rare as the clear manly style in which they are narrated."—*Literary Gazette.*

"Col. Bourchier has given a right manly, fair, and forcible statement of events, and the reader will derive much pleasure and instruction from his pages."—*Athenæum.*

# 𝔏egal.

---

## Annals of British Legislation :
### A Classified Summary of Parliamentary Papers.

### *Edited by Leone Levi.*

The yearly issue consists of 1,000 pages, super-royal 8vo, and the Subscription is Two Guineas, payable in advance. The Thirty-fifth Part is just issued, commencing the Third Year's Issue. Vols. I. to IV. may be had. Price 4*l*. 4*s*. cloth.

"A series that will, if it be always managed as it now is by Professor Levi, last as long as there remains a Legislature in Great Britain. These Annals are to give the essence of work done and information garnered for the State during each legislative year, a summary description of every Act passed, a digest of the vital facts contained in every Blue Book issued, and of all documents relating to the public business of the country. The series will live, while generations of men die, if it be maintained in its old age as ably and as conscientiously as it is now in its youth."—*Examiner.*

"The idea was admirable, nor does the execution fall short of the plan. To accomplish this effectively, and at the same time briefly, was not an easy task; but Professor Levi has undertaken it with great success. The work is essentially a guide. It will satisfy those persons who refer to it merely for general purposes, while it will direct the research of others whose investigations take a wider range."—*Athenæum.*

---

## A Handbook of Average.
### With a Chapter on Arbitration.

### *By Manley Hopkins.*

Second Edition, Revised and brought down to the present time. 8vo. Price 15*s*. cloth ; 17*s*. 6*d*. half-bound law calf.

---

## Manual of the Mercantile Law
### Of Great Britain and Ireland.

### *By Leone Levi, Esq.*

### 8vo. Price 12*s*. cloth.

" It is sound, clear, and practical. . . . Its contents are strictly those of a manual—a hand-book for law chambers, offices, and counting-houses; requisite in most of such places, and superfluous in none."—*Athenæum.*

"Its simplicity and faithfulness make it an extremely serviceable book."—*Examiner.*
"An admirable work of the kind."—*Law Times.*
"It presents a fair summary of the law on the great subject of which it treats."—*Law Magazine.*

---

## Laws of War
### Affecting Commerce and Shipping.

### *By H. Byerly Thomson.*

### Second Edition, greatly enlarged. 8vo. Price 4*s*. 6*d*. boards.

"Mr. Thomson treats of the immediate effects of war; of enemies and hostile property; of prizes and privateers; of license, ransom, re-capture, and salvage of neutrality, contraband of war, blockade, right of search, armed neutralities, &c., &c."—*Economist.*

B

# Fiction.

# Against Wind and Tide.

### By Holme Lee,
#### Author of "Sylvan Holt's Daughter." 3 vols.

"The reputation which 'Kathie Brande' and 'Sylvan Holt's Daughter' won for their author will be crowned by 'Against Wind and Tide.' A more charming novel has not proceeded of late years from the press."—*Morning Herald.*

"This novel is by many degrees the best specimen of fiction that has been placed in our hands."—*Literary Gazette.*

"This is one of the few good novels that deserve permanent life."—*Examiner.*

"Full of animated scenes and rich in clever description."—*Press.*

"To all who appreciate a powerfully concentrated work, this one may be fairly recommended."—*Sun.*

# The Cousins' Courtship.

### By John R. Wise.
#### Two vols.       [*Now ready.*

"The 'Cousins' Courtship' is a kind of prose idyll, in which an earnest, pure, simple love is developed without any hysterical romance. To a decided talent for satirical illustration and comment, Mr. Wise unites a nice observation, delicate reflections, and a sympathy for what is beautiful. Its cleverness, its genial tone, its playful satire, its scholarly yet perfectly easy and natural language, with its vivid portraiture of scenery, entitle the 'Cousins' Courtship' to a grateful recognition."—*Spectator.*

"We are well pleased with Mr. Wise's novel. Those who begin to read the 'Cousin's Courtship' will finish it. We rarely meet with one possessed of so many good qualities."—*Morning Post.*

"A very clever novel: it possesses some excellent qualities. The merits of the book are great. It is thoroughly true: we take it, indeed, that it is a collection of personal experiences. Mr. Wise can fairly lay claim to the merit of vivid and powerful description of what he has seen."—*Morning Herald.*

# The Fool of Quality.

### By Henry Brooke.
New and Revised Edition, with Biographical Preface by the Rev. C. KINGSLEY, Rector of Eversley.

#### Two vols, post 8vo, with Portrait of the Author, price 21s.

"If the 'Fool of Quality' be perused with reference to the period at which it was written, as well as from its author's point of view, and if it be considered as the earnest, heartfelt production of an accomplished gentleman and a sincere philanthropist, whose life was devoted to efforts to do good, its excellences, which are many, will be admitted."—*Illustrated London News.*

# Phantastes :

### A Faerie Romance for Men and Women.
### By George Macdonald.
#### Post 8vo.    Price 10s. 6d. cloth.

"The work is one which will form a source of agreeable reading to many. It is replete with wild imagery, strange flights of fancy, and beautiful descriptions of nature."—*Daily Telegraph.*

"The whole book is instinct with poetry, with delicate perception of the hidden emotions of the soul, with thought, and with ideal truth. The story is in fact a parable—an allegory of human life, its temptations and its sorrows."—*Literary Gazette.*

# Esmond.

### By W. M. Thackeray.
A New Edition, being the third, in 1 vol. crown 8vo. Price 6s. cloth.

"The book has the great charm of reality. Queen Anne's colonel writes his life—and a very interesting life it is—just as a Queen Anne's colonel might be supposed to have written it, Mr. Thackeray has selected for his hero a very noble type of the cavalier softening into the man of the eighteenth century, and for his heroine, one of the sweetest women that ever breathed from canvas or from book since Raffaelle painted and Shakspeare wrote."—*Spectator.*

"Once more we feel that we have before us a masculine and thoroughly English writer, uniting the power of subtle analysis, with a strong volition and a moving eloquence—an eloquence which has gained in richness and harmony. 'Esmond' must be read, not for its characters, but for its romantic plot, its spirited grouping, and its many thrilling utterances of the anguish of the human heart."—*Athenæum.*

# Recent Publications.

## VOYAGES AND TRAVELS.

### Visit to Salt Lake.

Being a Journey across the Plains to the Mormon Settlements at Utah.

*By William Chandless.*

Post 8vo, with a Map. 2s. 6d. cloth.

" Mr. Chandless is an impartial observer of the Mormons. He gives a full account of the nature of the country, the religion of the Mormons, their government, institutions, morality, and the singular relationship of the sexes, with its consequences."—*Critic.*

"Those who would understand what Mormonism is can do no better than read this authentic, though light and lively volume."—*Leader.*

" It impresses the reader as faithful."—*National Review.*

### Memorandums in Ireland.

*By Sir John Forbes.*

Two vols. post 8vo. Price 1l. 1s. cloth.

### The Argentine Provinces.

*By William McCann, Esq.*

Two vols. post 8vo, with Illustrations. Price 24s. cloth.

### Germany and the Tyrol.

*By Sir John Forbes.*

Post 8vo, with Map and View. Price 10s. 6d. cloth.

" Sir John Forbes' volume fully justifies its title. Wherever he went he visited sights, and has rendered a faithful and extremely interesting account of them."—*Literary Gazette.*

### The Red River Settlement.

*By Alexander Ross.*

One vol. post 8vo. Price 5s. cloth.

" The subject is novel, curious, and not without interest, while a strong sense of the real obtains throughout."—*Spectator.*

"The history of the Red River Settlement is remarkable, if not unique, among colonial records."—*Literary Gazette.*

"One of the most interesting of the romances of civilization."—*Observer.*

### Fur Hunters of the West.

*By Alexander Ross.*

Two vols. post 8vo, with Map and Plate. Price 10s. 6d. cloth.

" A well-written narrative of most exciting adventures."—*Guardian.*

"A narrative full of incident and dangerous adventure."—*Literary Gazette.*

### Campaign in Asia.

*By Charles Duncan, Esq.*

Post 8vo. Price 2s. 6d. cloth.

### The Columbia River.

*By Alexander Ross.*

Post 8vo. Price 2s. 6d. cloth.

### Travels in Assam.

*By Major John Butler.*

One vol. 8vo, with Plates. 12s. cloth.

## BIOGRAPHY.

### Life of Sir Robert Peel.

*By Thomas Doubleday.*

Two vols. 8vo. Price 18s. cloth.

### Women of Christianity

Exemplary for Piety and Charity.

*By Julia Kavanagh.*

Post 8vo, with Portraits. Price 5s. in embossed cloth.

### Woman in France.

*By Julia Kavanagh.*

Two vols. post 8vo, with Portraits. Price 12s. cloth.

### The Novitiate;

Or, the Jesuit in Training.

*By Andrew Steinmetz.*

Third Edition, post 8vo. 2s. 6d. cloth.

# RELIGIOUS.

## Historic Notes

On the Old and New Testament.
*By Samuel Sharpe.*
Third and Revised Edition. Post 8vo.
Price 7s. cloth.

"An inestimable aid to the clergyman, reader, city missionary, and Sunday-school teacher."
—*Illustrated News of the World.*
"A learned and sensible book."—*National Review.*

## Tauler's Life and Sermons.

*Translated by Miss Susanna Winkworth.*
With a Preface by the Rev. CHARLES KINGSLEY.
Small 4to, printed on Tinted Paper, and bound in Antique Style, with red edges, suitable for a Present.
Price 7s. 6d.

"Miss Winkworth has done a service, not only to church history and to literature, but to those who seek simple and true-hearted devotional reading, or who desire to kindle their own piety through the example of saintly men, by producing a very instructive, complete, and deeply interesting life of Tauler, and by giving to us also a sample of Tauler's sermons tastefully and vigorously translated."—*Guardian.*
"No difference of opinion can be felt as to the intrinsic value of these sermons, or the general interest attaching to this book. The Sermons are well selected, and the translation excellent."
—*Athenæum.*

## Signs of the Times;

Or, The Dangers to Religious Liberty in the Present Day.
*By Chevalier Bunsen.*
Translated by Miss SUSANNA WINKWORTH.
One vol. 8vo. Price 5s. cloth.

"Dr. Bunsen is doing good service, not only to his country but to Christendom, by sounding an alarm touching the dangers to religious liberty in the present state of the world."—*British Quarterly.*

## Testimony to the Truth of Christianity.

Fourth Edition, fcap 8vo. 3s. cloth.

## Sermons on the Church.

*By the Rev. R. W. Evans.*
8vo. Price 10s. 6d.

## Sermons.

*By the Rev. C. B. Taylor.*
Author of "Records of a Good Man's Life."
12mo. Price 1s. 6d.

# MISCELLANEOUS.

## Goethe's Conversations with Eckermann.

*Translated by John Oxenford.*
Two vols. post 8vo. Price 5s. cloth.

## The True Law of Population.

*By Thomas Doubleday.*
Third Edition, 8vo. Price 6s. cloth.

## Poetics:

An Essay on Poetry.
*By E. S. Dallas.*
Post 8vo. Price 2s. 6d. cloth.

## Juvenile Delinquency.

The Prize Essays.
*By M. Hill and C. F. Cornwallis.*
Post 8vo. Price 6s. cloth.

## The Endowed Schools of Ireland.

*By Harriet Martineau.*
8vo. Price 3s. 6d. cloth boards.
"The friends of education will do well to possess themselves of this book."—*Spectator.*

## The Principles of Agriculture;

Especially Tropical.
*By B. Lovell Phillips, M.D.*
Demy 8vo. Price 7s. 6d. cloth.

## European Revolutions of 1848.

*By E. S. Cayley, Esq.*
Crown 8vo. Price 6s. cloth.

"Mr. Cayley has evidently studied his subject thoroughly, he has consequently produced an interesting and philosophical, though unpretending history of an important epoch."—*New Quarterly.*
"Two instructive volumes."—*Observer.*

## MISCELLANEOUS—*continued.*

### The Bombay Quarterly Review.

Nos. 1 to 9 at 5s.; 10 to 14, 6s. each.

### The Court of Henry VIII.:

Being a Selection of the Despatches of Sebastian Giustinian, Venetian Ambassador, 1515-1519.

*Translated by Rawdon Brown.*

Two vols. crown 8vo. Price 21s. cloth.

"It is seldom that a page of genuine old history is reproduced for us with as much evidence of painstaking and real love of the subject as in the selection of despatches made and edited by Mr. Rawdon Brown."—*Times.*
"Very interesting and suggestive volumes."—*British Quarterly Review.*
"Most ably edited."—*Fraser's Magazine.*

### Hints for Investing Money.

*By Francis Playford.*

Second Edition, post 8vo. 2s. 6d. cloth.

### Men, Women, and Books.

*By Leigh Hunt.*

Two vols. Price 10s. cloth.

### Table Talk.

*By Leigh Hunt.*

Price 3s. 6d. cloth.

### Austria.

*By Thompson.*

Post 8vo. Price 12s.

## INDIA AND THE EAST.

### Suggestions towards the Government of India.

*By Harriet Martineau.*

Second Edition, demy 8vo. 5s. cloth.

"Genuine honest utterances of a clear, sound understanding, neither obscured nor enfeebled by party prejudice or personal selfishness. We cordially recommend all who are in search of the truth to peruse and reperuse these pages."—*Daily News.*

### Lectures on New Zealand.

*By William Swainson, Esq.*

Crown 8vo. Price 2s. 6d. cloth.

### Australian Facts and Prospects;

With the Author's Australian Autobiography.

*By R. H. Horne,*

Author of "Orion," "The Dreamer and the Worker," &c.

Small post 8vo. Price 5s. cloth.

### New Zealand and its Colonization.

*By William Swainson, Esq.*

Demy 8vo. Price 14s. cloth.

"This is the most complete and comprehensive account of the colonization of New Zealand which has yet been laid before the public."—*Globe.*

### Victoria,

And the Australian Gold Mines in 1857.

*By William Westgarth.*

Post 8vo, with Maps. 10s. 6d. cloth.

"Mr. Westgarth has produced a reliable and readable book well stocked with information, and pleasantly interspersed with incidents of travel and views of colonial life. It is clear, sensible, and suggestive."—*Athenæum.*
"A lively account of the most wonderful bit of colonial experience that the world's history has furnished."—*Examiner.*
"We think Mr. Westgarth's book much the best which has appeared on Australia since the great crisis in its history."—*Saturday Review.*
"A rational, vigorous, illustrative report upon the progress of the greatest colony in Australia."—*Leader.*

### The Commerce of India with Europe,

And its Political Effects.

*By B. A. Irving, Esq.*

Post 8vo. Price 7s. 6d. cloth.

"Mr. Irving's work is that of a man thoroughly versed in his subject. It is a historical handbook of the progress and vicissitudes of European trade with India."—*Economist.*

### The Cauvery, Kistnah, and Godavery:

Being a Report on the Works constructed on those Rivers, for the Irrigation of Provinces in the Presidency of Madras.

*By R. Baird Smith, F.G.S.,*

Lieut.-Col. Bengal Engineers, &c. &c.

Demy 8vo, with 19 Plans. 28s. cloth.

"A most curious and interesting work."—*Economist.*

## INDIA AND THE EAST—*continued.*

### The Bhilsa Topes;

Or, Buddhist Monuments of Central India.

*By Major Cunningham.*

One vol. 8vo, with Thirty-three Plates. Price 30s. cloth.

"Of the Topes opened in various parts of India none have yielded so rich a harvest of important information as those of Bhilsa, opened by Major Cunningham and Lieut. Maisey; and which are described, with an abundance of highly curious graphic illustrations, in this most interesting book."—*Examiner.*

### The Chinese and their Rebellions.

*By Thomas Taylor Meadows.*

One thick volume, 8vo, with Maps. Price 18s. cloth.

"Mr. Meadows' book is the work of a learned, conscientious, and observant person, and really important in many respects."—*Times.*

### Traits and Stories of Anglo-Indian Life.

*By Captain Addison.*

With Eight Illustrations. 2s. 6d. cloth.

"Anecdotes and stories well calculated to illustrate Anglo-Indian life and the domestic manners and habits of Hindostan."—*Observer.*

### Infanticide in India.

*By Dr. John Wilson.*

Demy 8vo. Price 12s.

### Grammar and Dictionary of the Malay Language.

*By John Crawfurd, Esq.*

Two vols. 8vo. Price 36s. cloth.

### WORKS OF DR. FORBES ROYLE.

### Culture and Commerce of Cotton in India.

8vo. Price 18s. cloth.

### Fibrous Plants of India.

Fitted for Cordage, Clothing, and Paper.

8vo. Price 12s. cloth.

### The Resources of India.

Super-royal 8vo. Price 14s. cloth.

### Review of the Measures

Adopted in India for the Improved Culture of Cotton.

8vo. Price 2s. 6d. cloth.

### Rangoon.

*By Lieut. W. F. B. Laurie.*

Post 8vo, with Plates. 2s. 6d. cloth.

### Pegu.

*By Lieut. W. F. B. Laurie.*

Post 8vo. Price 14s. cloth.

### The Theory of Caste.

*By B. A. Irving, Esq.*

8vo. Price 5s. cloth.

### Indian Exchange Tables.

*By J. H. Roberts.*

8vo. Second Edition, enlarged. Price 10s. 6d. cloth.

### The Turkish Interpreter:

A Grammar of the Turkish Language.

*By Major Boyd.*

8vo. Price 12s.

### Indian Commercial Tables.

*By James Bridgnell.*

Royal 8vo. Price 21s., half-bound.

# NAVAL AND MILITARY.

## Gunnery in 1858:

### A Treatise on Rifles, Cannon, and Sporting Arms.

*By William Greener,*
Author of "The Gun."

Demy 8vo, with Illustrations.
Price 14s. cloth.

"A very comprehensive work. Those who peruse it will know almost all, if not all, that books can teach them of guns and gunnery."—*Naval and Military Gazette.*
"The most interesting work of the kind that has come under our notice."—*Saturday Review.*
"We can confidently recommend this book of Gunnery, not only to the professional student, but also to the sportsman."—*Naval and Military Herald.*
"Mr. Greener's treatise is suggestive, ample, and elaborate, and deals with the entire subject systematically."—*Athenæum.*
"A work of great practical value, which bids fair to stand, for many years to come, the chief practical authority on the subject."—*Military Spectator.*
"An acceptable contribution to professional literature, written in a popular style."—*United Service Magazine.*

## Russo-Turkish Campaigns of 1828–9.

*By Colonel Chesney,*
R.A., D.C.L., F.R.S.

Third Edition. Post 8vo, with Maps.
Price 12s. cloth.

"The only work on the subject suited to the military reader."—*United Service Gazette.*
"In a strategic point of view this work is very valuable."—*New Quarterly.*

## The Native Army of India.

*By Brigadier-General Jacob, C.B.*
8vo. Price 2s. 6d.

## The Militiaman.

With Two Etchings, by JOHN LEECH.
Post 8vo. Price 9s. cloth.

"Very amusing, and conveying an impression of faithfulness."—*National Review.*
"A very lively, entertaining companion."—*Critic.*
"The author is humorous without being wilfully smart, sarcastic without bitterness, and shrewd without parading his knowledge and power of observation."—*Express.*
"Quietly, but humorously, written."—*Athenæum.*

## Military Forces and Institutions of Great Britain.

*By H. Byerly Thompson.*
8vo. Price 5s. cloth.

"A well-arranged and carefully digested compilation, giving a clear insight into the economy of the army, and the working of our military system."—*Spectator.*

## Sea Officer's Manual.

*By Captain Alfred Parish.*
Second Edition. Small post 8vo.
Price 5s. cloth.

"A very lucid and compendious manual. We would recommend youths intent upon a seafaring life to study it."—*Athenæum.*
"A little book that ought to be in great request among young seamen."—*Examiner.*

---

# LEGAL.

## Handbook of British Maritime Law.

*By Morice.*
8vo. Price 5s. cloth.

## Commercial Law of the World.

*By Leone Levi.*
Two vols. royal 4to. Price 6l. cloth.

## Land Tax of India.

According to the Moohummudan Law.
*By N. B. E. Baillie, Esq.*
8vo. Price 6s. cloth.

## Moohummudan Law of Sale.

*By N. B. E. Baillie, Esq.*
8vo. Price 14s. cloth.

---

## Moohummudan Law of Inheritance.

*By N. B. E. Baillie, Esq.*
8vo. Price 8s. cloth.

# ILLUSTRATED SCIENTIFIC WORKS.

## Results of Astronomical Observations
Made at the Cape of Good Hope.

*By Sir John Herschel.*

4to, with Plates. Price 4*l.* 4*s.* cloth.

## Geological Observations
On Coral Reefs, Volcanic Islands, and on South America.

*By Charles Darwin, Esq.*

With Maps, Plates and Woodcuts. Price 10*s.* 6*d.* cloth.

## Zoology of South Africa.
*By Dr. Andrew Smith.*

Royal 4to, cloth, with Coloured Plates.

| | |
|---|---|
| MAMMALIA | £3 |
| AVES | 7 |
| REPTILIA | 5 |
| PISCES | £2 |
| INVERTEBRATÆ | 1 |

## THE Botany of the Himalaya.
*By Dr. Forbes Royle.*

Two vols. roy. 4to, cloth, with Coloured Plates. Reduced to 5*l.* 5*s.*

---

## MEDICAL.

### The Vital Statistics
Of the European and Native Armies in India.

*By Joseph Ewart, M.D.*

Bengal Medical Service.

Demy 8vo. Price 9*s.* cloth.

"A valuable work, in which Dr. Ewart, with equal industry and skill, has compressed the essence and import of an immense mass of details."—*Spectator.*

"One main object of this most valuable volume is to point out the causes which render the Indian climate so fatal to European troops."—*Critic.*

### On Disorders of the Blood.
*Translated by Chunder Coomal Dey.*

8vo. Price 7*s.* 6*d.* cloth.

### On the Treatment of the Insane.
*By John Conolly, M.D.*

Demy 8vo. Price 14*s.* cloth.

"Dr. Conolly has embodied in this work his experiences of the new system of treating patients at Hanwell Asylum."—*Economist.*

"We most earnestly commend Dr. Conolly's treatise to all who are interested in the subject."—*Westminster Review.*

### On Abscess in the Liver.
*By E. J. Waring, M.D.*

8vo. Price 3*s.* 6*d.*

### Manual of Therapeutics.
*By E. J. Waring, M.D.*

Fcap 8vo. Price 12*s.* 6*d.* cloth.

---

## FICTION.

### Cousin Stella;
Or, Conflict.

*By the Author of "Violet Bank."*

Three volumes.

"An excellent novel, written with great care; the interest is well sustained to the end, and the characters are all life-like. It is an extremely well-written and well-conceived story, with quiet power and precision of touch, with freshness of interest and great merit."—*Athenæum.*

"'Cousin Stella' has the merit, now becoming rarer and rarer, of a comparative novelty in its subject; the interest of which will secure for this novel a fair share of popularity."—*Saturday Review.*

### Confidences.
*By the Author of "Rita."*

"This new novel, by the author of 'Rita,' displays the same combination of ease and power in the delineation of character, the same life-like dialogue, and the same faculty of constructing an interesting story."—*Spectator.*

"Decidedly both good and interesting. The book has a fresh and pleasant air about it; it is written in an excellent tone, and there are touches of pathos here and there which we must rank with a higher style of composition than that usually attained in works of this class."—*New Quarterly Review.*

## Trust for Trust.

*By A. J. Barrowcliffe,*
Author of "Amberhill."

Three volumes.

"It is seldom we find, even in this great age of novel writing, so much that is pleasant and so little to object to as in 'Trust for Trust.' It contains much original thought and fresh humour."—*Leader.*

"The story is admirably developed. The interest never flags, the incidents are natural without being commonplace, and the men and woman talk and act like human beings."—*Press.*

---

## Ellen Raymond;
### Or, Ups and Downs.

*By Mrs. Vidal,*
Author of "Tales for the Bush," &c.

Three volumes.

"The characters are good, the style pure, correct, brisk, and easy."—*Press.*

"Mrs. Vidal displays resource, imagination, and power in no common degree. * * * There is more power and strength put forth in 'Ellen Raymond' than perhaps in any lady's book of this generation."—*Saturday Review.*

"This novel will find a great many admirers."—*Leader.*

---

### THE
## Dennes of Daundelyonn.

*By Mrs. Charles J. Proby.*

Three volumes.

"This is a novel of more than average merit. There is considerable knowledge of character, power of description, and quiet social satire, exhibited in its pages."—*Press.*

"'The Dennes of Daundelyonn' is a very readable book, and will be immensely popular. . . . It has many beauties which deservedly recommend it to the novel reader."—*Critic.*

---

## The Two Homes.

*By the Author of "The Heir of Vallis."*

Three volumes.

"There is a great deal that is very good in this book—a great deal of good feeling and excellent design. . . . There are some good pictures of Madeira, and of life and society there; and there are evidences of much painstaking and talent."—*Athenæum.*

"'The Two Homes' is a very clever novel. . . Madeira furnishes Mr. Mathews with a fertile theme for his descriptive powers. The dialogue is good: the characters all speak and act consistently with their natures."—*Leader.*

---

## The Moors and the Fens.

*By F. G. Trafford.*

Three volumes.

"This novel stands out much in the same way that 'Jane Eyre' did. . . . The characters are drawn by a mind which can realize fictitious characters with minute intensity."—*Saturday Review.*

"It is seldom that a first fiction is entitled to such applause as is 'The Moors and the Fens,' and we shall look anxiously for the writer's next essay."—*Critic.*

---

## Lost and Won.

*By Georgiana M. Craik,*
Author of "Riverston."

One volume. Second Edition.

"Nothing superior to this novel has appeared during the present season."—*Leader.*

"Miss Craik's new story is a good one and in point of ability above the average of ladies' novels."—*Daily News.*

"The language is good, the narrative spirited, the characters are fairly delineated, and the dialogue has considerable dramatic force."—*Saturday Review.*

"This is an improvement on Miss Craik's first work. The story is more compact and more interesting."—*Athenæum.*

---

## An Old Debt.

*By Florence Dawson.*

Two volumes.

"A powerfully written novel; one of the best which has recently proceeded from a female hand. . . . The dialogue is vigorous and spirited."—*Morning Post.*

"There is an energy and vitality about this work which distinguish it from the common herd of novels. Its terse vigour sometimes recals Miss Brontë, but in some respects Miss Florence Dawson is decidedly superior to the author of 'Jane Eyre.'"—*Saturday Review.*

"This novel is written with great care and painstaking; it evinces considerable powers of reflection. The style is good, and the author possesses the power of depicting emotion."—*Athenæum.*

"A very good seasonable novel."—*Leader.*

---

## My Lady.
### A Tale of Modern Life.

Two volumes.

"'My Lady' is a fine specimen of an English matron, exhibiting that union of strength and gentleness, of common sense and romance, of energy and grace, which nearly approaches our ideal of womanhood."—*Press.*

"'My Lady' evinces charming feeling and delicacy of touch. It is a novel that will be read with interest."—*Athenæum.*

"The story is told throughout with great strength of feeling, is well written, and has a plot which is by no means common-place."—*Examiner.*

"There is some force and a good deal of freshness in 'My Lady.' The characters are distinctly drawn, and often wear an appearance of individuality, or almost personality. The execution is fresh and powerful."—*Spectator.*

"It is not in every novel we can light upon a style so vigorously graceful—upon an intelligence so refined without littleness, so tenderly truthful, which has sensibility rather than poetry; but which is also most subtly and searchingly powerful."—*Dublin University Magazine.*

---

## Gaston Bligh.

*By L. S. Lavenu,*
Author of "Erlesmere."

Two volumes.

"The story is told with great power; the whole book sparkles with *esprit*; and the characters talk like gentlemen and ladies. It is very enjoyable reading."—*Press.*

"'Gaston Bligh' is a good story, admirably told, full of stirring incident, sustaining to the close the interest of a very ingenious plot, and abounding in clever sketches of character. It sparkles with wit, and will reward perusal."—*Critic.*

# Sylvan Holt's Daughter.

*By Holme Lee,*
Author of "Kathie Brande," &c.

### Second Edition. 3 vols.

"The well-established reputation of Holme Lee, as a novel writer, will receive an additional glory from the publication of 'Sylvan Holt's Daughter.' It is a charming tale of country life and character."—*Globe.*

"There is much that is attractive in 'Sylvan Holt's Daughter,' much that is graceful and refined, much that is fresh, healthy, and natural."—*Press.*

"The conception of the story has a good deal of originality, and the characters avoid commonplace types, without being unnatural or improbable. The heroine herself is charming. It is a novel in which there is much to interest and please."—*New Quarterly Review.*

"A novel that is well worth reading, and which possesses the cardinal virtue of being extremely interesting."—*Athenæum.*

"A really sound, good book, highly finished, true to nature, vigorous, passionate, honest, and sincere."—*Dublin University Magazine.*

# The Professor.

*By Currer Bell.*

### Two volumes.

"We think the author's friends have shown sound judgment in publishing the 'Professor,' now that she is gone. . . . It shows the first germs of conception, which afterwards expanded and ripened into the great creations of her imagination. At the same time her advisers were equally right when they counselled her not to publish it in her lifetime. . . . But it abounds in merits."—*Saturday Review.*

"Anything which throws light upon the growth and composition of such a mind cannot be otherwise than interesting. In the 'Professor' we may discover the germs of many trains of thinking, which afterwards came to be enlarged and illustrated in subsequent and more perfect works."—*Critic.*

"There is much new insight in it, much extremely characteristic genius, and one character, moreover, of fresher, lighter, and more airy grace."—*Economist.*

# Below the Surface.

### Three volumes.

"The book is unquestionably clever and entertaining. The writer develops from first to last his double view of human life, as coloured by the manners of our age. . . . It is a tale superior to ordinary novels, in its practical application to the phases of actual life."—*Athenæum.*

"There is a great deal of cleverness in this story; a much greater knowledge of country life and character in its various aspects and conditions than is possessed by nine-tenths of the novelists who undertake to describe it."—*Spectator.*

"This is a book which possesses the rare merit of being exactly what it claims to be, a story of English country life; and, moreover, a very well told story."—*Daily News.*

"A more pleasant story we have not read for many a day."—*British Quarterly.*

# Eva Desmond ;

Or, Mutation.

### Three volumes.

"A more beautiful creation than Eva it would be difficult to imagine. The novel is undoubtedly full of interest."—*Morning Post.*

"There is power, pathos, and originality in conception and catastrophe."—*Leader.*

# The Three Chances.

*By the Author of "The Fair Carew."*

### Three volumes.

"Some of the characters and romantic situations are strongly marked and peculiarly original. . . . It is the great merit of the authoress that the personages of her tale are human and real."—*Leader.*

"This novel is of a more solid texture than most of its contemporaries. It is full of good sense, good thought, and good writing."—*Statesman.*

# The Cruellest Wrong of All.

*By the Author of "Margaret; or, Prejudice at Home."*

### One volume.

"The author has a pathetic vein, and there is a tender sweetness in the tone of her narration."—*Leader.*

"It has the first requisite of a work meant to amuse; it is amusing."—*Globe.*

# Kathie Brande.

A Fireside History of a Quiet Life.

*By Holme Lee.*

### Two volumes.

"'Kathie Brande' is not merely a very interesting novel—it is a very wholesome one, for it teaches virtue by example."—*Critic.*

"Throughout 'Kathie Brande' there is much sweetness, and considerable power of description."—*Saturday Review.*

"'Kathie Brande' is intended to illustrate the paramount excellence of duty as a moving principle. It is full of beauties."—*Daily News.*

# The Noble Traytour :

A Chronicle.

### Three volumes.

"The story is told with a graphic and graceful pen, and the chronicler has produced a romance not only of great value in a historical point of view, but possessing many claims upon the attention of the scholar, the antiquary, and the general reader."—*Post.*

"An Elizabethan masquerade. Shakespeare, the Queen, Essex, Raleigh, and a hundred nobles, ladies and knights of the land, appear on the stage. The author has imbued himself with the spirit of the times."—*Leader.*

# Riverston.

*By Georgiana M. Craik.*

### Three volumes.

"Miss Craik is a very lively writer: she has wit, and she has sense, and she has made in the beautiful young governess, with her strong will, saucy independence, and promptness of repartee, an interesting picture."—*Press.*

"Miss Craik writes well; she can paint character, passions, manners, with considerable effect; her dialogue flows easily and expressively."—*Daily News.*

"The author shows great command of language, a force and clearness of expression not often met with. . . . We offer a welcome to Miss Craik, and we shall look with interest for her next work."—*Athenæum.*

## Perversion ;

Or, the Causes and Consequences of Infidelity.

*By the late Rev. W. J. Conybeare.*

Three volumes.

"This story has a touching interest, which lingers with the reader after he has closed the book."—*Athenæum.*

"It is long, very long, since we have read a narrative of more power than this."—*British Quarterly Review.*

"This is a good and a noble book."—*New Quarterly.*

## Maud Skillicorne's Penance.

*By Mary C. Jackson,*

Author of "The Story of my Wardship."

Two volumes.

"The style is natural, and displays considerable dramatic power."—*Critic.*

"It is a well concocted tale, and will be very palatable to novel readers."—*Morning Post.*

## The Roua Pass.

*By Erick Mackenzie.*

Three volumes.

"It is seldom that we have to notice so good a novel as the 'Roua Pass.' The story is well contrived and well told; the incidents are natural and varied; several of the characters are skilfully drawn, and that of the heroine is fresh, powerful, and original. The Highland scenery, in which the plot is laid, is described with truth and feeling —with a command of language which leaves a vivid impression."—*Saturday Review.*

"The peculiar charm of the novel is its skilful painting of the Highlands, and of life among the Highlanders. Quick observation and a true sense of the poetry in nature and human life, the author has."—*Examiner.*

## The White House by the Sea :

A Love Story.

*By M. Betham-Edwards.*

Two volumes.

"A tale of English domestic life. The writing is very good, graceful, and unaffected; it pleases without startling. In the dialogue, people do not harangue, but talk, and talk naturally."—*Critic.*

## Extremes.

*By Miss E. W. Atkinson,*

Author of "Memoirs of the Queens of Prussia."

Two volumes.

"A nervous and vigorous style, an elaborate delineation of character under many varieties, spirited and well-sustained dialogue, and a carefully-constructed plot; if these have any charms for our readers, they will not forget the swiftly gliding hours passed in perusing 'Extremes.'"—*Morning Post.*

"'Extremes' is a novel written with a sober purpose, and wound up with a moral. The purpose is to exemplify some of the errors arising from mistaken zeal in religious matters, and the evil consequences that flow from those errors."—*Spectator.*

## Farina :

A Legend of Cologne.

*By George Meredith.*

One volume.

"A masque of ravishers in steel, of robber knights; of water-women, more ravishing than lovely. It has also a brave and tender deliverer, and a heroine proper for a romance of Cologne. Those who love a real, lively, audacious piece of extravagance, by way of a change, will enjoy 'Farina.'"—*Athenæum.*

## Friends of Bohemia ;

Or, Phases of London Life.

*By E. M. Whitty,*

Author of "The Governing Classes."

Two volumes.

"Mr. Whitty is a genuine satirist, employing satire for a genuine purpose. You laugh with him very much; but the laughter is fruity and ripe in thought. His style is serious, and his cast of mind severe. The author has a merriment akin to that of Jaques and that of Timon."—*Athenæum.*

## The Eve of St. Mark.

A Romance of Venice.

*By Thomas Doubleday.*

Two volumes.

"'The Eve of St. Mark' is not only well written, but adroitly constructed, and interesting. Its tone is perhaps too gorgeous; its movement is too much that of a masquerade; but a mystery is created, and a very loveable heroine is portrayed."—*Athenæum.*

## Stories and Sketches.

*By James Payn.*

Post 8vo. Price 2s. 6d. cloth.

"Mr. Payn is gay, spirited, observant, and shows no little knowledge of men and books."—*Leader.*

"A volume of pleasant reading. Some of the papers have true Attic salt in them."—*Literary Gazette.*

## Undine.

*From the German of " De La Motte Fouqué."*

Price 1s. 6d.

## The Rectory of Valehead.

*By the Rev. R. W. Evans.*

Fcap, cloth. Price 3s.

## Social Evils.

*By the Rev. C. B. Tayler.*

In Parts, each complete. 1s. each, cloth.

I.—THE MECHANIC.
II.—THE LADY AND THE LADY'S MAID.
III.—THE PASTOR OF DRONFELLS.
V.—THE COUNTRY TOWN.
VI.—LIVE AND LET LIVE; OR, THE MANCHESTER WEAVERS.
VII.—THE LEASIDE FARM.

# Cheap Series of Popular Works.

## Life of Charlotte Brontë
(Currer Bell),
Author of " Jane Eyre," &c.

### By Mrs. Gaskell.
Price 2s. 6d.

" We regard this record as a monument of courage and endurance, of suffering and triumph. . . . . All the secrets of the literary workmanship of the authoress of 'Jane Eyre' are unfolded in the course of this extraordinary narrative."—*Times.*

" Mrs. Gaskell has done her work well. Her narrative is simple, direct, intelligible, unaffected. She dwells on her friend's character with womanly tact, thorough understanding, and delicate sisterly tenderness. Many parts of the book cannot be read without deep, even painful emotion; still it is a life always womanly."—*Fraser's Magazine.*

## Lectures on the English Humourists
Of the Eighteenth Century.

### By W. M. Thackeray,
Author of " Vanity Fair," " Esmond," " The Virginians," &c.
Price 2s. 6d. cloth.

" What fine things these lectures contain; what eloquent and subtle sayings; what wise and earnest writing; how delightful are their turns of humour; with what a touching effect in the graver passages the genuine feeling of the man comes out, and how vividly the thoughts are *painted*, as it were, in graphic and characteristic words."—*Examiner.*

" This is to us by far the most acceptable of Mr. Thackeray's writings. His graphic style, his philosophical spirit, his analytical powers, his large heartedness, his shrewdness, and his gentleness, have all room to exhibit themselves."—*Economist.*

## British India.
### By Harriet Martineau.
Price 2s. 6d. cloth.

" Lucid, glowing, and instructive essays."—*Economist.*
" A good compendium of a great subject."—*National Review.*
" As a handbook to the history of India it is the best that has yet appeared."—*Morning Herald.*

## The Town.
### By Leigh Hunt.
With Forty-five Engravings.
Price 2s. 6d. cloth.

" We will allow no higher enjoyment for a rational Englishman than to stroll leisurely through this marvellous town, arm in arm with Mr. Leigh Hunt. The charm of Mr. Hunt's book is, that he gives us the outpourings of a mind enriched with the most agreeable knowledge: there is not one page which does not glow with interest. It is a series of pictures from the life, representing scenes in which every inhabitant of the metropolis has an interest."—*Times.*

## Jane Eyre.
### By Currer Bell.
Price 2s. 6d. cloth.

" ' Jane Eyre ' is a remarkable production. Freshness and originality, truth and passion, singular felicity in the description of natural scenery and in the analyzation of human thought, enable this tale to stand boldly out from the mass, and to assume its own place in the bright field of romantic literature."—*Times.*

" ' Jane Eyre ' is a book of decided power. The thoughts are true, sound, and original; and the style is resolute, straightforward, and to the purpose. The object and moral of the work are excellent."—*Examiner.*

## Shirley.
### By Currer Bell.
Price 2s. 6d. cloth.

" ' Shirley ' is the anatomy of the female heart. It is a book which indicates exquisite feeling, and very great power of mind in the writer. The women are all divine."—*Daily News.*

" ' Shirley ' is very clever. It could not be otherwise. The faculty of graphic description, strong imagination, fervid and masculine diction, analytic skill, all are visible. . . . Gems of rare thought and glorious passion shine here and there."—*Times.*

## Villette.
### By Currer Bell.
Price 2s. 6d. cloth.

" ' Villette ' is a most remarkable work—a production altogether *sui generis*. Fulness and vigour of thought mark almost every sentence, and there is a sort of easy power pervading the whole narrative such as we have rarely met."—*Edinburgh Review.*

" The tale is one of the affections, and remarkable as a picture of manners. A burning heart glows throughout it, and one brilliantly distinct character keeps it alive."—*Athenæum.*

## Political Economy of Art.
### By John Ruskin, M.A.
Price 2s. 6d. cloth.

" A most able, eloquent, and well-timed work. We hail it with satisfaction, thinking it calculated to do much practical good, and we cordially recommend it to our readers."—*Witness.*

" Mr. Ruskin's chief purpose is to treat the artist's power, and the art itself, as items of the world's wealth, and to show how these may be best evolved, produced, accumulated, and distributed."—*Athenæum.*

## Italian Campaigns of General Bonaparte.
### By George Hooper.
With a Map. Price 2s. 6d. cloth.

" The story of Bonaparte's campaigns in Italy is told at once firmly, lightly, and pleasantly. The latest and best authorities, the Bonaparte correspondence in particular, appear to have been carefully and intelligently consulted. The result is a very readable and useful volume."—*Athenæum.*

## Cheap Series—*continued.*

# Wuthering Heights and Agnes Grey.

### By Ellis and Acton Bell.
#### With Memoir by CURRER BELL.
#### Price 2s. 6d. cloth.

"There are passages in this book of 'Wuthering Heights' of which any novelist, past or present, might be proud. It has been said of Shakespeare that he drew cases which the physician might study; Ellis Bell has done no less."—*Palladium.*

"There is, at all events, keeping in the book; the groups of figures and the scenery are in harmony with each other. There is a touch of Salvator Rosa in all."—*Atlas.*

# A Lost Love.

### By Ashford Owen.
#### Price 2s. cloth.

"'A Lost Love' is a story full of grace and genius. No outline of the story would give any idea of its beauty."—*Athenæum.*

"A tale at once moving and winning, natural and romantic, and certain to raise all the finer sympathies of the reader's nature."—*Press.*

# Deerbrook.

### By Harriet Martineau.
#### Price 2s. 6d. cloth.

"This popular fiction presents a true and animated picture of country life among the upper middle classes of English residents, and is remarkable for its interest, arising from the influence of various characters upon each other, and the effect of ordinary circumstances upon them. The descriptions of rural scenery, and the daily pursuits in village hours, are among the most charming of the author's writings; but the way in which exciting incidents gradually arise out of the most ordinary phases of life, and the skill with which natural and every-day characters are brought out in dramatic situations, attest the power of the author's genius."

# Tales of the Colonies.

### By Charles Rowcroft.
#### Price 2s. 6d. cloth.

"'Tales of the Colonies' is an able and interesting book. The author has the first great requisite in fiction—a knowledge of the life he undertakes to describe; and his matter is solid and real."—*Spectator.*

"It combines the fidelity of truth with the spirit of a romance, and has altogether much of De Foe in its character and composition."—*Literary Gazette.*

# Romantic Tales
### (Including "Avillion")
### By the Author of "John Halifax, Gentleman."
#### A New Edition. Price 2s. 6d. cloth.

"'Avillion' is a beautiful and fanciful story, and the rest make very agreeable reading. There is not one of them unquickened by true feeling, exquisite taste, and a pure and vivid imagination."—*Examiner.*

"In a nice knowledge of the refinements of the female heart, and in a happy power of depicting emotion, the authoress is excelled by very few story tellers of the day."—*Globe.*

# Domestic Stories.

### By the Author of "John Halifax, Gentleman."
#### Price 2s. 6d. cloth.

"In a nice knowledge of the refinements of the female heart and in a happy power of depicting emotion, the authoress is excelled by very few story-tellers of the day."—*Globe.*

"There is not one of them unquickened by true feeling, exquisite taste, and a pure and vivid imagination."—*Examiner.*

# After Dark.

### By Wilkie Collins.
#### Price 2s. 6d. cloth.

"Mr. Wilkie Collins stands in the foremost rank of our younger writers of fiction. He tells a story well and forcibly, his style is eloquent and picturesque; he has considerable powers of pathos; understands the art of construction; is never wearisome or wordy, and has a keen insight into character."—*Daily News.*

"'After Dark' abounds with genuine touches of nature."—*British Quarterly.*

# Paul Ferroll.

#### Fourth Edition. Price 2s. cloth.

"We have seldom read so wonderful a romance. We can find no fault in it as a work of art. It leaves us in admiration, almost in awe, of the powers of its author."—*New Quarterly.*

"The art displayed in presenting Paul Ferroll throughout the story is beyond all praise."—*Examiner.*

# School for Fathers.

### By Talbot Gwynne.
#### Price 2s. cloth.

"'The School for Fathers' is one of the cleverest, most brilliant, genial, and instructive stories that we have read since the publication of 'Jane Eyre.'"—*Eclectic Review.*

"The pleasantest tale we have read for many a day. It is a story of the *Tatler* and *Spectator* days, and is very fitly associated with that time of good English literature by its manly feeling, direct, unaffected manner of writing, and nicely-managed, well-turned narrative. The descriptions are excellent; some of the country painting is as fresh as a landscape by Alfred Constable, or an idyl by Tennyson."—*Examiner.*

# The Tenant of Wildfell Hall.

### By Acton Bell.

*Preparing for Publication.*

# Kathie Brande:
### The Fireside History of a Quiet Life.
### By Holme Lee,
Author of "Sylvan Holt's Daughter."

# Below the Surface.
### By Sir A. H. Elton, Bart., M.P.

# Juvenile and Educational.

## NEW BOOKS FOR YOUNG READERS.
# The Parents' Cabinet
Of Amusement and Instruction for Young Persons.

New Edition, carefully revised, in Twelve Shilling Volumes, each complete in itself, and containing a full page Illustration in Oil Colours, with Wood Engravings, in ornamented boards.

### CONTENTS.
AMUSING STORIES, all tending to the development of good qualities, and the avoidance of faults.
BIOGRAPHICAL ACCOUNTS OF REMARKABLE CHARACTERS, interesting to Young People.
SIMPLE NARRATIVES OF HISTORICAL EVENTS, suited to the capacity of children.
ELUCIDATIONS OF NATURAL HISTORY, adapted to encourage habits of observation.
FAMILIAR EXPLANATIONS OF NOTABLE SCIENTIFIC DISCOVERIES AND MECHANICAL INVENTIONS.
LIVELY ACCOUNTS OF THE GEOGRAPHY, INHABITANTS, AND PRODUCTIONS OF DIFFERENT COUNTRIES.

MISS EDGEWORTH'S *Opinion of the* PARENTS' CABINET:—
"I almost feel afraid of praising it as much as I think it deserves. . . . There is so much variety in the book that it cannot tire. It alternately excites and relieves attention, and does not lead to the bad habit of frittering away the mind by requiring no exertion from the reader. . . . Whoever your scientific associate is, he understands his business and children's capabilities right well. . . . Without lecturing, or prosing, you keep the right and the wrong clearly marked, and hence all the sympathy of the young people is always enlisted on the right side."

\* \* The work is now complete in 4 vols. extra cloth, gilt edges, at 3s. 6d. each; or in 6 vols. extra cloth, gilt edges, 2s. 6d. each.

By the Author of "Round the Fire," &c.

## Unica :
A Story for a Sunday Afternoon.

With Four Illustrations. 2s. 6d. cloth.
"This tale, like its author's former ones, will find favour in the nursery."—*Athenæum.*
"The character of Unica is charmingly conceived, and the story pleasantly told."—*Spectator.*

### II.
## Old Gingerbread and the Schoolboys.

With Four Coloured Plates. 2s. 6d. cl.
"'Old Gingerbread and the School-boys' is delightful, and the drawing and colouring of the pictorial part done with spirit and correctness."—*Press.*
"This tale is very good, the descriptions being natural, with a feeling of country freshness."—*Spectator.*

### III.
## Willie's Birthday :
Showing how a Little Boy did what he Liked, and how he Enjoyed it.

With Four Illustrations. 2s. cloth.

### IV.
## Willie's Rest :
A Sunday Story.
With Four Illustrations. 2s. cloth.
"Extremely well written story books, amusing and moral, and got up in a very handsome style."—*Morning Herald.*

### V.
## Uncle Jack, the Fault Killer.

With Four Illustrations. 2s. 6d. cloth.

### VI.
## Round the Fire :
Six Stories for Young Readers.
Square 16mo, with Four Illustrations. Price 2s. 6d. cloth.
"Simple and very interesting."—*National Review.*
"True children's stories."—*Athenæum.*

## The King of the Golden River ;
Or, the Black Brothers.
*By John Ruskin, M.A.*
Third Edition, with 22 Illustrations by Richard Doyle. Price 2s. 6d.
"This little fancy tale is by a master-hand. The story has a charming moral."—*Examiner.*

## Investigation ;
Or, Travels in the Boudoir.
*By Miss Halsted.*
Fcap cloth. Price 3s. 6d.

## Rhymes for Little Ones.
With 16 Illustrations. 1s. 6d. cloth.

### Stories from the Parlour Printing Press.
*By the Authors of the "Parent's Cabinet."*
Fcap 8vo. Price 2s. cloth.

### Religion in Common Life.
*By William Ellis.*
Post 8vo. Price 7s. 6d. cloth.
"A book addressed to young people of the upper ten thousand upon social duties."—*Examiner.*
"Lessons in Political Economy for young people by a skilful hand."—*Economist.*

### Books for the Blind.
Printed in raised Roman letters, at the Glasgow Asylum.
A List of the books, with their prices, may be had on application.

### Little Derwent's Breakfast.
Price 2s. cloth.

### Juvenile Miscellany.
Six Engravings. Price 2s. 6d. cloth.

### Elementary Works on Social Economy.
*By William Ellis.*
Uniform in foolscap 8vo, half-bound.
I.—OUTLINES OF SOCIAL ECONOMY. 1s. 6d.
II.—PROGRESSIVE LESSONS IN SOCIAL SCIENCE.
III.—INTRODUCTION TO THE SOCIAL SCIENCES. 2s.
IV.—OUTLINES OF THE UNDERSTANDING. 2s.
V.—WHAT AM I? WHERE AM I? WHAT OUGHT I TO DO? &c. 1s. sewed.
\*\* These works are recommended by the Committee of Council on Education.

# Poetry.

### Homely Ballads
For the Working Man's Fireside.
*By Mary Sewell.*
Ninth Thousand. Post 8vo, cloth, 1s.
"Very good verses conveying very useful lessons."—*Literary Gazette.*
"Simple poems, well suited to the taste of the classes for whom they are written."—*Globe.*
"There is a real homely flavour about them, and they contain sound and wholesome lessons."—*Critic.*

### Wit and Humour.
*By Leigh Hunt.*
Price 5s. cloth.

### Jar of Honey from Hybla.
*By Leigh Hunt.*
Price 5s. cloth.

### Sketches from Dover Castle, and other Poems.
*By Lieut.-Col. William Read.*
Crown 8vo. Price 7s. 6d. cloth.
"Elegant and graceful, and distinguished by a tone of sentiment, which renders Colonel Read's volume very pleasant reading for a leisure hour."—*Daily News.*
"It is not often that the heroic couplet is in these days so gracefully written. Colonel Read is to be congratulated on his success in bending this Ulyssean bow. His little volume contains some very fine lyrics."—*Leader.*

### Ionica.
Fcap 8vo. Price 4s. cloth.
"The themes, mostly classical, are grappled with boldness and toned with a lively imagination. The style is rich and firm, and cannot be said to be an imitation of any known author. We cordially recommend it to our readers as a book of real poetry."—*Critic.*

### The Six Legends of King Goldenstar.
*By the late Anna Bradstreet.*
Fcap 8vo. Price 5s.
"The author evinces more than ordinary power, a vivid imagination, guided by a mind of lofty aim."—*Globe.*
"The poetry is tasteful, and above the average."—*National Review.*
"This is a posthumous poem by an unknown authoress, of higher scope and more finish than the crowd of poems which come before us. The fancy throughout the poem is quick and light, and musical."—*Athenæum.*

### National Songs and Legends of Roumania.
*Translated by E. C. Grenville Murray, Esq.*
With Music, crown 8vo. Price 2s. 6d.

### Poems of Past Years.
*By Sir A. H. Elton, Bart., M.P.*
Fcap 8vo. Price 3s. cloth.
"A refined, scholarly, and gentlemanly mind is apparent all through this volume."—*Leader.*

## Poetry—continued.

### Magdalene: a Poem.

Fcap 8vo. Price 1s.

"Rarely have we been more deeply touched than in reading this wonderful little book. Its author is a poet such as we have not read for many a day. There is nothing more sweet, more touching in the English language than this exquisite poem."—*Morning Herald.*

### Poems.

*By Ada Trevanion.*

Price 5s. cloth.

"There really is a value in such poems as those of Ada Trevanion. They give an image of what many women are on their best side. Perhaps nowhere can we point to a more satisfactory fruit of Christian civilization than in a volume like this."—*Saturday Review.*

### Poems.

*By Henry Cecil.*

Price 5s. cloth.

"He shows power in his sonnets, while in his lighter and less restrictive measures the lyric element is dominant. . . . If Mr. Cecil does not make his name famous, it is not that he does not deserve to do so."—*Critic.*

"There is an unmistakeable stamp of genuine poetry in most of these pages."—*Economist.*

### England in Time of War.

*By Sydney Dobell,*

Author of "Balder," "The Roman," &c.

Crown 8vo. Price 5s. cloth.

"That Mr. Dobell is a poet, 'England in time of War' bears witness."—*Athenæum.*

### The Cruel Sister,

And other Poems.

Fcap 8vo. Price 4s. cloth.

"There are traces of power, and the versification displays freedom and skill."—*Guardian.*

### Balder.

*By Sydney Dobell.*

Crown 8vo. Price 7s. 6d. cloth.

"The writer has fine qualities; his level of thought is lofty, and his passion for the beautiful has the truth of instinct."—*Athenæum.*

### Poems.

*By Mary Maynard.*

Fcap 8vo. Price 4s. cloth.

"We have rarely met with a volume of poems displaying so large an amount of power, blended with so much delicacy of feeling and grace of expression."—*Church of England Quarterly.*

### Poems.

*By William Bell Scott.*

Fcap 8vo. Price 5s. cloth.

"Mr. Scott has poetical feeling, keen observation, deep thought, and command of language."—*Spectator.*

### Stilicho: a Tragedy.

*By George Mallam.*

Fcap 8vo.

### Poems.

*By Mrs. Frank P. Fellows.*

Fcap 8vo. Price 3s. cloth.

"There is easy simplicity in the diction, and elegant naturalness in the thought."—*Spectator.*

### Poetry from Life.

*By C. M. K.*

Fcap 8vo, cloth gilt. Price 5s.

"Elegant verses. The author has a pleasing fancy and a refined mind."—*Economist.*

### Poems.

*By Walter R. Cassels.*

Fcap 8vo. Price 3s. 6d. cloth.

"Mr. Cassels has deep poetical feeling, and gives promise of real excellence. His poems are written sometimes with a strength of expression by no means common."—*Guardian.*

### Garlands of Verse.

*By Thomas Leigh.*

Price 5s. cloth.

"One of the best things in the 'Garlands of Verse' is an Ode to Toil. There, as elsewhere, there is excellent feeling."—*Examiner.*

### Poems.

*By Currer, Ellis, and Acton Bell.*

Price 4s. cloth.

### Select Odes of Horace.

In English Lyrics.

*By J. T. Black.*

Fcap 8vo. Price 4s. cloth.

"Rendered into English Lyrics with a vigour and heartiness rarely, if ever, surpassed."—*Critic.*

### Rhymes and Recollections

Of a Hand-Loom Weaver.

*By William Thom.*

With a Memoir. Post 8vo, cloth, 3s.

### King Rene's Daughter.

Fcap 8vo. Price 2s. 6d. cloth.

### Maid of Orleans,

And other Poems.

*Translated from Schiller.*

Fcap 8vo. Price 2s. 6d.

London: Printed by SMITH, ELDER and Co., Little Green Arbour Court, E.C.

www.ingramcontent.com/pod-product-compliance
Lightning Source LLC
Chambersburg PA
CBHW032027120726
47901CB00004BA/1173